Singapore

timeout.com/singapore

Published by Time Out Guides Ltd, a wholly owned subsidiary of Time Out Group Ltd.
Time Out and the Time Out logo are trademarks of Time Out Group Ltd.

© **Time Out Group Ltd 2007**

10 9 8 7 6 5 4 3 2 1

This edition first published in Great Britain in 2007 by Ebury Publishing
Ebury Publishing is a division of The Random House Group Ltd,
20 Vauxhall Bridge Road, London SW1V 2SA

Random House Australia Pty Limited 20 Alfred Street, Milsons Point, Sydney, New South Wales 2061, Australia
Random House New Zealand Limited 18 Poland Road, Glenfield, Auckland 10, New Zealand
Random House South Africa (Pty) Limited Isle of Houghton, Corner Boundary
Road & Carse O'Gowrie, Houghton 2198, South Africa

Random House UK Limited Reg. No. 954009

Distributed in USA by Publishers Group West
1700 Fourth Street, Berkeley, California 94710

Distributed in Canada by Publishers Group Canada
250A Carlton Street, Toronto, Ontario M5A 2L1

For further distribution details, see www.timeout.com

ISBN 1-84670-051-5
ISBN 9781846700514

A CIP catalogue record for this book is available from the British Library

Colour reprographics by Wyndeham Icon, 3 & 4 Maverton Road, London E3 2JE

Printed and bound by Firmengruppe APPL, aprinta druck, Wemding, Germany

The Random House Group Limited makes every effort to ensure that the papers used in our books are made from trees
that have been legally sourced from well-managed and credibly certified forests. Our paper procurement policy can
be found on www.randomhouse.co.uk.

Time Out Guides Limited
Universal House
251 Tottenham Court Road
London W1T 7AB
Tel + 44 (0)20 7813 3000
Fax + 44 (0)20 7813 6001
Email guides@timeout.com
www.timeout.com

Editorial

Editor Cath Phillips
Deputy Editor Hugh Graham
Consultant Editor Ben Slater
Listings Editor Nizhen Hsieh, Angelina Hue,
June Lee, Ang Song Ming, Lam Yisham
Proofreader Simon Cropper
Indexer Anna Norman

Managing Director Peter Fiennes
Financial Director Gareth Garner
Editorial Director Ruth Jarvis
Deputy Series Editor Dominic Earle
Editorial Manager Holly Pick

Design

Art Director Scott Moore
Art Editor Pinelope Kourmouzoglou
Senior Designer Josephine Spencer
Graphic Designer Henry Elphick
Junior Graphic Designer Kei Ishimaru
Digital Imaging Simon Foster
Ad Make-up Jenni Prichard

Picture Desk

Picture Editor Jael Marschner
Deputy Picture Editor Tracey Kerrigan
Picture Researcher Helen McFarland

Advertising

Sales Director Mark Phillips
International Sales Manager Fred Durman
International Sales Executive Simon Davies
International Sales Consultant Ross Canadé
Advertising Sales (Singapore) Ink Publishing
Advertising Sales Manager (North America) Rani Vavilis
Advertising Assistant Kate Staddon

Marketing

Group Marketing Director John Luck
Sales & Marketing Director (North America)
Lisa Levinson
Marketing Manager Yvonne Poon

Production

Group Production Director Mark Lamond
Production Manager Brendan McKeown
Production Coordinator Caroline Bradford

Time Out Group

Chairman Tony Elliott
Financial Director Richard Waterlow
Time Out Magazine Ltd MD David Pepper
Group General Manager/Director Nichola Coulthard
Time Out Communications Ltd MD David Pepper
Time Out International MD Cathy Runciman
Group Art Director John Oakey
Group IT Director Simon Chappell

Contributors

Introduction Cath Phillips. **History** Paul Rae. **Singapore Today** Paul Rae. **Culture, Race & Religion** Theresa Tan (*Got Singlish, lah!* Ben Slater). **Architecture** Thomas Woon. **Where to Stay** Charlene Fang. **Sightseeing Introduction** Cath Phillips (*Singapore by numbers* Hugh Graham). **Colonial District** Paul Rae. **Chinatown & the CBD** Ben Slater. **Little India & the Arab Quarter** Ben Slater. **Orchard Road & Around** Amy Van. **Sentosa & Around** Marguerita Tan. **Eastern Singapore** Amy Van, Marguerita Tan. **Western Singapore** Marguerita Tan. **Central & Northern Singapore** Marguerita Tan. **Restaurants** Daven Wu. **Bars** Anita Kapoor. **Shops & Services** Jacqueline Tan (*Super spas* Marianne Wee). **Festivals & Events** Jacqueline Tan. **Children** June Wan. **Clubs** Anita Kapoor. **Film** Ben Slater. **Galleries** Rachel Farnay Jacques. **Gay & Lesbian** *Gay* Darren Ho, *Lesbian, Island queen* Jamie Nonis. **Music** Chris Toh. **Sport & Fitness** June Lee. **Theatre & Dance** Rachel Farnay Jacques. **Getting Started** Cath Phillips. **Malaysia** June Lee. **Bintan & Batam** Chris Toh. **Getting Around** Angelina Hue. **Resources A-Z** Lam Yisham. **Further Reference** Paul Rae.

Maps maps@tribalwerks.com.ar.
MRT & LRT system map on p256 reproduced with the kind permission of the Land Transport Authority of Singapore.

Photography Elan Fleisher, except: page 12 Getty Images; page 17 Bettmann/Corbis; page 18 Topham Picturepoint; page 20 Time Life Pictures/Getty Images; page 25 Tan Peng Koon; page 200 Theatreworks (S) Ltd; page 163 Photolibrary; page 164 Empics/AP; page 175 Doris Young and Bobby A Suarez; page 177 National Arts Council.

The following photographs were supplied by the featured establishments/ artists: pages 124, 156, 183, 192, 203.
The Editor would like to thank the staff of the Singapore Tourist Board (especially Tangie Kay, Sara Chua, Raphael Lee) and Wong Wee Tee; Abby Hillier at Keene; Billie Cohen and the staff of Ink Publishing (especially Clare Brundle, Theresa Tan, Gerry Ricketts, Michael Keating); Kelvin Ang; Tang Fu Kuen and Philip Cornwel-Smith in Bangkok; Aun Koh and Tan Su-Lyn; Tay Tong; Dawn Mok at CityScoops; Jonathan Lobban; Simon Richmond; Tom and Fran Drake; Gareth Evans; Katy Attfield; Mike Harrison.

Contents

Introduction

Thirty-five million passengers passed through Singapore's Changi Airport in 2006, but the vast majority of them got no further than the transit halls. Changi is a pretty flash airport, it's true, and it's easy to get bewildered among the miles of florid carpets, too-bright lighting and icy air-conditioning, but that's no excuse. And many of those who did venture out into the not-so-mean streets of Singapore probably got no further than the gleaming shopping malls along Orchard Road and a few kitsch souvenir shops in Chinatown.

They're missing out.

There's a lot crammed into this tiny island-state, measuring barely 42 kilometres (26 miles) by 22.5 kilometres (14 miles). OK, so the beaches aren't up to much, and some of the museums are little more than displays of dated waxwork mannequins with uninformative labelling, but there's plenty to keep even the most jaded traveller occupied and interested. And although it's not as cheap as other countries in South-east Asia, the standard of living – and of tourist amenities and services – is much, much higher.

Its small size makes it easy to get about, as does the inexpensive and super–efficient public transport network. Some of the world's swankiest hotels are here, along with an increasing number of ultra-stylish boutique hotels. And the mega shopping malls (along Orchard Road mainly, but elsewhere too) are pretty astonishing in the variety and scope of their merchandise: shopaholics will be more than happy.

In many ways, Singapore is a microcosm of the region in which it sits. There's the mind-boggling variety of races, religions and languages, for a start, evident in the faces and voices in the streets, and the array of temples, mosques and churches on almost every other corner. And let's not forget the food, surely Singapore's greatest gift to the world. Chinese, Indian, Malay, Indonesian and other cuisines have merged over the years to provide one of the globe's richest and most varied eating cultures. Even after a year of feasting, the greediest gourmand would still find new dishes and dining experiences to delight in.

Singapore is highly urbanised, of course – and all those high-rise housing blocks can look very samey after a while – but it's not nicknamed the Garden City for nothing. Outside the city centre are are nature reserves and pockets of rainforest, and even some farmland.

So forget the clichés about the banning of chewing gum and *Playboy* magazine; while clichés have some relation to reality, this 'little red dot' is much more complicated than such simplifications allow. And the only way to find out is to leave the confines of Changi Airport and explore.

ABOUT TIME OUT CITY GUIDES

This is the first edition of *Time Out Singapore*, one of an expanding series of Time Out guides produced by the people behind the successful listings magazines in London, New York and Chicago. Our guides are all written by resident experts who have striven to provide you with all the most up-to-date information you'll need to explore the city or read up on its background, whether you're a local or a first-time visitor.

THE LIE OF THE LAND

Singapore is an easy place to get around, partly because it's so small. The key sightseeing areas are all near one another in the city centre, and are compact enough to negotiate on foot. The efficient and inexpensive MRT underground network makes getting between districts a doddle, though you'll need to use buses or taxis for some areas.

To make both this guide and Singapore easier to navigate, we've divided the island into areas and assigned each one its own chapter in our Sightseeing section. While many are official names (Chinatown, Little India, the Arab Quarter, the CBD), some are a simplification (Orchard Road & Around), but we hope they'll help you to understand the island's layout and to find its most interesting sights. We have used area names in addresses throughout the guide – except for venues located actually on Orchard Road.

We've given addresses starting with the floor or unit number followed by the building, street and area of the city; in Singapore itself, addresses tend to be written with some of this information reversed (*see p222* for an explanation). We've also included phone numbers, websites, postcodes for those venues to which you might want to write and map

references that point to the street maps at the back of the guide. For further orientation information, see p54.

ESSENTIAL INFORMATION

For all the practical information you might need for visiting Singapore – including visa and customs information, details of local transport, a listing of emergency numbers, information on local weather and a selection of useful websites – turn to the Directory at the back of this guide. It begins on page 218.

THE LOWDOWN ON THE LISTINGS

We have tried to make this book as easy to use as possible. Addresses, phone numbers, transport information, opening times and admission prices are all included in the listings. However, businesses can change their arrangements at any time. Before you go out of your way, we'd strongly advise you to phone ahead to check opening times and other particulars. While every effort and care has been made to ensure the accuracy of the information contained in this guide, the publishers cannot accept responsibility for any errors it may contain.

PRICES AND PAYMENT

We have noted where venues such as shops, hotels, restaurants and theatres accept the following credit cards: American Express (AmEx), Diners Club (DC), JCB (Japanese Credit Bank) MasterCard (MC) and Visa (V).

The prices we've listed in this guide should be treated as guidelines, not gospel. If prices vary wildly from those we've quoted, ask whether there's a good reason. If not, go elsewhere. Then please let us know. We aim to give the best and most up-to-date advice, so we want to know if you've been badly treated or overcharged.

TELEPHONE NUMBERS

The code for Singapore is 65 (you don't need to use the code if you're phoning from within Singapore). Land lines begin with a 6, while mobile (hand phone) numbers begin with a 9. Toll-free lines (which work only in Singapore) start with 1800. For more on telephones and codes, see p230.

MAPS

The map section at the back of this book includes a map of Singapore Island, an overview map of the main sightseeing areas, detailed street maps of the city centre and Sentosa island, a map relating to the Trips Out of Town section, and a map of the MRT system. The maps start on page 242, and the street maps pinpoint the specific location of hotels (❶), restaurants (❶) and bars (❶).

LET US KNOW WHAT YOU THINK

We hope you enjoy the *Time Out Singapore Guide*, and we'd like to know what you think of it. We welcome tips for places that you consider we should include in future editions and take note of your criticism of our choices. You can email us at guides@timeout.com.

There is an online version of this book, along with guides to over 100 international cities, at **www.timeout.com**.

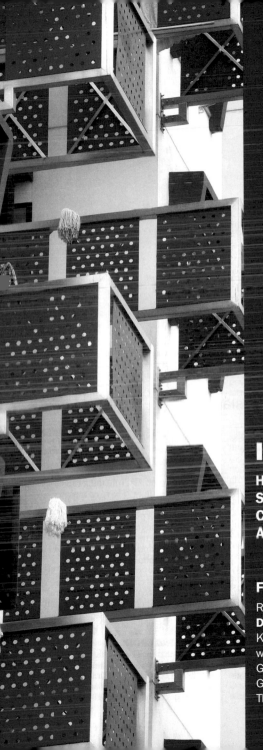

In Context

Features

Opium may have been the most profitable commodity, but it wasn't the only one. Before Raffles arrived, there were Chinese on the island growing pepper and gambier (a key ingredient in the tanning process) and mining for tin. As the 19th century developed, Singapore became a goods yard for regional and international trade, a plantation, and a shipping centre for produce from the Malayan mainland. As such, its fortunes ebbed and flowed with the globalising world economy. The advent of fast clipper ships in the mid 19th century meant that Singapore could be bypassed on the Europe-China run, but the opening of the Suez Canal in 1869 gave access to new markets. The invention of the canning process meant a surge in demand for tin, particularly from the US. And the discovery of how to vulcanise rubber, coupled with the rise of the motor car in the 20th century, enabled the region's rubber plantations – which the British established with Indian labour – to thrive; although Singapore was not itself a large producer of rubber, Firestone, Dunlop and Goodyear all established offices on the island to oversee their regional operations and shipments.

The peak of Singapore's colonial economy was 1926, with more than half its exports going to the West. But as the Great Depression kicked in, Singapore felt the pinch: it would not reach similar levels of trade again until the 1950s. Japan might have helped out, but preferential trade agreements with the colonial powers meant that Japan was not able to import much. The discrimination that Japanese traders encountered in British Malaya only fuelled their resentment – an added reason for the support they offered the Imperial Army when Japan invaded during the Pacific War.

TOILERS OF THE FAR EAST, UNITE!

The flurry of global economic activity on the island fuelled the idea of Singapore as a homeland. It was the two ethnic groups who considered themselves 'natives' of Malaya who began to agitate for a greater say in the running of the place. Prominent Malays and Straits Chinese sought positions on the Legislative Council and argued for senior jobs within the British-dominated Malayan civil service.

At the same time, social issues such as education and workers' rights began to be addressed by several politically motivated groups. Events in China were particularly influential. Between 1904-7, eight Chinese schools were established by groups sympathetic to political reform in China, while from 1906 the revolutionary Sun Yat Sen visited Singapore repeatedly to garner

support for the overthrow of the Chinese Emperor. In the 1920s, reading rooms and night schools circulated revolutionary material relating to Dr Sun's Kuomintang party. The British moved to close down the party and censor propaganda. But this only strengthened anti-colonial sentiment, prefigured in the Sepoy Mutiny of 1915, when disgruntled Indian soldiers guarding German prisoners of war freed their captives and went on a rampage, killing 40 British soldiers and local civilians before being executed. In 1919 the Comintern (Third International) was established in Moscow to support revolution in the colonies. In 1922 it formed the Congress of the Toilers of the Far East to mastermind a unified proletarian uprising.

By the late 1920s, this heady mix of communism, Chinese nationalism and anti-imperialism was coming to the boil. In 1927 a gathering to mark the anniversary of the death of Dr Sun led to a riot in Kreta Ayer where panicky policemen opened fire, leaving six dead. A trolleybus boycott ensued, causing the *Straits Times* to fulminate against social disorder. In response, Special Branch, initially founded after the Sepoy Mutiny, was given more funds to battle subversive activities – one of their agents, the deeply enigmatic Lai Teck, rose to become secretary-general of the Malayan Communist Party (banned in 1930).

Chinese activism got a boost with the outbreak of the Sino-Japanese war in 1937. Galvanised by anti-Japanese feeling, many Chinese boycotted Japanese goods and helped fund the war, a move that would prove costly.

ENTER THE JAPANESE

On 15 February 1942, Lieutenant-General AE Percival surrendered British Malaya to Lieutenant-General Yamashita Tomoyuki of the Japanese 25th Army at the Ford Motor Factory on Upper Bukit Timah Road. At the surrender meeting, the Japanese general was bullish, shouting 'No!' in English when Percival requested more time to organise the surrender of his troops. Yamashita later claimed that he shouted out of concern that if he granted Percival extra time, the vulnerable state of his own army would be revealed. Nevertheless, for the British Empire, the surrender marked the end of a humiliatingly swift attack.

The Japanese had come ashore in southern Thailand and northern Malaya early on 8 December local time, a couple of hours before the bombing of Pearl Harbour. Having sunk the battleships of Britain's Force Z and taken the nearby airfields, they had swept through the peninsula forcing the British, Australian, Indian, and Malayan troops into a fighting retreat. On 8 February they crossed the causeway to Singapore. The Allied defence was fierce and brave in parts, but suffered from poor planning and communications breakdowns. Contrary to popular belief, the guns of Sentosa were not facing the wrong way, but with the Japanese advancing rapidly, the Allies were soon destroying their own key installations, so as to deny them to the invaders. A week of bloody battles later (including Butik Batok, Bukit Timah and Pasir Panjang), with the Japanese themselves running low on resources, the island was within their grasp.

'Churchill would never forgive Percival for displaying the Union Jack alongside the flag of surrender.'

Prime Minister Winston Churchill was unambiguous about the threat to the honour of the Empire and with the fall of Singapore imminent instructed that 'the battle must be fought to the bitter end and at all costs... Commanders and senior officers should die with their troops'. 'The order,' as the historians Christopher Bayley and Tim Harper dryly put it, 'was not well received.' Churchill would never forgive Percival for displaying the Union Jack alongside the flag of surrender as they made their way towards the Ford Motor Factory in a now-iconic image. But in later years, Churchill's own actions and decisions would be implicated in the fall of Singapore, as much as those of officers on the ground.

The surrender marked the beginning of a dark period for Singapore. British civilians and Empire forces were interned in camps, most notoriously Changi prison, or dispatched, along with tens of thousands of locals, to Burma and Thailand to work on the so-called 'death railway'. Meanwhile, the Japanese renamed the island Syonan ('Light of the South') and set about turning it into a virtual Japanese colony.

Eager to instill Japanese values and culture in the local population, the occupiers changed the clocks to Tokyo time, changed the calendar (so that 1942 became 2602) and changed the *Straits Times* to the *Syonan Shimbun*. Everyone was encouraged to learn Japanese and to revere the Emperor by singing the national anthem, while cultural practices such as bowing to elders were strictly enforced. With Japanese resources going into the war effort, Singapore was left to become self-sufficient, and all available land was

Bumboats on the Singapore River, 1950s.

given over to growing staple crops such as tapioca and sweet potato, used to bulk out the meagre diet of rice porridge and scraps of fish and vegetables. A new currency was introduced, but inflation was rampant and the Japanese 'banana' money practically worthless.

The Japanese treated the various ethnic groups of Singapore differently, depending on their conduct in advance of and during the war. The invasion had been assisted by a group of nationalist Malays, and although a Malay regiment of the British army had fought with distinction during the invasion (at the Battle of Pasir Panjang), they were treated relatively well under the occupation. Many Indians were caught in conflicting loyalties between the British, for whom they had previously fought, and the Japanese, who promised to help them in their anti-colonial struggle. In 1943 the charismatic Indian fascist Subhas Chandra Bose arrived in Singapore to take control of the Indian National Army, which would fight alongside the Japanese for Indian independence. One third of the soldiers taken prisoner by the Japanese signed up; the rest were interned in Seletar Camp, or sent north.

The Japanese were particularly hostile towards the Chinese for reasons that combined historical resentment, suspicion of resistance

Round one: British troops surrender to the Japanese in February 1942. *See p16.*

and racism. Early in the occupation, between 25,000 and 50,000 Chinese were massacred in the Sook Ching ('purification through purge') campaigns. All able-bodied males were required to register with the authorities, and suspicion of anti-Japanese sentiment was enough to secure a death warrant. Meanwhile, rape and torture at the hands of the feared Kempeitai intelligence agency was common. In addition, the Chinese community was obliged to pay $50 million to the Japanese, which they could only do by borrowing heavily from a Japanese bank. In the 1950s, after the Japanese were absolved of paying further reparations, this 'blood debt' to the Chinese would continue to cause tensions between Japan and the ascendant city state.

RE-ENTER THE BRITISH, LIMPING

Following the bombing of Hiroshima and Nagasaki in August 1945, the Japanese began to surrender throughout Pacific Asia. On 5 September, the 5th Indian Division was the first Allied force back into Singapore, and on 12 September, Lord Louis Mountbatten oversaw the surrender of Japanese forces in South-east Asia at the City Hall. Union Jacks were waved, Japanese imperial swords were surrendered to skeletal former prisoners of war and war criminals were hanged. But neither Singapore nor the British Empire would be the same again.

Decolonisation in Asia began promptly, but in Malaya it took two decades of power struggles. The war had reshaped the political landscape: of particular concern to the British was the rise of the communists. The Malayan Communist Party and the Malayan People's Anti-Japanese Army had been the most effective resistance during the occupation

and were primed to take over an independent Malaya. When by 1948 it became evident that this would not be possible by constitutional means, they took to the jungle to engage in the bloody and intractable conflict known as the Malayan Emergency.

Meanwhile, numerous other political organisations pressed for decolonisation. In 1956 a delegation from Singapore went to London to argue for self-determination as part of the Federation of Malaya. They were led by David Marshall, a flamboyant Jewish lawyer who was the colony's first Chief Minister but wary of being closely linked to the British. Also present were two key members of the opposition People's Action Party (PAP): the Chinese-educated, unionist firebrand Lim Chin Siong and the brilliant, Cambridge-educated lawyer Lee Kuan Yew. The PAP adopted a socialist anti-colonial position and refused to accept the limited form of self-government offered by the British. The talks broke down and David Marshall resigned. In 1957, new Chief Minister Lim Yew Hock hammered out a deal that would lead to elections in 1959 and a chance of independence. But by clamping down on Chinese left-wing activists, Lim was seen as a stooge of the British and lost the '59 election.

He was beaten decisively by the PAP. Led by Lee Kuan Yew, it called for a merger with the rest of Malaya and independence from the British. The PAP succeeded by combining the political nous of Lee and his English-educated associates with the ground-level appeal of Lim and other unionists. However, the political tensions between Lee's Fabian socialism and Lim's militant left-wing populism caused a rift within the party, which split. The left-wing faction formed a rival party called the Barisan Sosialis, but it collapsed following the detention without trial of key members – including Lim – for communist sympathies. By 1963, the PAP was free to pursue its vision of a 'non-communist' socialist Malaya.

On 16 September 1963 Singapore and the Borneo colonies of Sabah and Sarawak united with Malaya to form Malaysia. But tensions soon arose between Singapore and the Malaysian government under Tengku Abdul Rahman. These concerned economic issues textile quotas, access to resources and trade agreements – and questions of ethnic representation. The Tengku wanted legislation that favoured Malays, but Singapore, with a majority Chinese population, argued for a 'Malaysian Malaysia'. Weakened by deep distrust between the Tengku and Lee, the federation could not hold. On 9 August 1965, Lee proclaimed Singapore's independence.

GOING SOLO

A commonly voiced perception among the 'post-1965' generation of Singaporeans is that they missed out on history: by the time they were born, all the hard work had been done It's certainly true that the history of independent Singapore had a different character. The PAP has governed continuously since 1959, and looks set to do so for the foreseeable future. As such, although Singapore has undergone eye-popping economic and physical changes since 1965, its politics have become sober – some say numbing. A legacy of the PAP has been to depoliticise politics: it is now an exercise in administration and governance, shorn of the cut and thrust of debate. As Carl Trocki somewhat contentiously – puts it, the history of modern Singapore is about how the PAP 'allied with international capitalism to create a workers' paradise'.

> **'The history of Singapore is also one of increasing censorship and social control.'**

Lee Kuan Yew gathered around him highly capable men who set about building a nation: Yusof Ishak became the first president and national figurehead; Goh Keng Swee lured multinational corporations to take advantage of a well-educated workforce; Lim Kim San initiated a massive programme of housing construction, clearing cemeteries and villages to build the Housing Development Board (HDB) blocks where 83 per cent of Singaporeans now live; S Rajaratnam oversaw foreign

Don't miss
War sites

Singapore may have changed out of all recognition in the 60 years since the end of World War II, but it's littered with reminders of the events leading up to the British surrender and afterwards. Many sites have been preserved or turned into museums; these are the main ones.

The Battle Box
The underground headquarters of the Allies, in Fort Canning Park. *See p60.*

Changi Chapel & Museum
Tells the story, by turns chipper and horrific, of life in the notorious internment camp. Includes a re-creation of its mural-covered chapel. *See p94.*

Fort Siloso
A 19th-century fort on Sentosa that was also used in World War II. Contains the most comprehensive exhibition on the war. *See p84.*

Kranji War Memorial
A tranquil cemetery (*pictured*) remembering the thousands of Allied and Empire deaths. *See p101.*

Labrador Secret Tunnels
Nineteenth-century tunnels in Labrador Park used in the British defence. *See p82.*

Memories at Old Ford Factory
The site of the British surrender to the Japanese. *See p98.*

Reflections at Bukit Chandu
Commemorates the bravery of the Malay Regiment in the dying days of the defence of Singapore. *See p98.*

Father figure: **Lee Kuan Yew** in 1965.

policy, carving out a place for his fledgling nation on the world stage and fostering an official ideology of 'multiracialism' at home; and CV Devan Nair took the unions in hand, establishing a 'tri-partite' system of co-operation between business, the PAP and the National Trades Union Congress. And Lee Kuan Yew had a hand in everything.

The motivation behind all these achievements was national survival. Against a backdrop of tensions with Indonesia and Malaysia (even today, you won't find a Malaysian newspaper in Singapore) and without a unified ethnic or religious identity to fall back on, or even a heroic independence struggle to lionise, the government sought to invent a nation – both as place and idea – as it went along. The small size of the state and the legacy of colonial structures helped. The 1966 Land Acquisitions Act enabled the state to annex large swathes of land for infrastructure like roads and housing; social engineering initiatives soon followed. Only Singaporeans who are married or over 35 may apply for an HBD flat, for instance, one of the few things (along with medical insurance and certain stocks and shares) that can be paid for with their Central Provident Fund accounts, made up of the 20 per cent of income deducted monthly at source and supplemented by a contribution from the employer. Such measures were matched with initiatives to promote a sense of national identity. These include two years of National Service for men (introduced in 1967), the annual National Day Parade, and hundreds of campaigns advising citizens on everything from hygiene to procreation to 'civil defence'.

Lee Kuan Yew believed that the fate of the nation lay in the hands of a tiny elite, so talented youngsters from all classes were groomed for jobs in the civil service and government-linked companies that ran key national industries. Meritocracy ensured social mobility, while state patronage encouraged political obedience. Indeed, given its dominance in parliament (from 1965 to 1981, there were no opposition MPs in Singapore, and since then only a sprinkling), a challenge to the PAP was seen as a challenge to Singapore itself.

So the history of Singapore is also one of increasing censorship and social control; the banning of independent print media; the detention without trial of leftists and 'Marxist conspirators'; the disbanding of bodies (such as the Chinese-language Nanyang University) seen to be promoting undesirable political or ethnic agendas; PAP politicians bankrupting opposition figures by suing them for libel; of film censorship; and of stringent control of the political content of websites. This continued throughout the prime ministership of Goh Chok Tong (1990-2004), though he was seen to govern in a softer style than his predecessor.

After the millennium, two events triggered forceful professions of the need for national cohesion. In 2001, documents detailing planned terrorist attacks on American and local targets in Singapore were discovered, and 31 local members of Jemaah Islamiah (JI), an Al-Qa'eda-linked group instrumental in the 2002 Bali attacks, were detained without trial under the Internal Security Act; as of early 2007, not all have been released. Then, in 2003, an outbreak of Severe Acute Respiratory Syndrome (Sars) killed 32 people. Building on existing programmes of social control and environmental management, strict hygiene and quarantine measures were introduced to curtail the spread of the disease.

In 2004, Singapore's third prime minister, Lee Hsien Loong (Lee Kuan Yew's son) came to power promising a more 'open and inclusive' society. The jury is out on that one, but it is easy to forget that Singaporeans have continued to live lives as open and inclusive as possible under the circumstances. From the 1950s to the '70s, a Malay and Chinese film industry flourished; in more recent decades, artists and theatre-makers explored the complexities of Singaporean identity; and civil society groups dealing with social and environmental topics have continued to emerge – albeit sporadically. A people's history of the republic remains to be written – although the new National Museum of Singapore on Stamford Road, which opened at the end of 2006, has made a valuable start.

Key events

c300 Early Chinese account of Singapore describes the island of 'Pu Luo Chung'.
c1300 Sang Nila Utama founds Singapura, on the island of Temasek.
1349 The Chinese traveller Wang Dayuen writes his account of Temasek, noting the cohabitation of Chinese and Malays.
c1400 Iskandar Shah, fifth king and possible usurper of the throne, flees to Malacca.
1511 Portuguese attack Malacca; Temasek becomes part of Sultanate of Johor.
1603 The Dutch and Portuguese fight a sea battle off the coast of Singapore.
1819 Sultan Hussain and Temenggong Abdul Rahman grant Sir Stamford Raffles permission to establish a 'factory' on Singapore for the British East India Company.
1824 The Anglo-Dutch Treaty signed, the Dutch withdraw all objections to British occupation of Singapore and return Malacca to the British.
1826 Dr John Crawfurd renegotiates with the Sultan and Temenggong to claim all of Singapore for the Straits Settlements.
1852 A new deep harbour called New Harbour (later Keppel Harbour) is built.
1867 Straits Settlements become a crown colony of British Empire.
1869 The Suez Canal opens; Singapore benefits economically.
1877 William Pickering appointed Protector of the Chinese; dismantling of Triads begins.
1887 The Raffles Hotel is built.
1906 Dr Sun Yat Sen establishes the Singapore branch of the Tongmeng Hui to work towards revolution in China.
1915 The Sepoy Mutiny.
1922 Singapore becomes the main British naval base in East Asia.
1927 Kreta Ayer riots and trolleybus boycott.
1941 Japan begins Pacific War and attacks Malaya; air raids on Singapore.
1942 The British surrender and the Japanese 'Syonan' occupation begins; 25,000-50,000 killed in Sook Ching massacre.
1945 Japanese surrender to the British.
1946 Straits Settlements dissolved; Singapore becomes a separate crown colony.
1948 Limited elections. Communists initiate an armed insurgency; Malayan Emergency is declared by the British.
1950 Ethnic riots following a custody battle between Dutch parents and Malay-Muslim foster parents: 18 killed.

1953 Rendel Commission established to recommend structures for self-government; proposes finance, administration, internal security and law to remain with the British.
1954 Hock Lee bus riots exemplify left-wing unrest: four killed.
1955 Electoral success of Singapore Labour Front: David Marshall first chief minister.
1957 Lim Yew Hock gains full self-government for Singapore.
1959 People's Action Party (PAP) wins general election: Lee Kuan Yew becomes first prime minister.
1962 Referendum approves merger with Malaysia.
1963 Operation Coldstore: 107 left-wingers detained by Internal Security Department. Singapore joins an independent Malaysia. The PAP wins the state elections.
1965 Ejected from Malaysia, Singapore becomes independent and is admitted into the United Nations as its 117th member.
1967 National Service begins. Singapore a founding member of the Association of South east Asian Nations (ASEAN).
1968 PAP wins clean sweep in a general election boycotted by the Barisan Sosialis.
1971 Reneging on a commitment to remain, British military forces leave Singapore.
1972 PAP wins clean swoop in general election. Singapore Airlines launched.
1981 Changi International Airport opens. Workers' Party JB Jeyaretnam wins by-election to break PAP monopoly of parliament.
1990 After 31 years as PM, Lee Kuan Yew is replaced by Goh Chok Tong.
1993 PAP preferred candidate Ong Teng Cheong becomes the first directly elected president.
1994 American teenager Michael Fay caned for vandalism.
1999 PAP candidate Sellapan Ramanathan becomes president. Asian financial crisis triggers recession.
2000 Speaker's Corner launched at Hong Lim Park. Speakers must register with the police.
2001 15 suspected militants of Jemaah Islamiah are arrested for alleged bomb plot.
2003 Sars virus outbreak in Singapore.
2004 Lee Hsien Loong sworn in as PM.
2005 Government breaks with tradition and approves plan to legalise casino gambling.
2006 The PAP wins 82 of 84 seats in the general election.

Singapore Today

Size doesn't matter: this tiny city-state has big ambitions.

No, Singapore is not part of China; yes, the commercial import of chewing gum is banned (although the chewing of it isn't); ye-e-es, the sci-fi writer William Gibson had a point when, in the early 1990s, he described the place as 'Disneyland with the death penalty'; and right you are – it is very, very clean.

Oh, and did you know foreign reports on Singapore are given to cliché? Barring 'part of China', even the most lazy Western journalistic saws about Singapore have some truth to them, but that tends to be where the descriptions end, rather than begin. A shame. Not only is the reality much more complicated, but – and here's where the hacks miss a trick – it's often much more bizarre.

Nicknames are one way of getting a grip on modern Singapore: Lion City, Garden City, 'Fine' City, New Asia. Comparisons (a popular journalistic pastime) are another: Sparta, Manchester, Israel, Switzerland, Beirut, Cuba – where would you like to go today? But there have been so many, they soon start to cancel one other out. Singapore is, after all,

an inadvertent nation, which has made itself up as it has gone along.

It proudly proclaims its Asianness and denounces 'decadent Western values' – in English. It routinely tops world globalisation indexes, while languishing alongside North Korea and Iran near the bottom of press freedom surveys. Its markets are open, its politics closed. Its people are brainy and cosmopolitan, but its public culture parochial (as evidenced daily by the stultifying letters page of the *Straits Times*). Its propaganda and nationalistic mass displays are straight out of Maoist China, its housing policies and pervasive government involvement in business recall the ruling People's Action Party's (PAP) socialist roots, while its anti-welfarism and celebration of materialism are true-blue Thatcherite. In short, the city-state's small size, densely packed and driven population, colonial history, multicultural make-up and strategic location – all subjected to the singular vision and authoritarian genius of its 'founding father', Lee Kuan Yew – combine to sweep the Tourist

Board guff aside and stake a claim on what is really 'uniquely Singapore'.

There are, in consequence, two ways of finding out what makes Singapore tick. The first is to put down this book and talk to somebody, then somebody else, then somebody else. Daily life is conspicuously absent from most representations of Singapore. Its arts are abstract, idealised or deal with the privileged anxieties of the leisure classes; its television mistakes product placement for reality and consuming for living; public space is first and foremost a retail commodity. The blogosphere aside (*see p24* **www.blog.sg**), Singaporeans seem to have adopted a 'don't ask, don't tell' policy towards local life. This can make even the most casual chat an education you won't get anywhere else.

Then there's the second way of getting to know Singapore from the inside-out. Start with an event, or a place or a person, and work your way through the degrees of separation that link everything up. The republic is small and centrally controlled, so the connections aren't hard to make.

GLOBAL ASPIRATIONS

Take, for instance, 'Singapore 2006: Global City, World of Opportunities', an event whose all-encompassing title perfectly suits the task at hand. Taking place over a week in September 2006, this was the name given to the annual meetings of the boards of governors of the International Monetary Fund (IMF) and the World Bank. Despite the scale of the event – 16,000 delegates descended on a newly fortified Suntec Exhibition Centre, near Raffles City – it was in most regards unremarkable. No major breakthroughs in world trade negotiations were made, nor did protestors strike any headline-grabbing blows. However, in its very unremarkableness, it was a typically Singaporean event, one born of the mix of competence and constraint that characterises many aspects of local life.

For example, it reaffirmed Singapore's global position as a financial centre and as an international player that boxes above its weight. Located within a politically volatile region and with few natural resources of its own, Singapore has long looked beyond the neighbourhood to build its economy; and as its increasingly educated workforce has been priced out of the mass-production market, the government has aggressively promoted a 'knowledge-based economy'. Now that major cities worldwide have pretty much equal access to the same financial information and technological know-how, Singaporeans realise that the challenge is to be more innovative

or efficient – which is to say, profitable. This attitude, on top of running the world's busiest port, leading the way in industries ranging from semiconductor manufacturing to oil-rig installation, and investing heavily in biomedical research and new media, is what makes Singapore so globalised, and a place where the good people of the IMF and the World Bank would feel right at home.

Meanwhile, Singapore's diplomats have long sought to raise their nation's international political profile. They have persuaded several world powers – most notably the US – that it is in their strategic interests to look out for the security of the island. Although highly militarised and heavily defended (20 per cent of Singapore's scarce land is reserved for military use, while, at US$25.3 billion, its 2006 defence budget was ten times that of massive Indonesia), it is nevertheless vulnerable simply by virtue of being so small.

Singapore 2006 not only highlighted these global aspirations, but cemented a growth industry: MICE (Meetings, Incentives, Conventions & Exhibitions). With Changi Airport among the world's best, Singapore has long been a transit centre and favoured stopover point. But the advent of long-range planes that don't need to refuel means people have to be persuaded to get off here. Along with so-called 'health tourism' (for a price, Singapore offers excellent healthcare), MICE is key to this aim. It informed the government's decision in 2005 to do away with a long cherished sacred cow, and permit the development of two large scale casino complexes – or 'integrated resorts' (IRs), as they are euphemistically known – due to be operational by 2009.

'Singaporeans are reluctant to participate in activities perceived as "political".'

No major government initiative in Singapore is complete without its attendant campaigns. Since independence in 1965, these have been rolled out in their hundreds to instruct the public in everything from hygiene to courtesy to curbing the birth rate (during the 1970s and '80s, the last proved so successful that a counter-campaign had to be introduced: 'Stop at two' was replaced with the not-so-snappy 'Have three or more if you can afford it'). Singapore 2006 was no exception, with the 'Go the extra mile for service' campaign aimed at getting the nation's perennially inept waiting staff and shop assistants to buck up, while the

Meanwhile, the 'anchor cultural event' for Singapore 2006 was the nation's first Biennale. Taking place in numerous sites across town, it was an epic undertaking that aimed to establish Singapore on the international art map, but many in the Singapore arts community have been asking, with some justification, whether high-profile investments in infrastructure and signature events might more meaningfully be spent on the artists themselves.

If there's one thing, however, that Singapore 2006 is not so well placed to illustrate, it's the everyday concerns of ordinary Singaporeans. These are poorly represented in the arts and media, so the best way to learn more is to live it, if only for a while. Head out of town, park yourself in a coffeeshop, and these are some of things you might learn. Race and ethnicity is far more complicated than the conventional 'Chinese, Malay, Indian, Other' classification suggests – people's official designation often doesn't map on to the language they speak, the religion they profess, or who, deep down, they

feel themselves – and others – to be; food tastes nicer when the place is a little bit dirty; there is resentment of the 'elite', and anxiety about an influx of foreigners taking local jobs; they know what they're told is propaganda, but they believe it anyway; there is no end to what can be said about local food; old superstitions run deep – offerings are left out, rituals are carefully observed, and any significant combination of figures, from the patterns on a fish to the licence plate of a crashed car, may be the answer you need to get lucky in the lottery; there is no limit to how far people will travel for a good chilli crab; Korean soap operas are all the rage; the vast majority of people have complicated family histories, and skeletons in the closet; Chinese dialects – despite the best efforts of the 'Speak Mandarin' campaign – are not dead; Singlish – despite the best efforts of the 'Speak Good English' campaign – is everywhere; some people squat on the toilet seat; the best biryani is in Tekka Market – you have to queue for 45 minutes, but it's worth it.

Growing pains

While Singapore is often described by people from more history-barnacled places as 'futuristic', it too has a future, and it's called Downtown at Marina Bay. In the pipeline since the early 1980s, this massive new development – set to expand the CBD by 70 per cent – comes courtesy of a huge land reclamation project. Extending from Shenton Way to the large swathe of empty land across the bay from the Merlion, the scheme's first couple of skyscrapers have already gone up. Subsequent years will see the opening of one of two casino complexes (the other is on

Sentosa), a green corridor running the length of the main precinct, a bridge to the Esplanade area, and a marina.

Even by Singapore standards, building an entirely new downtown from scratch is ambitious. However, the government is counting on a population increase of two million within 20 years (from the current 4.5 million) to keep the economy ticking over – and, given falling birth rates, a yuppie paradise is just the kind of bait it needs to reel in so-called 'foreign talent'. Not scheduled for completion until 2025, the development is clearly a risky business. The addition of so much more office space is less about meeting current demands than stimulating future need; and it will make Singapore even more vulnerable to the vicissitudes of the global markets. Nevertheless, the sheer scale of the plan puts even moderately ambitious cities like London in the shade; and if anyone can turn a 'can-do' attitude into tangible results, it's Singapore Inc.

Culture, Race & Religion

Welcome to the ultimate melting pot.

The population of Singapore is predominantly Chinese (76.7 per cent), with significant numbers of Malays (14 per cent) and Indians (7.9 per cent). Eurasians and other minority groups make up the remaining 1.4 per cent.

The Chinese arrived in the Malay archipelago as early as the 14th century, from southern China. A unique Chinese sub-group are the Peranakans (also called the Straits Chinese) – the product of intermarriage between Chinese and Malay immigrants and locals. The Malays are the indigenous people, of course, but some Malays from Indonesia also made Singapore their home. The Indians trace their roots back to southern India, with most being Tamil speakers. The Eurasians resulted from colonial rule and the many European trading enterprises that settled in the region: Portuguese, British and Dutch settlers intermarried with local Indians, Malays, Chinese, Bataks and other races. One distinct Eurasian group is descended from the Luso-Malay or Kristang in Malacca (now Melaka), which was conquered by Portugal in 1511.

There's also a significant foreign element: about 18 per cent are non-resident foreigners, and another seven per cent permanent residents. The largest communities are Malaysian, American, British, Australian, French, German, Japanese, Swiss, Filipino, Thai and Indonesian, while rapidly growing groups include Nigerians, South Africans, Russians, and Chinese and Indian nationals. Since the 1960s, and increasingly in recent decades, overseas companies have set up offices and regional headquarters in Singapore, a move that has added significantly to the cultural mix. But the largest numbers of foreigners are domestic helpers (many from the Philippines, Indonesia and Sri Lanka) and construction workers (largely from India, with pockets of Koreans, Thais and Malaysians).

TALK, TALK, TALK

So it's not surprising that Singapore is a modern-day Babel. There are with four official languages (English, Chinese, Tamil and Malay, which is also the national language), and many unofficial languages, including Bengali, Gujarati, Javanese and Madurese, dialects such as Hokkien, Teochew, Cantonese, Hakka, Hainanese and Hockchew, and creoles such as Baba Malay and Malaccan Portuguese. And, of course, Singlish, Singapore's unique gift to the English-speaking world (*see p29* **Got Singlish, lah!**). And that's just the locals. If you include the languages spoken by expats and foreign workers, the number is multiplied many times and added to by the day.

English being the linguistic common denominator helps hugely: foreigners visiting Singapore rarely have difficulty communicating what they need as long as they speak English. It's common for Chinese, Indian and Malay taxi drivers, hawkers and others in the service sectors to speak more than one language on a casual basis – a smattering of English (enough to get you from the airport to your hotel), a touch of Mandarin (enough to get food) and phrases in Malay (enough to get a smile).

And to streamline communication, give the Chinese a common identity and ease business with China, the government strongly encourages the use of standard Mandarin. Chinese Singaporeans used to segregate themselves by dialect (traditionally, even marriage between dialect groups was frowned upon), but with the government's eradication of dialect from media and education, such distinctions have all but disappeared. (This move has also been

MRT sign in English, Chinese and Tamil.

blamed for a widening generation gap, as the young and the dialect-speaking old find it hard to communicate.)

CULTIVATING COLOUR BLINDNESS

Historically, Singapore was geographically determined by race. The Jackson Plan of 1822 divvied the chief areas into European Town, housing European traders, Eurasians and wealthy Asians; Chinese Kampong for the ethnic Chinese; Chulia Kampong for the Indians; and Kampong Glam for the Muslims (ethnic Malays and Arabs). Even suburban areas were occupied by subgroups; for example, the Teochews settled in Hougang and the Peranakans in Katong.

> **'You can't stop a Singaporean from talking about money, but religion is a taboo topic.'**

Today, many of these areas still betray their ethnic origins, but are far from homogenous: city planners have deliberately engineered things so that no one area belongs exclusively to one race. Where you find a mosque, you'll find a Buddhist or Hindu temple or a church within a two-kilometre radius – sometimes all three. Every Housing Development Board (HDB) estate has a quota for each of the main races. Flat-owners wanting to sell their property are obliged to sell to their own race, to maintain the desired quota. (Not always a good deal for the seller, since it may be difficult to find a buyer of the same minority race, and returns are limited.) Expats are also renting HDB apartments, adding even more diversity.

While these policies are sometimes clumsy and may seem intrusive, it can be argued that they have done the job rather well. Incidences of explicit interracial hostility are extremely rare. Whether this 'big happy family' extends to all is a point of debate: only 7.4 per cent of HDB occupants surveyed in 2004 said they made an effort to talk to neighbours of other races (though this may just mean that HDB dwellers prefer to mind their own business).

Why all this effort to make everyone get along? History has been the greatest teacher. Singapore began as part of Malaya (now Malaysia), and its ejection in 1965 has affected the tiny nation in many ways. One of the reasons for the split was the objection by Lee Kuan Yew (who became first prime minister of newly independent Singapore) to Malaysia's 'bumiputra' practice, which segregated the Malays from other races by giving them positions and privileges. Race riots between

Got Singlish, lah!

From the 1960s to the early '80s, most Singaporeans grew up in multilingual households and kampongs (villages), where Chinese dialects, English and Malay were all freely spoken (and sung), and it was natural to switch rapidly between languages and modes of address depending on who you were chatting to. This, in part, led to the rise of what was then called Singapore English, but is now commonly known as Singlish – a pidgin English that draws heavily from Chinese grammar translated back into English, spoken with the fluid cadences and speed of Malay, and peppered with earthy Hokkien, Malay and some Tamil expressions.

The powers that be viewed the form as corrupted English, potentially unintelligible to outsiders, and although that's partly true (much of Singlish derives from the mispronunciation of English words), it's an oft-observed irony that with all the state's promotion of racial harmony, it actively discourages the one mutual language in which all Singaporeans can communicate. Singlish, along with Chinese dialects, was effectively banned from radio and TV, although these days you'll sometimes hear TV presenters and DJs speak a very mild version of it.

There are, crudely speaking, two kinds of Singlish – the version spoken by less-educated Singaporeans, for whom it really is the only 'English' they know (which can be indecipherable for visitors); and the kind used by people who speak English as

a first language but code-switch to Singlish with friends, or when they want to break the ice. 'Speak Good English' campaigns may have tried to counter the prevalence of Singlish, but it remains in rude health, and is the source of much Singaporean humour.

CLASSIC SINGLISH

● Adding lah to the end of sentences or exclamations for emphasis, such as telling an impatient person to 'Wait, lah!'. There are other versions of this, lor, meh and mah being favourites.

● Abbreviating sentences until all that's left is the verb. In answer to a query about driving to the airport, a taxi driver might reply 'can', or 'cannot'. A more elaborate version would be 'want' (I want to do it) and 'don't want' (I don't want to do it), which might sound like 'wan' and 'donwan', as the t will usually be dropped.

● Many Malay and Hokkien nouns are used, regardless of the race of the person being addressed. So, when ordering Chinese dishes a Singaporean might say 'no sotong' (Malay for squid); or when ordering fried noodles from a Malay stall 'don't want taugeh' (Hokkien for beansprouts).

● Over the years English expressions and verbs have taken on new, very specific meanings in Singlish. For instance, 'spoilt' means broken, as in 'this camera is spoilt', and 'to keep' literally means 'to put away' – thus 'keep the clothes' would mean 'put the clothes away'.

the Malays and the Chinese accompanied this tumultuous period. Lee stuck to his belief in a non-segregated society; and the nation today is the result of his vision. Four decades of efforts and programmes to promote interracial and interreligious peace are accompanied by swift and uncompromising punishment of anyone and anything that threatens this peace.

THE GOD FACTOR

There's a saying that two things never to bring up in civilised conversation are money and religion. You couldn't stop a Singaporean from talking about money, but religion is a taboo topic. Public discussion of religious matters, especially outspoken criticism, is not encouraged. People may discuss religion casually, but if there is any hint that you are being insulting, it could constitute an offence.

But that's not to say religion is not important. Just over 85 per cent of residents say they have a faith: 42.5 per cent are Buddhist, 14.0 per cent Muslim, 14.6 per cent Christian, 8.5 per cent Taoist, 4 per cent Hindu, and the remaining 0.6 per cent Jews, Mormons and other minority beliefs. Buddhism is, by default, the main religion because of the predominance of the Chinese, but the country is not overwhelmingly Buddhist – unlike, say, Thailand. It's common to find amalgamations of Buddhism, Taoism and ancestor worship, and several of the 242 Chinese temples on the island are 'combined'. Many Singapore Buddhists would be hard pressed to tell you what form of Buddhism they practise.

Only half the Indian population are Hindu, the rest being Muslims, Sikhs, Jains, Buddhists and Christians. Hindus may not be strong in numbers, but their presence is felt in loud and flamboyant festival processions and in the spectacular, colourful Dravidian architecture of their 24 temples.

Malays dominate the Muslim population, though Indian Muslims are not uncommon and the occasional Chinese, Eurasian or Caucasian marries into the faith. There are 70 mosques, and the Islamic Religious Council of Singapore (MUIS) pretty much determines how Muslims live their lives, with a sharia court established since the 1950s to deal specifically with Muslim divorce proceedings.

Christianity entered Singapore shortly after Raffles. The first Roman Catholic mission was in 1821, and Catholicism developed a stronghold in the region thanks to the influence of Portuguese-occupied Malacca. Thirty-two of Singapore's 292 churches are Catholic, serving 210,000 followers, mostly Chinese, Eurasians and Indians. There are twice as many Protestants, divided into numerous denominations (including Anglican, Baptist, Presbyterian, Lutheran and Methodist). Christianity has been on the rise in the past two decades, with evangelical megachurches, in particular, multiplying at a blistering rate. While lacking anything like the political clout of their US counterparts, these are set to play an increasingly prominent role in shaping social attitudes. City Harvest Church, which holds

services at the Singapore Expo to accommodate its 22,000-strong congregation, is the second largest church in Asia.

The government also has a banned list of religions (including Jehovah's Witnesses and the Unification Church), based on their potential to hurt racial or religious harmony and thus threaten social stability. In 2002, 30 Jehovah's Witnesses were imprisoned for refusing to perform National Service (a legal obligation for all male citizens). A handful of school students, also Jehovah's Witnesses, have been suspended for refusing to sing the national anthem, recite the pledge or salute the flag. The authorities also keep their eye on the Chinese spiritual sect of Falun Gong; recently, two women were arrested for protesting without a permit.

In general, the different races and religions mix happily. Chinese and Indians, for example, will join in Hari Raya celebrations at a Malay friend's house. And Christmas is a holiday celebrated by many as a time of gift-giving.

What constitutes common ground for all is the superstitious nature of your average Singaporean, most evident during the Chinese Hungry Ghost Festival. Malay folk culture has an equally strong influence, with myths such as the Pontianak, a beautiful but deadly female demon. Bestselling books include the *True Singapore Ghost Stories* series (750,000 copies sold to date). Note to women visitors: if you have long black hair, don't try flagging a cab alone at night during Ghost Month, particularly in suburban areas. Female ghost passengers are a popular urban myth, and superstitious drivers don't take chances.

FOR THE COMMON GOOD

Sceptics feel the government's heavy-handed style has discouraged the kind of creativity and natural-born vibrancy that is evident in other multiracial cities, such as London and New York. On the other hand, many appreciate the peaceful coexistence of Singapore's numerous cultures and races. What's hard to argue against is that such stability is good for economic growth, as shown by the country's attractiveness to foreign investors, and its ability to bounce back quickly from disasters like the 1997 Asian financial crisis.

Like a protective parent, Singapore's government works hard to inculcate practices that have kept the youthful country relatively free from race- and faith-related strife. In 2006, two young Chinese men found guilty of inciting hatred against another race through their blogs were swiftly caught, tried and jailed, and made a public spectacle of in the *Straits Times* to demonstrate just how serious the government is about keeping the peace. Get along, or else.

A 19th-century **Peranakan** family. *See p27.*

Architecture

The building blocks of Singapore.

Thanks to Stamford Raffles, who devised the first Singapore Town Plan in 1822, Singapore became a planned city barely three years after its founding. The plan laid out the fabric of the city centre by defining government and business districts, as well as ethnic enclaves for the different migrant communities. Its imprint can still be seen today in the form of the civic district, the business area around Shenton Way, and the ethnic areas of Little India, Chinatown, and the Arab Quarter.

Flourishing trade brought with it rapid population growth (from 150 residents in 1819 to 185,000 in 1911) and expansion of the city. The colonial government set up the Singapore Improvement Trust (SIT) in 1927 to alleviate urban congestion and look after public infrastructure. This included the first public housing schemes; of the five remaining SIT estates, the most notable is the art-deco inspired Tiong Bahru estate (1936-54, *see p95*).

The Housing & Development Board (HDB) replaced the SIT in 1960, and set about providing affordable mass housing for the ever-growing population. While the HDB was busy building homes and resettling people, the Urban Redevelopment Authority (URA), form in 1974, was given the task of reshaping and transforming the city centre. Today, it's the planning authority for the whole nation.

The relentless growth and building boom experienced from the 1960s to the '80s result in the demolition of many colonial buildings and shophouses. Many significant structure have disappeared, including the National Theatre, Amber Mansions on Orchard Roa Court on Stamford Road and the famous M Polo Hotel. Except for the occasional outcr most Singaporeans – a pragmatic lot – have accepted the fate of their rapidly changing city.

But it's not all doom and gloom. The Preservation of Monuments Board (PMB) was established in the '70s to safeguard historical landmarks. To date, it has listed 55 buildings, mainly religious ones, as national monuments. The URA has also identified areas deemed worthy of conservation; around 6,000 buildings (mostly shophouses) are located within

The high life

Over 80 per cent of Singaporeans live in (and own) high-rise, high-density flats – a solution to the problems of overcrowding and limited land resources – all built by the Housing & Development Board and concentrated within seven large public housing estates and 23 new towns. Visitors used to associating public housing with poverty, neglect and social unrest will be astonished by how well it can work. Numerous rules and regulations covering eligibility, racial quotas and so on, and a hefty dollop of social engineering, play their part, but Singapore's public housing progamme is certainly one of its greatest achievements.

In the beginning, the HDB erected one- to three- room utilitarian flats to house low-income families, many from squatter settlements and urban slums. By the late 1970s, when basic housing needs had been met, more spacious flats with four to five rooms were built. In the '80s and '90s, the programme extended to the development of integrated townships. Enormous new towns were built further away from the city centre, each equipped with a central bus and rail terminus and a network of new roads and expressways.

To improve community cohesiveness, the new towns were divided into smaller neighbourhoods of 1,000-5,000 families, each with its own park and neighbourhood centre with a wet market, mini food court, shops, clinics and banks. Each neighbourhood was in turn subdivided into smaller precincts of 600-1,000 families, containing a car park, a communal building, a playground and garden.

To differentiate the new towns, each was given a thematic identity, based on cultural and historical roots, and a set of design guidelines. An example of this is Pasir Ris, which is designated a 'Seaside Town'. Stylised elements resembling wave forms, seashells and nautical ornaments have been incorporated into building exteriors, as well as the streets and landscaping, to evoke a marine environment.

Such details can get lost, however. Ironically, the sheer scale of the HDB's achievement – row upon row of identical blocks, stretching off into the distance – is also its most dispiriting aspect.

designated conservation zones, such as Little India, Chinatown, Boat Quay and Emerald Hill. These buildings are marked either for protection or 'envelope control'; the latter allows the building to be demolished and rebuilt in accordance with strict design guidelines.

For an overview of Singapore's urban fabric, visit the **Singapore City Gallery** (*see p66*), inside the URA's headquarters in Chinatown. The highlight is a massive scale model of the city, showing existing buildings as well as proposed developments. Below is a very abbreviated look at some of the key elements of Singapore's architectural make-up.

COLONIAL BUILDINGS

Singapore's colonial architecture owes much to Irish architect George Drumgoole Coleman, who helped shape the city's early skyline. Adopting the Palladian style, popular in 18th-century England, he cleverly modified it to suit tropical conditions. Classical orders were combined with traditional local design elements such as wide verandas, deep roof overhangs and louvred windows to keep out the sun and rain. Of the key buildings he designed, a few still stand, including the **Armenian Church** (1835, *see p59*) and Old Parliament House, now the **Arts House** (1827, *see p202*).

Coleman was succeeded by various surveyors, architects and engineers, notably John Turnbull Thompson, Major JFA McNair and Regent Alfred John Bidwell, who designed the city's first public and commercial buildings, schools and churches. McNair was responsible for the **Istana** (*see p79*). Built in 1869 as Government House, it was the official residence of the colonial governor; now it's the official residence of the president of Singapore. Another landmark is the Fullerton Building, now the **Fullerton Hotel** (*see p41*), designed by Keys & Dowdeswell in 1928. With its imposing Doric columns, it represented the heights of Palladian architecture and was Singapore's biggest building. It was also the centre of social, official and commercial life, occupied by such major institutions as the Singapore Club, the Chamber of Commerce and the General Post Office.

Most of Singapore's significant colonial buildings are in the civic district, on the north bank of the Singapore River, as dictated in Raffles' original Town Plan. Many are described in more detail in the Sightseeing chapters (*see p54-106*).

SHOPHOUSES

For visitors, the multicoloured, ornately decorated, low-rise shophouse is perhaps Singapore's most distinctive and attractive type of building. The earliest shophouses were built in Chinatown, Little India and the Arab Quarter, on narrow, elongated plots of land subdivided to maximise the number of units that could face the road. These utilitarian terraced timber structures with pitched attap roofs – a design originating in China – had deep interiors with business premises on the ground floor and dwelling quarters above. Airwells brought in light and ventilation. The 'five-foot way' – a continuous covered passage providing sheltered access next to the street – is a notable feature, and a design requirement imposed by Raffles himself.

'A distinctively Singaporean shophouse style evolved: Singapore Eclectic.'

From the 1850s to the 1930s, improvements were made to the original design. Red clay tiles replaced attap on the roof; plastered brick walls, instead of timber, permitted elaborate ornamentation on the façade. With the rise of wealthy Chinese merchants in the late 19th century, the shophouse developed a residential counterpart: the terrace house. And a distinctively Singaporean shophouse style evolved: Singapore Eclectic. A hybrid of Chinese, Malay and European features, it reflected the colonial community's rich and

Suntec City. See p34.

diverse cultural heritage, and was as eclectic and cosmopolitan as the city itself. Fine examples can be seen around Ann Siang Hill and Neil Road in Chinatown.

At its peak, Singapore Eclectic exhibited a profusion of styles and extravagance of decorations that challenged the imagination, inventiveness and skill of its plasterwork craftsmen. The curious mix of Renaissance motifs such as festoons and garlands, with animals, flowers and mythical creatures from Chinese folklore, plus other quirky ornaments, echo Chinese baroque. However, the use of classical orders on the exterior remained fairly repetitive. Such flamboyant designs are evident in the Geylang district and Joo Chiat Road.

In the 1930s, improved technology, the advent of modernism and changes in the social, economic and political climate brought an end to the shophouse. The nation woke up to its heritage rather late in the day, but since the 1980s, thanks to the URA's conservation efforts, many shophouses have been saved. Now designer offices occupy the upper floors, stylish restaurants, bars and shops the ground floor; others house hip boutique hotels.

BLACK AND WHITES
Bungalows and villas built before World War II are an endangered species in urbanised Singapore. Many beautiful houses have been torn down in the name of progress. Most of the survivors are 'black and whites', built mainly during the 1920s rubber boom to house senior British civil servants and, later, army officers.

Their distinctive black-painted timber frames and white plasterwork and walls are nostalgic reminders of mock Tudor houses in the Home Counties, but they also include features typical of traditional Malay kampong dwellings, such as wide roof overhangs, balconies, verandas and bamboo blinds, timber louvred screens and shutters to protect against the weather. Now owned by the government, they are often leased to overseas corporations or rented to expats.

Fine examples can be found near Orchard Road, on Goodwood Hill, Ridley Park, Nassim Road and Dalvey Road. Further afield, several are located at Adam Park, off Alexandra Road and off Sembawang Road.

RELIGIOUS BUILDINGS
Even the most jet-lagged visitor can't fail to notice the great number and variety of religious buildings in Singapore. The Hindu temples with their multicoloured gopurams (entrance towers) and kitsch sculptures, and the Buddhist temples with their rich, ornate decorations, are probably the most striking; but there are mosques and churches galore too. Even

minority races like the Jews, Armenians and Sikhs erected their own buildings for worship.

We've highlighted many of the key edifices in the Sightseeing chapters. Notable ones include **Thian Hock Keng Temple** (*see p67*), the oldest Chinese temple, completed in 1842; the **Sultan Mosque** (*see p75*), the only existing example of Saracenic architecture (a mix of Persian, Turkish, Moorish and Indian elements); **Sri Mariamman Temple** (*see p67*), the oldest Hindu temple, begun in 1827; English-Gothic **St Andrew's Cathedral** (*see p58*); and the **Armenian Church**, the oldest church.

Two recent religious buildings are also worth mentioning because of their progressive and contemporary approach. The Assyafaah Mosque (2004, 1 Admiralty Lane) – its large prayer hall defined by huge arches and clad in aluminium screens adorned in arabesque motifs – breaks from traditional mosque design; while the Church of St Mary of the Angels (2003, 5 Bukit Batok East Avenue 2) is a complex of finely crafted modernist volumes.

MODERN ARCHITECTURE

The Singapore skyline has changed hugely since the 1960s. Along with hundreds of high-rise public housing schemes, office buildings and shopping malls, barren reclaimed land has been turned into large-scale developments in the Marina area, namely Marina Square (1986), Suntec City (1997) and Millenia Singapore (1997). The conservation of old buildings and districts has also given rise to interesting developments where the new embraces the old – as at Far East Square (1998), China Square Central (2003) and Clarke Quay (2006). For the latter, British architect Will Allsop created oversized futuristic 'umbrellas' to shelter the open spaces between the old warehouses, now housing bars and restaurants.

Alsop's involvement is typical of how the recent architectural scene has been greatly influenced by foreign architects, thanks to the government's open-door policy of the 1970s. IM Pei's 50-storey OCBC Centre (1976) paved the way for a host of star names, including Kenzo Tange (UOB Centre, NTU campus, UE Square), Paul Rudolph (The Concourse, The Colonnade), Murphy Jahn (Hitachi Tower, Caltex House), Zaha Hadid (Biopolis), Richard Meier (Camden Centre), and Toyo Ito (VivoCity).

Joint ventures between local and foreign architects are also common, such as Esplanade – Theatres on the Bay (2002), the National Library (2005), the new Supreme Court (2005) and the Singapore Management University (2006). Strange, though, that despite their glittering reputations, these luminaries have not tended to create their best works in Singapore.

Although the island may appear to be a playground for overseas firms, a new generation of local architects is on the rise. Firms such as SCDA, WOHA, Forum Architects and W Architects have created a variety of contemporary buildings that suit local conditions using modernist design elements. Noteworthy residences are the Loft (Nassim Hill), 33 Robin (Robin Road), Lincoln Modern (20 Lincoln Road), River Place (60 Havelock Road), the Caribbean (Keppel Bay) and 1 Moulmein Rise.

THE FUTURE

As other cities in South-east Asia, such as Kuala Lumpur, Shanghai and Taipei, exert themselves in a global context, the pressure is on Singapore to promote itself as a vibrant, well designed, world city.

Key to this is a new-found awareness of the importance of landscaping and green design to soften the effects of the dense urban environment. The 'garden city' is already known for its tree-planting efforts, but now roof gardens, sky terraces, high-level courtyards and landscaped atriums will complement the vegetation found at ground level. Such green design concepts will feature in many of the high-profile, large-scale projects slated for completion in the next five years.

The most prominent and publicly debated new developments are the two 'integrated resorts', with a combined investment of $10 billion: one at Marina Bay (*see p26* **Growing pains**), the other on Sentosa (*see p86* **More, more, more**). Also eagerly awaited is the 50-storey Pinnacle at Duxton Plains, by local firm ARC Studio. Featuring seven residential blocks with sky gardens on the 26th and 50th levels, it will be Singapore's tallest and most densely populated public housing complex.

Other high-rise residences in the pipeline include the Sail at Marina Bay (Peter Pran) and the Reflections at Keppel Bay (Daniel Libeskind). The latter has six towers varying in height from 26 to 41 storeys, crowned with luxuriant gardens on sloping rooflines and linked by skybridges. The Sail will be the tallest residential development in the country, with two 'supertowers' of 63 and 70 storeys. Located in a mainly commercial district, it's a prime example of the URA relaxing time-tested rules to inject more life into the city centre.

One new structure that will be greeting most visitors to Singapore is Changi Airport's Terminal 3, scheduled to open in 2008. Featuring a huge cantilevered roof and, internally, natural lighting, patterns and textures, it will be a high-tech version of a giant rainforest canopy – a most appropriate introduction to this modern tropical metropolis.

Where to Stay

Shangri-La Hotel. *See p49*.

Where to Stay

From colonial gems to 72-storey giants, Singapore hotels are on the up and up.

The number of visitors to Singapore reached a record 9.7 million in 2006, with tourists staying an average of 4.2 days and spending a total of S$12.4 billion. The country's strategic location, right in the heart of South-east Asia, and the rise of low-cost airlines (making regional travel not just convenient but affordable) were partly responsible, along with a number of prominent global business events – IOC, ASEAN, IMF – held in the country that year.

As a result, the average hotel occupancy rate roared to 86 per cent, with room rates increasing by up to 20 per cent across the board. Singapore currently has 36,000 hotel rooms – pretty healthy for the 'little red dot', one of the smallest countries in the world – but the Singapore Tourism Board (STB) has stated the number of rooms needs to double by 2015.

New upmarket properties will certainly arrive to cope with the influx of high-rollers hoped to be drawn to Singapore's two new 'integrated resorts' (IRs) in Marina Bay and on Sentosa island – but they're some years away. Hotels in the pipeline include the prestigious St Regis on Cuscaden Road, three new resorts on Sentosa and the Boutique Hotel@Tiong Bahru, together adding another 700 rooms by the end of 2007. The Tiong Bahru establishment proves that the boutique hotel trend – as in the rest of the world – is here to stay.

Boutique hotels, however, are just one portion of the overall market. Singapore's accommodation choices are plentiful – from five-star, big-name luxury hotels to mid-priced options, budget joints and backpacker hostels. Prices are not as cheap as elsewhere in South-east Asia, of course, but travellers from Europe and North America will be pleasantly surprised by what their money will buy. At least for the moment: it's likely that prices will rise further, particularly if the current tourist taxes go up.

One thing is for sure: hotels will have to go the extra mile to win over customers. Already impressive service standards will have to be improved; facilities will need to be constantly upgraded; and personalised in-room extras and

bonuses will have to be extended to ensure long-lasting loyalty. In short, it will be the visitor who reaps the benefits in the long run.

WHERE TO STAY

The vast majority of Singapore's hotels are in the city centre. The biggest and swankiest hotels are found on and around Orchard Road, next to the city's shopping heart; and in the Marina area, on the edge of the Colonial District and near the CBD (Central Business District). Chinatown seems to have cornered the boutique hotel market, while Little India and the Arab Quarter are the best choice for visitors counting their pennies. There's also a cluster of good-value hotels at the eastern end of Orchard Road. For a beachside retreat, try the resorts on Sentosa.

BOOKING AGENCIES

The Singapore Tourism Board has a hotel directory/search facility on its website, **www.visitsingapore.com**, and also publishes a handy booklet with details, photos and maps for about 200 hotels, in all price brackets and areas. You can also book online via the Singapore Hotel Association's dedicated website, **www.stayinsingapore.com**; or, if you've arrived without somewhere to sleep, visit the SHA counters at terminals 1 and 2 at Changi Airport; there are four counters, two of which operate 24 hours a day. Useful online booking sites include **www.asiarooms.com**, **www.asiatravel.com** and **www.wotif.com**.

There are no high/low seasons as such, though June, July, October and November are traditionally busy months, as are public holidays such as Chinese New Year. December and January are also increasingly popular.

ABOUT THE LISTINGS

Price categories given below are based on the hotel's 'rack' rates for a standard double room: deluxe means $400 or above; expensive $300-$400; moderate $150-$300; budget under $150. Note that these rates are often higher than what you'll pay; and it's always worth asking for standby rates, website deals and other special offers. Rates are often written +++, meaning you will pay an extra ten per cent service charge, five per cent GST (Goods & Services Tax) and one per cent local tax. We've given hotels' postcodes, in case you need to write to them.

➊ Green numbers given in this chapter correspond to the location of each hotel as marked on the street maps.
See pp246-252.

Colonial District

Deluxe

Conrad Centennial

2 Temasek Boulevard, 038982 (6334 8888/ fax 6333 9166/http://conradhotels1.hilton.com). City Hall MRT then 10mins walk. **Rooms** 509. **Rates** $500 standard; $540-$580 deluxe; $700 suite. **Credit** AmEx, DC, JCB, MC, V. **Map** p251 M7 ❶

One of a cluster of hotels in the Marina/Suntec area, the Conrad Centennial stands out from the crowd. The 31-storey exterior is sleek and futuristic; the striking, tree-filled lobby is centred around a curved marble staircase and a postmodern sculpture. And the spacious bedrooms are decorated with taste and flair – an artful mix of minimalist and ornate styles. The creamy marble bathrooms ooze luxury. Business amenities include broadband and video/ audio conferencing. A palm-fringed pool and three restaurants complete the picture.

Bar. Business centre. Concierge. Disabled-adapted rooms. Gym. Internet (high-speed/wireless). No-smoking floors. Parking (free). Pool (outdoor). Restaurants (3). Room service. Spa. TV (pay movies/ cable/DVD).

Marina Mandarin Singapore

6 Raffles Boulevard, 039594 (6845 1000/fax 6845 1001/www.marina-mandarin.com.sg). City Hall MRT then 10mins walk. **Rooms** 575. **Rates** $450 deluxe; $550 premier; $700 suite. **Credit** AmEx, DC, JCB, MC, V. **Map** p251 L8 ❷

After a $25 million revamp, the Marina Mandarin positively sparkles. The rooms are crisp and elegant – done up in creams, beiges and browns – and all have balconies; some suites have views of the harbour. Meritus Club rooms come with extras such as coffeemakers, a six-jet power shower and plush pillow-top mattresses. The three restaurants (Italian, Chinese and international) are stylishly designed, and the lounge offers a soundtrack of tropical Asian birds. Other features include a 25m mineral water pool, the Open Studio (an artist-in-residence programme) and *dendrobium Marina Mandarin*, a local orchid that is scattered throughout the hotel in floral arrangements and as a decorative motif.

Bars (2). Business centre. Concierge. Disabled-adapted room. Gym. Internet (high-speed/wireless). No-smoking floors. Parking (free). Pool (outdoor). Restaurants (3). Room service. Spa. TV (pay movies/ music/DVD).

The Oriental

5 Raffles Avenue, 039797 (6338 0066/fax 6339 9537/www.mandarinoriental.com/singapore). City Hall MRT then 10mins walk. **Rooms** 527. **Rates** $430 standard; $520-$630 deluxe; $690-$3,000 suite. **Credit** AmEx, DC, JCB, MC, V. **Map** p251 M8 ❸

With its unusual fan-shaped structure and chic, glossy interiors, the Oriental makes a long-lasting impression. Rooms are decorated in neutral tones, complemented by polished hardwood floors and floor-to-ceiling windows. Features include sumptuous Jim Thompson bed covers, oversized bathtubs and laptop safes with charge points. For a view towards Pulau Ubin, ask for the deluxe ocean view room; the Club Harbour suite overlooks the harbour and the city. Restaurants include acclaimed steakhouse Morton's (*see p112*) – with potent Martinis in the adjoining bar (*see p131*) – and poolside Dolce Vita for scrumptious Italian cuisine.

Bar. Business centre. Concierge. Disabled-adapted rooms. Gym. Internet (high-speed/wireless/web TV). No-smoking floors. Parking (free). Pools (2, outdoor). Restaurants (5). Room service. Spa. TV (music/cable/DVD).

Pan Pacific Singapore

7 Raffles Boulevard, 039595 (6336 8111/fax 6339 1861/www.singapore.panpacific.com). City Hall MRT then 10mins walk. **Rooms** 750. **Rates** $480 standard; $510-$580 deluxe; $700 suite. **Credit** AmEx, DC, JCB, MC, V. **Map** p251 M7 ❹

Designed by acclaimed American architect John Portman in 1986, the Pan Pacific is a real showpiece. There's a groovy, retro-tinged lobby, a striking exterior dotted by bubble lifts, a 34-storey atrium (the tallest in town) and a public art gallery. The curious disc-like structure on the 37th floor houses top-notch Cantonese restaurant Hai Tien Lo; haute Indian cuisine is on offer at Rang Mahal (*see p112*). Deluxe rooms come with ergonomic Herman Miller chairs and glossy marble bathrooms. The Pacific Floor

 The best **Hotels**

For bathing beauties

The **Fullerton Hotel**'s infinity pool – with a backdrop of neo-classical columns – offers breathtaking views across the river and Colonial District. *See p41.*

For a room with a view

Enjoy unblocked harbour or city views at the **Oriental** (*see left*), or gaze as you bathe at the **Ritz-Carlton Millenia** (*see p39*).

For style and content

Boudoir glamour at the **Scarlet Hotel** (*see p42*) or idiosyncratic, individually designed rooms at the **New Majestic Hotel** (*see p42*)? It's a tricky choice.

For the lap of luxury

Princesses and presidents prefer the **Shangri-La** (*see p49*), **Grand Hyatt** (*see p50*) and **Four Seasons** (*see p47*).

For a superior hostel

Extras galore at the **Inn Crowd Hostel** (*see p46*).

rooms (on the 33rd and 34th floors) are even more luxurious, with a Hansgrohe massage shower, free broadband access and butler service.

Bar. Business centre. Concierge. Gym. Internet (high-speed/wireless/web TV). No-smoking floors. Parking (free). Pool (outdoor). Restaurants (6). Room service. Spa. TV (pay movies/music).

Raffles Hotel

1 Beach Road, 189673 (6337 1886/fax 6339 7650/http://singapore-raffles.raffles.com). City Hall MRT. **Rooms** 103. **Rates** from $1,000; presidential suite $6,000. **Credit** AmEx, DC, JCB, MC, V. **Map** p249 L6 ❺

The grand dame of colonial hotels, Raffles needs no introduction. Established in 1887, it still evokes an era when travel and romance went hand in hand, even if droves of tourists now flock here for a Singapore Sling at the Long Bar. Despite the clichés, the Raffles legend endures, thanks to its fusion of timeless elegance, classical architecture and tropical gardens. Buildings are linked by cool verandas, and rattan furniture and oriental rugs still dot the rooms. Refurbished in 1991, all 103 rooms are now suites; 12 are named after famous guests such as Rudyard Kipling, Noel Coward and Somerset Maugham. The seven Grand suites are the most nostalgic, with lofty ceilings, polished wooden floors, opulent drapes and balconies overlooking the garden. Among the numerous bars and restaurants are the traditional Raffles Grill and Long Bar Steakhouse, plus Asian offerings at Royal China and Doc Cheng's.

Bars (3). Business centre. Concierge. Disabled-adapted rooms. Gym. Internet (high-speed). No smoking rooms. Parking (rates vary). Pool (outdoor). Restaurants (10). Room service. Spa. TV (cable).

Raffles The Plaza

80 Bras Basah Road, 189560 (6339 7777/fax 6337 1554/www.rafflescityhotels.com). City Hall MRT. **Rooms** 769. **Rates** $520 standard; $580 deluxe; $4,200 suite. **Credit** AmEx, DC, JCB, MC, V. **Map** p251 K6 ❻

Not to be confused with the colonial legend opposite, this modern giant is nonetheless famous in its own right. Despite its colossal size, it has won awards galore. The swish rooms have chic decor, ultra comfortable beds and Bose sound systems; balconies offer skyline views. Bathrooms boast rainforest showerheads and marble tubs. The two pools are surrounded by lush greenery. And the Raffles Amrita Spa (*see p156* **Super spas**) pampers patrons silly.

Bar. Business centre. Concierge. Disabled-adapted rooms. Gym. Internet (high-speed/wireless). No-smoking floors. Parking (89). Pools (2, outdoor). Restaurants (8). Room service. Spa. TV (pay movies/music/DVD).

Ritz-Carlton Millenia

7 Raffles Avenue, 039799 (6337 8888/fax 6337 5190/www.ritzcarlton.com/hotels/singapore). City Hall MRT then 10mins walk. **Rooms** 608. **Rates** $550-$600 standard; $600-$650 deluxe; $700-$875 suite. **Credit** AmEx, DC, JCB, MC, V. **Map** p251 M8 ❼

Splash out at the **Ritz-Carlton Millenia**.

The Ritz-Carlton is a luxury hotel for culture vultures: Frank Stella's stunning sculpture, *Cornucopia*, sits in the lobby; and the rest of the building houses a 4,200-piece collection of modern art by the likes of Dale Chihuly and David Hockney (a catalogue is available). The large, glossy rooms come with raised beds, flatscreen TVs, DVD players and – a definite selling point – gorgeous bathrooms with Bulgari toiletries and a panoramic view (of the city or harbour) from the bathtub. Lavish tropical gardens surround the swimming pool. Four high-end restaurants include the Summer Pavilion (*see p112*), serving haute Cantonese cuisine.

Bar. Business centre. Concierge. Disabled adapted rooms. Gym. Internet (high-speed/wireless). No-smoking floors. Parking (rates vary). Pool (outdoor). Restaurants (4). Room service. Spa. TV (pay movies/music/cable/DVD).

Swissôtel The Stamford

2 Stamford Road, 178882 (6338 8585/fax 6338 2092/http://singapore-stamford.swissotel.com). City Hall MRT. **Rooms** 1,261. **Rates** $480 standard; $520-$560 deluxe; $1,300 suite. **Credit** AmEx, DC, JCB, MC, V. **Map** p251 K7 ❽

Designed by IM Pei, the legendary modernist architect, this skyscraper is a behemoth, comprising 72 storeys and over 1,200 rooms, along with numerous bars and restaurants, a helipad and its own entrance to City Hall MRT station. A popular choice with

flight crews and big tour groups, it has an air of hustle and bustle. The rooms are nothing to write home about – especially those on the lower levels – though the upper floors provide spectacular views. As does the New Asia Bar (*see p131*) on the 71st floor. The Stamford is part of the same complex as sister hotel Raffles The Plaza, and shopping centre Raffles City. *Bars (3). Business centre. Concierge. Gym. Internet (high-speed). No-smoking floors. Parking (free). Pool (2, outdoor). Restaurants (5). Room service. Spa. TV (pay movies/music/cable/DVD).*

Moderate

Novotel Clarke Quay

177A River Valley Road, 179031 (6338 3333/fax 6339 2854/www.novotel.com). Clarke Quay MRT.
Rooms 398. **Rates** $250-$275 standard; $325-$345 deluxe; $350-$410 suite. **Credit** AmEx, DC, JCB, MC, V. **Map** p250 I8 ⑨
Although the Novotel Clarke Quay was recently renovated, little about the property stands out. The rooms are clean and comfortable, but nothing special; bathrooms are smallish and the fixtures could do with an overhaul. The main attraction is its location – on tourist hotspot Clarke Quay, and near Boat and Robertson Quays.
Bar. Business centre. Concierge. Disabled-adapted room. Gym. Internet (high-speed/wireless). No-smoking floors. Parking (free). Pool (outdoor). Restaurant. Room service. TV (pay movies/music/DVD).

Chinatown & the CBD

Deluxe

Fullerton Hotel

1 Fullerton Square, 049178 (6733 8388/fax 6735 8388/www.fullertonhotel.com). Raffles Place MRT.
Rooms 399. **Rates** $620 standard; $670 deluxe; $1,080 suite. **Credit** AmEx, DC, JCB, MC, V.
Map p251 K9 ⑩
Built in 1928, the former General Post Office was transformed into an award-winning luxury hotel in 2001. The Palladian building is a striking landmark on the edge of the Singapore River; inside, the grand, soaring atrium makes the most of the unusual, wedge-shaped floorplan. The room aesthetics are cool, clean and serene; creams, beiges and browns, with dark wood furnishings and fresh flowers. All come with the latest gizmos and gadgets for staying connected. Request one of the Quay rooms, which have spectacular views over the river and colonial civic area. The splendid outdoor pool faces the same way; it's almost like you're swimming in the city. The slap-up buffet breakfast is one of the best in town, and classy cocktails are served in the fashionable Post Bar (*see p133*).
Bar. Business centre. Concierge. Disabled-adapted rooms. Gym. Internet (high-speed/wireless/web TV). No-smoking floors. Parking (free). Pool (outdoor). Restaurants (2). Room service. Spa. TV (pay movies/ cable/DVD).

Stamp of approval: award-winning post office-turned-luxury hotel the **Fullerton**.

Expensive

M Hotel Singapore

81 Anson Road, 079908 (6224 1133/fax 6227 9267/www.mhotel.com.sg). Tanjong Pagar MRT. **Rooms** 413. **Rates** $330-$390 standard; $430-$460 deluxe; $700-$800 suite. **Credit** AmEx, DC, JCB, MC, V.

Combining form and function, M Hotel is geared towards style gurus and business travellers alike. The innovative decor is themed around wood, fire, earth, metal and water, and the offices of the CBD are a walk away (as is the bustling port area; corner rooms overlook it). The chic, minimalist rooms boast sleek bathrooms, flatscreen TVs, mood lighting and high-speed internet access. A spa, gym and pool are located on the 11th floor: the spa comes with state of the art hydrotherapy facilities; two outdoor massage pools are equipped with 12 hydro-jets. The cool Café 2000 serves Asian fusion fare.
Bar. Business centre. Concierge. Disabled-adapted rooms. Gym. Internet (high-speed/wireless/web TV). No-smoking floors. Parking (free). Pool (outdoor). Restaurants (3). Room service. Spa. TV (pay movies).

New Majestic Hotel

31-37 Bukit Pasoh Road, 089845 (6511 4700/fax 6222 3379/www.newmajestichotel.com). Outram Park MRT. **Rooms** 30. **Rates** $310 standard; $370 aquarium room; $600 attic suites. **Credit** AmEx, MC, V. **Map** p250 G12 ⑪

M Hotel: a triumph of form and function.

Under the same ownership as nearby Hotel 1929 (*see below*), the New Majestic opened to great acclaim in 2006. From the big white lobby with its vintage fans and designer chairs to the idiosyncratic themed guest rooms – each one different – the whole place is a style statement. Brightly coloured wall murals, created by local artists and designers, are a feature, as are claw-footed bathtubs (perhaps encased in glass in the middle of the room, or set outside in a mini garden). Some rooms are two-level, others have hanging beds. There's a small pool, with portholes in the bottom that overlook the in-house Cantonese restaurant, Majestic (*see p113*). **Photo** *p43*.
Business centre. Concierge. Internet (high-speed/wireless). No-smoking rooms. Pool (outdoor). Restaurant. TV (cable).

Moderate

Berjaya Hotel

83 Duxton Road, 089540 (6227 7678/fax 6227 1232/www.berjayaresorts.com). Tanjong Pagar MRT. **Rooms** 47. **Rates** $257 standard; $292 deluxe; $467 suite. **Credit** AmEx, DC, JCB, MC, V. **Map** p250 H12 ⑫

This chic 47-room property was one of Singapore's earliest boutique hotels. Housed in an old Straits Chinese trading house, it has a shophouse exterior and an atmospheric, colonial-style interior (double-glazed french windows, wooden fixtures and magnificent chandeliers). No two rooms are alike; the duplex rooms come with a spiral staircase, while the garden suites offer guests their own indoor patch of greenery. Upmarket restaurant Casa Mediterranea serves traditional Ital-Med cuisine.
Bar. Concierge. Internet (high-speed/shared terminal/pay terminal). Restaurant. Spa. TV (pay movies).

Hotel 1929

50 Keong Saik Road, 089154 (6347 1929/fax 6327 1929/www.hotel1929.com). Outram Park MRT then 10mins walk. **Rooms** 32. **Rates** $160 standard; $225 deluxe; $280 suite. **Credit** AmEx, MC, V. **Map** p250 H11 ⑬

In 2002, owner Loh Lik Peng (who also owns the New Majestic – *see above*) turned five colonial shophouses into this 32-room boutique property. A vast collection of designer chairs – including vintage Verner Panton, and Charles and Ray Eames designs – decorate different corners of the hotel. Suites come with an outdoor bathtub, and there's a Jacuzzi on the rooftop. Admittedly, the rooms are a little on the small side, but they're equipped with flatscreen TVs, broadband and designer Marimekko bedspreads.
Business centre. Internet (high-speed). No-smoking rooms. Restaurant. TV (cable).

Scarlet Hotel

33 Erskine Road, 069333 (6511 3333/fax 6511 3303/www.thescarlethotel.com). Tanjong Pagar MRT then 10mins walk. **Rooms** 84. **Rates** $250 standard; $330 executive; $950 suite. **Credit** AmEx, DC, JCB, MC, V. **Map** p250 I11 ⑭

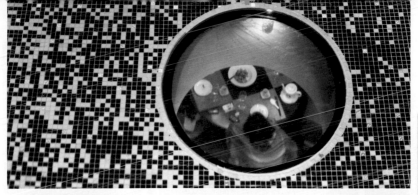

New Majestic Hotel. *See p42.*

The Scarlet is indeed scarlet – and gold and black; dramatic furniture, chandeliers and polished surfaces add to the sexy, boudoir-glam vibe. Occupying a series of shophouses at the top of Erskine Road, it's much favoured by media and design types. The public areas (especially the bar, lobby and lovely rooftop bar Breeze – *see p133*) are the best; rooms are small and some are windowless, though beds are comfortable. Opt for a suite, if you can. There's a tiny outdoor Jacuzzi and mini gym. **Photo** *p45*. *Bars. Business centre. Concierge. Disabled-adapted room. Gym. Internet (high-speed/wireless). No smoking. Restaurants (2). Room service. TV (cable).*

Budget

Inn at Temple Street

36 Temple Street, 058581 (6221 5333/fax 6225 5391/www.theinn.com.sg). Chinatown MRT. **Rooms** 42. **Rates** $110-$150 standard; $120-$170 deluxe; $150-$190 suite. **Credit** AmEx, DC, MC, V. **Map** p250 I10 ⑮

Bang in the heart of Chinatown, the Inn at Temple Street is a small hotel with big character. Owned by the sons of the late Kho Beng Kang (aka 'the Nutmeg King'), the hotel tries to revive the era when Kho was the region's largest spice trader. Hence there are plenty of decorative antique objects, along with intricately carved wooden furniture and murals. But rooms are small and some don't have windows (ask to see your room before checking in). *Internet (high-speed/shared terminal/pay terminal). No-smoking floor. TV.*

Royal Peacock Hotel

55 Keong Siak Road, 089158 (6223 3522/fax 6221 1770/www.royalpeacockhotel.com). Outram Park MRT then 10mins walk. **Rooms** 74. **Rates** $145 standard; $165 deluxe; $185 suite. **Credit** AmEx, DC, JCB, MC, V. **Map** p250 H11 ⑯

This boutique hotel, created out of ten beautifully refurbished shophouses, exudes character. The mood-lit lobby sets the stage for the sumptuous decor: dark wooden furnishings, dramatic red walls and drapes, plush purple carpets and gilt-edged

antique mirrors. Rooms are on the small side, but rates are very reasonable. The location, in a red-light district, adds to the frisson of decadence.
Bar. Disabled-adapted room. Internet (high-speed/ wireless/shared terminal/pay terminal). No smoking. Room service. TV.

Little India & the Arab Quarter

Expensive

InterContinental Singapore
80 Middle Road, 188966 (6338 7600/fax 6338 7366/www.ichotelsgroup.com). Dhoby Ghaut MRT. **Rooms** 409. **Rates** $370 deluxe; $400 shophouse; $450 club suite. **Credit** AmEx, DC, JCB, MC, V. **Map** p249 L6 ⑰
Situated in a clutch of restored 1920s shophouses, the InterContinental is a luxurious nostalgia kick. The elegant rooms fuse Peranakan and colonial decor: think oriental rugs, wooden floors and hand-painted lampshades, along with ornate tapestries. The old stuff contrasts with modern gadgetry (nifty iPod docking stations), and everything has a contemporary sheen. The rooftop pool has a tropical vibe with its palms. The traditional Victoria Bar evokes old Singapore; there's live jazz and Latin in the Lounge Bar; choose from Mediterranean, Japanese or Chinese food in the three restaurants. *Bars (2). Business centre. Concierge. Disabled-adapted rooms. Gym. Internet (high-speed). No-smoking rooms. Parking ($2 per entry.). Pool (outdoor). Restaurants (3). Room service. TV (cable/pay movies).*

Moderate

Albert Court Hotel
180 Albert Street, 189971 (6339 3939/fax 6339 3252/www.albertcourt.com.sg). Bugis MRT then 10mins walk. **Rooms** 210. **Rates** $160 standard; $180 deluxe; $190 suite. **Credit** AmEx, DC, JCB, MC, V. **Map** p248 K4 ⑱
The Albert Court Hotel is at the southern end of Little India, just over Rochor Canal. The building, a refurbished pre-war shophouse complete with a tropical courtyard, has got plenty of character. The epitome of 'old meets new', the rooms come with all mod cons – including broadband – but retain an authentic feel thanks to Peranakan touches. Extras include a gym, steam room and Jacuzzi. Good value. *Bar. Business centre. Disabled-adapted rooms. Gym. Internet (high-speed/wireless/shared terminal/ pay terminal). No-smoking floors. Parking (free). Restaurants (2). Room service. TV (cable).*

Golden Landmark
390 Victoria Street, 188061 (6297 2828/fax 6298 2038/www.goldenlandmark.com.sg). Bugis MRT. **Rooms** 393. **Rates** $210 standard; $250 executive club. **Credit** AmEx, DC, JCB, MC, V. **Map** p249 M4 ⑲

Located above an ageing shopping mall and accessed by an escalator, the Golden Landmark is not easy to find. But the rooms are spacious and well equipped (including cable TV and broadband), though the bathrooms could be spruced up. If the hotel lacks character, its location doesn't: the colourful shopping and eating options of Bugis and Arab Streets are nearby. Honeymooners and older guests might find it all a bit noisy, though the greenery around the pool provides some tranquility.
Bar. Business centre. Concierge. Disabled-adapted rooms. Internet (high-speed/wireless). No-smoking floors. Parking (free). Pool (outdoor). Restaurants (2). Room service. TV (cable).

Park Royal on Kitchener Road
181 Kitchener Road, 208533 (6428 3000/fax 6297 2827/http://kitchener.singapore.parkroyalhotels.com). Farrer Park MRT. **Rooms** 530. **Rates** $160 standard; $225 suite. **Credit** AmEx, DC, JCB, MC, V. **Map** p249 L2 ⑳
Located next to the Mustafa Centre and its 24-hour bustle, this chain hotel is a popular choice with Indian tourists. The ambience is, well, chain-like, but the 341 rooms have been refurbished and there are practical advantages (a self-service laundry, for instance, for long-term stays). The lap pool is large and enticing, and the Spice Brasserie serves local and international cuisine until 1am.
Bar. Concierge. Gym. Internet (high-speed/ wireless). No-smoking floors. Parking (rates vary). Pool (outdoor). Restaurants (2). Room service. TV (cable).

Boudoir glam at the sexy **Scarlet**. *See p42.*

Hangout@Mt Emily

Rendezvous Hotel

9 Bras Basah Road, 189559 (6336 0220/fax 6337 3773/www.rendezvoushotels.com). Dhoby Ghaut MRT. **Rooms** 299. **Rates** $240-$270 standard; $320-$395 deluxe; $500-$770 suite. **Credit** AmEx, DC, JCB, MC, V. **Map** p248 J5 ㉑

With its central location, the Rendezvous is easy for just that; it's handy for both the CBD and Orchard Road shopping, as well as the National Museum and Singapore Art Museum. The architecture is a curious hybrid: a three-storey colonial building backed by a modern 11-storey edifice. The fern-fringed lobby strikes an elegant note with its marble floor mosaics. Rooms are polished but plain: a quiet mix of white bedding and pastel hues. But the glass-roofed courtyard leaves the biggest impression, along with the Balinese-style swimming pool and the well-regarded Straits Café (try the nasi padang), which overlooks Bras Basah Park.
Bar. Concierge. Disabled-adapted rooms. Gym. Internet (high-speed/wireless/web TV). No-smoking floors. Parking ($5). Pool (outdoor). Restaurant. Room service. TV (pay movies).

Budget

Broadway Hotel

195 Serangoon Road, 218067 (6292 4661/fax 6235 1416/www.geocities.com/broadwayhotel/). Little India or Farrer Park MRT then 10mins walk. **Rooms** 63. **Rates** $80 double. **Credit** AmEx, MC, V. **Map** p248 K2 ㉒

There's nothing particularly spectacular about this three-star hotel with 63 modestly furnished rooms, but its location is great – bang in the heart of Little India. It's also good value for money, and rooms come with all the usual mod cons: cable TV, air-conditioning, a safe and even a hairdryer. Rollaway beds cost an extra $25.
Internet (shared terminal/pay terminal). No smoking. Parking (free). Restaurant. Room service. TV (cable).

Fragrance Hotel – Selegie

183 Selegie Road, 188329 (6337 7888/fax 6345 3433/www.fragrancehotel.com). Little India MRT. **Rooms** 98. **Rates** $88-$98 standard; $118 deluxe; $128 executive. **Credit** MC, V. **Map** p248 J4 ㉓

Despite the evocative name, this is not a decadent oasis. Instead, Fragrance is about getting a bang for your buck. True, this branch of the local chain boasts luxuries such as a rooftop swimming pool, broadband access and LCD TVs with DVD players. But the rooms are tiny – steer clear if you are either tall or claustrophobic. And the hotel can get noisy. Still, the location is tough to beat.
Business centre. Disabled-adapted rooms. Internet (shared terminal/pay terminal). Parking (free). Pool (outdoor). Room service. TV (cable).

Hangout@Mt Emily

10A Upper Wilkie Road, 228119 (6438 5588/fax 6339 6008/www.hangout-hotels.com). Little India MRT then 10mins walk. **Rooms** 6 dorm; 59 rooms. **Rates** $35 dorm; $140 twin; $240 quad. **Credit** MC, V. **Map** p248 J4 ㉔

A stylish little hotel-cum-hostel, perched atop Mount Emily Park, near the Istana. Rooms are basic, but clean and bright, with Ikea-style furniture; most are doubles, but a handful sleep three or more. The rooftop terrace is a bonus, with barbecue pit, 'standing shower pool' and loungers. Breakfast is served in the ground-floor dining area, which becomes the funky Wild Rocket restaurant at lunch and dinner. The Hangout is a short walk from Little India, but the steep steps make carrying luggage a no-no. Staff are friendly and obliging.
Internet (high-speed/shared terminal/pay terminal). Laundry room. No smoking. Parking (free/limited). Payphone. Restaurant. TV room.

Inn Crowd Hostel

73 Dunlop Street, 209401 (6296 9169/www.the-inncrowd.com). Bugis or Little India MRT. **Rooms** 70 dorm; 7 double. **Rates** $18 dorm; $48 double. **Credit** AmEx, DC, JCB, MC, V. **Map** p248 K3 ㉕

If you can get past the cheesy name, the Inn Crowd is an excellent hostel. The vibe is friendly and relaxed, the decor cheerful and stylish, and the mattresses top quality. There is a wealth of extras too: a travel library, rooftop garden, open-air showers and a hearty breakfast (Marmite included). Skylights and full windows let in plenty of natural light, and the owner – who stays in the house – keeps the place spick and span. Little India is just outside your door.
Bars. Internet (high-speed/shared terminal). Kitchen. Laundry. No smoking. TV (double rooms only). TV room.

New 7th Storey Hotel

229 Rochor Road, 188452 (6337 0251/fax 6334 3550/www.nsshotel.com). Bugis MRT. **Rooms** 40. **Rates** $18 dorm; $56 double shared bath; $80-$83 double en suite. **Credit** MC, V. **Map** p249 M5 ②

Singapore's answer to the Leaning Tower of Pisa, this budget hotel is famous for tilting slightly (don't worry – it is structurally safe). Built in 1953, it used to be a party haunt for British officers. These days the exterior is run-down, but there are charming old-fashioned touches such as a cage lift and dramatic spiral staircase. The rooms are clean and simply decorated; all come with a TV, and some have DVD players and en suite bathrooms. The backpacker brigade appreciates the beer garden, sun deck, games room, internet access and bike rental.
Internet (high-speed/shared terminal/pay terminal). Laundry. Parking (free). Payphone. Room service. TV.

Perak Hotel

12 Perak Road, 208133 (6299 7733/fax 6392 0919/www.peraklodge.com). Little India MRT. **Rooms** 35. **Rates** $128-$138 standard; $158-$168 superior; $178-$188 deluxe. **Credit** AmEx, DC, MC, V. **Map** p248 K4 ②

Tucked behind the Little India Arcade, the Perak Hotel is ideal for soaking up local colour, while simultaneously offering a respite from the area's hectic vibe. Housed in a restored, Peranakan-style building, it is small but characterful; all 35 rooms are tastefully done up and come with a safe. High-speed internet is available and breakfast is included.
Business centre. Internet (high-speed/shared terminal/pay terminal). No smoking. Parking (free). TV (DVD).

Sleepy Sam's

55 Bussorah Street, 119471 (9277 4988/ www.sleepysams.com). Bugis MRT then 10mins walk. **Rooms** dorm 6; rooms 59. **Rates** $25 dorm; $45 single; $69 double; $90 triple. **Credit** V. **Map** p249 M4 ②

Situated just a stone's throw from the Sultan Mosque, in what used to be the Sultan's palace grounds – not bad for $25 a night – Sleepy Sam's has character by the bucketload. The hostel's rustic charms are complemented by contemporary decorative touches. Some of the dorms rooms are set aside for women only, and there are private rooms too. But keeping to oneself isn't the done thing: the living room and barbecue area make meeting other guests easy.
Internet room. Laundry. No smoking. Restaurant. TV room.

Strand Hotel

25 Bencoolen Street, 189619 (6338 1866/fax 6338 1330/www.strandhotel.com.sg). Dhoby Ghaut MRT. **Rooms** 100. **Rates** $120 deluxe; $160 family. **Credit** AmEx, DC, MC, V. **Map** p248 J5 ②

For a budget hotel, the Strand is surprisingly stylish. The rooms, fashionably decorated in rich colours and simple woods, are a good size, though the bathrooms are short on toiletries. For a memorable stay, ask for a 'special' room; these come with flamboyant decor – leopard print walls, anyone? – and glass-walled bathrooms (not ideal for the bashful). The central location is great for exploring Little India, Orchard Road or the Colonial District.
Internet (high-speed). Laundry. Parking (free). Payphone. Room service. TV (pay movies).

Orchard Road & Around

Deluxe

Four Seasons Hotel Singapore

190 Orchard Boulevard, 248646 (6734 1110/ fax 6733 0682/www.fourseasons.com/singapore). Orchard MRT then 10mins walk. **Rooms** 254. **Rates** $480 standard; $510-$730 deluxe; $945-$5,300 suite. **Credit** AmEx, DC, JCB, MC, V. **Map** p246 D3 ③

When the stars come to Singapore, they stay at the Four Seasons. Located just off Orchard Road, it's more intimate than many of Singapore's luxury hotels. Guest rooms are decorated in an understated luxurious style, but with local touches such as tropical plants, colonial-style furnishings and Asian art. The custom-designed beds are comfortable enough to cure insomniacs. The swimming pool is a sultry retreat, and the air-conditioned tennis courts make matches bearable in the Singapore heat. The Sunday champagne brunch in One-Ninety restaurant is a lavish affair.
Bar. Business centre. Concierge. Disabled-adapted rooms. Gym. Internet (high-speed/wireless/shared terminal/pay terminal). No-smoking floors. Parking (free). Pool (2, outdoor). Restaurants (2). Room service. Spa. TV (pay movies/music/cable/DVD).

Goodwood Park Hotel

22 Scotts Road, 228221 (6737 7411/fax 6732 8558/www.goodwoodparkhotel.com.sg). Orchard or Newton MRT then 10mins walk. **Rooms** 235. **Rates** $425 standard; $5,000 suite. **Credit** AmEx, DC, JCB, MC, V. **Map** p247 F2 ③

The distinguished Goodwood Park boasts a deeply romantic castle-style tower and a rich history. Built in 1900 as the Teutonia Club, an exclusive retreat for German expats, it became a hotel in 1929; the

Paradise found at the **Shangri-La**. See p49.

grounds were used for war crimes trials after World War II. It still has a majestic air, with elegant columns and classical archways. Rooms are mostly done up in the tropical colonial uniform of creams, beiges and creams. Highlights include the wooden-shuttered poolside suites, and classy Sichuan restaurant Min Jiang (*see p120*). High-rollers stay in the aristocratic Brunei Suite, which includes a spacious lounge, study and grand dining room with rooftop garden – all accessed by its own private lift.
Bar. Business centre. Concierge. Gym. Internet (high-speed/wireless). Parking (rates vary). Pool (2, outdoor). Restaurants (4). Room service. Spa. TV (pay movies).

Meritus Mandarin Singapore
333 Orchard Road, 238867 (6737 4411/fax 6732 2361/www.mandarin-singapore.com). Somerset MRT. **Rooms** 1,050. **Rates** $480-$4,000. **Credit** AmEx, DC, JCB, MC, V. **Map** p247 G4 ⑫
The award-winning Meritus Mandarin had a $52 million refurb in 2003, so it's looking pretty smart these days. Popular with business travellers, it's a big place – with two 40-storey towers, South and Grand, housing more than 1,000 rooms – so not exactly cosy. But the rooms, decorated in soothing neutral colours, marry elegance with comfort; and there are recreational facilities galore, including tennis and squash courts, a gym, sauna and a big outdoor pool. Shoppers will enjoy the Mandarin Gallery (stores to note are the Link, Quintessential and Chokri), while the street-level Chatterbox restaurant (*see p119*) is famed for its chicken rice. For panoramic city views, head up for dinner at the revolving restaurant Top of the M.
Bars (2). Business centre. Concierge. Disabled-adapted room. Gym. Internet (high-speed/shared terminal/pay terminal/). No-smoking floors. Parking (free). Pool (outdoor). Restaurants (4). Room service. TV (pay movies/music).

Regent Singapore
1 Cuscaden Road, 249715 (6733 8888/fax 6732 8838/www.regenthotels.com). Orchard MRT then bus 36, 105, 111 or 15mins walk. **Rooms** 430. **Rates** $400 standard; $425 deluxe; $525-$2,500 suite. **Credit** AmEx, DC, JCB, MC, V. **Map** p246 C4 ⑬
The Regent oozes class and elegance. It makes liberal use of marble, plush furnishings, elaborate flower arrangements and dazzling chandeliers. Rooms are spacious and tastefully styled, with ferns and potted palms adding a sense of tropical allure. The cocktail bar – adorned with overstuffed armchairs and polished wood – is one of Singapore's most underrated watering holes, while Modern European restaurant Iggy's (*see p122*) is one of its best eateries. Burn off the calories in the large, kidney-shaped pool.
Bar. Business centre. Concierge. Disabled-adapted room. Gym. Internet (high-speed/wireless/pay terminal). No-smoking floors. Parking (free). Pool (outdoor). Restaurants (2). Room service. Spa. TV (pay movies/music/DVD).

Royal Plaza on Scotts

25 Scotts Road, 228220 (6737 7966/fax 6737 6646/www.royalplaza.com.sg). Orchard MRT. **Rooms** 511. **Rates** $450 standard; $500-$530 deluxe; $730-$2,500 suite. **Credit** AmEx, DC, JCB, MC, V. **Map** p247 E3 ③④

The Royal Plaza has always been sought after, thanks to its reputation for excellent service, affordable rates and convenient location on Scotts Road. But some upgrading was needed to keep up with the competition; the hotel reopened – as a no-smoking property – in early 2007. The grand marble lobby with its twin curving staircases sets the scene for a host of luxurious touches, even in the standard rooms (32in LCD TV, ultra-comfortable beds with hypo-allergenic pillows). Notable additions include a brand-new lounge bar, Heat, and the all-buffet restaurant Carousel. Business travellers will appreciate the free wireless internet access.

Bar. Business centre. Concierge. Disabled-adapted rooms. Gym. Internet (high-speed/wireless). No smoking. Parking (free). Pool (outdoor). Restaurant. Room service. TV (pay movies/music).

The Shangri-La

22 Orange Grove Road, 258350 (6737 3644/fax 6737 3257/www.shangri-la.com). Orchard MRT then 15mins walk/bus 190. **Rooms** 750. **Rates** $640 standard; $740 deluxe; $875 suite. **Credit** AmEx, DC, JCB, MC, V. **Map** p246 C2 ③⑨

It's not quite paradise on earth, but the Shangri-La provides a super-luxurious retreat from the real world. Located off Orchard Road in spacious, landscaped grounds, it's got all the marble flooring, dripping chandeliers, soaring ceilings, grand artworks, sumptuous furnishings and polished staff you'd expect of a five-star hotel. There are three sections: the Valley Wing is the most exclusive, with its own entrance, lobby and lifts. Rooms in the low-rise Garden Wing have bougainvillea draped balconies overlooking the freeform swimming pool, while the extra-large Horizon Club rooms in the Tower Wing are popular with business travellers. Enjoy a lavish buffet breakfast in fashionable poolside restaurant the Line (*see p120*). The Shangri-La hotel group also owns the Rasa Sentosa Resort (*see p52*) on the western tip of Sentosa. **Photos** *p48*.

Bar. Business centre. Concierge. Disabled adapted rooms. Gym. Internet (high-speed). No-smoking floors. Parking (free). Pool (outdoor). Restaurants (6). Room service. Spa. TV (music/DVD).

Singapore Marriott Hotel

320 Orchard Road, 238865 (6735 5800/fax 6735 9800/http://marriott.com). Orchard MRT. **Rooms** 392. **Rates** $460 standard; $530-$570 deluxe; $750-$2,000 suite. **Credit** AmEx, DC, JCB, MC, V. **Map** p247 E3 ③⑥

With a prime position on the corner of Orchard and Scotts Roads, and a green-roofed, pagoda-style tower, the Marriott definitely stands out. But the Asian-style façade belies the contemporary interior. The ten pool terrace rooms are the most enticing

options: they come with private verandas and in-room bathtubs bathed in sunlight; the pool suite comes with its own private dip pool. Nightlife options are good: there's the Crossroads Café (a people-watching hotspot); the late-opening Living Room cocktail bar (*see p136*); and lively music venue Bar None (*see p187*).

Bars (2). Business centre. Concierge. Disabled-adapted rooms. Gym. Internet (high-speed/wireless/pay terminal). No-smoking floors. Parking ($18). Pool (outdoor). Restaurants (4). Room service. Spa. TV (pay movies/music).

Expensive

Furama Riverfront Singapore

405 Havelock Road, 169633 (6333 8898/fax 6733 1588/http://riverfront.furama.com). Bus 16, 51, 64, 75, 608, 970. **Rooms** 525. **Rates** $320-$380 standard; $450-$500 deluxe; $880-$1,080 suite. **Credit** AmEx, DC, JCB, MC, V.

A short walk from Chinatown and Clarke Quay, this four-star property is well sited, but is looking rather tired these days. Still, the good-sized swimming pool, landscaped grounds and extensive buffet breakfast are a draw, and there's wireless broadband in all rooms. Service is decent, and the bellboys, many of whom have been working here for over 30 years, are well informed – the hotel is right next to the neon-lit Tiananmen KTV (a notorious 'entertainment' spot), so you can be sure they'll have plenty of interesting stories to tell. The Waterfall Lounge is a soothing place for a drink. Practise your backhand on the tennis court and ease your muscles after wards in the Jacuzzi.

Business centre. Concierge. Disabled-adapted room. Gym. Internet (high-speed/wireless/pay terminal). No-smoking floors. Parking (free). Pools (2, outdoor). Restaurants (2). Room service. TV (movies).

Grand Copthorne Waterfront Hotel

392 Havelock Road, 169663 (6733 0880/fax 6233 1122/www.grandcopthorne.com.sg). Bus 16, 51, 64, 75, 608, 970. **Rooms** 539. **Rates** $360-$450 standard; $600-$650 deluxe; $800-$2,500 suite. **Credit** AmEx, DC, JCB, MC, V.

Though located at the end of Robertson Quay, this riverside hotel is more suited to corporate travellers than tourists. In addition to a business centre, there are 25 fully furnished offices and a complimentary shuttle bus service to the CBD (and Orchard Road). Many of the rooms have gorgeous views over the river. For a scenic jog, guests can run along the riverbank or in nearby Kim Seng Park. Night owls can whoop it up next door at mega dance club Zouk (*see p172*). The downside? The swimming pool is tiny for such a big hotel.

Bar. Business centre. Concierge. Disabled-adapted rooms. Gym. Internet (high-speed/wireless/ web TV). No-smoking floors. Parking (free). Pool (outdoor). Restaurants (2). Room service. TV (pay movies/music).

Grand Hyatt Singapore

10 Scotts Road, 228211 (6738 1234/fax 6732 1696/http://singapore.grand.hyatt.com). Orchard MRT. **Rooms** 663. **Rates** $320-$380 standard; $400-$460 deluxe; $720-$6,170 suite. **Credit** AmEx, DC, MC, V. **Map** p247 E3 ③

Following a recent face-lift, the Grand Hyatt has been given the feng shui treatment, from the carefully angled lobby doors to the tranquil water features (including a lavish waterfall). Rooms are decorated in soothing neutral tones with liberal use of blond wood; each has a small patio. The Grand Wing rooms are highly indulgent: think goose-down beds, luxury bed linens and Bang & Olufsen entertainment systems. For a garden view, ask for a Cabana room; each comes equipped with a balcony. Other highlights include the free-form swimming pool and deck, the poolside barbecue (on weekends only) and the classy cocktails served up at the Martini Bar (*see p136*).
Bars (2). Business centre. Concierge. Disabled-adapted rooms. Gym. Internet (high-speed/wireless). No-smoking floors. Parking (free). Pool (outdoor). Restaurants (4). Room service. Spa. TV (pay movies/music).

Holiday Inn Park View Singapore

11 Cavenagh Road, 229616 (6733 8333/fax 6734 4593/www.singapore.holiday-inn.com). Somerset MRT then 10mins walk. **Rooms** 315. **Rates** $300 standard; $400 deluxe; $700-$900 suite. **Credit** AmEx, DC, JCB, MC, V. **Map** p247 H4 ③

Off Orchard Road, tucked away behind Centrepoint Shopping Centre, the Holiday Inn Park View is often overlooked because of its hidden location and bland chain reputation. But it's a cut above the norm. The chandelier-filled lobby is a glam extravaganza and, for a Holiday Inn, the rooms are surprisingly tasteful; many offer lush green views. And the rooftop pool is the stuff of romance. In fact, the hotel regularly hosts Bollywood stars, who frequent its award-winning Indian restaurant Tandoor. For an exclusive experience, ask for the Park View suite, which overlooks the home of the president of Singapore, in Istana Park.
Bar. Business centre. Concierge. Disabled-adapted rooms. Gym. Internet (high-speed/wireless). No-smoking floors. Parking (free). Pool (outdoor). Restaurants (3). Room service. Spa. TV.

Orchard Hotel Singapore

442 Orchard Road, 238879 (6734 7766/fax 6733 5482/www.orchardhotel.com.sg). Orchard MRT then 15mins walk. **Rooms** 653. **Rates** $355 standard; $435 club; $900 suite. **Credit** AmEx, DC, JCB, MC, V. **Map** p246 D3 ③

One of a long string of hotels along Orchard Road, the Orchard has a few distinguishing features: a putting green, a 25m pool and a lifesize poolside chess set. Inside, the aesthetic is East meets West; luxuries include an extensive pillow menu and an IT butler service. For a bird's-eye view of Orchard Road, ask for an upper floor in the Orchard Wing. Signature Club rooms are sumptuous oriental extrav-aganzas featuring green, red or blue colour schemes, and lots of extras including evening cocktails and a hydro-massage rain shower.
Bar. Business centre. Concierge. Disabled-adapted rooms. Gym. Internet (high-speed/web TV). No-smoking floors. Parking (free). Pool (outdoor). Restaurants (4). Room service. Spa. TV (cable/pay movies).

Moderate

Gallery Hotel

1 Nanson Road, 238909 (6849 8686/fax 6836 6666/www.galleryhotel.com.sg). Bus 32, 54, 143, 195. **Rates** 221. **Rates** $295 standard; $345-$395 deluxe; $470-$570 suite. **Credit** AmEx, DC, JCB, MC, V. **Map** p250 G8 ④

Billed as Singapore's first design hotel, this hip riverside hotspot cuts a striking figure with its postmodern, neon-lit exterior. The stylish rooms fuse minimalism with flamboyance: white bedding dotted with vibrant cushions, for instance, or metal shelving offset by gaudy wall murals. To get a feel for the Singapore arts scene, book yourself into one of the CYX rooms, which have been refurbished by local artists; the in-house photo gallery also reflects the hotel's edgy spirit. For underwater views of the city, take a swim in the glass-sided pool.
Bars (4). Business centre. Concierge. Gym. Internet (high-speed/shared terminal). No-smoking floors. Parking (free). Pool (outdoor). Restaurant. Room service. Spa. TV.

SHA Villa

64 Lloyd Road, 239113 (6734 7117/fax 6736 1651/www.sha.org.sg). Somerset MRT. **Rooms** 40. **Rates** $165 standard; $185 deluxe. **Credit** AmEx, DC, JCB, MC, V. **Map** p247 G6 ④

In a refurbished colonial bungalow just off Orchard Road, SHA Villa boasts an alluring setting. But it is not the lap of luxury. Run by the Singapore Hotel

Association, the place is staffed by hospitality students, which is a double-edged sword: the students are eager to please, but service is rough around the edges. With polished wood floors and teak beds, the place has character, but be warned: the standard rooms do not have windows. Breakfast is included. *Concierge. Internet (shared terminal). TV.*

Budget

Lloyd's Inn

2 Lloyd Road, 239091 (6737 7309/fax 6737 7847/ www.lloydinn.com). Somerset MRT then 10mins walk. **Rooms** 33. **Rates** $80 standard; $90 deluxe. **Credit** MC, V. **Map** p247 H6
Housed in an old, fort-style bungalow, Lloyd's looks characterful from the outside. The interior is less impressive: rooms are clean and spacious, but bland. The proprietor has not yet mastered the art of exchanging pleasantries, but the place has been going for 16 years; the central location – a short walk from Orchard Road – and low rates must have something to do with it. Booking is advisable; it fills up fast. For an extra $10, you'll get a fridge (useful, as there's no room service)
Parking (free). TV.

Robertson Quay Hotel

15 Merbau Road, 239032 (6735 3333/fax 6738 1515/www.robertsonquayhotel.com.sg). Clarke Quay MRT then 10mins walk/bus 64, 123, 143. **Rooms** 150. **Rates** $150 standard, $200 quad. **Credit** AmEx, DC, JCB, MC, V. **Map** p250 H8
This compact riverside hotel stands out for two reasons: its unconventional, cylindrical shape and affordable prices. Rooms are small and simply decorated with white bedding and soft colours; all come with en suite bathroom and cable TV; many have water views. The small rooftop pool is landscaped with rockery and palms, and there's also a spa and

gym. You can eat and drink alfresco at the Riverside Beach Bar; alternatively, fashionable Robertson Quay is teeming with bars and restaurants.
Bar. Business centre. Concierge. Disabled-adapted rooms. Gym. Internet (high-speed). No-smoking floors. Parking (free). Pool (outdoor). Restaurants (2). Room service. TV (cable).

Sloane Court Hotel

17 Balmoral Road, 259803 (6235 3311/fax 6733 9041). Bus 48, 66, 170. **Rooms** 32. **Rates** $128 standard; $158 deluxe. **Credit** AmEx, MC, V.
Calling all anglophiles: this red-roofed, mock Tudor-style property, built in the 1950s, is like a slice of Britannia transplanted to the tropics. All the reasonably sized rooms are decorated in English country house style, and come with black and white tiled bathrooms. It has a traditional pub that serves a popular weekend roast lunch; rates are good; and it's handy for exploring the shops on Orchard Road.
Bar. Internet (wireless/shared terminal). No-smoking rooms. Parking (free). Restaurant. Room service. TV.

YMCA International House

1 Orchard Road, 238824 (6336 6000/fax 6337 3140/www.ymcaih.com.sg). Dhoby Ghaut MRT. **Rooms** 111. **Rooms** $30 dorm; $150 standard; $230 suite. **Credit** AmEx, DC, JCB, MC, V. **Map** p248 J6
Despite the onslaught of budget designer hotels, the YMCA is sticking to its successful formula: comfortable accommodation at reasonable prices. All rooms come equipped with air-conditioning, TV and telephone. Most are doubles or twins, but there's dozen family rooms with three or four beds, plus a handful of four-bed dorms. There's also a gym, snooker room, cute little rooftop pool, internet café and outdoor terrace. The Y Café's fish head and chicken curries pack a punch. The central location is handy for the east end of Orchard Road, Fort Canning Park and the National Museum.
Business centre. Concierge. Disabled-adapted rooms. Gym. Internet (broadband/shared terminal/pay terminal). No smoking. Parking (free). Pool (outdoor). Restaurant. TV.

Sentosa

Deluxe

Sentosa Resort & Spa

2 Bukit Manis Road, 099891 (6275 0331/fax 6275 0228/www.thesentosa.com). HarbourFront MRT then Sentosa Express. **Rooms** 215. **Rates** $420 standard; $600 suite; $2,000 villa. **Credit** AmEx, DC, JCB, MC, V. **Map** p252 D3
Perched on a cliff overlooking the South China Sea, the Sentosa Resort & Spa is tailor-made for honeymoons. The lush tropical grounds and beautiful landscaped water gardens cry out for a romantic stroll. Sunsets are a spectacle, best watched from the bar at the Cliff restaurant (*see p124*) or the wooden walkway leading down to Palawan Beach. After a

Gallery Hotel

Introduction

On your marks, get set – go.

The city of Singapore sits on the southern tip of the island, centred around the Singapore River. The basic division of districts still reflects the the original Town Plan, as laid out by Stamford Raffles in 1822. The areas of most interest to visitors are small and self-contained enough to make walking the best way to get about (though the heat and humidity can be exhausting). To get from one district to the next, jump on the MRT – Singapore's cheap, efficient and comfortable underground train system – or grab a taxi (short trips never cost more than a few dollars). For leaflets, maps and more information, pop into one of the Singapore Tourist Board's visitor centres (*see p231*).

Don't miss Highlights

Animal magic
Get in touch with your wild side at **Jurong BirdPark** (*see p100*), the **Night Safari** (*see p105*) and **Singapore Zoo** (*see p105*).

Eat, eat, eat
Food, Singapore's greatest asset. You can eat your way around the world here, but don't miss the hawker centres. *See p114* **Grub hubbub**.

Get cultural
Delve into Singapore's past at the new **Singapore National Museum** (*see p60*), and its artistic heritage at the **Asian Civilisations Museum** (*see p58*).

Get religion
Singapore is stuffed with temples, mosques, shrines and churches. Hindu **Sri Mariamman Temple** and Buddhist **Thian Hock Keng Temple** (for both, *see p67*) are good starting points.

Island life
Find family fun and beach amusements on **Sentosa** (*see p83*) or the Singapore of yesteryear on **Pulau Ubin** (*see p94*).

Only in Singapore
Don't miss bizarre and bloodthirsty sculpture park **Haw Par Villa** (*see p97*).

Arranged by area, our Sightseeing chapters start with the **Colonial District**. Nestled on the northern riverbank, this housed the early colony's major civic institutions; many of these still stand (some have been turned into museums or arts centres), alongside their newer incarnations. Also here is one of three waterfront nightlife spots – **Clarke Quay** – and, occupying reclaimed land to the north-east, the offices, hotels, shopping malls and convention centres of the **Marina** district.

Opposite, on the south side of the river, in stark contrast to the low-rise, red-roofed colonial area, stand the streamlined skyscrapers of the **CBD** (Central Business District), the nation's business and financial heart. Adjacent, and further south, is **Chinatown**, with its conservation shophouses, temples, mosques, shops and hawker centres. The bars, clubs and restaurants of **Boat Quay**, now looking rather tawdry, line the riverfront. The city's two other main ethnic enclaves – **Little India**, with its busy streetlife and numerous temples, and the **Arab Quarter**, the focus for Malay and Muslim life (also known by its Malay name, Kampong Glam) – are north of the colonial district. Nearby lie **Bras Basah** and **Bugis**, now cleansed of its sin city reputation.

The long sweep of **Orchard Road**, the main shopping belt, heads west from Fort Canning and the colonial area. Orchard Road itself is served by three MRT stops, but you'll need to jump in a cab or take a bus to reach areas off the main drag, such as Tanglin and Dempsey Road. South of the Orchard Road area, along the river, is **Robertson Quay**, the third and newest of the nightlife hubs. And off the southern tip of Singapore is the resort island of **Sentosa**, popular for its family-friendly attractions and man-made beaches.

Don't stop there, though. The further reaches of the country are worth exploring too. **Eastern Singapore** combines cultural vibrancy in Katong with coastal recreation at East Coast Park and Changi Village, plus charmingly untouched Pulau Ubin. In the other direction, **Western Singapore** encompasses expat strongholds (including much-loved Holland Village), World War II sites and nature reserves, while **Central & Northern Singapore** features primary rainforest habitats and a couple of must-see sights.

Singapore by numbers

697 Singapore's size in square kilometres (269 square miles). By size, it's ranked 189 out of 228 countries.
4,492,150 Singapore's population in 2006.
6,430 The number of people per square kilometre. It's the world's second most densely populated country, after Monaco.
4 Singapore is the fourth largest foreign exchange trading centre after London, New York City and Tokyo.
22 Singapore is the 22nd wealthiest country in the world (GDP per capita).

1 The ranking of Singapore's port, the world's busiest. In 2006, 1.3 billion gross tonnes and 24.8 million container loads were handled.
31 The average maximum temperature, in celsius (88°F).
90 The average percentage humidity in the morning.
1,000 The number of species of orchids found in Singapore Botanic Gardens (plus 2,000 hybrids).
1,000 The maximum fine for first offenders, in Singapore dollars, for littering.

Tours

Duck Tours

Tickets from Duck Counter, Suntec City Mall Galleria, 3 Temasek Boulevard, Marina (6333 3825/ www.ducktours.com.sg). City Hall MRT then 10mins walk or Suntec shuttle bus. **Open** 9.30am 7pm daily. **Tickets** $33; $17 concessions. **Map** p249 M6.
See the sights by Duck, a converted amphibious craft that once served in the Vietnam War. The 1hr tour explores the historic civic district, takes a bash through the woods, then plunges into Kallang Bay for a scenic harbour tour, right up to the open mouth of the Merlion. Tours run daily; the first is at 10am, the last at 6pm. It's all relentlessly jokey, so not recommended for adults without children.

Original Singapore Walks

6325 1631/www.singaporewalks.com. **Tickets** $18; $12 concessions.
Operating daily, these guided walking tours are an in-depth way to visit Singapore's heritage areas, such as Chinatown, Little India, the Colonial District and Fort Canning, taking in haunted houses, wet markets and other offbeat places. The Chinatown night walk, for example, evokes the old sin city with tales of brothels, opium dens and gambling. Further afield, the Changi Museum War Trails tour ($30, $20 concessions) relives the brutal days of the Japanese occupation. Booking is not necessary for most tours; just turn up at the designated meeting point (usually an MRT station).

SH Tours

6734 9923/www.asiatours.com.sg. **Tickets** $29-$54.
Variety is the name of the game with this company. Start off with a straightforward greatest hits medley of Singapore, by land and water. Then pick a niche: perhaps a night tour with alfresco dining by the Singapore River, or a feng shui tour. The Eastern Homelands tour visits the Malay enclave of Geylang Serai, Changi Chapel & Museum and Tampines New Town, the epitome of Singapore suburbia.

Singapore Explorer

6339 6833/www.singaporeexplorer.com.sg. **Tickets** $10 $15.
If you can't bear the idea of sightseeing from a monstrous modern coach, go for nostalgia with an old-fashioned red trolley bus. Tours take in Orchard Road, the Colonial District, Clarke Quay and the Botanic Gardens. Trishaw tours also available.

Singapore River Cruise

6336 6111/19/www.rivercruise.com.sg. **Tickets** $12; $6 concessions.
See the city from the water on a no-frills 30mins journey aboard a bumboat. You can buy tickets, and board or alight, at any of the jetties along the Singapore River: near the Esplanade, Merlion Park, Fullerton, Boat Quay, Raffles Landing Site, Riverside Point, Liang Court, Robertson Quay and Grand Copthorne Waterfront Hotel. Boats run daily (9.30am-10.30pm); it's quite a sight at night when the skyscrapers are lit up. The bizarrely accented recorded commentary is uniquely irritating.

Trishaw Tours

Alphaland Travel Services 9100 4276(T)ishaw Tours 6545 6311/Triwheel Tours 6336 9025/6. **Tickets** $25.
A colourful, if noisy, way to see Singapore is by trishaw: an open-air trike with two passengers sitting behind a driver. Most tours operate in Chinatown and Little India. Rides last from 30 to 45mins, and you should book with a licensed operator (call or go to at ticket kiosk); avoid casual street pick-ups.

Watertours

1F HarbourFront Centre, HarbourFront (6533 9811/www.watertours.com.sg). HarbourFront MRT. **Tickets** from $26; $12 concessions. **Map** p252 B1.
Take a leisurely 2.5hr cruise past Sentosa and the Southern Islands of Kusu, St John, Sisters and Lazarus aboard an ornate replica of a Ming dynasty Chinese junk. There are two regular cruises a day (10.30am, 3pm) and two more expensive dining cruises (3pm, 6.30pm).

Sightseeing

Colonial District

Take a walk on the old side.

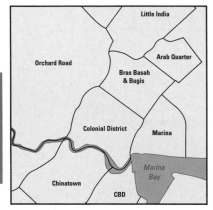

Civic District

The northern bank of the Singapore River is where the Singapore you see today began. No river, no Stamford Raffles – who allegedly first stepped ashore here, on 29 January 1819, as marked by the imposing white statue (with fawning inscription) at **Raffles' Landing Site**. Across the river, the red-roofed shophouses of Boat Quay front the soaring skyscrapers of the CBD (Central Business District), providing an iconic 'city of contrasts' snapshot of Singapore. Towards the mouth of the river on the left is attractive **Cavenagh Bridge**, the oldest (and only suspension) bridge in the country; built in Glasgow, it was shipped over to Singapore and reassembled in 1869. Real versions of Singapore's distinctive 'drain cats' can often be seen hanging around their bronze counterparts on the corner of the bridge. In 1910 it was pedestrianised, on the opening of the adjacent **Anderson Bridge**.

From here, you can take in many of the most significant buildings of the civic district, several of which have been transformed into arts and cultural centres. Across Cavenagh Bridge, on the south bank, lie the grand granite columns of the recently restored **Fullerton Hotel** (*see p39*), built in 1928 as the General Post Office; while behind the bridge is the impressive neo-Palladian **Asian Civilisations Museum** (ACM, *see p58*), designed in the

1860s to house governnment offices. Behind the ACM, also on Empress Place, is the 1862 **Victoria Theatre** (*see p204*), which saw the addition of the **Victoria Concert Hall** (*see p192*) and a 54-metre (177-foot) clock tower in 1905. And next to that is Old Parliament House, parts of which date from 1827; it was built by Irish architect George Drumgoole Coleman, one of the key creators of the city's early skyline. Originally a private house, then a court house, it is now the **Arts House** (*see p202*), used for assorted cultural events.

The 1919 bronze statue of Raffles (from which the white one was cast in 1972) outside the Victoria Theatre was made to mark the 100th anniversary of modern Singapore's

Victoria Concert Hall

founding, while nearby Dalhousie Obelisk is a typical monument to colonial pomp. Commemorating the 1850 visit to Singapore of the Marquis of Dalhousie, governor-general of British India (of which the colony was then a part), it includes an enduringly resonant statement of Singapore's commitment to liberating commerce from all restraints.

Later civic structures include **City Hall** (1929) and the old **Supreme Court** (1939) – testament to the economic boom experienced by Singapore during the first third of the 20th century. Sited just to the north of the Arts House, flanking the western edge of the open grassy area known as the Padang, the two buildings are no longer in use, but are slated (in keeping with a recent trend) to become a massive national art gallery by 2012.

The civic district has been the focal point for many key events in Singapore's history: during the Japanese occupation (1942-45), the clock tower was set to Tokyo time and tapioca was grown on the Padang, and City Hall was the site of the Japanese surrender to the Allies, and also of the various proclamations of self-government, merger with Malaysia and then independence between 1959 and 1965. Today, all the administrative action has moved round the back: the judiciary into the new **Supreme Court** (designed by Norman Foster in 2005, and topped by a UFO-like update of the St Paul's Cathedral-style dome of its precursor); and the MPs into the bunker-like new **Parliament House** (1999), which runs along the river bank opposite Boat Quay. A gallery just inside the Supreme Court's main entrance charts the history of law in Singapore, and is open to the public, as are all parliament sittings. Adjacent to City Hall, standing on a spot that was designated as a site of worship by Raffles in 1823, is bright, white **St Andrew's Cathedral** (*see p58*).

The **Padang** ('flat field' in Malay, **photo** *p58*) was marked out in Raffles' original town plan as a recreation area, and so it remains, being the site of regular cricket matches and big public events. The grand structure at the southern end, with a red-tiled roof and green bamboo shutters, is the **Singapore Cricket Club** (www.scc.org.sg, established in 1852). It's the third clubhouse on the site, constructed in 1884, with the wings added in 1922. At the other end is the **Singapore Recreation Club** (www.src.org.sg), set up by Eurasians in 1883 in response to the SCC's all-white policy.

Across Connaught Drive is **Esplanade Park** and shady **Queen Elizabeth Walk**, which features a string of memorials, pragmatically gathered together from diverse original sites to provide a snapshot of key

Asian Civilisations Museum. *See p58.*

A green and pleasant land: the playing fields of the **Padang.** *See p57.*

events and personalities in Singapore's history. These include the Chinese memorial to World War II resistance hero Lim Bo Seng, the solemn Cenotaph and the fussily Victorian Tan Kim Seng Fountain, erected to mark the businessman's contributions to improving Singapore's water supply. A nearby marker identifies the former site of a monument to the Indian National Army (which collaborated with the Japanese in World War II to fight for Indian independence). Built during the occupation, it was destroyed by the British shortly afterwards, in a bid, it is said, to erase evidence of anti-colonial sentiment.

Recent years have seen the scribes of the Tourist and Heritage Boards spring into action, and the civic district might now be diagnosed as suffering a severe build-up of plaque. Some plaques celebrate other plaques, while outside the Fullerton Hotel there's one to Joseph Conrad (unveiled in 2004 by the Polish president, no less), who spent five months in Singapore in 1887-88 and featured the Supreme Court in his novel *Lord Jim.* Selectively reading your way around the area can enhance a sense of place and history, and the two trails mapped out at various spots take in most local sites of interest.

Asian Civilisations Museum
1 Empress Place (6332 7798/www.acm.org.sg). Raffles Place MRT. **Open** *1-7pm Mon; 9am-7pm Tue-Thur, Sat, Sun; 9am-9pm Fri.* **Admission** *$5-$8; $2.50-$4 concessions; free under-7s.* **Credit** *AmEx, JCB, MC, V.* **Map** *p251 K10.*
The ACM contains a great concentration of beautiful artefacts from numerous parts of Asia, representing a range of historical periods – a reminder of the immense complexity and diversity of cultures and practices that make up the Asian region. The Mary and Philbert Chin Gallery displays

striking jewellery and textiles from South-east Asia; the West Asia Gallery holds stunning Islamic calligraphy; and the Singapore River Gallery shows how crucial the river was to the island's fortunes. There are weaknesses; one of the museum's implicit agendas is to reconnect Singapore – often accused of cultural sterility – with its cultures of origin: hence no Japan or Korea, and not much Central Asia. Similarly, artefacts from very different eras are set alongside one other to create a generic sense of rich civilisational heritage, with scant regard for historical nuance. Still, the ACM is a must-see, and there's a fun kids' activity corner in every gallery, as well as a pleasant riverside café and good gift shop. **Photos** *p57.*

St Andrew's Cathedral
11 St Andrew's Road (6337 6104/www.living streams.org.sg). City Hall MRT. **Open** *Guided tours 10.30am-4.30pm Mon, Tue, Thur-Sun; 2.30-4.30pm Wed.* **Map** *p251 K7.*
This impressive Gothic edifice was built by Indian convict labourers and consecrated in 1862. The original church (another of George Drumgoole Coleman's creations) was replaced by a neo-classical building that was pulled down in 1855. In 1870, St Andrew's became a cathedral, and has played a central role in Anglican mission work in the region ever since. Despite the flashy new glass Welcome Centre, it's not really a showpiece. The transepts are more redolent of small-town English church halls than a grandiose cathedral, while the nave, with its ceiling fans and scattered supplicants, gives the sense that this is a working church. Brass wall plaques tell tales of personal suffering and professional sacrifice (it is striking how many of those commemorated died young), and guided tours highlight distinctive features, such as the Coventry Cross behind the pulpit (made from nails from the bombed ruins of Coventry Cathedral in 1940).

Raffles City to Fort Canning

This relatively small area – stretching from City Hall MRT to Dhoby Ghaut MRT – reveals the full variety of people, places and periods that have made modern Singapore. Civic institutions, historic buildings, shopping centres and green spaces give on to each other in a fascinating jumble.

Surfacing from City Hall MRT, **Raffles City Shopping Centre** (not to be confused with Raffles Place, across the river in the CBD) is, in terms of size, location and orientation, one of the more manageable malls. It's attached to Asia's tallest hotel, **Swissôtel The Stamford** (*see p39*); the **New Asia Bar** (*see p131*) on the 71st floor offers unrivalled views over the island, and as far as Indonesia. On the other side of Bras Basah Road, **Raffles Hotel** (*see p39*) is of modest size, but even more of a landmark, whose opulence, in typically contrasting Singapore style, backs on to streets selling cheap, unpretentious eats.

These include Purvis Street's **Chin Chin Eating House** (No.19) and **Hock Lam Street Popular Beef Kway Teow** (No.27, 6339 9641). On Seah Street, there's the **Soup Restaurant** (No.39), which specialises in the hearty food of the female immigrant labourers from China who were known as Samsui women. Also on Seah Street is the **Mint Museum of Toys** (*see p166*).

Across North Bridge Road – which leads south to Elgin Bridge and across the river to Chinatown, and north to the Arab Quarter is **Chijmes** (pronounced 'chimes'), a drinking and dining complex located in an atmospheric former convent. The name refers to the Convent of the Holy Infant Jesus, which is associated with several of Singapore's top girls schools. Inside the compound is a beautiful and painstakingly renovated Anglo-French Gothic style chapel, dating from 1904; now deconsecrated, it's mainly used for private functions. Restaurants cover a range of cuisines, with the pricier places - including the dependable Cantonese **Lei Garden** (6339 3822), popular with extended families – clustered around the central cobbled courtyard. Bars and pubs, ersatz, Oirish and otherwise, are to be found downstairs in the Fountain Court.

Numerous historic churches and other places of worship are located in the area, including the striking **Cathedral of the Good Shepherd** (1847, the oldest Roman Catholic church in Singapore), on the other side of Victoria Street. From here, if you look back towards Chijmes, you can see the slot where babies would be abandoned to the nuns' care.

Back on North Bridge Road, opposite the grassed area containing St Andrew's Cathedral, the art deco façade of the 1929 **Capitol Building** hides a huge, iconic and now defunct cinema. A block further south, **Peninsula Plaza** is the main hangout for Burmese foreign workers (*see p76* **Little Everywhere**), and the upper floors offer cheap Burmese food, CDs and other paraphernalia. In the basement, **Inle Myanmar Restaurant** (#B1-07A, 6333 5438, www.inlemyanmar.com.sg), is less rough and ready than most, with an extensive and inexpensive menu. The tattoo parlour on the third floor with the Bhudda figurines in the window is staffed by three elderly Chinese men who specialise in the kinds of religious and mythical imagery often associated with local gangsters. Further south still, the **Funan DigitaLife Mall** (*see p145*) is good for all things electronic.

Hill Street runs parallel to North Bridge Road, crossing the Singapore River via Coleman Bridge. Near the bridge, the 911 colourful shutters of the former Hill Street police station and barracks (1934) signal the presence of the **MICA Building**, home to the Ministry of Information, Communications & the Arts, and a cluster of art galleries (*see p178*). The distinctive red-brick and white plaster bands of the 1909 **Central Fire Station** (*see p166*), with its free **Civil Defence Heritage Gallery**, stands just to the north, on the corner of Coleman Street. As the name suggests, the gallery offers equal parts information and propaganda about the devastation caused in the past by fires in a densely populated city, and the need to remain in a state of militarised preparedness against future threats.

Next door is the 1879 **Freemasons Hall** (Raffles was said to have been a member of the esoteric brotherhood), followed by the **Singapore Philatelic Museum** (*see p61*), and the **National Archives** (6332 7973, www.nhb.gov.sg/NAS). The reference room is open to the public (9am-5.30pm Mon-Fri, 9am-1.30pm Sat), and guided tours are available.

On the opposite side of Coleman Street, the Orthodox **Armenian Church** (full name: the Armenian Apostolic Church of St Gregory the Illuminator) dates from 1836, and is an oasis of calm in the city. Designed by the ubiquitous GD Coleman, the white building is Palladian in style, but adapted to the tropical climate, with wide verandas and timber-louvred windows. The spire was added in 1853. Information on the walls, along with the gravestones in the grounds – including that of Agnes Joaquim (1844-99), after whom Singapore's national orchid, the Vanda Miss Joaquim is named –

Singapore swings at **Clarke Quay**. *See p61.*

(3E River Valley Road, 6338 1146, www.gmax. co.nz) may be fun, but at $35 a pop, it's a serious business too. For those seeking a more sedate form of transport, Clarke Quay is the northernmost point for boarding a bumboat for the **Singapore River Cruise** (*see p54*). River taxis are also available for a short hop ($5 from Clarke Quay to the Merlion, for example).

Marina

The site of numerous mega-malls, office blocks and five-star hotels, the reclaimed land east of Nicoll Highway and north of Marina Bay exemplifies consumerist, corporate, deluxe Singapore at its most undiluted. Shopaphobics might give it a wide berth, but there is still a perverse appeal in wandering trance-like through the miles of interlinking byways and skyways of shops and restaurants.

There's no MRT station nearby; it's a ten-minute walk from City Hall MRT. Head overground, and you can stop by the elegant and imposing **Civilian War Memorial**, nicknamed 'the chopsticks' because of its four slender pillars, each 67 metres (220 feet) high, which represent the four 'races' of Singapore (Chinese, Malays, Indians and 'Others') who suffered under the Japanese. Alternatively, plunge headlong into a consumerist reverie by

taking the underground Citylink Mall, which leads from the MRT stop to One Raffles Link, next to the huge shopping/office/convention complex of **Suntec City**.

The main tourist draw here is the massive bronze **Fountain of Wealth**. At 13.8 metres (45 feet) in height and spreading over a huge area, it's the largest fountain in the world – and, boy, do they milk it. Designed to feng shui principles, the ring of the fountain apparently represents the palm of the hand – with the fingers symbolised by surrounding office towers – and, as such, draws wealth-generating forces into its centre. Visitors are encouraged to perform a special ritual to harness these forces, while the gullible can buy take-home-and-cherish (but presumably don't drink) test tubes of the lucky water. A free multimedia laser show takes place every evening (8-9pm): a deafening disco inferno of Asian techno and Western chart-toppers. You can input a message into a computer, which will then be laser-written on to a wall of water spraying out from the fountain's centre. Neat.

Beyond Suntec, **Millenia Walk** is nothing special, although if you're looking for a Sunday blowout, Oscar's restaurant at the **Conrad Centennial hotel** (*see p38*) does a fine champagne brunch. Across Raffles Boulevard towards Marina Bay, the **Marina Square** mall (*see p141*) is vast, bland and yet dazzling in the abundance of goods for sale. Of most appeal is the **Marina Food Loft** on level four: it's the best appointed food court in Singapore, where the local mantra of cheap and good applies not only to the grub, but also to the bay views.

Further south, over Raffles Avenue and on the waterfront, sit the dramatic, spiky domes of **Esplanade – Theatres on the Bay** (*see p204*), Singapore's main performing arts centre. It has its own mall, of course, and adjacent is open-air hawker centre **Makansutra Gluttons Bay** (*see p111*). Pedestrianised **Marina Promenade**, heading east from here around the edge of the bay, is for a stroll and a waterside picnic.

With the advent of the huge new Downtown at Marina Bay development (*see p26* **Growing pains**), the whole area, including the vast empty Marina South district on the other side of the water, is set for big changes in coming years. The **Singapore Flyer** ferris wheel (www.singaporeflyer. com.sg), modelled on the London Eye, launches in March 2008 and, adjacent to the Esplanade complex, a rugby pitch-sized floating stage, with bleachers for 30,000, appeared practically overnight in early 2007. It will be used for the **National Day Parade** (*see p163*) and other large-scale public events.

Chinatown & the CBD

Shophouses and street markets, skyscrapers and stock markets.

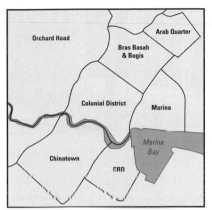

Chinatown

Chinatowns traditionally spring up in cities where the Chinese are a minority. So it's strange that Singapore, a country where the Chinese outnumber all other races by far, should have a Chinatown. The reasons for this date back to the colonial era, when Raffles organised the influx of immigrants based on their cultural origins. He gave the Chinese one of the largest portions of land – just south-west of the Singapore River – realising that they comprised many dialect groups and would need their own separate enclaves. Fresh water was drawn into the area by ox and buffalo, so Chinatown was known to locals as niu che shui (Chinese for 'ox-drawn cart') or kreta ayer (Malay for 'water cart').

As the construction of shophouses and the street-naming began, it became clear where immigrants from different parts of China were settling. Each group had their own temples, food shops and welfare support in the form of clan associations and, more worryingly, secret societies. Called Triad organisations, they offered protection, and also organised most of the criminal activity in the area, including gambling, prostitution, slavery and opium dens. The majority of Chinese travelling to Singapore were labourers, and so Chinatown became a place of poverty, abject conditions and vice – it would be a constant problem for the colonial authorities.

After World War II, when the British were struggling to keep hold of power, Chinatown became a centre for political agitation and rioting, and after Independence, the PAP came down hard on communist activists based in the area. Gradually, the old trades and businesses (ship chandlery, remittance, carpentry, coolies) wound down and the area was redeveloped: families were moved out and into HDB estates in other parts of the island, and the 'big clean up' of slums and crime improved conditions. But the fundamental character of the area had changed, and old-timers are quick to lament its passing. Many of the old shophouses were demolished or gaudily restored and the area is now geared to tourists. Yet traces of its immigrant history remain.

Chinatown still covers a large swathe of territory. Beginning south of the river, it stretches down to Cantonment Road and the Ayer Rajar Expressway in the south. On the west it is bordered by Chin Swee Road; it abuts the CBD (Central Business District) to the east. There are three MRT stops in the area: Tanjong Pagar, Outram Park and Chinatown. If the area has a main drag it is the twin-road thoroughfare of New Bridge Road (going south) and Eu Tong Street (going north). A long, frantically busy stretch through the whole district, it contains almost as many shopping centres as Orchard Road. Most of the malls have virtually identical wares: cheap clothes, mobile phones, Chinese music and movies, as well as travel agents and Chinese medicine halls (a great source of interesting gifts).

Next to Outram Park MRT station is **Pearl's Centre** (100 Eu Tong Sen Street), which sells food and clothing. Further north is the mighty **People's Park Complex** (1 Park Road), which, aside from dozens of standard shops, has stalls selling old photos, Chinatown memorabilia and nostalgic street snacks like muah chee, a sweet gooey paste dipped in crushed peanuts. Across the two roads lies the entrance to Chinatown MRT station, with a mural by local artist Tan Swee Hian. It depicts heroic coolies and craggy rocks turning into skyscrapers – a colourful mix of kitsch and propaganda.

For some respite from the urban grind, walk north along New Bridge Road to **Hong Lim Park**, a calm patch of greenery and benches.

Architectural digest: classic shophouse buildings line **Mosque Street**.

It was designated a Speakers' Corner in 2000, but with so many restrictions on orators (who must register at a police post before they begin), you'll be lucky to hear any rousing speeches.

A network of back streets is lined with classic Chinatown shophouse architecture. Mosque Street, quietly gentrified with spas and restaurants, leads to the **Jamae Mosque** (*see p66*) on South Bridge Road, practically next door to **Sri Mariamman Temple** (*see p67*). Both these places of worship stand at the edge of Chinatown's most touristy, central area – Pagoda Street, Temple Street and Smith Street, with Trengganu Street cutting across them. Numerous shops are filled with Chinese 'antiques' and all manner of Buddha-shaped merchandise, from car ornaments to plastic radios. Another local curiosity: stores that specialise in paper money, clothes and even paper cars – all burned as offerings on auspicious days for deceased ancestors.

Pagoda Street, once known for its opium dens, now attracts shopaholics; the pedestrianised market comprises stalls laden with fashion and accessories, mostly cheap imports of designer goods. For a drink with a view of the streets, climb the stairs to the no-frills **Roof Bar** (32A Pagoda Street, closed Sun). At No.48, the **Chinatown Heritage Centre** (*see p66*) vividly tells the story of Singapore's early immigrants; next door is the Singapore Heritage Restaurant, which specialises in mid-priced 'authentic' Chinese food by celebrity chef Alvin Koh. The glass Chinatown MRT entrance is next door.

Smith Street is filled with Chinese music and movie stalls, digital camera shops and Indian tailors sitting on stools touting for trade. Come

evening, one section of Smith Street is furnished with tables and roadside stalls that sell classic and tasty Singaporean hawker fare. Behind the stalls, inside the shophouses, are several good restaurants. A night market, along Trengganu Street and into Sago Street, also brings the district to life. You can buy gifts and snacks, including roast chestnuts, aloe vera juice and, of all things, German wurst. Look out for the **Lai Chin Yuen** building (36 Smith Street, at Trengganu), a flamboyant, three-storey Chinese opera theatre dating from 1887. You'll also notice extravagant balconies on some of the shophouses: prostitutes used to display themselves here a century ago, when Chinatown was packed with brothels.

Around the corner is Kreta Ayer Square, a modest civic space with a stage for events. Trishaw drivers sleep here when not shuttling package tourists around, and the elderly male residents of the nearby HDB flats while away their days playing draughts. Next door is a popular food market and hawker centre, **Chinatown Complex** (335 Smith Street); currently closed for major 'upgrading', it should re-open at the end of 2007.

Aside from the sago factories that gave them their names, Sago Street and Sago Lane were dotted with 'death houses' – to which Chinese workers without families would pay a regular stipend until they could no longer work, then be given floor space on which to end their days. These buildings were razed in 1961, and the site (adjoining South Bridge Road) will soon be occupied by the enormous **Buddha Tooth Relic Temple**. Designed around the Buddhist mandala (map of the universe), it promises to be one of the biggest temples in Singapore.

Local colour: browsing the bric-a-brac on **New South Bridge Road**.

To experience a modern hawker centre, cross South Bridge Road and visit the ever bustling **Maxwell Food Centre** (*see p113*); afterwards, head inside the URA Centre, the offices of the Urban Redevelopment Authority, to visit the **Singapore City Gallery** (*see p66*), which documents the city-state's changing landscape. Halfway down Maxwell Road (which leads to Tanjong Pagar MRT) is the massive crimson building that is **Red Dot Traffic** (*see p66*). Nearby is Duxton Hill, a stretch of rough and ready bars, eateries, wedding boutiques and the new **Kay Ngee Tan Architects Gallery** (16-17 Duxton Hill, 6423 0198, www.kayngee tanarchitects.com), displaying work by local photographers.

Up the steep-for-Singapore Erskine Road, you'll find the sumptuously designed **Scarlet Hotel** (*see p42*). This leads to Ann Siang Road and Ann Siang Hill, once a centre for 'remittance' companies that helped Chinese labourers to send their wages to their families in China; in the same area, a high concentration of professional letter writers would help illiterate workers send news back home. These days, it is better known for its gay bars and trendy boutiques. It connects to another key nightlife spot, Club Street, named after the profusion of clan associations that had their premises there. Some of these old organisations remain amid the upmarket bars and eateries.

Cut through Ann Siang Park to reach the parallel streets of Telok Ayer Street and Amoy Street, once the centre of the large community of Hokkien immigrants from China's Fujian province. On the corner you'll find another fine hawker centre, **Amoy Street Food Centre**. Amoy Street has been gentrified by the advertising agencies, publishing companies and recording studios that occupy the converted shophouses (M&C Saatchi and Getty Images are here, among others). History endures on Telok Ayer Street in the form of two historical places of worship – Buddhist temple **Thian Hock Keng** (*see p67*), and the currently closed Muslim shrine **Nagore Durgha** (*see p66*) – and **Ying Fo Fui Kun** (*see p67*), a well-preserved Chinese clan building. At the north end, over Cross Street, lies **Far East Square** which links to **Capital Square** and **China Square**, part of a glass-roofed complex full of restaurants catering to the lunch-time office crowd. Despite the preservation of the original streets inside, there's little sense of history apart from a few token 'heritage' photographs of Chinatown and the **Fuk Tak Chi Museum** (*see p66*).

One street that has escaped development and heritage embalming is Keong Saik Road. At the intersection with Kreta Ayer Road, look for the **Sri Layan Sithi Vinayagar Temple** (*see p66*). As you wind your way up the hill you'll pass a number of great Chinese coffee shops selling freshly cooked, modestly priced food. Try **Foong Kee** (No.6) for wonton mee (dumpling and pork noodles) or **Kok Seng** (No.30) for prawn bee hoon (thin noodles). For more sophisticated (and air conditioned) dining, boutique **Hotel 1929** (*see p42*) boasts the acclaimed **Ember** (*see p115*). Further up, there's cult organic café and yoga 'healing space' **Whatever** (*see p116*) and a crop of dimly lit bars. Finally, you'll reach the remains of Chinatown's once-famed red-light district, a dozen shophouses with big numbers on the doors and, yes, red lanterns.

Glittering **Thian Hock Keng**. *See p67.*

Chinatown Heritage Centre

48 Pagoda Street (6325 2878/www.chinatown heritage.com.sg). Chinatown MRT. **Open** 9am-8pm daily. **Admission** $8; $5.30 concessions. **Credit** AmEx, DC, JCB. MC, V. **Map** p250 I10.

Occupying a Tardis-like shophouse, the Chinatown Heritage Centre is full of engaging stuff. It documents the poverty-induced flight of immigrants from China, and their early days in Singapore during the 19th century. As you ascend, the centre presents information and tableaux about coolie life; the descent reconstructs the shophouse to illustrate the cramped, hot and unsanitary conditions endured by generations of labourers and their families. Guides paint a vivid picture; the shop is a good source of souvenirs.

Fuk Tak Chi Museum

#01-01 76-78 Telok Ayer Street (6532 7868). Chinatown MRT then 10mins walk. **Open** 10am-10pm daily. **Map** p250 J10.

This building was originally a Buddhist shrine, built in 1824 and said to be the oldest Chinese temple on the island; it later became a centre for the Hakka and Cantonese communities. The religious functions were eventually moved elsewhere as the building became dilapidated, and in the 1990s the place was restored and converted into a 'street museum'. Don't expect much – there's some historical information, a few artefacts and a small glass-cased model portraying 19th-century street life.

Jamae Mosque

218 South Bridge Road (6221 4165/www.mosque. org.sg). Chinatown MRT. **Open** 5.45am-9.30pm daily. **Map** p250 I10.

One of Singapore's earliest mosques, the Jamae was founded in 1827 by Muslim Indian entrepreneurs from southern India (the Chulias – it's also known as the Chulia Mosque). In contrast to so many 19th-century religious sites, it hasn't been renovated, but the curious architecture – a medley of South Indian, neoclassical and Muslim influences – still shines through, and the interior is well maintained.

Nagore Durgha

140 Telok Ayer Street. Tanjong Pagar MRT. Currently closed. **Map** p250 J10.

This shrine was built to honour an Indian Muslim holy man from Chulia who visited Singapore in the early 19th century. Thanks to its striking, palatial design – characterised by 14-storey minarets topped by onion domes – it was given national monument status in the 1970s. But in the '90s the building was deemed structurally unsound and closed. It's slated for restoration and should open at the end of 2007.

Red Dot Traffic

28 Maxwell Road (6534 7194/www.reddottraffic. com/www.red-dot.sg). Tanjong Pagar MRT. **Open** *Design museum* 11am-8pm Mon, Tue, Fri-Sun. **Admission** $5; $3 concessions. **No credit cards.** **Map** p250 I12.

Red Dot desperately wants to be the centre for Singapore's hip young media and designer types. The setting is striking: a massive rectangular colonial building, formerly the headquarters of the traffic police, now painted a flamboyant shade of red. Inside, the independent venture combines cafés, bars and office space for 'creative industries' with a sleek and airy design museum. It is usually quiet, except for the popular MAAD (Market of Artists & Designers) on Sunday.

Singapore City Gallery

URA Centre, 45 Maxwell Road (6321 8321/ www.ura.gov.sg). Tanjong Pagar MRT. **Open** 9am-5pm Mon-Sat. **Map** p250 I12.

Sharing a building with architects and city planners, this gallery documents Singapore's changing urban landscape. Temporary exhibitions are a mixture of self-congratulatory, 'look-how-we've-progressed' showcases and interesting explorations of Singapore's urban fabric. The centrepiece is a permanent 3D scale model of the whole island, a revealing reminder of how small the place is and how much land has yet to be reclaimed.

Sri Layan Sithi Vinayagar Temple

73 Keong Saik Road (6221 4853/www.sttemple.com). Outram Park MRT. **Open** 7.30am-noon, 5.30-8.30pm daily. **Map** p250 H11.

Constructed in 1925 by Hindu Chettiers from South India, who came to Singapore mainly as moneylenders, this temple was intended as a shrine for Vinayagar – another name for Ganesha, the Elephant

God. It was frequented by workers from the nearby hospital (which is still there) and prison (which is not). It's still popular with worshippers at weekends, as is evident from the hundreds of pairs of shoes left in the street.

Sri Mariamman Temple

244 South Bridge Road (6223 4064/www.heb. gov.sg). Chinatown MRT. **Open** 7am-noon, 6-9pm daily. **Map** p250 I11.

Oddly enough, the oldest Hindu temple in Singapore is smack in the middle of Chinatown. It was built (as a humble shed) in 1827 by Naraina Pillai, the first recorded Indian immigrant to enter colonised Singapore (he travelled with Raffles from Penang). Completed in 1863, it's famous for its staggeringly detailed gopuram (tower gateway). It is also the site of Theemidhi (*see p164*), a remarkable fire-walking ceremony held a week before the Hindu festival Deepavali, usually in October. If you want to take photos, you have to pay $3 ($6 for video cameras).

Thian Hock Keng Temple

158 Telok Ayer Street (6423 4616/www.thian hockkeng.com.sg). Tanjong Pagar MRT. **Open** 7.30am-5.30pm daily. **Map** p250 I11.

A century ago, Telok Ayer Street was right up against the sea. And this temple, known as the Temple of Heavenly Happiness, was popular with newly arrived immigrants, who came here to burn incense in thanks to Ma Cho Po (a Taoist deity and protector of seafarers) for their safe arrival. Some of the materials used in the temple were taken from the boats, including the rooftop mosaic. Inside, the main altar features a statue of Ma Cho Po, and other deities of luck, war and punishment. **Photo** *p66*.

Ying Fo Fui Kun

98 Telok Ayer Street (6533 6726). Chinatown MRT then 10mins walk. **Open** 9am-5pm Mon-Sat; 11am-5pm Sun. **Map** p250 I11.

As you wander around Chinatown, you'll see many signs for clan associations. But this one, for the Hakka community from eastern Guangdong, is the oldest still-functioning clan building on its original site. It began life as a temple, but gradually took on more functions as a welfare centre, and was rebuilt for that purpose in the late 19th century; later, it was a Chinese school. Inside are historical artefacts and antique furniture imported from China.

CBD

Singapore is driven by the financial industries, and the place where the largest amounts of money are shifted is the CBD. Relatively small and dull (compared to the ethnic enclaves) it may be, but it's the beating heart of Singapore. No surprise, then, that most postcards feature the same cluster of skyscrapers towering over the CBD. These banking headquarters are as much a symbol of Singapore as the Merlion or a plate of chicken rice.

Wedged up against the Singapore River, the CBD is on the fringes of Chinatown. Although the main body of the CBD around Raffles Place doesn't extend further south than Cross Street, offices continue to dominate Shenton Way, a main road that runs down past the Marina Bay developments to the south-east of Chinatown. But Raffles Place MRT station is the middle of the action.

Raffles Place

Cultural ramblings

Combine the CBD's vast wealth with the Chinese belief in feng shui – and the use of artworks as receptacles for good fortune and prosperity – and it's easy to see why the financial district has become a veritable public art gallery.

Start your walking tour underground in **Raffles Places MRT station (1)**. On the wall opposite the ticket barriers are large silk-screen panels depicting colonial history on one side, and the modern city on the other. Workers, children and soldiers gaze defiantly towards Singapore's future; this untitled piece of 'nation-building' propaganda, from the 1980s, is by Thang Kiang How.

Exit the station on to **Raffles Place (2)**. Behind each of the station's two main exits are large sculptures by Aw Tee Hong: *Struggle For Survival* and *Pioneering Spirit* (both 1987), works which continue the theme of Singapore's success in the face of adversity. For some classic corporate art, cross Almeida Street into **Republic Plaza (3)**, site of Yu Yu Yang's sculpture *Harmony* (1993). A reflective silver ball, topped with the Chinese character for man (ren), it depicts the conjoining of man and heaven. Head north and cross Chulia Street to **UOB Plaza (4)**, where you will encounter Salvador Dalí's imposing *Homage to Newton* (1985), a later work by the famous surrealist. It shows an opened-up figure whose heart is a gravity-defying, suspended ball (meant to depict an open-hearted spirit).

Head west down Chulia Street until you hit the **OCBC Centre (5)** on your left. IM Pei, the building's modernist architect, recommended that OCBC purchase Henry Moore's bronze sculpture *Reclining Figure* (1983) to offset the centre's 'masculine' qualities. Said to be Moore's largest work, it comprises fragmented female shapes that are monumental and mercurial. Turn right off Chulia Street towards the quayside, and follow the river back to the **UOB Building (6)**, where you can't miss *Bird* (1990), by Colombian artist Fernando Botero. Typical of the artist's outsized forms, the work is meant to exude 'peace and optimism'; it's also a favourite photo-spot for tourists.

Continue along the river towards Cavenagh Bridge. In front of the **Maybank Tower (7)** is a clutch of realistic bronze men, apparently in conversation. This is *The River Merchants* (2003, also by Aw Tee Hong), depicting an English businessman talking to Chinese and Malay traders, a made-for-tourists illustration of the river's history. Further up, in front of the **Fullerton Hotel (8)**, is the more dynamic and mischievous *First Generation* (2000) by Chong Fah Cheong. A gang of naked boys is freeze-framed as they prepare to jump into the water below.

For the finale, walk down the side of the Fullerton Hotel towards the main road, Collyer Quay, cross over to One Fullerton, descend the steps and go left. **Merlion Park (9)** features Singapore's national icon, half sea creature, half lion. Invented in the late 1960s as a logo for the first Singapore Tourism agency, it was given shape in 1972 in this eight-metre (26-foot) water-spewing sculpture, *The Merlion*, by Lim Nang Seng. Originally sited overlooking Marina Bay near the Esplanade, it was moved in 2002 (not without complaint) to its current position, which it shares with a mini Merlion. It's the most famous, most kitsch and weirdest piece of public art on the island – and a fitting end to the walk.

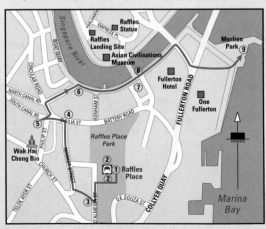

Originally called Commercial Square but renamed Raffles Place in 1858, this zone was established by Raffles in collaboration with George Drumgoole Coleman, one of Singapore's leading colonial architects; both saw the commercial value of its proximity to the river and docks. Although commerce and development have been unbroken throughout its history, it wasn't until after World War II that the increasingly high-profile tenants of Raffles Place began to build upwards, shaping the dramatic skyline seen today. More recently, the square was pedestrianised and the MRT interchange (with numerous exits/entrances) was built, with many older buildings being demolished in the process.

The Place itself is an open square with several small patches of lawn and low walls; office workers congregate here to socialise and escape from their cubicles. With such a captive audience, commercial or promotional events are frequent here. During the 2006 general election, for instance, the prime minister used it to make a memorable campaign speech. Similarly, veteran opposition figure JB Jeyaretnam regularly pitches up outside the Arcade Building on Collyer Quay, one of the older offices, to sell his books critiquing the PAP.

If you're impressed by height, then the tower blocks to look for are **Republic Plaza** (9 Raffles Place), **UOB Plaza** (No.80) and **OUB Centre** (No.1) – all 280 metres (920 feet) high. UOB Plaza's 'sky lobby' is closed for the time being, and none of the other skyscrapers allows the public on to the upper floors to enjoy the views – a sign of the security conscious times. Other notable high-risers are the **Bank of China** (4 Battery Road), one of the oldest, built in a classical-modern style in the late 1950s; and **OCBC Centre** (65 Chulia Street) designed in 1975 by IM Pei (the Chinese-American architect behind the Louvre pyramid in Paris).

The shops around the CBD cater mainly to the lunchtime crowds; there's a proliferation of chain cafés, coffee shops and sandwich shops (including Singapore's first Pret A Manger, at 35 Robinson Road). The basements of many buildings are connected by **Raffles Express**, an underground shopping and eating zone that's linked to the MRT system. Above ground, Hitachi Tower (16 Collyer Quay) contains **Change Alley**, two floors of stalls and boutiques, including 'express' spas and massages for the stressed-out. Across the road is **Clifford Pier**, a charmingly dilapidated meeting point for tourist boats running sightseeing cruises; at the time of writing, it's closed for the inevitable 'upgrade'.

The only real hawker centre in the CBD is **Lau Pa Sat** (18 Raffles Quay), a grandiose cast-iron Victorian structure dating from 1894; formerly a market, it's now known for the satay stalls that spring up outside in the evening. For lunch, try **Gourmet Corner** (15 Philip Street): its mouth-watering char siew and roast pork is so popular with the white-collar crowd that queues spill into the street. Opposite is **Wak Hai Cheng Bio Temple** (*see below*), also known as Yueh Hai Ching, a haven amid the banks and skyscrapers.

Wak Hai Cheng Bio Temple

30B Philip Street (www.ngeeann.com.sg).
Raffles Place MRT. **Open** 6am-6pm daily.
Map p250 J10.
Also known as the Calm Sea Temple, built in 1826 by Teochew fisherman. Set back from the road, the temple's wide forecourt is dominated by incense coils hung on wires. Note the large kilns for burning 'hell money' and other offerings to the dead.

Boat Quay

Boat Quay may be unabashedly touristy, but it's still a quintessential Singapore experience. Set on the northern edge of Chinatown, the riverside promenade and surrounding streets have a hint of oriental flavour with their array of colourful shophouses, though any historical authenticity is overshadowed by touristy shops, bars and restaurants. Still, the place comes alive at night as pleasure seekers stroll by the river.

Boat Quay has always been a hive of activity: in the 19th century, it handled three-quarters of Singapore's shipping business, and bumboats would jostle for berths at the water's edge. The Chinese traders chose to build their shophouses here because the south bank of the river resembled the belly of a carp – a symbol of wealth and prosperity. Materials traded included rubber, tin, steel and foodstuffs such as rice and coffee. Boat Quay's river trade declined in the 1960s when bumboats fell out of favour; by the '80s, when the government built a mechanised container port in Pasir Panjang, its commercial demise was complete. Later that decade, the URA started restoring shophouses and luring businesses.

Amid the chains and tourist traps, there are a few decent eating and drinking spots: Italian deli **Ricciotti** (*see p116*), a popular spot for dessert by the river; **Archipelago Craft Beer Hub** (*see p132*), a smart bar for beer experts; and **Molly Malone's** (*see p133*), an Irish pub beloved of expats. And a trip along the river, on an old-fashioned wooden bumboat, is a good way to see the skyline, especially at night. There are nine jetties along the river, and boats run until 10.30pm daily.

Sightseeing

Little India & the Arab Quarter

Teeming streets, bustling bazaars and an abundance of temples and mosques.

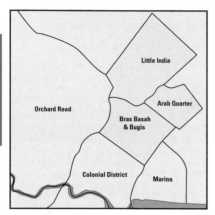

Little India

Under colonial rule, the area east of the Singapore River was designated as a settlement for Indian immigrants and workers, a legacy that has been enshrined in the district's more recent name, Little India. Today, it's one of the most distinctive places in Singapore, a bustling, chaotic sensory overload of people, shops, traffic, colours, smells and tastes, and largely unchanged for decades. To some extent it has retained its status as cultural centre for the Indian and Hindu community in Singapore – the majority Tamils from South India – but there are other races and religions in Little India, and a day spent wandering its streets will confirm how rich and fascinating the area is.

And it is fairly little. Starting north of the Colonial District, it covers only the first couple of miles of Serangoon Road, extending into the side streets that branch out to Race Course Road and Bukit Timah Road on one side, and Jalan Besar on the other. The main MRT station is Little India, which brings you to the heart of the area, beside Race Course Road – the site of Singapore's first stables and race course (and also where the first planes landed on the island).

Nearby are Buffalo Road and Kerbau Road. Both are named after the cattle (kerbau means

'water buffalo') that used to be sold here – a hugely successful business run by European merchants. Now, Buffalo Road's 'five-foot ways' (narrow, semi-sheltered pavements) are packed close with grocery stalls selling all kinds of fruit, vegetables and spices as well as the obligatory Hindi flower garlands.

Kerbau Road is, by comparison, an oasis of calm. The street was designated an 'Arts Belt' in 2002 by the National Arts Council, and several of the shophouses are rented out at a subsidised rate to visual and performing arts groups. Open to the public are the Indian art gallery at **Bhaskar's Arts Academy** (No.19, 6396 4523 – *see also p203*); contemporary arts space **Plastique Kinetic Worms** (*see p179*); and **spell#7** (*see p201*), which has created *Desire Paths*, an 'audio walking tour' of the area that combines music, soundscapes and voice (available on Saturday mornings, but call in advance). As you walk down Kerbau you can't miss **Tan Teng Ngiah House**, at No.37, a wonderful old Peranakan abode. Once a private residence (built by a confectionery businessman for his wife), it now houses shops and offices, but most of its original features are intact.

From there it's a short walk to the pungent smells and sights of **Tekka Centre** (*see p73*), and the noisy intensity of Serangoon Road. Little India's main strip, it is overwhelmingly busy with vehicles and human traffic (and has been for a long time: in early colonial maps it is marked as 'The Road Across the Island'). On each side of the road, you'll find yourself negotiating the shop displays that spill on to the cramped pavements. Clothing shops (either with traditional Indian saris and fabrics, or just cheap clothes) are interspersed with Tamil and Bollywood music and movie stores; there's also a mix of Indian goldsmiths, jewellers and more flower garlands, along with cafés and restaurants.

Little India Arcade, on the corner of Serangoon Road and Campbell Lane, is a touristy warren of traditional shops and services (including a henna tattoo artist), with a Singapore Tourist Board rep on hand to answer your questions. Several budget hotels

Little India

and backpacker hostels have sprung up in the last few years along Campbell Lane, and now there are pubs and cafés catering to this influx of younger tourists, including the **Prince of Wales** (*see p133*) on Dunlop Street. Also on Dunlop is the splendid **Abdul Gafoor Mosque** (*see below*), and **P Govindasamy Pillai** (PGP, No.153) a provisions and supplies shop founded by (and named after) one of Little India's most respected businessmen and benefactors. Walk further from Serangoon Road and you'll see backstreets teeming with an alternative economy of second-hand goods traders in paper, furniture, computers, washing machines and other cast-off items.

Near the corner of Serangoon Road and Upper Dickson Road is a fortune-teller accompanied by two 'psychic' parrots, who's been plying her trade here for 40 years – a living example of how little the area has changed. For a few dollars, one of the birds will pick you a fortune card. Continue northwards and the next side road is Cuff Road, a street that became famous for selling freshly ground spices. **Khan Mohamed Bhoy & Sons**

Sakya Muni Buddha Gaya. *See p73.*

(No.20) still sells a vast selection of packet spices, but the only grinder left is at No.2 – you can smell the turmeric outside the door. Further up Serangoon, on the opposite side of the road, is the **Sri Veeramakaliamman Temple** (*see p73*), Little India's most famous and ornate place of worship for Hindus.

When you get peckish, Race Course Road is the food street, where legendary curry houses **Banana Leaf Apolo** (*see p117*) and **Muthu's Curry** (*see p118*) can be found, along with many other South and North Indian restaurants. There are also branches of **Komala Vilas** (12 Buffalo Road, 6293 3664; 76 Serangoon Road, 6293 6980; www.komala vilas.com.sg), a vegetarian Indian eatery that is highly recommended (and cheap).

Heading north up Serangoon Road, you eventually hit Syed Alwi Street and the mammoth **Mustafa Centre** (*see p139*), known locally as Mustafas, the one-stop, 24-hour department store that sells everything from imitation Singapore Airlines uniforms to cars. For those curious about the dark underbelly of Singapore, behind Desker Road there is a back alley of cut-price brothels catering largely to foreign construction workers.

At the top end of Race Course Road is Farrer Park MRT, and many shops selling crystals, jade, Buddhas and other kitschy Chinese objets d'art. Nearby are several historical temples and places of worship, including **Sri Srinivasa Perumal Temple** (*see p73*) – the starting point for the annual **Thaipusam** procession (*see p165*) – and two Buddhist temples, **Leong San See** and **Sakya Muni Buddha Gaya** (for both, *see p73*).

Running parallel to Serangoon Road, but on the opposite side to Race Course Road, is Jalan Besar (literally 'big road' in Malay), which sports a number of shops specialising in bathroom fittings, lights and electronic appliances. More interestingly, it runs adjacent to a stretch of open space that's the site for the glamorously named **Thieves Market** (between Sungei Road and Jalan Besar), a set of makeshift stalls laid out on the ground. They flog bric-a-brac of all kinds, little of which is likely to be stolen these days.

Abdul Gafoor Mosque

41 Dunlop Street (6295 4209/www.mosque.org.sg/ abdulghafoor). Little India or Bugis MRT then 10mins walk. **Open** *7am-noon, 2.30-4.30pm daily.* **Map** *p249 L4.*

This side of Little India was historically the area where the Indian Muslims settled, and the original mosque on this site was founded by Shaik Abdul Gaffoor, a legal clerk in the late 19th century. The current building was a replacement, started in 1907 but not completed until the 1920s. Its architecture is a combination of South Indian, Moorish and Roman styles with a number of unique features such as the sundial in the entrance to the main prayer hall, which is decorated with 25 sunbursts that denote the 25 prophets in calligraphy.

Leong San See Temple

371 Race Course Road (6298 9371). Farrer Park MRT. **Open** 6am-6pm daily. **Map** p249 L1.
Supposedly dating from the early 19th century, the name of this incense-filled Taoist Buddhist temple translates as Dragon Mountain. You'll see plenty of fearsome-looking dragons among the swastikas and relief paintings on its exterior. Inside is an altar to Confucius and behind that an ancestral hall dedicated to the deceased.

Sakya Muni Buddha Gaya Temple

366 Race Course Road (6294 0714). Farrer Park MRT. **Open** 8am-4.30pm daily. **Map** p249 L1.
Founded by a Thai monk in the 1920s, this temple is decorated in a style unlike traditional Buddhist temples elsewhere in Singapore. The first thing you'll notice are the brightly coloured (and cartoon-ish) tiger statues that flank the doorway. The interior contains an impressive 15m (50ft) statue of Buddha, illuminated with dozens of lights – hence the building's other name, Temple of 1,000 Lights. In the back chambers are an image of the elderly reclining Buddha, and a wheel of fortune that you can spin for a small donation. **Photo** *p72.*

Sri Srinivasa Perumal Temple

397 Serangoon Road (6928 5771). Farrer Park MRT. **Open** 6.30am-noon, 6-9pm daily.
Map p249 L1.
The original temple was built in 1885. It has been renovated several times, particularly in the 1960s, with the gopuram erected only as recently as 1979. Dedicated to Lord Vishnu, the temple features decorations of the deity in his many incarnations. Statues of him, his consorts and Garuda (the bird he flies on) can be seen inside.

Sri Veeramakaliamman Temple

141 Serangoon Road (6295 4538/6/ www.sriveeramakaliamman.com). Little India MRT. **Open** 5.30am-12pm, 4-9pm daily.
Map p248 K3.
Little India's most popular Hindu temple is dedicated to the goddess Kali, often misrepresented in the West as a deity of destruction, but actually a benevolent (if powerful) figure. The building was apparently constructed by Bengali immigrants, and completed in 1881, but like all such monuments in Singapore has gone through many extensions and renovations over the years. The gopuram (tower entrance) is strikingly decorated with multicoloured depictions of numerous Hindu deities, while the main shrine houses a jet black statue of Kali, flanked by her sons Ganesha and Murugam. You can spot those who have been blessed at this temple: they have white ash on their forehead, rather than the usual dark colours.

Colourful **Sri Srinivasa Perumal Temple**.

Tekka Centre

Corner of Buffalo, Bukit Timah & Serangoon Roads. Little India MRT. **Open** approx 6.30am-9pm daily.
Map p248 K3.
At the start of Serangoon Road, on the corner facing Bukit Timah and the Rochor Canal, stands the perennially popular Tekka Centre. Built in 1981, it replaced the original food market that gave the place its name (tek khia ka is Hokkien for 'at the foot of the bamboo'). It's always been a famous place to buy a vast selection of vegetables, fruit, herbs and, especially, meat. The new complex also houses a hawker centre, while upstairs is a bazaar selling cheap clothes, jewellery, watches and more.

Arab Quarter

South-east of Little India is an enclave of streets and landmarks between Rochor Canal Road and Beach Road that has come to be known as the predominantly Arab area of Singapore. It is still referred to by its original name, Kampong Glam, named after the gelam trees that grew in the area, or the Gelam tribe, or both. It was designated by Raffles as the site for Sultan Husain Shah's palace after the Sultan had relinquished the island to the Brits. And it soon became a gathering point for Malays, Indonesians from Java and merchants from the Middle East. The street names reflect this:

Sightseeing

Sultan Mosque

you'll find yourself wandering down Arab Street, Kandahar Street and Baghdad Street. The nearest MRT is Bugis, but it's not that close: if you don't fancy the 15-minute walk, get a bus (48 or 57 if you're coming from Little India) or jump in a cab.

The area is still an important centre for the Malay and Muslim communities because of the **Sultan Mosque** (*see p75*), the largest and most imposing in Singapore. Other mosques in the area include the **Hajjah Fatimah Mosque** (*see below*), on Beach Road next to Kampong Glam Park, and **Malabar Muslim Jamaah Mosque** (*see p75*), on Victoria Street. By day the Arab Quarter is ideal for a quiet and pleasant stroll; at night (especially at weekends) it starts to buzz with its own smoky atmosphere. The cafés and restaurants may not serve alcohol, but there is live music to enjoy, hearty Middle Eastern food and shisha pipes to be puffed in joints like **Café Samar** (*see p133*).

The Sultan Mosque is at the heart of the Arab Quarter, and its pre-eminence as a tourist attraction is reflected in Bussorah Street in front of it: a pedestrianised lane of gift shops selling antiques, postcards and coloured cloth. If you really want to go shopping, head to the Beach Road end of Arab Street where there's greater choice – an array of silk, cloth and carpet dealers, along with the superb **Café Le Caire** (*see p118*), whose iced mint tea takes the edge off a hot day. Parallel to Arab Street is much-hyped Haji Lane, home to a handful of trendy boutiques, vintage clothing shops and quirky cafés (*see p146* **Beyond the mall**). Behind it is the mostly gentrified Bali Lane, a vision of what Haji Lane could be in a few years.

The Sultan's palace (Istana Kampong Glam) and its grounds were closed for many years, but have now been transformed into the **Malay Heritage Centre** (*see p75*) and are open to the public. For those curious about Malay and Islamic culture, there are several specialist bookshops on Kandahar Street.

The major thoroughfare of Beach Road was, as its name suggests, once a coast road fronting the sea, lined with impressive villas, hotels and bars. Land reclamation began in the 1880s and gradually pushed it further inland: Nicoll Highway and the Marina area beyond it are all built on reclaimed land. At the northern end of Beach Road is the **Golden Mile Complex**, a classic 1970s building that, in its fusion of residential and commercial space, was designed to represent a futuristic vision of the city. The apartments, which come with gardens, are pretty run-down these days. Underneath the complex, the **Golden Mile Shopping Centre** has become an enclave for Thai food and entertainment. It also houses the Golden Theatre, a soft-porn cinema, and is a meeting point for holiday coaches off to Malaysia.

Hajjah Fatimah Mosque

4001 Beach Road (6297 2774). Lavender MRT then 10mins walk. **Open** 9am-9pm daily. **Map** p249 N4. Named after a Malaccan woman shipping entrepreneur who donated her home to become the site for the mosque. Distinct because of its European style, and for being skewed against the lines of the road grid, the 1846 building was designed by John Turnbull Thomson, an influential colonial civil engineer. Other notable features include the high minaret tower and the stained-glass dome roof, visible from the prayer hall.

later, the population of the area had swelled, and it was rebuilt. Designed by Irish architect Dennis Santry and influenced by monuments like the Taj Mahal, it's a striking structure, crowned with an immense golden dome. Visitors are welcome to wander freely (except into the prayer hall), though it's often busy with worshippers. During Ramadan, local Muslims come to the grounds to break their fast at the end of the day, and a cooked food market springs up outside.

Bugis & Bras Basah Road

Flanked by Prinsep Street and the middle section of Beach Road, and extending from Rochor Canal Road south to Bras Basah Road, Bugis is a thriving shopping zone (it gets packed at weekends) that is centred around a large mall, **Bugis Junction** (see p141), built above Bugis MRT station. Though Bugis Road is named after the tribe of nomadic Malays who used to sail into Singapore to trade, land reclamation has wiped away all traces of that era.

Bugis' famous night market is another piece of history that has been erased. Originating after World War II, it grew to become one of Singapore's most infamous tourist attractions. At night the narrow lanes around Bugis Street would fill with (pre-hawker centre) street food stalls serving customers on makeshift furniture. Then, around midnight, scores of transvestites and transsexuals would descend on the punters – flirting, soliciting, dancing and generally behaving outrageously. A favourite spot for soldiers and sailors on shore leave, it was such an institution that the 'girls' even had their own postcards. Sadly, the area was cleaned up in the early 1980s, and the development around the MRT drastically altered the geography of Bugis. The original Bugis Street was absorbed into Bugis Junction, along with adjoining Hylam Street – these are now glass roofed, vaguely preserved shopping 'streets' that are essentially part of the mall.

On the other side of Victoria Street, New Bugis Street houses a pedestrianised covered street market filled with low-end tourist tat, cheap watches and 'Singapore is a Fine City' T-shirts. The adjacent shophouses have become Bugis Village, two storeys of boutiques selling low-price clothes and accessories; in keeping with the area's history, there's also a sex shop. Keep heading up pedestrianised Albert Street and you'll hit **Sim Lim Square** (see p146), a legendary treasure trove of cheap electronics and the latest gizmos from Japan and South Korea. Across the canal is **Sim Lim Tower**, which has more specialised shops for professional audio equipment.

Malabar Muslim Jamaah Mosque
471 Victoria Street (6294 3862/www.mosque.org sg/malabar). Lavender MRT. **Open** 5.30am-10.30pm daily. **Map** p249 M3.
Beautiful blue patterned walls are topped with a golden sphere, earning this building the nickname 'Golden Dome Mosque'. But the real name refers to its origins: it was Singapore's only mosque built by Indian Muslims from the Malabar coastal region of Kerala. It was completed in 1963.

Malay Heritage Centre
85 & 73 Sultan Gate (6391 0450/www.malay heritage.org.sg). Bugis MRT then 10mins walk. **Open** *Grounds* 8am-9pm daily. *Museum* 1-6pm Mon; 10am-6pm Tue-Sun. **Admission** *Grounds* free. *Museum* $3; $2 concessions; free under-7s. **Credit** MC, V. **Map** p249 M/N4.
This heritage centre tells the story of Singapore's place in the Malay world. It has a reasonable number of historical objects and, a couple of dubious murals aside, the ground floor display successfully evokes the complex political, cultural and religious worlds that shaped the Malay experience until the end of the 19th century. Upstairs is patchier, perhaps because the 20th-century story is more sanitised and politically selective. Nevertheless, there's enough to give the visitor a valuable perspective on Singapore's most significant 'minority' ethnic group. Ask about cultural performances on Wednesday and Sundays.

Sultan Mosque
3 Muscat Street (6293 4405/ www.mosque.org.sg/ sultan). Bugis MRT then 10mins walk. **Open** 9am-4.30pm Mon-Thur, Sat, Sun; 9am-noon, 2.30-4.30pm Fri. **Map** p249 M4.
The original mosque was constructed in 1826 under the instructions of Sultan Husain, who wanted a mosque for his family close to his palace. A century

Sightseeing

On the western end of Bugis is Waterloo Street, containing (on the pedestrianised stretch near Albert Street) side-by-side Hindu and Buddhist temples. In fact, many Buddhist Chinese also pray at the **Sri Krishnan Temple**, while **Kwan Im Thong Hood Cho Temple** (for both, *see below*) is always frenetically busy.

On the same road is **Sculpture Square** Middle Road, 6333 1055, www.sculpture sq.com.sg), a former Methodist church that has been converted into a gallery specialising in contemporary sculpture and installations. For more art, head up Middle Road to the **Nanyang Academy of Fine Arts** (NAFA, Bencoolen Street, 6512 4000, www.nafa.edu.sg), which houses some public galleries. The government has a master plan to turn this district into an 'Arts Education' hub, with the new LaSalle-SIA College of the Arts on Prinsep Street due to be ready in 2007, and the Arts School (a secondary school specialising in arts education) under

construction at Selegie Road. All will be in reasonably close proximity to the **Singapore Art Museum** (*see below*) on Bras Basah Road, the country's largest visual arts gallery.

Between Victoria Street and North Bridge Road, you can't miss the impressive, 16-storey **National Library Building** (*see below*), opened in 2005. Sitting next to it is the **Bras Basah Complex**, an open-air shopping centre that specialises in second-hand books, stationery and arts equipment.

Kwan Im Thong Hood Cho Temple

178 Waterloo Street (6337 3965/ 6337 9227). Bugis MRT then 10mins walk. **Open** 6am-6pm daily. **Map** p248 K5.

This Buddhist temple, built in 1884, is dedicated to Kwan Im (also called Guanyin), the goddess of mercy, and was used as a refuge for the sick and destitute during the Japanese occupation. Today, hundreds of worshippers flood in every day; the main prayer hall is a flurry of activity as people take turns to kneel on the prayer carpet in front of the golden Buddha, where they shake i-ching sticks.

National Library Building

100 Victoria Street (6332 3255/www.nlb.gov.sg). Bugis MRT. **Open** *Central Lending Library* 10am-9pm daily. **Map** p249 L6.

Showered with architectural awards before it had even opened, the new building (a replacement for the old National Library on Stamford Road) is designed as two towers, linked by walkways and walled almost entirely with glass. The spacious reference section on the upper floors offers great views across the city. There are some small exhibition spaces, and it also houses the Drama Centre (*see p203*).

Singapore Art Museum

71 Bras Basah Road (6332 3222/www.nhb.gov.sg/ sam). City Hall MRT. **Open** 10am-7pm Mon-Thur, Sat, Sun; 10am-9pm Fri. **Admission** $5; $2.50 concessions; free under-6s. Free for all 6-9pm Fri. **No credit cards. Map** p248 K6.

This former Catholic boys' school, a striking white building with two wings and long verandas, was revamped in the early 1990s when there was a policy of converting old colonial buildings into public museums. Because of its small, unusual and hidden gallery spaces, it has never held blockbuster shows. Instead, it specialises in smaller exhibitions, mostly 20th-century Asian visual art, often drawn from its own collection of South-east Asian 'pioneer' art.

Sri Krishnan Temple

152 Waterloo Street (6337 7957). Bugis MRT then 10mins walk. **Open** 6am-2.30pm, 5.30-9pm daily. **Map** p248 K5.

What began in 1870 as a banyan tree with a few deities placed next to it has evolved into a vivid, colourful temple dedicated to Lord Krishna, the supreme god in Hindu cosmology. Much of the current building was constructed in the 1980s.

Little Everywhere

With over half a million low-income foreign migrant workers doing the jobs that Singaporeans prefer not to do, it's hardly surprising that some of them have transformed parts of the island into homes away from home – with their own distinct atmospheres and cheap grub.

The most famous is Little India on Sunday evening, when Indian construction workers, many from Bangladesh, head for the streets and open spaces around Serangoon Road to catch up and take a breather before another week of back-breaking grind. Thais flock to Golden Mile Shopping Centre (Golden Mile Complex on Beach Road), where there are numerous Thai eateries, pubs, karaoke joints and discos, running the gamut from charming to sleazy. You'll also find locals here letting off steam.

Peninsula Plaza on North Bridge Road is another elderly shopping centre, but it's also a centre for Burmese workers over from Myanmar, and there are a few genuine provisions shops, cafés and a book and music shop. On Sundays, Lucky Plaza mall on Orchard Road fills up with hordes of laughing and gossiping Indonesian and Filipino women. It's the maids' one day off a week, and there are a number of shops and food stalls catering to their needs.

Orchard Road & Around

Shop till you drop and lie down in luxury.

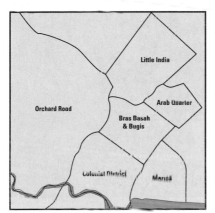

Orchard Road is the island's most famous shopping district, but it's also a popular eating and sleeping destination with a slew of excellent restaurants and many of Singapore's grandest hotels. It runs from Dhoby Ghaut in the east – site of the Istana, home of Singapore's president – to the Tanglin area in the west, where you'll find numerous embassies and the Singapore Botanic Gardens. Three MRT stations serve the main drag: Orchard, Somerset and Dhoby Ghaut. To the south, off Killiney Road, is River Valley, which leads to the entertainment belt around Robertson Quay and Mohamed Sultan Road; northwards are the districts of Newton and Novena.

For more information, maps and brochures, pop into the STB's **Singapore Visitors Centre@Orchard**, at the junction of Orchard and Cairnhill Roads.

Orchard Road

Singapore's vibrant shopping drag is a wide, one-way street flanked by tree-lined walkways. The road's name was derived from the nutmeg, pepper and fruit plantations found here in the 19th century. Cemeteries also existed in the 1840s: a large Chinese graveyard once occupied the site of the **Meritus Mandarin** hotel (*see p46*), and a Jewish cemetery was located in the Dhoby Ghaut area (and not demolished until 1984). The first malls appeared in the 1970s, and it's been non-stop development ever since.

The area around Orchard MRT station is the heart of the shopping district. Notable malls include gargantuan **Ngee Ann City** (*see p141*), which houses **Kinokuniya** (*see p143*), Southeast Asia's largest bookstore, and Japanese department store **Takashimaya** (*see p139*). Other shopping centres nearby are **Wisma Atria** (*see p142*), known for its large food court and aquarium; fashionable and iconic **Tangs** (*see p139*); **Wheelock Place**, containing **Borders** (*see p143*); and the swanky **Paragon** (*see p141*). Teens flock to the **Heeren Shops** (*see p141*) and **Far East Plaza** (on Scotts Road, *see p141*) for the latest streetwear, and to **Cathay Cineleisure Orchard** (on Grange Road) for fast food, more shops and the 12-screen Cathay cinema. You can escape the heat (or the rain) via an extensive network of underground passageways linking the malls. You can't flag a cab along Orchard Road, but there are taxi ranks at strategic points.

Orchard is always a bustling spot, but it gets positively rammed with shoppers during holiday periods. The over-the-top 'Christmas Light Up' event at the end of the year, and the Chingay Parade of Dreams, a colourful street and float parade to celebrate Chinese New Year, also attract the masses.

Though retail therapy is the area's raison d'être, there's a plethora of swanky restaurants and luxury hotels too, including the pagoda-shaped **Marriott Hotel** (*see p49*) and the **Grand Hyatt** (*see p50*) on Scotts Road, whose floors were redesigned by a feng shui specialist to usher in more wealth. The **Hilton Hotel** (581 Orchard Road, 6737 2233) is flanked by two outdoor ceramic statues representing two Tang-era generals. Known as 'doorway guardians', the generals were meant to protect the brutal Chinese emperor Tang from haunting spirits at night; the 'ghostbuster' statues perform the same function for the hotel.

Directly opposite the Hilton is the **Thai Embassy** (370 Orchard Road), purchased by the King of Siam in the early 1890s. Although run-down, the white building oozes character and is surrounded by a pretty garden. The embassy also hosts the occasional Thai fair: you'll know when it's on, as you can smell the durians from miles away. West of the embassy is the infamous **Orchard Towers** (400 Orchard Road). Known by day as a regular

Christmas crowds and lights along **Orchard Road**, Singapore's main shopping strip.

shopping mall, by night it is transformed into an unofficial red-light district, where scantily clad ladies and lady boys tout for trade in the many pubs and clubs.

This area is due for a face-lift as part of Singapore's urban renewal plan. Besides a new crop of shopping and entertainment complexes, the two-kilometre (1.2-mile) main strip will include a 218-metre (715-foot) skyscraper with a 360-degree public observation deck. Called Orchard Turn, the massive project will contain luxury apartments and eight storeys of shops – and will take over the last patch of greenery on Orchard Road, adjacent to Orchard MRT.

If you tire of trawling the malls, take a walk around the picturesque enclave of Emerald Hill, located on the north side of Orchard Road, across from Somerset MRT station. At the front is **Peranakan Place**, a crop of carefully restored shophouses with bustling cafés and boutiques on the ground level, and **Rouge** nightclub (9738 1000) above. To get to Emerald Hill proper, walk up the pedestrian alley past the musty 'One Price Shop' (selling oriental knick-knacks) and a string of popular bars: **Alley Bar** (2 Emerald Hill Road, 6732 6966); and **No.5, Que Pasa** and **Ice Cold Beer** (for all three, *see p136*). To soak up the flavour, meander and take in the early 20th-century, double-storey terrace houses. Built by affluent Peranakans, they are now primarily occupied by well-heeled expats. The façades are well preserved; look for intricate ceramic tiles with

flower motifs, and carved swing doors with gold patterns. No.83, with its white tiles and pastel blue woodwork, and No.73, with wooden shutters and gold paintwork, are charmers.

The neighbourhood's roots date back to 1819, when Chinese squatters started clearing the jungle to provide fuel for the boiling of gambier leaves. In 1837, Emerald Hill was turned into a nutmeg plantation by William Cuppage, its first owner. In 1901, the land was subdivided for residential development. But the neighbourhood maintains its tropical allure, covered as it is by frangipani trees and multi-hued bougainvillea.

On block east, on Cairnhill Road, is another row of lovely 1920s terrace houses. No.56, with gargoyles perched on the fence, is the **Whisky Store** (6732 3452), while No.82 is the **Art Forum** gallery (*see p179*) a showcase for South-east Asian art. Cuppage Terrace, east of Peranakan Place, is where to go to chow down. It has several alfresco eateries and a food court serving nosh around the clock.

Adjacent, at 176 Orchard Road, is **Centrepoint Shopping Centre**, containing branches of Robinsons department store, Marks & Spencer and Cold Storage, the oldest supermarket in town. Yet another super-mall is opening opposite in 2007: the 12-storey Orchard Central is planned to be even bigger than Ngee Ann City. Further east, near Dhoby Ghaut MRT, is **Plaza Singapura** (No.68), which houses the French hypermarket Carrefour and a cineplex. Behind it are the tropical gardens of the **Istana** (*see below*), the office and official residence of the president of Singapore.

On the other side of Orchard Road, across Istana Park, is Penang Road and the **House of Tan Yeok Nee**, a traditional mansion built in 1885 for a wealthy Chinese merchant. Used as the Salvation Army headquarters from 1940 to the '80s, it now houses the Asian campus for the University of Chicago's graduate business school – but is not open to visitors. Other buildings of interest are **YMCA International House** (*see p51*). Now a good choice for budget travellers looking for a cheap bed, during the Japanese occupation it was the headquarters of the Kempcitai (Japanese secret police), while the **Cathay Building** across the road housed the Japanese propaganda and military intelligence departments. Next to the YMCA is **Orchard Road Presbyterian Church**, which dates back 150 years. Used as an issuing store for Japanese civilians during World War II, it was also where the gruesome (and still unsolved) 'curry murder' took place in 1984: an Indian caretaker was clubbed to death, chopped up and cooked in a pot of curry.

More shopping centres and first-class hotels line Scotts Road, running north from Orchard MRT station. Historic **Goodwood Park Hotel** (*see p47*) is a splendid throwback to the colonial era: built in 1900, the elegant building rivals Raffles Hotel in the charm stakes. And it's rich in history: it was the Teutonia Club for German expats until World War I, then a performance venue. In 1929, it was converted to a hotel, frequented by celebs and royalty. During the Japanese occupation it became an army headquarters; later, its grand tower was declared a national monument. These days, local foodies come here for steaks, Taiwanese porridge and durian puffs.

Further north, just past Newton MRT, is **Newton Hawker Centre** (*see p121*), built in 1971 and newly renovated. Although touristy, it serves typical hawker food in a convivial open-air setting. One stop after Newton is Novena MRT (which some locals believe is haunted) and the Catholic **Novena Church** (300 Thomson Road), a neo-classical landmark built in 1950. To the west lies the district of Balestier, site of the former Shaw Brothers film studios, and worth exploring for its temples, art deco shophouses and old-fashioned coffeeshops.

Istana

www.istana.gov.sg. Dhoby Ghaut MRT. Map p248 H3.
Set in sprawling, lush grounds, the Istana ('palace' in Malay) is the setting for state and ceremonial occasions. Built in 1869, the elegant building (a mix of Palladian and Anglo Indian styles) was once the British colonial governor's residence, and during

World War II was occupied by Japanese army commanders. There are two entrances: a main one with an imposing driveway along Orchard Road, and a smaller gate on Cavenagh Road. The latter is used by VIPs (George Bush zoomed through it with his motorcade in 2006). The Istana is open to the public on selected public holidays (usually 8.30am to 6pm), such as New Year's Day, Hari Raya Puasa, Chinese New Year, National Day and Deepvali – there are always queues, and foreigners have to pay $1 admission. On the first Sunday of the month, a changing of the guard ceremony takes place at the main gate at 6pm; a good viewing spot is Istana Park, on the other side of Orchard Road.

Tanglin & Dempsey Road

Orchard Road becomes Tanglin Road at the **Orchard Parade Hotel** (6737 1133); next door is the **Tanglin Shopping Centre** (No.19), which marks the end of the Orchard Road shopping belt. Despite the centre's dated exterior, great antique stores can be found here. More Asian arts and crafts shops are housed in **Tudor Court** (No.123), along with French food shop **Hediard** (*see p139*). Adjacent **Tanglin Mall** (No.163) is stuffed with kids' toy and clothes shops, plus Tanglin Market Place, a gourmet supermarket beloved of expats. There aren't any MRT stations here, so catch a bus, or take a short taxi ride or a long walk.

Emerald Hill.
See p78.

Sightseeing

The neighbourhood is crawling with diplomats: the streets around Napier and Tanglin Roads contain embassies and high commissions for numerous countries, including Australia, Indonesia, China, the UK and the US (unmissable – it's a massive, grey, fort-like complex). South of Napier Road is Minden Road, a nutmeg estate until 1860 and later purchased by the British for military use. Today, it is home to the Ministry of Foreign Affairs, small **Tanglin Golf Course** (6473 7236, open to the public) and the Anglican **St George's Church**, a popular spot for weddings. Built in 1911 as a garrison church, the squat, red-brick building was used by the Japanese as an ammunition dump in World War II. To the north is the long green sprawl of **Singapore Botanic Gardens** (*see below*) with its orchids, palm trees and lakes. There's an entrance on Napier Road, but the main gate and visitor centre are off Cluny Road.

Further west, south of Holland Road, is the characterful and tree-lined Dempsey Road area – recently renamed **Tanglin Village** (www.tanglinvillage.com.sg). Originally a plantation, then a British army camp, it has become a thriving cultural enclave filled with Asian antiques shops and galleries. The colony of wine bars, cafés and restaurants is the toast of the town; hotspots include **PS Café** (*see p123*), **Oosh** (*see p136*) and **Hacienda** (*see p135*). In durian season, a stall located in a car park near the Hacienda sells good-quality specimens of the odiferous fruit. The colonial buildings near the Dempsey Road entrance will soon be resuscitated. One of them already has been: Block 25A, which used to be the Civil Service Club, is home to the ever-popular **Samy's Curry Restaurant** (*see p121*), going strong for more than two decades. The Dempsey Road area is dark at night, and not easy to explore on foot – best to take a cab.

Singapore Botanic Gardens

1 Cluny Road (6471 7361/www.sbg.org.sg).
Bus 7, 75, 77, 105, 123, 174. **Open** 5am-midnight
daily. *National Orchid Garden* 8.30am-7pm daily.
Admission free. *National Orchid Garden* $5;
$1 concessions; free under-12s. **Credit** (shop only)
AmEx, DC, JCB, MC, V. **Map** p246 A2.

The first 'Botanical and Experimental Garden' was set up by Raffles in 1822, on Fort Canning. Thirty years later, the Singapore Botanic Gardens were established to collect, grow and distribute poten-tially useful plants; in the early days, botanist Henry Ridley experimented with South American rubber tree seeds, paving the way for the region's rubber industry. These days it's a major research centre and a lovely tranquil retreat from the urban grind. Paths wind past grassy slopes, towering rain trees, stat-ues and fountains; on weekends, crowds practise

Singapore Botanic Gardens

yoga and tai chi at the gazebos, and children feed black Australian swans at Swan Lake. Highlights include the Evolution Garden Walk, a cleverly designed, Jurassic-style garden containing the fossilised remains of ancient trees; and the National Orchid Garden, the world's largest display of orchids, with over 1,000 species and 2,000 hybrids (including the blowsy national flower, Vanda Miss Joaquim). There's also a patch of rainforest, a bougainvillea garden and Symphony Lake, where outdoor concerts are sometimes held.

Around Robertson Quay

Killiney Road runs south-west from Somerset MRT station. It's notable for its string of eateries in a row of shophouses, including **Killiney Kopitiam** (67 Killiney Road, 6734 9648), a coffeeshop that has been serving its famous charcoal-grilled kaya toast, a local breakfast delicacy, since 1919. To the south is River Valley Road, a middle-class residential stretch that runs eastwards to the foot of Fort Canning. To the west is Zion Road, site of the **Zion Riverside Food Centre** (see p122), a popular hawker centre that's known for its char kway teow. Singapore's favourite nightspot **Zouk** (see p172) is nearby – off Kim Seng Road, parallel to Zion Road.

Along the riverbank is Robertson Quay, the newest of Singapore's waterfront nightspots, lined with condominiums, restaurants and bars. Quieter and more upmarket than Boat and Clarke Quays, it stands to gain more character in the long run. Highlights include the relaxed **Book Café** (#01-02 Seng Kee Building, 20 Martin Road, 6887 5430); manga-tastic Japanese restaurant **Bon Goût** (see p119); and the seriously stylish **Gallery Hotel** (see p50). One block back from the water, Mohamed Sultan Road was dominated by noisy bars and clubs in the 1990s, but these have been replaced by restaurants in recent years. The latest residential site, the Pier@Robertson (No.80), is dotted with trendy eateries such as chocolatier/café **Chocolate Factory** (6235 9007) and Belgian bar and bistro **Brussels Sprouts** (6887 4344). Amid the nightspots is Buddhist temple **Hong San See** (see below).

Cultural offerings in the area include **Singapore Repertory Theatre** (see p201), one of Asia's leading English-language theatre companies; the **Singapore Tyler Print Institute** (see p177), a renowned gallery focusing on printed works that also houses much-praised Australian restaurant, the **Rivercafé** (6733 4414, www.rivercafe.com.sg); and **72-13**, a multi-disciplinary arts space run by Singapore's foremost experimental theatre group, **TheatreWorks** (see p201).

For a cluster of religious sites, head up Tank Road, off River Valley Road. First comes Hindu temple **Sri Thandayuthapani** (see below), then the Catholic **Church of Sacred Heart** and, around the corner on Oxley Rise, **Chesed-El Synagogue**. The last was built in 1905 by Sir Reuben Menasseh Meyer, who was Singapore's municipal commissioner from 1893 to 1900.

Hong San See Temple

31 Mohamed Sultan Road (6737 3683/3866). Bus 32, 54, 143, 195. **Open** *7am-5pm daily.* **Map** *p250 G7.*
Dedicated to the god of filial piety, Hong San See was constructed by Fukien immigrants in 1829 in Tanjong Pagar; it was moved to its present location in 1907. Set on a hill for good feng shui, it is surrounded by lush gardens. The flamboyant red and gold interior features granite columns festooned with dragons and flowers.

Sri Thandayuthapani Temple

15 Tank Road (6737 9393/www.sttemple.com). Dhoby Ghaut MRT then 10mins walk. **Open** *8am-noon, 5.30-8.30pm daily.* **Map** *p250 H7.*
One of the largest temples in Singapore, built in 1859 by Nattukkotai Chettiars (merchants and money lenders from Tamil Nadu), and rebuilt in the 1980s. Its unique feature is the lavishly decorated painted glass ceiling; each of the 48 panels represents a different deity and is angled to reflect the sunrise and sunset. The temple's busy festival calendar includes a three-day event in April and July, during which 100,008 recitals are performed. It's also the final destination for the annual Thaipusam procession (see p165), which starts in Little India. Watch exhausted but exhilarated kavadi-carrying devotees mark the end of their ordeal with the smashing of a coconut, whose white flesh represents spiritual purity.

Green retreats

Bukit Timah Nature Reserve
Singapore's only surviving area of primary rainforest. *See p98.*

Kranji Countryside
Frogs, goats and vegetables. *See p101* **Down on the farm.**

MacRitchie Reservoir
The lush, forested heart of the island. *See p104.*

Singapore Botanic Gardens
A tranquil escape in the city centre. With orchids. *See p80.*

Sungei Buloh Wetland Reserve
Mangrove swamps and birdwatching. *See p101.*

Sightseeing

Sentosa & Around

A self-contained island resort, alongside the world's busiest port.

Some of Singapore's most popular attractions can be found at the island's southern tip. The area comprises the district of Telok Blangah (where Singapore's *temenggong* or village chief once lived) dominated by Mount Faber; Keppel Harbour; and the island resort of Sentosa. There's also the HarbourFront precinct, which houses the country's largest mall, biggest nightspot complex, cruise centre and only cable car system. Just 15 minutes from the city centre, it's all easily accessible by bus and MRT.

HarbourFront & Mount Faber

The **HarbourFront** precinct is a designated business and lifestyle hub along Singapore's southern waterfront. HarbourFront MRT station opens into the $400-million **VivoCity** (*see p84*), Singapore's largest shopping mall. The white, wave-like structure (by Japanese techno-futurist architect Toyo Ito) includes a waterfront promenade, rooftop amphitheatre and over 300 shopping, entertainment and dining options. You'd have thought Singapore would have enough malls, but no: almost a million visitors came during its first week of operations in October 2006.

To the west is the HarbourFront Centre, a busy shopping centre with a striking two-storey rotunda. It also houses the **Singapore Cruise Centre** (6513 2222, www.singaporecruise.com), which handled 850,000 cruise and ferry passengers in 2006 alone. Here, you can catch a ferry to the Indonesian islands of Batam and Bintan, and pick up free maps, brochures and information on local tours and events from the Singapore Visitors Centre in the arrival hall. The weekend taxi queues outside are notoriously long.

Head to **HarbourFront Tower Two** in the Office Park next door to catch the **cable car** (*see p84*) to the top of **Mount Faber** (*see p83*). At 105 metres (345 feet), it's the second highest point in Singapore after Bukit Timah Hill and offers breathtaking views of the southern coastline and northern cityscape. You can also get to the peak on bus 409 from the HarbourFront bus interchange. Alternatively, climb up via any of the two roads and eight footpaths through the park's rich flora and fauna. The easiest and most popular route with

joggers and dog walkers is along the road off Kampong Bahru Road. On this route, you'll see lovely black and white colonial houses as well as a small kramat (shrine) to a Javanese princess. If you go by Morse Road, you'll pass the striking red and white striped Danish Seamen's Church, one of five seafarers' missions in Singapore.

Taking the cable car in the opposite direction from Mount Faber will bring you to Sentosa – also accessible via the Sentosa Express light rail system or by road, over the Sentosa Causeway. To the east of the causeway is the red-brick **St James Power Station** (*see p172*). Built in 1927, the country's first coal-fired power station is now heating up as the largest nightclub hotspot in the land, with nine different themed spaces under its roof. It also houses **TigerLIVE** (6376 9339, www.tigerlive.com.sg), a multi-media entertainment centre showcasing everything you could ever possibly want to know about Singapore's famous lager, Tiger Beer.

The view to the east is dominated by towering container cranes and, sometimes, a colossal container ship or two. This is **Keppel Harbour**, a natural port with deep and sheltered waters, which enabled the tiny island of Singapore to become a vital global trading port. Formerly known as New Harbour, it was renamed Keppel Harbour in 1900 after British Admiral Sir Henry Keppel. Its three container terminals – Keppel and Tanjong Pagar on the mainland, and Brani on the island just off the harbour – are part of the collective facilities that make the Port of Singapore the world's busiest; it's arguably Singapore's biggest asset.

A hidden gem worth seeking out west of HarbourFront (catch bus 408) is lovely, coast-hugging **Labrador Park**. A former defence battery known as Fort Pasir Panjang used by the British Army in the late 19th century, its promenade is great for picnicking, cycling and fishing, and within its luscious nature reserve, next to several nature and history trails, you'll find World War II relics such as gun emplacements and war bunkers, including the **Labrador Secret Tunnels** (*see p83*).

From the park, walk up Alexandra Road till you see a bridge that leads to **Gillman Village**. Formerly known as Gillman Barracks, a British military camp during World War II, it is today a cosy enclave with pubs, restaurants and antiques furniture stores.

Labrador Secret Tunnels

Labrador Villa Road, Carpark A (6339 6833)
HarbourFront MRT then bus 408. **Open** 9am-
7pm daily. **Admission** $8; $5 concessions.
No credit cards.

These tunnels are actually part of a casemate (war
bunker) built by the British Army in 1886 for the
defence of Singapore, but were used extensively
during World War II. Though not as historically
vital as Sentosa's Fort Siloso, the two dark, damp
tunnels do provide an eerie feeling of what soldiers
had to endure during the Fall of Singapore. Hourly
guided tours are available.

Mount Faber

Mount Faber Road (6270 8855/www.mountfaber.
com.sg). HarbourFront MRT then Sentosa cable
car or bus 409 (Sat, Sun only).

Covered by lush rainforest and with landscaped
slopes, Mount Faber is a lovely spot, especially at
dawn and dusk. Formerly part of Telok Blangah
Hill, it was renamed in 1845 after British engineer
Captain Charles Edward Faber, who built the narrow winding road that leads to the summit. A joggers' haven, it is also popular with tourists because
you can stand next to the Merlion for that quintessential Singapore souvenir shot. Next to the cable
car station is the Jewel Box, a glass-walled complex
of souvenir shops, bars and restaurants, including
the Altivo Bar (*see p137* The Jewel Box) – one of the
best sunset viewing spots in Singapore.

Sentosa

Sentosa, which means 'peace and tranquility' in
Malay, is anything but. Once a fishing village,
it served as a British military fortress from
the 1800s to 1967 when it was known as Pulau
Blakang Mati ('Island of Death from Behind').
In 1968 it began a new lease of life as a holiday
resort. Today's Sentosa is a far cry from its
20th-century counterpart, which was burdened
with lame attractions and inadequate facilities.
After a $8-billion redevelopment plan rolled
out in 2002, the island – covering five square
kilometres (two square miles) – now has
pristine man-made beaches, waterfront eating
and drinking outlets, first-class resorts and a
ream of attractions. Controlled and manicured
it may be – this is Singapore, after all – but
it's a gamble that worked: a record 5.2 million
visitors turned up in 2006.

Some think Sentosa is the bee's knees
among Singapore's sights; others deem it a
poor Disneyland wannabe. The best way to
tackle the island is to embrace its tackiness
along with the decent offerings. There is plenty
to see – exhaustively described on the island's
own website, www.sentosa.com.sg – so prepare
to spend at least half a day here. Avoid visiting,
if you can, at weekends and school and public

The best Viewpoints

Carlsberg Sky Tower

Take in the mainland, Sentosa and
the outlying islands, from 131 metres
(430 feet) up. *See p85.*

Changi Point Coastal Walk

Views of the sea, Pulau Ubin and parts
of Malaysia. *See p94.*

Mount Faber

Glorious sunsets, and great harbour
and city views. *See p83.*

New Asia Bar

A city centre vista from the 71st-level
bar inside Swissôtel The Stamford,
South-east Asia's tallest hotel at 226
metres (740 feet). *See p131.*

Ritz-Carlton Millenia

All guest rooms offer breathtaking
views of either the Singapore skyline
or Marina Bay. *See p39.*

Singapore Cable Car

To the north, Mount Faber; to the south,
Sentosa and the Southern Islands.
See p84.

Top of the M

The revolving restaurant (reservations
6831 6258/88) perched atop the
Meritus Mandarin hotel (*see p48*)
overlooks bustling Orchard Road from
173 metres (567 feet) up.

Siloso Beach

holidays, when crowds are immense. You can reach the island by foot, car, the Sentosa bus (HarbourFront Interchange), cable car (HarbourFront Tower Two or Mount Faber) or the Sentosa Express, a brand-new $140-million light rail system that links the island to VivoCity and HarbourFront MRT station. All visitors must pay a $2 entrance fee. Free buses ply set routes between the major attractions, and trams service the beaches.

A slew of family-friendly attractions are based at the **Imbiah Lookout** (*see p85*), where the cable car station is located. From here you can experience something of the island's lush greenery on the Dragon Trail Nature Walk, which leads downhill towards two other must-visit sights: **Underwater World** (*see p86*) and **Fort Siloso** (*see p85*).

The string of beaches along the island's southern edge – artificial-looking though they are, with the view out to sea dominated by hundreds of container ships waiting to get into port, and distant oil refineries – are a draw too. Wi-fi enabled Siloso Beach is popular with partying youths, thanks to its sports facilities and trendy beach bars. It has also hosted Singapore's annual beach rave, **ZoukOut** (*see p165*), which pulled in a record 20,000 partygoers in December 2006. Next to Siloso, family-oriented Palawan Beach offers kid-friendly play areas, dolphin shows and plenty of eating outlets. A suspension bridge leads

to a tiny sandy spur: the southernmost point of continental Asia. East of Palawan, tranquil Tanjong Beach is for those who prefer to be away from the maddening crowds.

For the upwardly mobile, **Sentosa Golf Club** (6275 0090, www.sentosagolf.com), home to the prestigious annual Singapore Open, has one of the country's finest golf courses, plus a classy Italian restaurant, **Il Lido**, and adjoining **Lounge Bar** (*see p137*).

If you would like to stay overnight (beach camping is not allowed) there's a number of resorts from which to choose. The five-star **Sentosa Resort & Spa** (*see p51*) houses the ultra-pampering **Spa Botanica** (*see p156* **Super spas**); while most of the rooms at the classy **Rasa Sentosa Resort** (*see p52*) offer ocean views. Newcomer **Siloso Beach Resort** (*see p52*), bang next to the island's most popular beach, has a curving pool with a four-storey-high waterfall at one end.

Singapore Cable Car

From the Jewel Box, 109 Mount Faber Road or HarbourFront Tower Two, 3 HabourFront Place to Imbiah Lookout (6270 8855/www.mountfaber. com.sg). **Open** 8.30am-11pm daily. **Tickets** *One-way* $9.90; $4.50 concessions. *Return* $10.90; $5.50 concessions. *Glass cabin return* $15; $8 concessions. **Credit** AmEx, DC, JCB, MC, V. **Map** p252 B1/B2.

The most enjoyable way to get to Sentosa. Take in the great views as you swing sedately 70m/230ft above the water; night views are not as spectacular, but the façade of the Jewel Box atop Mount Faber does change colour between 8pm and 10pm, as does the Merlion on Sentosa. You can opt for a glass-bottomed cabin or even dine in one (for a price).

Fort Siloso

Siloso Point, near Underwater World (6279 3264/ www.fortsiloso.com). **Open** 10am-6pm daily. **Admission** $8; $5 concessions. **Credit** AmEx, JCB, MC, V. **Map** p252 A2.
If you visit only one World War II-related site, make it this one. The main story of Japan's victory is punchily told, alongside displays on resistance hero Lim Bo Seng and Force 136, and on the local civilian experience during the Japanese occupation. The 'Surrender Chambers', containing exact waxwork replicas of the main players, are surprisingly effective at reconstructing the British surrender to the Japanese, and vice versa. But the main attraction is the sprawling structure of the fort itself. Wandering around the gun emplacements and underground complexes at your own pace gives a material sense of a place lived in and fought for that is just as striking (if not more so) than any number of theatricals.

Imbiah Lookout

Map p252 B2.
Butterfly Park & Insect Kingdom
6275 0013. **Open** 9am-6pm daily. **Admission** $10; $6 concessions. **No credit cards.**
Featuring specimens of more than 3,000 species of butterflies and rare insects, this living organism museum is a real eye-opener. The highlight is the netted conservatory where 1,500 beautiful butterflies flutter freely around you.
Carlsberg Sky Tower
6279 3291/www.skytower.com.sg. **Open** 9am-9pm daily. **Admission** $10; $6 concessions. **Credit** AmEx, JCB, MC, V.
The revolving, air-conditioned cabin of Asia's tallest observation tower rises to a height of 131m/430ft, providing the best 360° views of Singapore's southern coastline, Sentosa itself, the Southern Islands and parts of Malaysia and Indonesia – accompanied by a rather twee recorded commentary. Day and night views are equally striking, even when the weather is stormy. Despite the name, no alcohol is allowed on board.
Images of Singapore
6279 3280. **Open** 9am-7pm daily. **Admission** $10; $7 concessions. **Credit** AmEx, JCB, MC, V.
Housed in a former 19th-century British military hospital, this 'museum' lets you in on Singapore's history, cultures and values via a series of multimedia exhibits in under an hour. Overall it's a bit of a muddle; the best displays include stirring footage of the Japanese Surrender in 1945, events leading to the independence of Singapore in 1965, and the displays showcasing various ethnic cultures and traditions (ugly wax mannequins notwithstanding). The place also houses a restaurant and an extensive souvenir shop.

Sentosa Luge. *See p86.*

Merlion. *See p86.*

Sightseeing

Merlion

6279 3255. **Open** 10am-7.30pm daily. **Admission** $8; $5 concessions. **Credit** AmEx, JCB, MC, V.

At 37m/121ft, this is the tallest version of the half-lion, half-fish Singapore icon. Skip the downright silly video presentations about Merlion myths on the ground level and proceed straight to the viewing gallery at the top for a breathtaking unobstructed view of Sentosa, the mainland and surrounding islands. At night, there's a multicoloured laser and musical fountain show (7.40pm, 8.40pm daily) – kitsch, yes, but fun for children.

Sentosa 4D Magix

6274 5355/www.sentosa4dmagix.com.sg. **Open** 10am-8.45pm daily. **Admission** $16; $9.50 concessions. **Credit** MC, V.

As the 3D film Pirates (starring Leslie Nielsen and Eric Idle) plays on the screen, the 4D element comes from the vibrating seats and sensory effects such as water sprays and leg ticklers. It's strictly for children – and expensive, considering that the effects are hardly thrilling.

Sentosa Luge & Skyride

6274 0472. **Open** 10am-6pm Mon-Thur; 10am-7pm Fri-Sun. **Admission** *Luge & Skyride* $8. *Skyride* $4 (one-way), $6 (return). **Credit** MC, V.

Cruise in a leisurely fashion – or race down, if you prefer – a long paved, curving track in a luge cart that is remarkably easy to manoeuvre. When you reach the bottom of the track, scramble on to the chairlift for a treetop ride back to the starting point, and do it all over again. Sheer fun for young and old.

Underwater World

80 Siloso Road (6275 0030/www.underwaterworld. com.sg). HarbourFront MRT then Sentosa bus. **Open** *Underwater World* 9am-9pm daily.

Dolphin Lagoon 10am-6pm daily. **Admission** $19.50; $12.50 concessions; free under-3s. **Credit** DC, JCB, MC, V. **Map** p252 A2.

Sentosa's pioneering aquarium is still a big draw after 15 years in business. New features include an interactive stingray feeding pool, a marine reef display and Singapore's first 'fish reflexology spa' (where Turkish spa fish nibble at the dead skin on visitors' feet in a pool). The highlight is the travellator ride through an 83m (270ft) acrylic tunnel while sharks, rays, eels and schools of fish swim above you. There are feeding sessions, and you can even dive with sharks or a dugong. Admission includes Dolphin Lagoon at Palawan Beach, where pink humpback dolphins perform tricks in the water. Come 2010, Underwater World looks set to be dwarfed by Quest Marine Life Park, part of Sentosa's new Resorts World (*see below* **More, more, more**) and supposedly the world's largest oceanarium, with 700,000 marine creatures in a huge lagoon. **Photos** *p87.*

Other islands

Singapore has 63 outlying islands, scattered mainly off the southern coast, of which Sentosa is the most famous. Many are uninhabited, while those used for military training (such as Pulau Tekong) or petrochemical plants (Jurong Island) are off limits to tourists. Those accessible by ferry or water taxi include the **Southern Islands** (*see p87*) near Sentosa, **Pulau Hantu** (*see p87*) in the south-west, and **Pulau Ubin** (*see p94*) in the north-east. For permits to camp on Hantu or Sisters Islands, write to Sentosa Leisure Group, 33 Allanbrooke Road, Sentosa, Singapore 099981.

More, more, more

Being Singapore's top tourist destination is not enough for Sentosa: a slew of upcoming developments aims to double revenue and boost visitor numbers to eight million by 2010.

Plans include a $31-million water and light show (opening mid 2007) and three additional luxury resorts by 2008: Amara Sanctuary Resort, Capella Singapore and the Knolls. The affluent, yacht-owning set is being wooed by Sentosa Cove, an exclusive oceanfront residential enclave at the eastern end of the island, which will provide 2,500 residences, a quayside village, hotel and a 204-berth marina. Residents are assured that they will have as much privacy as possible (read: no accidental tourist walk-ins).

Overshadowing all these is the much-hyped $5.2-billion **Resorts World at Sentosa**,

designed by US architect Michael Graves (a rival bid by Frank Gehry was rejected). Due to open in 2010, the 'integrated resort' will combine a host of family-friendly attractions including a Universal Studios theme park; Quest Marine Life Park oceanarium; a water park; a maritime museum; six hotels; and a plethora of shopping, dining and entertainment outlets. And, of course, a not-so-family-friendly casino – the reason for the resort in the first place (and a controversial move by the previously anti-gambling government). A $100 entry fee is meant to ensure that only high-rollers grace its premises, and not your ordinary Singapore Pools punter from the heartlands.

Success or failure is difficult to predict, but what's certain is that Sentosa is going to get a lot more crowded.

Venture into the deep, at **Underwater World**. *See p86.*

Pulau Hantu

Hantu (which means 'ghost' in Malay), is so named as it is believed that the spirits of two ancient Malay warriors, who duelled to their death here, still roam the island. Despite the spooky premise, the island is regarded as Singapore's best diving spot. Facilities are basic, so you should bring your own refreshments. You can only get to Hantu via water taxi from Marina South Pier.

Southern Islands

Popular with day-trippers, campers and scuba divers, the relatively unspoilt Southern Islands are about 30 minutes from the mainland. From Marina South Pier there's a regular ferry service ($11, $8 children) to Kusu and St John, with most ferries on Sunday; the other islands are only accessible by water taxi. A $1-billion plan is underway to turn these isles into 'getaways for the rich' by 2015, complete with resort, spa and entertainment facilities. Though there are promises to maintain the islands' rich flora and fauna, best pay them a visit before their natural charm is lost.

Kusu Island Kusu, which means 'turtle' in Chinese, is known for its annual pilgrimage during the ninth lunar month (usually falling in October or November – *see p162*), when thousands of Taoist devotees flock to its Da Bo Gong Temple (also called Tua

Pekong) to pray for good fortune. The rest of the year is thus a better time to visit the idyllic isle, which also has a popular Malay shrine, Kusu Kramat, and a turtle sanctuary. The island can be covered in under an hour, so pack a lunch and have a swim in the sheltered lagoons. Staying overnight is not allowed, so don't miss the last ferry.

St John's Island A former quarantine station and penal settlement just ten minutes from Kusu, St John's (also called Pulau Sakijang Bendera) is popular with campers, nature lovers and fishing enthusiasts. There are shelters, toilets, a basketball court and three lagoons, while overnight stays are allowed for holiday camps and bungalow occupants. Plans are under way to link St John's to three smaller nearby islands, Lazarus, Seringat and Kias. Of the three, Lazarus – currently accessible by water taxi – has waters good for snorkelling and diving, while its pristine kilometre-long beach now bears specially transported coconut trees and greenery to give it a more lush, tropical look.

Sisters Islands These two small islands (Pulau Subar Darat and Pulau Subar Laut) are ideal for diving and snorkelling, as they contain one of Singapore's richest coral reefs. Currents are very strong, so take care when swimming; and facilities are basic, so bring ample food and drink. Access is via water taxi; a return trip costs about $180.

Eastern Singapore

Go east: life is peaceful there.

'The east', as residents call it, is distinguished by its laid-back vibe. It's synonymous with balmy beaches, outdoor sports and excellent eateries, complemented by a smattering of historical sights. Each neighbourhood has its own distinct character, but all boast an abundance of good food. In short: Geylang is a red-light district, but also home to some of Singapore's most popular eating places; Katong mixes Peranakan and Eurasian culture with gorgeous traditional food; East Coast Park is known for sea sport activities as well as Singapore's signature chilli crab. On the north-east tip is Changi Village, from where bumboats leave for the old-fashioned island of Pulau Ubin.

Towns from Kallang to Pasir Ris are linked by the MRT's East West Line, while the sea-facing areas along East Coast Road and East Coast Parkway are only accessible by bus or taxi. From Orchard Road, bus 14 heads via Kallang to East Coast Road; bus 16 takes in Kallang and Marine Parade; and bus 36 goes directly to the Marine Parade area, en route to Changi Airport.

Kallang & Geylang

Mention Kallang and most locals think of the iconic **National Stadium**, south of Kallang MRT station. Built in 1973, it hosted National Day parades and big football matches, but was torn down in 2007 to make way for a new $650 million stadium, due for completion by 2010. Adjacent **Singapore Indoor Stadium** (*see p197*), the current venue of choice for sporting events, concerts and musicals, is still standing but is due for refurbishment. On its south side, facing Geylang River, **Stadium Waterfront** was designed for alfresco dining, but as it's difficult to get to – taxi only – most of the restaurants have gone. Two reputable eateries remain: **Vansh** (6345 4466), an ultra-modern Indian restaurant; and a branch of the popular **Jumbo Seafood** (6440 3435). The area only livens up when there are events at the Indoor Stadium.

Travel one stop east for a taste of sin city. Aljunied MRT is the gateway to **Geylang**, Singapore's legal red-light district. It consists of 42 perennially busy lorongs (streets), which are divided into even and odd numbers and

branch off the main Geylang Road. The local joke here is 'To eat meat, head to the odd-numbered streets; to meet flesh, head to the even-numbered streets!' On any given night, call girls – mainly from China, Thailand and Malaysia – lure punters beneath the glow of purple neon from Lorongs 4 to 22. To ensure that patrons don't go knocking on some unsuspecting family's door, brothels are marked with large red numbers. Once a deal is struck, the couple makes their way to one of the numerous 'transit' hotels to get down to business. But most strollers are curious tourists who turn up just to watch the street action.

Geylang is also famous for culinary pleasures. Foodie favourites include the flat rice noodles at **Beef Kuay Teow** (Lorong 9, 9388 0723) and the frogs' leg porridge at **Eminent Frog Porridge** (Lorong 19, 9842 2941). For peerless crab bee hoon, head to **Sin Huat Eating House** (Lorong 35, 6744 9755), but brace yourself for the prices: a plate for three costs $100. For dessert, try the durian stands along Lorong 11, 13 and 15 or on Sims Avenue. The unofficial national fruit, the durian is stinky to some, delicious to others.

Continuing east, you'll come to a more wholesome neighbourhood, **Geylang Serai** (a short distance south of Paya Lebar MRT). Originally a coconut, rubber and lemongrass plantation, the district was home to wealthy Malays and Arabs in the 1880s; it still has a large Malay population. Here you'll find the **Malay Village** (39 Geylang Serai, 6748 4700, open 10am-10pm daily), with shops selling traditional Malay art and fabrics and a cultural museum featuring artefacts (weaving tools, swords and a ceremonial wedding setting). Nearby is **Geylang Serai Market**, a busy wet market with all the ingredients for a sumptuous Malay feast – herbs, spices, lamb and mutton. During Ramadan, it is packed cheek by jowl with Muslim housewives jostling for fresh produce, while stalls in the street and Malay Village sell decorations, textiles and foodstuffs.

Katong & Joo Chiat

South-east of Geylang Serai is **Katong**, which gets its name from a species of sea turtle once found on Singapore. The area has a distinctive, laid-back charm and is the centre

of Eurasian and Peranakan culture (*see p90*
Peranakan pleasures). It's a ten-minute taxi
ride from Paya Lebar or Eunos MRT stations
and roughly bounded by Tanjong Katong
Road, East Coast Parkway and Still Road.
Alternatively, walk south from Paya Lebar
station down Joo Chiat Road towards East
Coast Road.

The district's character has its roots in the
early 19th century, when wealthy Portuguese
and Chinese settlers developed cotton, coconut
and gambier plantations here, building lavish

seaside villas (some still remain) along Meyer
Road, Mountbatten Road and East Coast Road.
The long, narrow, brightly coloured Peranakan
shophouses showcase a blend of southern
Chinese, Malay, Mediterranean and European
influences. Most have beautiful plasterwork
with flora and fauna motifs, and intricate tiles.
Other typical features are a pair of carved
pintu pagar (fence doors) and a five-foot way
(sheltered pathway) linking the units.

Some fine examples can be found around
Joo Chiat (notably on Koon Seng Road), which

Discover Singapore's Peranakan community in laid back **Joo Chiat**.

Sightseeing

Peranakan pleasures

The Peranakans, or Straits-born Chinese, are cultural sponges. Descendants of the early Chinese settlers who settled in Malaysia in the 17th century, their culture is a mish-mash of Chinese and Malay traditions, with added influences from Portuguese, Dutch, British, Thai, Indian and Indonesian cultures. The Peranakans are renowned for their exotic cuisine (a spicy fusion of Chinese and Malay dishes), exquisite fashion (especially ornate beading and embroidery) and distinctive architecture (mixing Corinthian columns, Mediterranean-style windows and Chinese detailing). To experience Peranakan culture, head to Katong and Joo Chiat and soak up some local colour at the following.

Katong Antique House

208 East Coast Road, Katong (6345 8544). Paya Lebar MRT then bus 40. **Open** by appointment only 11am-6.30pm daily. **Admission** free. *Tour* $15. **No credit cards**.
A chance to see a bona fide Peranakan house, perfectly preserved as it was in the old days. Curator and owner Peter Wee – who has been buying, restoring and selling Peranakan-related items since 1971 – has filled his family home with heirlooms: traditional Peranakan crockery, jewellery, beaded slippers, costumes, furniture and photographs of Singapore's earlier generations of Babas and Bibiks.

Kim Choo Kueh Chang

109 & 111 East Coast Road, Katong (6440 5590/www.kimchoo.com). Eunos MRT then bus 13. **Open** 8am-9pm daily. **Credit** DC, MC, V.
Established in 1949, this eaterie (*pictured*) is famed for its sweet and savoury Nonya glutinous rice dumplings. It also serves Peranakan and local favourites such as fish-head curry and Nonya kuehs (cakes), and offers curious condiments like belachan (prawn paste) and taucheo (bean paste).

Rumah Bebe

113 East Coast Road, Katong (6247 8781/ www.rumahbebe.com). Eunos MRT then bus 13. **Open** 9.30am-6.30pm Tue-Sun. **Credit** AmEx, MC, V.
Owned by Bebe Seet, a well-known Peranakan beadwork specialist, this elaborately designed 1928 shophouse showcases Peranakan artefacts, furnishings and porcelain. You can buy ready-to-wear and custom-made sarong kebayas (Nonya outfits), plus bags and beaded slippers, and also take classes in beading and embroidery.

True Blue Cuisine & St Francis Enterprise

117 East Coast Road, Katong (6440 0449). Eunos MRT then bus 13. **Open** 11.30am-3pm, 6-10pm Tue-Sat. **Credit** AmEx, DC, JCB, MC, V.
A restaurant-cum-shop where customers can dress up, then tuck in. Beautifully tailored Nonya outfits, made by owner Benjamin Seck, dominate the ground floor. On the upper floor, sample his mother's signature dishes at the formal Peranakan restaurant (*see p126*), where the family's collection of antique jewellery, fine old porcelain and framed ancestor pictures are displayed.

was designated a national heritage conservation area in 1993 and is also known for its excellent restaurants. In the last few years, however, the district has made the news for all the wrong reasons. Dodgy massage parlours and suspect karaoke joints sprang up, creating an atmosphere akin to Geylang's lorongs. In a rare show of civic initiative, residents demanded a 'clean up'. The authorities obliged, and Joo Chiat is on its way back to being a family-friendly neighbourhood.

Walk south down Joo Chiat Road to reach East Coast Road: a bustling dining and entertainment stretch, starting from the Katong Shopping Centre in the west (at the junction with Haig Road) all the way to Upper East Coast Road in the Siglap area. It's lined with numerous coffeeshops and shophouse restaurants (some are fine examples of Peranakan dining). At the intersection of Joo Chiat and East Coast Roads, west of Katong Mall, is the red façade of the **Red House Bakery** (aka Katong Bakery & Confectionery) at No.75. The bakery operated for over 80 years, but closed in 2003. Thanks to public demand, the building has been conserved.

Katong is famous for its laksa: a dish of rice vermicelli, cockles, shrimps, fish cake and chilli paste in thick, coconut-based broth. There are no fewer than four laksa stalls – at Nos.47, 49, 57 and 328 East Coast Road – each claiming to be the original and/or the best. For our money, No.49, just off Ceylon Road, is the true blue original. Magazine reviews and photos of its celebrity patrons are proudly displayed.

Just around the corner is the **Sri Senpaga Vinayagar Temple** (19 Ceylon Road). One of the oldest Hindu temples in Singapore (built in 1875), it's known for its striking architecture and murals. Further down, at No.139, is the **Eurasian Heritage Centre** (6447 1578, open 9.30am-6.30pm Mon-Fri). The Eurasians have strong roots in Katong, and the centre offers insight into their culture and achievements in the region. Best behave, though: the residence of SR Nathan, President of the Republic of Singapore, is just opposite (behind the guard house); though the **Istana** (*see p79*) is the official residence, the president spends much of his time here.

Back on East Coast Road, take time to sample the various eateries and food shops. **Yong's Teochew Kueh** (No.150) sells a variety of traditional, handmade savoury kuehs (cakes); across the road is **Glory Catering** (No.139, 6344 1749), known for its nasi padang, mee siam and Nonya popiah. For authentic Peranakan cuisine, **Peranakan Inn** (No.210, 6440 6195) serves a mean ayam buah keluak (chicken and stuffed Indonesian

keluak nuts braised in a thick gravy) and ngo hiang (deep-fried beancurd rolls stuffed with chicken, prawns and water chestnuts).

Chin Mee Chin bakery (No.204, *see p125*), going strong for 65 years, is a Singapore institution: its claim to fame is its kaya (egg and coconut jam), the best in town. But don't come for Sunday lunch: it will be crammed with parishioners from the nearby Holy Family Church, a 1932 landmark frequented by the area's large Catholic community. To the left of the church is a row of quaint terrace houses. These single-storey homes (Nos.150-152) were situated by the beach before reclamation works in the 1970s: their living areas were built on raised ground to protect against high tides.

Continue eastwards down Upper East Coast Road and you'll reach **Siglap**. This is the yuppie end of the stretch, where old and new worlds meet. It's known for its luxury condominiums with sea views, upmarket cafés and restaurants, and traditional coffeeshops and hawker centres.

On the left, before Siglap Road, is Frankel Avenue. This upmarket enclave houses top-notch foodie destinations, including bistro **Gourmet Plus** (117 Frankel Avenue, 6441 1120); bakeries **Cedele Depot** (No.115, 6243 2056) and **Swiss Bakerie** (No.97, 6441 8788); and noteworthy diners **Different Tastes** (No.111, 6241 6518) and **Baba Inn Peranakan Restaurant** (No.103, 6445 2404).

Upper East Coast Road (which starts at the junction with Siglap Road) contains another string of quality eating and drinking establishments. Visit **Werner's Oven** (No.6, 6442 3897) for authentic German fare and beer; **Big Fish Seafood Grill** (No. 85, 6441 6920) for Western-style seafood; and **Blooie's Roadhouse** (49 Jalan Tua Kong, 6442 0030) for tasty barbecue. The last is off the main road, on the way to the swanky Opera Estate, which has many striking houses and streets bearing such operatic names as Figaro, Carmen and Aida.

East Coast Park

Running parallel to and south of East Coast Road is Marine Parade Road, which serves the **Marine Parade** housing estate. Also developed on reclaimed land, it's one of the oldest and smallest estates in Singapore, yet property prices are sky-high – because most apartments boast sea views and are a short walk from the recreational and culinary attractions of **East Coast Park**.

At weekends, the park – which stretches for about 20 kilometres (12.5 miles) between Marina Bay and Changi Airport – teems with families cycling, rollerblading or picnicking. Amenities

Sightseeing

East Coast Park

include cycle paths, a jogging track, bowling alleys, tennis courts, barbecue pits and refreshment kiosks. There is also a 7.5km (4.5-mile) beach, but it slopes sharply into murky waters and is not recommended for swimming.

The easiest way to get there is to jump in a cab from Eunos, Kembangan or Bedok MRT stations. Or take bus 16 from Orchard Road to Marine Crescent and walk via the underpass (one of many beneath East Coast Parkway), located near HDB block 18. This will bring you to **Marine Cove** (Carpark C), a popular dining and recreation hub. Tenants include **Tung Lok Seafood** (6246 0555) and a skate-through McDonald's. Kiosks renting rollerblades and bikes are nearby, as is the **Singapore Tennis Centre** (*see p193*).

Further east lies one of the reasons many people visit the park: the chilli and pepper crabs at the **East Coast Seafood Centre (**1206 East Coast Parkway) are perfectly executed and draw diners from all corners of the island. Among the top-notch restaurants are **Jumbo Seafood** (6442 3435) and **Long Beach Seafood** (*see p126*). Next door, the recently refurbished East Coast Lagoon features Singapore's first waterski track, at **Ski 360 Cableski Park** (*see p196*). Beside it is the **East Coast Lagoon Food Village** (Carpark E2), popular for its satay and wonton noodles. Along the beach, there are canoes for rental, fitness and camping areas, and the Bedok jetty where people stroll, fish and relax.

Changi

Dominating the eastern end of Singapore is massive Changi Airport, but there are a number of other sights in Changi that are worth a visit. Top of the list is **Changi Chapel & Museum** (*see p94*), dedicated to the victims and survivors of World War II. Built by the British in the 1930s, Changi Prison became a notorious prisoner of war camp, where the Japanese interned 50,000 civilians and soldiers (many British and Australian). The original prison was demolished in 2000, leaving only the entrance gate and a high outer wall with two turrets. The huge new prison complex – which you pass on bus 2 from Tanah Merah MRT – holds serious criminal offenders and death-row inmates, who are executed by hanging (traditionally at dawn on Fridays).

A short distance down the road, opposite Selarang Camp, is **Johore Battery**, a gun emplacement site built by the British in 1939 to defend Singapore. Featuring a replica of the so-called 'Monster Gun' that the British used to pound Japanese forces across the Straits, it's a neglected and rather poorly conceived site.

Catch a bumboat to **Pulau Ubin** for a slower pace of life. *See p94.*

Bus 2 terminates at **Changi Village**, a seaside town dotted with holiday bungalows, chalets and camping sites, where residents are outnumbered by holidaymakers. Small but classy **Changi Village Hotel** (*see p52*) is in the area known as Changi Point, which also contains several shops, eateries and a bustling hawker centre, famous for its nasi lemak and Chinese noodle stalls. At the back of the centre is local legend **Charlie's Corner** (open 11.30am-2.30pm, 6pm-midnight Mon-Sat). This stall sells 100 types of beer and good pub grub (fish and chips with homemade gravy); it's a local tradition to drink and tuck in while watching planes descend towards the airport.

From **Changi Point Ferry Terminal** (6542 7944), you can hop on an antiquated bumboat to nearby **Pulau Ubin** (*see p94*), then hire a bike and explore. A reminder of old Singapore, the boomerang-shaped island is covered in trees (the remnants of rubber plantations) and dotted with beaches and characterful old Malay houses. It contains the country's last kampongs, where about 100 villagers still count on wells for water and diesel generators for electricity. The granite hills explain the abandoned quarries (granite mining was done by early settlers). The ten-minute trip costs $2 one way (pay on board). The bumboats depart when they have 12 passengers (but you usually don't have to wait very long), and there are plenty going to and fro during weekends.

The ferry terminal is also the start of the **Changi Point Coastal Walk**, a 2.6km (1.6-mile) boardwalk – heading west – that offers views of the open sea, yachts, Pulau Ubin and Malaysia. In the opposite direction is **Changi Beach Park**. Hire a canoe, fish at the pier or just enjoy the sea breeze and watch planes land (best spot: near Carpark 2). The beach is craggy, so don't be fooled by its 'soft' sandy look. Permits are required for overnight camping, but that doesn't deter the squatters.

If you crave a tropical getaway, eastern Singapore is the gateway to island life. From Tanah Merah station, bus 35 heads to **Tanah Merah Ferry Terminal** on the southern coast, from where ferries leave for Indonesia's Bintan and Batam islands (roughly 60 minutes) and Desaru in Johor, Malaysia (45 minutes). East from here is **Changi Naval Base**. Built on reclaimed land, its 6.2km (ten-mile) dock can accommodate massive ships and aircraft carriers, and is often used by visiting US Navy ships. The base currently houses Landing Ship Tanks (LSTs), Missile Gunboats (MGBs) and a Submarine Squadron. A new **Republic of Singapore Navy Museum** will open here in early 2008.

Changi Chapel & Museum

1000 Upper Changi Road North (6214 2451/ www.changimuseum.com). Tanah Merah MRT then bus 2. **Open** 9.30am-4.30pm daily. **Admission** free. *Tour* $8; $4 concessions.

The most iconic of Singapore's World War II sites, even though the museum is housed in a purpose-built venue, and the chapel is a reconstruction (the original was shipped to Australia after the war). The main interest lies in the stories of industry and ingenuity within the POW camp. The civilian and military internees essentially established an alternative, if somewhat surreal, society, catering for everything from entertainments to the manufacture of thousands of everyday items. Contact with the outside world was maintained through handmade and carefully disguised radios. The chapel, located in the courtyard of the museum, encourages quiet reflection. It also houses copies of the kitschy but affecting Changi murals, recreated by the original artist, Stanley Warren, after a widely publicised international effort to find him; the preponderance of blue and white is because of his reliance on billiard cue chalk. The $8 audio guide is pricey, but it is comprehensive and complements the displays well.

Pulau Ubin

6542 4108/www.nparks.gov.sg. Bumboat from Changi Point Ferry Terminal.

On reaching Ubin jetty, walk straight ahead for the National Parks information kiosk (open 8.30am-5pm daily), where you can pick up a map. To the left is the 'town', with a wayang (theatre) stage, a small shrine and some ramshackle houses that have been converted into bicycle rental shops, humdrum eateries and provisions shops (with stock that looks as if it hasn't been replenished for decades). Other villagers depend on farming and fishing for a livelihood. Many used to own chickens, but poultry was banned on the island after the 2005 bird flu epidemic.

The best way to explore is by bike; the island is too large, and the weather usually too hot, for walking. Bikes (available 8am-6pm) cost $3-$8 to rent; it's

wise to pick as new a model as possible. Less tiring (but less fun) is a taxi van – unmetered; negotiate the fare beforehand. There are three cycling trails (on paved and dirt roads), which lead past old fruit and rubber plantations, mangrove swamps, water-filled quarry pits and old wooden houses. Toilets and shelters are located at key points. The Chek Jawa wetlands area on Ubin's eastern tip is worth visiting, with marine life visible at low tide. Visitor numbers are restricted to protect the fragile ecosystem, so you have to pre-book a guided tour – contact the National Parks Board for more information.

If you want to stay overnight, permits are not required for camping, but note that the water from public toilets and wells is not suitable for drinking or bathing. The Marina Country Club Ubin Resort (6388 8388, www.marinacountryclub.com.sg) offers basic air-conditioned chalets. **Photos** *p93.*

Tampines & Pasir Ris

At Tanah Merah MRT, the East West Line splits in two: one route covers the satellite towns of Simei, Tampines and Pasir Ris; the other leads to Singapore Expo and Changi Airport.

Tampines is another huge housing estate, with more than 200,000 residents living in some 52,000 HDB flats; urban planners should make a pilgrimage, as it has won a prestigious UN World Habitat award for housing design. The estate was designed to be self-contained, thus relieving the pressure on central Singapore, but it is almost too successful: on weekends, the area is jam-packed with what the Chinese would call 'people mountain, people sea'. The bustling town centre contains shops, restaurants and two huge malls (Tampines Mall, Century Square), with three superstores soon to follow. During Chinese New Year, the hub is transformed into a mini Chinatown with 24-hour bazaars and cultural performances.

North of Tampines is **Pasir Ris**, a young town where the HDB flats bear interesting architectural designs and bold colour schemes. Thanks to its proximity to the sea, Pasir Ris has holiday chalets and resorts including **Costa Sands Resort Downtown East** (1 Pasir Ris Close, 6589 1865, www.costasands. com.sg). Next door are two theme parks, **Wild Wild Wet** and **Escape Theme Park** (for both, *see p68*). Also popular is waterfront **Pasir Ris Park** (*see p167*), a lovely green stretch with a great beachfront dining spot, **Fisherman's Village** (67 Pasir Ris Road, 6585 1211), which specialises in seafood. Kids can play on the giant space-net, explore the maze garden or ride ponies at **Gallop Stables** (*see p195*). On the mangrove boardwalk you can observe mudskippers and crabs, or birdwatch from the high observatory tower.

Western Singapore

Expat hangouts, Chinese demons and wartime ghosts.

Singapore's 'west end' – with the country's largest industrial estate in the south-west and vast spaces of seemingly uninhabited rural land in the north-west – is seldom explored by casual visitors. Yet it contains biodiversity-rich nature reserves, noteworthy World War II memorials, unique themed attractions and some of Singapore's few farms. Nearer the city centre are vibrant suurban enclaves such as Holland Village. The region is accessible by MRT, although many sights can only be reached by bus or taxi.

Tiong Bahru to Holland Village

Travelling west on the MRT's East West Line will bring you through some of Singapore's older housing estates, each with its own distinct charms and characteristics.

Just over the Central Expressway (CTE) from Chinatown is **Tiong Bahru**. Most of the sights are located east of the MRT station. Walk to the end of Tiong Bahru Road and you'll find the Tiong Bahru conservation area around Seng Poh Road and Eng Hoon Street. Singapore's very first public housing estate, begun in the 1930s, it's an exceedingly attractive array of low-rise blocks of flats, painted orange and white. The architecture is a mix of art deco and Straits Settlement styles, with distinctive flat rooftops, rounded balconies and spiral staircases (a shame that later developments didn't follow a similar design). An exclusive upper-class housing estate before World War II, it fell out of favour in the following decades, but the refurbished flats are now popular with young, trendy homeowners.

Here you'll also find the famous **Tiong Bahru Market** (*see p127*), which has a wet market and some of Singapore's best hawkers under its roof, and is a great place at which to try out local delicacies. Now bright and light after a revamp in 2006, it's usually jam-packed at weekends with hungry Singaporeans from all over the island. Nearby is the coffeeshop where elderly bird lovers gather every Sunday morning for a caffeine boost, while their birds chirp their hearts out in bamboo cages.

Next stop on the MRT is **Redhill** ('bukit merah' in Malay), one of Singapore's biggest estates with 153,000 residents. Legend has it

that the ground on the hilly area turned blood-red after a jealous king had a young village hero assassinated – hence the neighbourhood's name, Bukit Merah. In truth, it was probably coined because of the red soil, but the popular legend, with different variations, lives on. A short walk south of the MRT station is Bukit Merah Central, home to the Bukit Merah bus interchange, a hawker centre, supermarket, bakeries, banks and shops. Nearby Leng Kee Road is Singapore's premier car showroom strip, where the latest models from the likes of Porsche, Lexus and Chevrolet are displayed.

On Alexandra Road stands the blue and yellow building of Ikea, as popular here as in Europe (avoid it at weekends). Diagonally opposite is **Queensway Shopping Centre**; though it looks drab and old (which it is), it's a good source of quality branded sportswear, from tracksuits and trainers to NBA jerseys. If you buy jeans here, you can get them altered right away at the 'auntie/uncle' tailor shops.

Tiong Bahru: the first housing estate.

Three stops from Redhill is Buona Vista MRT station, from where it's a ten- to 15-minute walk to Singapore's most famous suburban enclave, **Holland Village**. Alternatively, from Orchard Road catch bus 7 or 77 along Holland Road. Popular with locals and especially expatriates, Holland V, as it's known, has modern restaurants, bars and shops alongside old-style coffeeshops and knick-knack stores. It's compact and walkable.

There are two malls – Holland Road Shopping Centre and Holland V Shopping Mall – a 24-hour supermarket, food court, banks, post office, convenience stores, spas, thrift shops, factory outlets, pet shops and Asian handicrafts and antiques galleries, including **Lim's Arts & Living** (*see p154*) – a great spot for souvenirs. At the 'mama shops' (stalls traditionally run by Indians), you'll find the widest range of local and international magazines outside the major bookstores, plus moneychangers offering good rates. The food is exceptional: one of the island's best laksa stalls is here, while upmarket restaurants – including those in Jalan Merah Saga, on the opposite side of Holland Avenue – range from French to Mexican, Lebanese to Cantonese. The cool bars, pubs and cafés on Lorong Mambong are great for chilling out, especially at night when the road is closed to traffic.

South of Buona Vista MRT and minutes from Holland Village, **One-North** is a government-devised, 'intellectually vibrant' hub where creative types can work, live and play. Although the biomedical research complex Biopolis and research and media hub Fusionopolis (due to open in 2008) are not open to tourists, the hub's two lifestyle enclaves are. Within walking distance is **Rochester Park**, where striking, black and white colonial houses, nestled within leafy surrounds, now house a series of smart restaurants and fashionable bar **One Rochester** (*see p137*).

The other, **Workloft@Wessex**, is located at Portsdown Road – not far, but best reached by taxi. With walk-up apartment blocks and 1940s' semi-detached houses surrounded by pretty trees and gardens, it's an artsy lifestyle-cum-residential hub. At Block 1 Aden, for instance, you'll find a cooking studio, art gallery and a handmade linen shop. Opposite Aden is old-fashioned eating house **Colbar** (9A Whitchurch Road, 6779 4859). Previously located on nearby Jalan Hang Jebat, it was due for demolition to make way for a highway but a campaign by (mostly expat) fans saved it. The present premises now have 'history boards' telling of its celebrated status in the former British Army barracks. It's one of the few places in Singapore for greasy spoon fare

(steak and chips, full English breakfast, great curry chicken), and fans are drawn to its old-world charms. No air-con, of course.

Pasir Panjang

West of HarbourFront MRT and best reached by bus, **Pasir Panjang** is primarily an industrial area. But it's also steeped in history, home to a few national institutions and has one quirky attraction that makes a trip worthwhile.

Haw Par Villa (*see p97*), on Pasir Panjang Road, is a bizarre outdoor park containing over 1,000 statues depicting Chinese myths, legends and morality tales that are either endearingly kitsch or downright grotesque. Once one of Singapore's main tourist attractions, it has slipped down the back of the cultural sofa in the last decade, and is now looking rather shabby – but that's part of its charm. Housed within the park is the new **Hua Song Museum** (*see p97*), which tells the story of the Chinese diaspora.

Nearby is sprawling **Kent Ridge Park**, which attracts fitness enthusiasts, nature lovers and history geeks in equal numbers. It has 20 fitness stations, as well as a tank and two artillery guns (the Singapore Army has adopted it as their Army Green Park). It is also the site of the last battle before the Fall of Singapore. The 48-hour Battle of Pasir Panjang, on 13 and 14 February 1942, between the 1,400-strong Malay Regiment and 13,000 Japanese soldiers, is detailed at **Reflections at Bukit Chandu** (*see p98*), which is linked to the park by a canopy walk from where you can spot birds, butterflies and lizards.

Haw Par Villa

In mid 2007, the new **HortPark**, a one-stop gardening hub, will link Kent Ridge Park eastwards to Telok Blangah Hill Park. As well as 20 themed gardens, planned attractions include a show flat that offers visitors ideas on how to create their own gardens at home and a HortMart selling gardening tools and plants.

North-west of Kent Ridge Park lies the campus of Singapore's leading university, the National University of Singapore (NUS), and beside it, the National University Hospital. The small **NUS Centre for the Arts Museum** (50 Kent Ridge Crescent, Queenstown, 6516 4616, www.nus.edu.sg/museums, closed Sunday) is worth a peek if you're interested in Asian arts.

Dominating the area's southern coastline is the huge **Pasir Panjang Container Terminal**, its wharves extending over two kilometres. Built in 2000, it also contains the Pasir Panjang and West Coast Ferry Terminals, which serve workers and visitors travelling to and from offshore islands and docked ships. Next to the container terminal, on the West Coast Highway, is the **Pasir Panjang Wholesale Centre**, where vegetables, fruits and dried goods, mostly from Malaysia and Thailand, are sold. In recent years, the place has been dogged by misfortune. In 2003 it was closed for 15 days after a SARS scare, and in 2005 an eight-year-old girl was murdered here, a horrific crime that shocked the country.

Next to the centre is the very popular **West Coast Park**, which contains a bird sanctuary, dog run, reflexology facilities, chess garden, bicycle obstacle course and an adventure play area for children and adults.

Haw Par Villa

262 Pasir Panjang Road, Queenstown (6872 2780). Bus 10, 51, 143, 188, 200. **Open** *9am-7pm daily. Ten Courts of Hell 9am-6pm daily.* **Admission** *free; Ten Courts of Hell $1; $0.50 concessions.* **Credit** (shop only) AmEx, JCB, MC, V.

Opened in 1937, this weird and wonderful park was named after its owners, Aw Boon Haw and Aw Boon Par, the brothers who made their fortune from the acclaimed cure-all ointment Tiger Balm (it's also known as Tiger Balm Gardens). Multicoloured statues and tableaux – some looking rather neglected– depict scenes from Chinese history and mythology. The highlight is the Ten Courts of Hell (responsible for childhood nightmares for generations of Singaporeans) where small-scale tableaux show human sinners being punished in a variety of hideous and bloodthirsty ways – in extremely gory and graphic detail. It's a safe bet that you will never see anything like it anywhere else. **Photos** *below.*

Hua Song Museum

Haw Par Villa, 262 Pasir Panjang Road, Queenstown (6339 6833/www.huasong.org). Bus 10, 51, 143, 188, 200. **Open** *noon-7pm Tue-Sun.* **Admission** *$8.40, $5.25 concessions.* **Credit** (restaurant only) AmEx, DC, JCB, MC, V

Opened in 2006, Hua Song, which means 'in praise of the Chinese' in Mandarin, details the histories of Chinese communities around the globe. Sections include the Popular Culture Hall, where famous Chinese songs and movies from the 1950s and '60s are played, and From China to Chinatown, which explains how Chinese migrants adapted to lives in foreign lands. It's spacious and nicely designed – with archive photos, multimedia displays, and the inevitable wax figures in tableaux (obligatory at every Singapore museum, it seems) – but not really worth the entrance fee.

Reflections at Bukit Chandu

31K Pepys Road, Queenstown (6375 2510/ www.s1942.org.sg). Bus 10, 30, 51, 143, 188. **Open** 9am-5pm Tue-Sun. **Admission** $2; $1 concessions; free under-6s. **No credit cards**.

The museum commemorates the brave defence given by the vastly outnumbered soldiers of the Malay Regiment against the Japanese in the Battle of Pasir Panjang. Downstairs, documentary material is gathered in display cases, while the upstairs rooms recreate the building's military past. Alongside familiar facts about how the Japanese swept down through Malaya, there's some intriguing information about the role of British racism in an initial reluctance to train and arm the local Malays. No one proved such prejudices more wrong than Lieutenant Adnan Saidi, and the display makes a heroic effort to cement his heroic reputation. That said, his diminutive projection in a natty multimedia replay of the final battle risks recalling Princess Leia's hologram rather than Luke Skywalker fighting off the forces of evil.

Bukit Timah

There are two sides to Bukit Timah. The areas around Bukit Timah Road, bounded by Clementi Road to the west and Newton Circus to the east, is located in the prestigious District 10. With its numerous luxury residential estates, this is one of Singapore's most sought after (and expensive) areas to live. Beyond the Pan Island Expressway, however, around Upper Bukit Timah Road, the residential areas consist of low-cost public housing. There's no MRT stop, but it's a 20-minute taxi ride (45 minutes by bus) from Orchard Road.

The main attraction is **Bukit Timah Nature Reserve** (*see below*), containing the only substantial area of primary rainforest left on the island, and Bukit Timah Hill, the island's highest peak at (a not very high) 164 metres (538 feet). Nearby is the former Ford Factory, the first automobile assembly plant in South-east Asia, and where the British forces surrendered Singapore to the Japanese Army on 15 February 1942. Designated a national monument in 2006, it now houses the **Memories At Old Ford Factory** exhibition (*see below*).

Reminders of World War II are also evident at nearby **Bukit Batok Nature Park**. The site where the MediaCorp transmission tower stands used to serve as a memorial for Japanese soldiers who died during the war; all that remains today are two pillars and 120 concrete steps. A small memorial dedicated to the end of the war is nearby. The similarly named **Bukit Batok Town Park**, located beside Bukit Gombak MRT station, is also worth a visit. It's nicknamed Xiao Guilin or Little Guilin as it resembles (albeit on a much smaller scale)

China's picturesque Guilin lake, which has a huge granite rock sitting in it. This is why local TV crews are often seen shooting Chinese period dramas here, complete with actors in full costume. Views of the lake and the surrounding housing estates can be seen at the lookout points along the Bukit Gombak Trail.

Bukit Timah Nature Reserve

177 Hindhede Drive, Bukit Panjang (1800 468 5736/www.nparks.gov.sg). Bus 67, 75, 171, 852, 961. **Open** 7am-7pm daily. **Admission** free.

This 1.64sq km (0.63sq mile) nature reserve is renowned for having one of the richest and most diverse ecosystems in the world. Besides hundreds of animal and insect species, it also contains more tree species than the whole of North America. Weekends are busy with walkers, nature lovers and mountain bikers, so come on a weekday if you prefer a quiet trek. There are four walking trails. A steep paved path takes you directly to the peak, but more interesting are the unpaved trails; route 3 (green) follows a winding forest path, past caves used by Japanese soldiers in World War II. Look out for long-tailed macaques, squirrrels and snakes, and listen for the incessant 'chonk-chonk' of the striped tit-babbler. Cyclists should wear protective gear as the biking trail is extremely rugged. The visitor centre has toilets and souvenirs, but no food.

Memories at Old Ford Factory

351 Upper Bukit Timah Road, Bukit Batok (6332 7973/6462 6724/www.s1942.org.sg). Bus 67, 171, 173, 184, 961. **Open** 9am-5.30pm Mon-Fri; 9am-1.30pm Sat. **Admission** $3; $2.50 concessions; $8 family; free under-6s. **No credit cards**.

The location of the British surrender to the Japanese languished in disrepair for years; MOFF only opened in February 2006. The actual room where the surrender took place is rather coyly barricaded off (suggesting some kind of inferiority complex in contrast with the showy 'Surrender Chambers' waxworks at Fort Siloso). And there's a lot of text in the too-busy exhibition. While this means that there's detailed information on aspects of the war overlooked elsewhere – such as the story of the pro-Japanese Indian National Army, and attempts by Chinese and Eurasian communities to build self-sufficient communities on nearby islands – if you've already visited other better-known World War II sites, you may want to save yourself the trip.

Jurong & Tuas

Jurong is one of the country's biggest housing estates (with 263,000 residents), its largest industrial powerhouse and the site of some of the island's most innovative attractions.

The Jurong East MRT interchange (which links the green East West Line to the red North South Line) is smack in the heart of bustling Jurong East town centre. Extremely crowded

Take wing to **Jurong BirdPark**, one of Singapore's best sights. *See p100.*

on weekends, the area often has a circus atmosphere, especially when trade fairs set up around the MRT station. A ten-minute walk west is the **Singapore Science Centre** (*see p166*), a family-friendly institution with an IMAX theatre. Next door is **Snow City** (*see p195*), the only place in Singapore where you can indulge in such untropical activities as skiing and snowball fights.

The next MRT stop is Chinese Garden, where a short walk up a footpath brings you to – surprise, surprise - the **Chinese Garden** (*see p100*), built in 1975 as part of the government's plans to inject greenery into Jurong's heavily industrialised landscape. South of the garden is **Jurong Lake Park**, popular with amateur anglers. Next door are the 'ruins' of the former Tang Dynasty City, a privately funded attraction that flopped despite being a rather remarkable re-creation of the ancient Chinese city of Chang-An, complete with 1,200 life-size terracotta warriors – which were auctioned off after its closure.

Jurong West, served by Lakeside and Boon Lay MRT stations, is the site of **Jurong Industrial Estate**, Singapore's first and largest centre of industry. In its midst lies, ironically enough, one of Singapore's greenest attractions, **Jurong BirdPark** (*see p100*), the largest bird park in the Asia Pacific region. Nearby is **Jurong Hill Park**; a tall lookout tower provides panoramic views of Jurong.

To the south lies **Jurong Port** – Singapore's second port, after Keppel Harbour – which deals mainly with the transport of raw materials and manufactured products. Offshore is **Jurong Island**, Singapore's biggest island, created by joining several smaller islands together. A petrochemical hub (off-limits to tourists), its refineries processes 1.3 million barrels of crude oil per day, putting Singapore

among the world's top three oil refining centres – despite not having any oil deposits itself.

At the mouth of the Jurong River is the **Jurong Fishery Port**. Fishing vessels and reefer boats unload their catch overnight, in time for thousands of fish merchants and retailers to start haggling at the daily (except Monday) market at 2am

Boon Lay MRT station, the last stop on the East West Line, is one of the most crowded points in the west: it's next to the always-packed Jurong Point shopping mall and the equally busy Boon Lay bus interchange. West of the MRT stop down Upper Jurong Road is the **Singapore Discovery Centre** (*see p166*), which examines milestones in Singapore's history via multimedia presentations. The new **Army Museum of Singapore** (*see p100*) is due to open nearby at the end of 2007. The extensive greenery visible to the west is the **SAFTI Live Firing Area**, a restricted area used by the Singapore military for training that covers the island's western coastline.

Beyond the long sweep of Raffles Golf Course (and the less appealing Tuas Industrial Estate, is **Tuas Second Link**, another causeway linking Singapore to Malaysia. Opened in 1998 to ease traffic on the Singapore-Johor Causeway in the northern suburb of Woodlands, it's a slightly longer route to Johor Bahru city centre, but most locals use it to get to other nearby towns, such as Gelan Putoh where they can purchase groceries and basic necessities at cheap prices.

Next to the checkpoint is the exclusive yachting club **Raffles Marina** (10 Tuas West Drive, 6861 8000, www.rafflesmarina.com.sg), which caters specially for luxurious 'mega yachts'. It hosts various events during the year, including sailing regattas, boardsailing and wakeboarding championships.

Army Museum of Singapore

500 Upper Jurong Road, Jurong West (6799 7277/ www.armymuseum.gov.sg). Boon Lay MRT then bus 182, 193.

Under construction at the time of writing, Singapore's very first army museum will have six galleries detailing the history of the Singapore Army and the contributions of National Service (NS) men. Displays will include personal mementos, a mock-up of a 1970s trainees' bunk, and multimedia shows depicting a modern army in battle, complete with the 'sounds and smells' of warfare. Visitors will also be able to play games on battle simulators.

Chinese Garden

1 Chinese Garden Road, Jurong East (6261 3632/ chinesegardens.com.sg). Chinese Garden MRT. **Open** 6am-10pm Mon-Fri; 6am-11pm Sat, Sun. **Admission** *Garden* free. *Turtle & Tortoise Museum* $5. **No credit cards**.

Popular with photographers and wedding couples, this tranquil garden has a good bonsai collection, and various pavilions and pagodas in the northern Chinese imperial style. The best times to visit are during Chinese New Year (usually January or February) and the Mid-Autumn Festival (September or October), when cultural performances are held and the gardens are lit up at night like a fairyland by hundreds of beautiful and ornate paper lanterns. Don't miss the unusual Live Turtle & Tortoise Museum, containing 180 turtles and more than 3,000 turtle-related items collected by the museum's owner and his daughter. The adjoining Japanese Gardens are currently undergoing renovation and should reopen some time in 2007.

Jurong BirdPark

2 Jurong Hill, Boon Lay (6265 0022/www.bird park.com.sg). Boon Lay MRT then bus 194, 251. **Open** 9am-6pm daily. **Admission** $16; $8 concessions. **Credit** AmEx, DC, JCB, MC, V.

This top-notch attraction contains 8,000 birds from 600 species. There's a multitude of exotic and endangered South-east Asian species, alongside pelicans, penguins, flamingoes, ibises, swans, toucans, birds of paradise – and more. Key attractions include the largest walk-in aviary in the world, where you'll find a 30m (98ft) man-made waterfall and 1,500 birds from Africa and South America flying freely within the huge compound. After a $10m revamp in 2006, the park now has a exhibit modelled on the Okvango River in Botswana, complete with storks, cranes, fish, frogs and African-style huts. Bird shows and feeding sessions take place throughout the day. Joint tickets for the BirdPark, Night Safari and Zoo ($40; $20 children) are available. **Photos** *p99*.

Kranji & Around

A hundred years ago, Kranji (named after the keranji tree, common in Singapore in the first half of the 19th century) used to serve as a transit stop between Singapore and mainland Malaysia for a steam tramway (1885-94), a railway (1903), an electric tram system (1905) and even a ferry connection. Today it's still a transit stop of sorts: Kranji MRT station is one of the biggest in the country, as it's designed to handle the thousands of horse-racing fans who visit the **Singapore Turf Club** (*see p199*) every weekend. On weekdays, this largely industrial area is relatively quiet – which is the best time to visit **Kranji War Memorial** (*see p101*), located near the Turf Club off Woodlands Road. This 1946 cemetery commemorates the members of the Allied Forces who died during World War II.

For another peaceful spot, take the 925 bus from the MRT stop to **Kranji Reservoir**. Its scenic park, which faces the Straits of Johor, attracts anglers daily and picnicking families at weekends. A plaque nearby marks the site of the 1942 Kranji Beach Battle.

Beyond the reservoir, hugging the coastline, is **Sungei Buloh Wetland Reserve** (*see p101*), a major birdwatching area: between November and March thousands of migratory birds transit here on route to Australia. Adjoining the reserve is what's known as the Kranji Countryside: a cluster of vegetable and livestock farms, some of which are open to visitors (*see p101* **Down on the farm**). This tranquil, rural area is a side of Singapore that not many foreign visitors see (nor many locals, for that matter).

Even more remote and less visited is **Choa Chu Kang Cemetery Complex** (head south about five kilometres down Lim Chu Kang Road), the only cemetery in Singapore still open for burials. There are plots for different religions (Christian, Muslim, Hindu, Jewish, Parsi and more) and a huge Chinese cemetery. East from the cemetery, along Old Choa Chu Kang Road, is **Sungei Tengah Argo Park**, where you'll find more farms, dealing mainly in ornamental plants and fish. Worth a visit is the **Farmart Centre** (67 Sungei Tengah Road, 6767 0070, www.farmart.com.sg, open 10am-7pm daily). There are prawn fishing ponds and more than 40 outlets selling local farm products ranging from organic juices and quail meat to delicate aquarium fish; puppies are also for sale. Located on a hill, the centre provides panoramic views of the north-western countryside.

South of the cemetery complex is **Thow Kwang Pottery** (85 Lorong Tawas, off Jalan Bahar, 6265 5808, www.tkpotteryjungle.com, open 9am-5pm daily), where hand-painted pottery and classic Chinese blue and whites are much cheaper than on Orchard Road. It's famous for its 44-metre (144-feet) long Dragon Kiln, an ancient-style clay firing stove, now designated a national heritage piece. In 2006

Down on the farm

Farms in Singapore? It seem unlikely in this highly urbanised city-state, but Singapore does have about 200 farms, mainly in the north-western region of Lim Chu Kang and Kranji. Dubbed the Kranji Countryside (www.kranjicountryside.com), some farms specialise in vegetables, fruit and orchids, while others breed livestock like quails, frogs and koi. Many welcome visitors; some offer tours, sell produce and have their own restaurant.

The easiest way to explore is to hire a car or taxi for half a day. Alternatively, the Kranji Express bus ($2; $1 children) runs hourly 9am-5pm daily from Kranji MRT, stopping at various farms, as well as **Sungei Buloh Wetland Reserve** (*see below*) and **Thow Kwong Pottery** (*see p100*). Walking is not advisable as most of the farms are far apart.

Aero-Green Technology

260 Neo Tiew Crescent (6792 4298/ www.aerogreentech.com.sg). **Open** 9am-5pm daily. **Admission** $4. **No credit cards.**
In order to grow temperate vegetables and fruits in tropical Singapore, Aero-Green uses the aeroponics technique whereby plants' roots are sprayed with nutrients via a sprinkler system, instead of being embedded in soil.

Bollywood Veggies

100 Neo Tiew Road (6898 5001/ www.bollywoodveggies.com). **Open** 9am-6pm Wed-Sun. **Admission** $2; $1 per person family. **No credit cards.**
This organic farm grows a variety of fruits and vegetables, from chill padi to bananas. You can buy herbs and plants, and eat the farm's produce at the cosy Poison Ivy Bistro.

Hay Dairies

3 Lim Chu Kang Lane 4 (6792 0931/ www.haydairies.com.sg). **Open** 9am-4pm daily. **Admission** free.
Over 1,000 goats of various breeds are kept at this dairy goat farm, the only one on the island. Milking sessions are from 9am to 11am, so arrive early. Kids can feed hay to the kids (the furry kind). Note: no entry to those who have visited European dairy farms recently.

Jurong Frog Farm

56 Lim Chu Kang Lane 6 (6791 7229/ www.jurongfrogfarm.com.sg). **Open** 7am-6pm daily. **Admission** free; $2 guided tour.
Singapore's only frog-breeding farm, with over 6,000 American bullfrogs, as well as soft-shell turtles and ornamental fish. Possibly not for the squeamish: the tour explains how the amphibians are slaughtered for their meat.

the kiln produced its first ceramic art pieces in years; it's used mainly by the Jalan Bahar Clay Studios, a local arts centre.

Kranji War Memorial

9 Woodlands Road. Kranji MRT. **Open** 7am-6pm daily. **Admission** free.
The long MRT trip to Kranji affords plenty of time to contemplate the serried rows of public housing that represent one of the Singapore government's greatest yet most perplexing drab achievements. By contrast, the serried rows of 4,000 white gravestones at this peaceful hillside cemetery have a serene, if solemn beauty. Dominated by the huge, wing-like Singapore Memorial, and fronted by a Sir Edwin Lutyens-designed memorial stone, the site includes several monuments for servicemen massacred in the early days of the Japanese Occupation, and one for those lying in 'unmaintainable graves' elsewhere in South-east Asia. The inscriptions tell countless tales of death and sacrifice, and you can easily spend an hour piecing together a picture of the British Empire in all its diversity. Also here are the tombs of the first two presidents of Singapore.

Sungei Buloh Wetland Reserve

301 Neo Tiew Crescent, Lim Chu Kang (6794 1401/ www.sbwr.org.sg). Kranji MRT then bus 925 then 15mins walk/Kranji MRT then Kranji Express bus. **Open** 7.30am-7pm Mon-Sat; 7am-7pm Sun. **Admission** free Mon-Fri; $1; $0.50 concessions Sat, Sun. **No credit cards.**
This wetland reserve of mangrove swamps, ponds and secondary forest is home to 140 species of birds. Thousands of egrets, sandpipers and plovers pass through in winter, but plenty of local species (king fishers, herons, bitterns) are visible all year round. Early morning is the best time for birdwatching; there are observation hides, and you can rent binoculars. There are three nature trails (3-7km/2-4 miles long), and you can also spot mudskippers, monkeys and climbing crabs on the mangrove boardwalks. Free guided tours are available on Saturday (9.30am, 3.30pm). On Sundays the 925 bus stops at the entrance; the rest of the week you have to walk from Kranji Reservoir car park – either via Kranji Way and Neo Tiew Crescent, or via the rugged and longer Kranji Nature Trail. Alternatively, you can catch the Kranji Express bus (*see above* **Down on the farm**).

Central & Northern Singapore

A lush nature reserve, bustling new towns and wildlife galore.

If the frenetic urban buzz of the city centre makes you crave greenery or the 'real Singapore', head for the island's central and northern regions. Bounded by three arteries – Bukit Timah Expressway to the west, Pan Island Expressway to the south and Central Expressway to the east – this is where you'll find Singapore's oldest suburbs and greenest spaces. The red North South Line of the MRT serves a string of satellite towns, from Toa Payoh to Woodlands (the jumping-off point for Malaysia), while the Central Catchment Nature Reserve contains reservoirs, rainforest, hiking trails and two of Singapore's major attractions: Singapore Zoo and the Night Safari.

Toa Payoh & Bishan

Three stops north of Orchard MRT is **Toa Payoh**, Singapore's first and oldest new town, established in 1969 and equipped with its own schools, markets, public library, sports facilities and industrial parks. A huge area of uninhabited swamp in the 1920s, Toa Payoh is aptly named: 'toa' means 'big' in Hokkien and 'payoh' comes from the Malay word 'paya' for swamp. It's a typical satellite town, and a frequent showcase for foreign dignitaries (Queen Elizabeth II has visited twice, no less, in 1972 and 2006).

Toa Payoh MRT station is bang-slap in the centre of town, adjacent to the country's first air-conditioned bus interchange, and surrounded by scores of shops. Also located here is the **HDB Hub**, the headquarters of the Housing & Development Board (HDB), the government agency in charge of the country's public housing – where around 84 per cent of Singaporeans live. Visit the **HDB Gallery** (*see p103*) to learn more about Singapore's 'pigeon-hole' housing.

Within walking distance of the MRT station is the Buddhist **Lian Sang Shuang Lin Temple** (*see p103*). Designated a national monument, this impressive 1908 temple commemorates Buddha's life. Another national monument nearby is the **Sun Yat Sen Nanyang Memorial Hall** (*see p104*),

dedicated to Dr Sun, the founding father of China's revolutionary activities in South-east Asia. He stayed at the magnificent 19th-century villa during his eight visits to Singapore between 1906 and 1911.

A 20-minute walk west of the MRT station is the prestigious **Singapore Polo Club** (*see p199*), founded in 1886. Most of the clubhouse facilities (gym, pool, spa) are for members only, but the restaurant, which has a good view of the polo field, is open to the public. Weekdays bring power-lunching businessmen, while weekends are popular with families.

The next stop on the MRT is **Bishan**. Once the site of a Cantonese cemetery, this satellite town, built in 1984, is one of the better-looking new towns, blessed with pleasant colours and wide spaces between apartment blocks. A short walk from the MRT station – which stands next to Junction 8 Complex, a popular mall – is the town's most beautiful asset, **Bishan Park**. One of the biggest parks in Singapore, it has lush greenery, lakes, cycling tracks, playgrounds and the country's first park-based spa, **Aramsa Garden Spa** (*see p156* **Super spas**).

A short bus or taxi ride from the town centre is the Buddhist **Kong Meng San Phor Kark See Monastery** (*see p103*), also known as Bright Hill Temple, the largest place of worship in Singapore. Walking south from here (via Sin Min Drive) will bring you to the famous **Upper Thomson Road food strip**. Between the Longhouse food centre – the char kway teow and goreng pisang are recommended – and Thomson Plaza, a popular shopping centre about 400 metres west, are more than 35 shophouse eateries (including two 24-hour joints) serving fare from chicken rice to pizzas, French crêpes to roti prata.

One stop after Bishan is **Ang Mo Kio**, one of Singapore's oldest estates, which looks set for rejuvenation thanks to the opening (in February 2007) of the AMK Hub mega-mall. Connected to the MRT station and a brand-new air-conditioned bus interchange, this four-storey complex houses more than 250 shops, a huge pharmacy and an eight-screen cineplex.

Sightseeing

HDB Gallery
Basement One, HDB Hub, 480 Toa Payoh
Lorong 6, Toa Payoh (6490 1111/www.hdb.gov.sg).
Toa Payoh MRT. **Open** 8.30am-5pm Mon-Fri.
Admission free.

The past, present and future of public housing in Singapore are mapped out at this multi-media gallery. Intriguing displays include 'before' and 'after' photographs of all the island's 24 new towns and housing estates, and a giant pin model showing 50 years of HDB block designs. The Future sector is a let-down, though: the 'virtual lift' that leads to the '50th storey skybridge' is extremely dull, as are the gadgets in the e-Home display.

Kong Meng San Phor Kark See Monastery
88 Bright Hill Road, Bishan (6849 5300/
www.kmspks.org.sg). Bishan MRT then bus 52,
410 (white plate only). **Open** 8.30am-4pm daily.
Admission free.

This hillside Buddhist complex, founded in the 1920s, contains classic Chinese temple structures, tranquil gardens, a tortoise pool, a crematorium and a majestic bell and drum tower. Housed in the Pagoda of 10,000 Buddhas are thousands of mini Buddhas (inside the main stupa) and one of the largest bronze Medicine Buddhas in South-east Asia. Bishan MRT stop is quite a distance away; you can catch a bus to the monastery, but the easiest option is to take a taxi.

Lian Sang Shuang Lin Temple
184 Jalan Toa Payoh, Toa Payoh (6259 6924).
Toa Payoh MRT then bus 8, 19, 26. **Open** 7.30am-5pm daily. **Admission** free.

This 1908 Buddhist monastery, Siong Lim Temple, for short, is the oldest in Singapore. An 11-year, $40m restoration project was completed in 2002 (using carpenters and artisans from China), but it still remains a fine specimen of classic Chinese style architecture. Highlights include the two magnificent

Sightseeing

Base concerns

It you need to escape the madding crowd, head to Seletar Base on Singapore's northern coast. Located off Jalan Kayu north of the Tampines Expressway, it's a tranquil enclave that is wonderfully undisturbed by Singapore's aggressive modernisation. At the far end is Selatar Airport, founded in 1929 and Singapore's first commercial airport. It's still in use today – as an immigration checkpoint for small aircraft, private jets and medical evacuation flights, and for scheduled flights for Pulau Tioman (West Malaysia) and Pulau Batam (Indonesia) – but planes are few and far between. In the 1940s it served as a British military airbase – which is why most of the streets bear London names: there's an Oxford Street,

Park Lane, Regent Street, Mornington Crescent, and even a roundabout called Piccadilly Circus.

Elsewhere are aerospace companies, flying schools, a military camp and recreational establishments including a country club, golf courses and a driving range. Yet the base still comes across like a country town, dotted with open fields, quaint old-fashioned lamp-posts and more than 300 lovely black and white colonial houses. Formerly officers' residences, the latter are now owned by the government and much in demand for renting by expats.

In the evenings, locals fish, picnic and enjoy views of the outlying islands from the Lower Seletar Reservoir Tidal Gates (along Yishun Avenue 1, west of the airport). Another favourite spot is the Republic of Singapore Flying Club's Sunset Grill & Pub (140B Piccadilly, East Camp, 6482 0244, open 4-10pm Mon, Wed-Sun), especially at sunset.

But hurry: the base is likely to lose its old world charm once the $60m Seletar Aerospace Park – a massive hub handling aircraft maintenance, repair and overhaul that's being built around Seletar Airport – is completed by 2015.

Getting there: from Serangoon MRT station, bus 103 runs along West Camp Road where Seletar Airport lies, while bus 103W follows East Camp via Piccadilly. If you want to check out every inch of the base, the best option is to hire a car or a taxi for the day.

9.1m (30ft) wooden entrance gates and the 29m (95ft) Dragon Light Pagoda built entirely of granite and topped with a golden spire.

Sun Yat Sen Nanyang Memorial Hall

12 Tai Gin Road, Novena (6256 7377). Toa Payoh MRT then bus 139, 145. **Open** 9am-5pm Tue-Sun. **Admission** $3; $2 concessions. **Credit** (shop only) AmEx, DC, MC, V.

A pioneer of China's revolutionary struggle in the early 20th century, Dr Sun Yat Sen made numerous trips to South-east Asia; a sympathiser, Teo Eng Hock, turned over this villa to the cause. It was here in 1906 that Dr Sun formed the Singapore branch of the Chinese Revolutionary Alliance, and he would return several more times before his success in deposing the emperor in 1911 – whereupon a new battle for the future of China began. The story told here fleshes out the political history of the Singapore Chinese, and makes a change from the more usual focus on migrant labour and World War II. While there are a few videos, replica objects and wax-works, the spacious halls and galleries are over-whelmingly reliant on captioned black and white archive photos. Next door is the Burmese Buddhist Temple, containing a 3m (11ft) marble Buddha, the largest Burmese Buddha image outside Burma.

Central Catchment Nature Reserve

The concrete jungle does have a green heart. Dominating the island's central region is the Central Catchment Nature Reserve, covering 18 square kilometres (7 square miles) of lush rainforest and home to more than 800 plant and 500 animal species.

The greenery that remains is but a small fraction of the original lowland tropical rainforest that covered much of the island before the early 19th century. Huge tracts of forest were cleared for cultivation and logging purposes between 1820 and 1870. Thankfully, the deforestation was halted after the powers that be realised that water-scarce Singapore badly needed its own water resources (Malaysia still provides about half the island's water needs). In 1868 the development of MacRitchie Reservoir saw its surrounding six square kilometres (2.3 square miles) of forest protected as a water catchment reserve. The forests around Pierce (1910) and Seletar Reservoirs (1920) were subsequently protected too.

MacRitchie Reservoir (*see below*) is the most popular of the three areas. Hiking trails run around the reservoir, and the nature park, located off Lornie Road, contains jogging trails, an exercise area, kids' playground, tea kiosk, fountain and a bandstand. Directly above

MacRitchie is **Pierce Reservoir**: after it was dammed in 1975, it became two reservoirs, Upper Pierce and Lower Pierce. Though not as easily accessible as MacRitchie, their idyllic parks still draw nature lovers and fishing fans. The area is best reached by car, but you can also take bus 167 from Orchard Road and alight just before Old Upper Thomson Road, which leads to Lower Pierce. Follow the long winding road north, then west, to get to Upper Pierce.

Upper Seletar Reservoir forms the head of the reserve, off Mandai Road. Its park has picnic areas, jogging tracks, a lookout tower, playground, sport fishing, paddle boating and a nine-hole public golf course. To get here, take bus 139 from Ang Mo Kio MRT station. Overlooking the eastern side of the reservoir, and adjacent to each other, are two of Singapore's top attractions: **Singapore Zoo** and **Night Safari** (for both, *see p105*) – reason enough to make the long trip to the remote north. The island's largest commercial orchid garden, **Mandai Orchid Garden** (*see p105*), is just ten minutes away.

MacRitchie Reservoir

Lornie Road, MacRitchie (6468 5736/www.nparks. gov.sg). Bus 132, 165, 640, 855, 980. **Open** *MacRitchie Reservoir* 9am-5pm Tue-Fri; 8.30am-5pm Sat, Sun. *TreeTop Walk* 9am-5pm Tue-Sun. **Admission** free.

Singapore's oldest and most popular nature park is a haven for joggers, families and weekend strollers; occasional free concerts are held on Sundays. Popular as it is, facilities are rather run-down and

Orang-utans galore, plus rare white tigers, at **Singapore Zoo**.

works (due to end March 2008) are under way to provide more user-friendly amenities. To get into the rainforest proper, the MacRitchie Trails around the reservoir offer easy boardwalk treks and ambitious hikes, ranging from 3-11km (1.8-7 miles) in length. Wildlife, from flying lemurs to tree frogs and pangolins, is abundant but rarely seen. Long-tailed macaque monkeys are more common, but be wary: some can be quite ferocious, as they're used to being fed by irresponsible visitors. A highlight is the HSBC TreeTop Walk, a suspension bridge positioned 25m (82ft) above the forest floor, which connects the two highest points in the reserve and offers splendid panoramic views. Depending on where you start, the round trip is 7-11km (4.3-7 miles, about 3-5 hours), and graded in parts as 'difficult' – so attempt it only if you're fit and properly equipped. Traffic on the bridge is one-way, so there's literally no turning back. There are toilets, but bring your own water, food and insect repellent.

Mandai Orchid Garden

200 Mandai Lake Road, MacRitchie (6269 1036/ www.mandai.com.sg). Bus 138, 927. **Open** 8am-6pm daily. **Admission** $3; $1-$1.50 concessions. **Credit** MC, V.

The highlight of this privately owned orchid garden, established in 1951, is the stunning view of an orchid-filled hillside. Over 200 varieties, including the national flower Vanda Miss Joaquim, are cultivated here, and its gift-wrapped orchids are cheaper than in the city centre. But it's probably only worth a trip if you're a keen horticulturist or also visiting nearby Singapore Zoo.

Night Safari

80 Mandai Lake Road, MacRitchie (6269 3411/ www.nightsafari.com.sg). Bus 138, 927. **Open** 7.30pm-midnight daily. **Admission** $20; $10 concessions. **Credit** AmEx, DC, JCB, MC, V.

Set in lush secondary rainforest, this is a must-see. The world's first night zoo (opened in 1991) allows you to see what over 900 nocturnal animals from 130 species get up to after dusk, in naturalistic habitats and without barriers, via the use of special lighting techniques. To see the zoo, take a 45-minute tram ride: observe majestic lions gnawing on their meat dinners, coy mountain deer striking poses and, if you're lucky, a noisy rhino taking a bath. You can get off the tram at designated points to follow three walking trails that let you get close to flying squirrels, dangling bats and a leopard or two. The hourly Creatures of the Night show is worth a look, but the ethnic performances are a bit lame. Don't use flash if you're taking photos as it may scare the animals. The Night Safari gets a million visitors a year, most of whom seem to turn up at the weekend; go late at night during the week to have a quieter time.

Singapore Zoo

80 Mandai Lake Road, MacRitchie (6269 3411/ www.zoo.com.sg). Bus 138, 927. **Open** 8.30am-6pm daily. **Admission** $15; $7.50 concessions. **Credit** AmEx, DC, JCB, MC, V.

Opened in 1973, this is one of the world's first 'open concept' zoos, where animals are kept in landscaped enclosures (instead of traditional cages) separated from visitors via ditches or moats. Even more popular than the Night Safari, it has more than just lions, tigers and bears: it's home to over 3,000 animals from all over the world, including giant tortoises, hamadryas baboons, penguins, the world's largest colony of orang-utans, and a good number of endangered species. You can have breakfast with the orang-utans (and meet the famous Ah Meng), while kids can get their kicks at the petting zoo. The elephant shows (11.30am and 3.30pm) and assorted feeding sessions are always fun. As the zoo is aiming to go 'tropical rainforest' in the next few years, do visit the polar bears (mother Sheba and son Inuka – the only ones in the tropics) before they are transferred to colder pastures. **Photos** *pp104-105*.

Woodlands & Sembawang

Located in the northern tip of Singapore, **Woodlands**, built in 1971, is one of the island's oldest and biggest new towns, with around 193,000 residents. It's served by three MRT stations: Marsiling, Woodlands and Admiralty. Its busiest hub is, hands down, the massive **Woodlands Checkpoint**, which fronts the Singapore-Johor Causeway that connects Singapore to Malaysia. Located north of Marsiling MRT station, the checkpoint regulates traffic into and out of Singapore – on foot or by bus, coach, car, taxi or rail. Thousands use the causeway daily, with traffic heaviest in the early mornings and evenings. On weekends and public holidays, the jams are hellish and can last for hours.

Woodlands MRT stop leads into the busy town centre, where the ever-crowded Causeway Point shopping mall and Woodlands Civic Centre stand; hugging the coastline near Admiralty MRT station is the **Senoko Industrial Estate**. Of little interest to visitors but of great importance to Singapore, this houses a power station, incineration plant, gasworks, numerous industries and Senoko Fishery Port, where frantic buying and selling of fish takes place at the wholesale market every day except Monday (2-6am).

Next stop on the MRT line is Sembawang, also mainly an industrial area. North of the station lies the massive **Sembawang Shipyard**. The former British Royal Naval Dockyard was 'sold' to the Singapore government for $1 in 1968, and is now the country's leading ship-repair facility, dealing with some 220 vessels annually. The sight of the 'Very Large' ships and carriers moored along its five docks – visible from Admiralty Road West bus terminal – is daunting.

Just west of the shipyard is **Sembawang Camp**, famously known by locals as the camp where 'our boys' reported for National Service (NS) training in the 1970s and '80s. Originally the British Navy's Terror Barracks (named

after HMS *Terror*), this was where the Japanese Navy surrendered to the British fleet on 6 September 1945. In 1971 the camp was named Terror Camp by the Singapore military, only to be renamed Sembawang Camp a year later after hundreds of NS men complained that life in the camp lived up to its name.

Now a Singapore Navy establishment, it houses the **Republic of Singapore Navy Museum** (32 Admiralty Road West, Endurance Block, 6750 5585, open 8.30am-5pm Mon-Fri) in a pre-World War II building renovated to resemble the interior of a ship, complete with narrow passageways and portholes in the walls. Bring your passport to get an entry pass at the camp gate – but note that the museum will have closed by September 2007, and will reopen early in 2008 in new premises at Changi Naval Base.

East of Sembawang Shipyard is the **PSA Sembawang Terminal**, which contains recreational facilities for visiting servicemen from the US, UK, Australia and New Zealand. The area also has plenty of exquisite black and white colonial houses.

East of the terminal is lovely **Sembawang Park**, often packed on weekends with locals swimming and camping besides its beach – one of Singapore's few naturally sandy beaches. It's also a popular fishing spot, with anglers staked out along the shoreline or where the former pier and jetty stood. Near the jetty is the stately 1910 **Beaulieu House**, a former residence for senior British naval officers that is now a seafood restaurant. Take care if using your mobile phone here: the park is so close to Johor that you may find yourself connected to a Malaysian phone network.

South of Sembawang MRT station, off Gambas Avenue, is **Sembawang Hot Spring**, – the only natural hot spring on the mainland (there's another on the island of Pulau Tekong). Discovered by a Chinese merchant on his pineapple estate in 1909, the waters – which are said to have healing properties – were later marketed as 'Seletaris' mineral water by local soft drinks company Fraser & Neave. The spring is now located within Sembawang Airbase grounds, but is fenced off from the restricted military premises and accessible to the public from 7am to 7pm daily.

The next MRT stop brings you to **Yishun**, which is also served by Khatib station. One of the bigger new towns, with 164,000 residents, Yishun has seen better days – though its park is great for jogging, fishing and picnics, and scenic Lower Seletar Reservoir is nearby. Another popular, surprisingly peaceful hangout is **Seletar Base** (*see p103* **Base concerns**), located on the eastern bank of the reservoir.

Eat, Drink, Shop

YOU KNOW WHO YOU ARE.
SINGAPORE • 50 CUSCADEN ROAD #05-01
656-2355232 • HARDROCK.COM

Restaurants

Sacred chow.

A common greeting in Singapore is not 'Hello', but 'Have you eaten?' – an indication of just how deep the nation's obsession with food runs. The national joke is that as Singaporeans are having lunch, they're discussing where and when to have dinner; when that's settled, they'll start workshopping tomorrow's meals.

Which isn't so surprising given the almost mind-bending number of eateries – around 40,000 on this tiny island. It seems as if a new restaurant opens, and another one closes, almost every other day: industry experts reckon that for every ten restaurants that open each year, seven will have closed in three years. All of which adds up to a very dynamic (and fickle) scene, where voracious appetites are rewarded and everyone is spoilt for choice.

For visitors – even those from cities with an established, multicultural dining scene, such as London and New York – this translates into a breathtaking array of eating options. Settings range from chi-chi restaurants to open-air hawker centres. Every imaginable cuisine is represented, from numbingly hot Thai tom yam, piquant Indian curries and dainty Japanese sushi to muscular Brazilian churrascarias and American steaks. And unlike the world cuisines offered by other metropolises in the region that might tweak flavours to local tastes – Tokyo comes to mind here – in Singapore, it's usually the real thing, whether it's a rosy pink vitello tonnato or a bowl of perfectly executed Belgian moules with a side of crisp frites.

It hasn't always been this way. Just a decade ago, the dining scene – the top end, at least – was decidedly more staid. The shift coincided with a returning diaspora of sexy twentysomethings from New York, Sydney and London, plugged into a vibe of great design and uncomplicated food. A tipping point was the opening of Marmalade on Purvis Street in 1999. The menu lured fussy gourmands with fresh Antipodean flavours, in a dramatic and sophisticated setting of steel strips, heavy drapery, deep brown woods and mood lighting.

Marmalade stirred an interest in good design, and simple but well prepared food. Although no longer open, it still casts a long shadow, as shown by the spate of copycats that continues to this day.

At about the same time, the Tung Lok group broke the dowdy, red lantern-themed Chinese restaurant mould by melding Western influences with traditional Chinese classics. Local diners, more used to the politically incorrect shark's fin soup, were knocked for six by peking duck pancakes paired with foie gras.

Attracted by all the moolah being thrown around and the increasingly sophisticated tastes of the population, chefs from all over the world have chown up on Singapore's doorstep armed with their spatulas, well-thumbed copies of *Larousse* and a great deal of creative brio – thanks, especially to the Australian contingent.

To get the most out of your gourmet tour of Singapore, sweep quickly through the Orchard Road belt. Here you'll find the big names, glossy interiors and expense-account menus. Good food, to be sure, but there's much more: some of the best eating places are tucked away in the outer suburbs. Hawker centres (*see p114* **Grub hubbub**), in particular, are a treasure trove of taste sensations, gathering under one roof an entire microcosm of cuisines – Chinese, Malay, Peranakan, Indian, Eurasian – that combine the two virtues near and dear to local diners' hearts: cheapness and quality.

But in this rosy gastronomic landscape rings a cautionary bell: service remains a thorny issue. Waiting staff are paid a pittance (tipping is not the norm, and restaurants almost always pocket the ten per cent mandatory service charge), so the turnover rate is embarrassingly high. The result is poorly trained – and very temporary – staff, who know little about the menu or the rudiments of table service. And that's just the high-end restaurants. But in the end, the quality of the cooking and sheer volume of eateries overwhelms all other considerations. Note that many restaurants are closed between lunch and dinner, so eating mid-afternoon can be tricky.

❶ Purple numbers given in this chapter correspond to the location of each restaurant as marked on the street maps. *See pp246-252.*

LOCAL CUISINES

The staggering range of cuisines in Singapore is a direct result of its history as a magnet for immigrants from all over Asia. Over the years, as the different races settled in and intermingled, they watched each other cook, exchanged recipes, cherry-picked techniques and ingredients and slowly adapted their own cuisines. It was the earliest form of fusion.

The Indians, for instance, thriftily plonked fish heads into saffron-tinged sauces and created the now iconic fish-head curry, a dish not found in Mother India. The Peranakans took the traditional Chinese spring roll of braised turnips and carrots, and filled it with meat, five-spiced powders and water chestnuts, deep fried it, and renamed it ngoh hiang. Meanwhile, the Eurasian community took a bit of everything from everyone else and came up with their own delightful mélange of aromatic stews and softly fragrant curries.

Today, the layered cuisines to be found in Singapore bear the imprint of this early mixing of ingredients and flavours, but in each can still be found the distinct features of the original. What follows is an outrageously abbreviated thumbnail of what to expect when you sit down and open the menu.

Chinese

It's the regional ingredients that give the different Chinese cuisines their uniqueness. For instance, the Shanghainese adore ginger, black vinegar, bamboo shoots and crabs. The Cantonese are renowned for dim sum, roasted meats and ambrosial soups laced with all manner of delicacies (abalone, fish maw, dried scallops). Sichuan cooking is marked by the use of dried red chillies and spicy soups; and the Hunanese are famed for their cold cuts. Steamed fish, congee and light soups are typical of Teochew cooking. Hokkien dishes include hokkien mee (thick wheat noodles with meat, seafood and vegetables) and oyster omelette.

Indian

Most Indians in Singapore originate from South India, so you'll find plenty of vegetarian dosais alongside coconutty Keralan seafood dishes. Strong, fragrant spices, such as cardamom, cloves, cumin, saffron, coriander, chillis and tamarind, are common. North Indian food features tandoor-cooked meats and milder, creamier sauces. Indian desserts tend to be incredibly sweet and milky. A local twist is provided by Indian Muslim Malaysian food, with its biryanis, pratas and murtabaks (prata stuffed with meat, onion and egg). Roti prata – fried flatbread with lentil curry – is a common breakfast dish.

Malay & Indonesian

Malay and Indonesian cuisines share ingredients and cooking styles. Ginger, chilli, lemongrass and dried shrimp paste are favoured spicings. Marinated freshwater fish is fried to a delicious crisp, while curries run the gamut from vegetables to chicken pieces bathed in thick, coconut-infused gravies. Curry puffs (pastries filled with egg, sardines or just potatoes) are favourite snacks, while satay with

peanut sauce is a byword for comfort food. Nasi padang stalls offer a buffet-selection of classic Malay dishes.

Peranakan

Combining the flavours of their Chinese and Malay heritage – with a fair amount of culinary plundering from Indian, Indonesian and Thai kitchens – the Peranakans blend fresh herbs and spices (including lemongrass and pandan leaves), shrimp paste, coconut, tropical fruits and vegetables to create a richly layered cuisine of stews, curries and spectacularly elaborate desserts. Expect a combination of tart, spicy, salty and chilli hot flavours.

Desserts

Local puddings tend to be very sweet and very colourful, and often soupy or gloupy. Favourites include chendol (mung bean jelly with shaved ice, coconut milk and brown palm sugar); ice kachang (a tower of shaved ice topped with assorted syrups, fruits and sweet beans); and herbal grass jelly – dark brown in colour – with syrup and fruit toppings.

Drinks

Alcohol is expensive in Singapore, and wine lists are often not as good as you'd find in Europe or North America. Local soft drinks include freshly

The best Restaurants

For bargain-priced Indian
Bombay Café (see p125), Samy's Curry Restaurant (see p121).

For super seafood
The Cliff (see p124), Long Beach (see p126), No Signboard Esplanade (see p111).

For dim sum
Imperial Treasure Nan Bei (see p119), Jade (see p112).

For non-Canto Chinese
Chef Heng's (Teochew, see p125), Din Tai Fung (Shanghainese, see p119), House of Hunan (Hunanese, see p129), Min Jiang (Sichuan, see p120).

For top-class Thai
A-roy Thai (see p111), P&P Thai (see p118).

For Modern European flair
Ember (see p115), Poppi (see p112).

For heavenly hawker fare
Maxwell Food Centre (see p113), Tiong Bahru Market (see p127).
See also p114 Grub hubbub.

squeezed juices from a staggering array of tropical fruits, sugar cane juice, and soy bean milk in various guises. Teh tarik ('pulled tea') is a distinctive Singaporean beverage: sweet, milky Indian tea that's aerated by pouring the liquid from one glass to another. Purists won't be impressed by the regular coffee served in local kopitiams (coffeeshops) – stale filter coffee, sugar and both evaporated and condensed milk – but lattes, cappuccinos et al are readily available in smarter cafés.

Colonial District

Asian

A-roy Thai

#04-06 Funan DigitaLife Mall, 109 North Bridge Road, Colonial District (6338 3880). City Hall MRT. **Open** 11.30am-3pm, 6-10pm daily. **Main courses** $9-$31. **Credit** AmEx, JCB, MC, V. **Map** p250 J8 **❶** Thai

A-roy Thai's nondescript interior (in the middle of an electronics mall) belies the superb quality of its kitchen. The flavours ring true, the high notes of sour, sweet, salty and chilli heat recalling all that is good in Thai cuisine. House specials include a nasal-clearing tom yam, jade-green curries perfumed with lemongrass, delicately stuffed chicken wings, rice crackers topped with a coconutty pork mince, and fish steamed in a red shower of chillis.
Other locations: 81 Upper East Coast Road, Katong (6443 0373).

Coriander Leaf

#02-03 3A Merchant Court, 3A River Valley Road, Clarke Quay (6732 3354/www.corianderleaf.com). Clarke Quay MRT. **Open** noon-2.30pm, 6.30-10pm Mon-Thur; noon-2.30pm, 6.30-10.30pm Fri; 6.30-10.30pm Sat. **Main courses** $23-$35. **Credit** AmEx, DC, MC, V. **Map** p250 H8 **❷** Pan-Asian
Pakistani born and ex-New Yorker Samia Ahad has been charming locals for years with her pan-Asian cooking. Dressed in a trademark starched white shirt, she effortlessly skates across a wonderland of subcontinental and South-east Asian cuisines, from golden Iranian pilafs and lamb kebabs to fresh Vietnamese rice-paper rolls, from melt-in-the-mouth garlic naans to saffron-scented snapper. Try to snag a table by the windows with views of the Singapore River. *See also p128* **Taste makers.**

Empire Café

Raffles Hotel, 1 Beach Road, Colonial District (6412 1101/www.singapore-raffles.raffles.com). City Hall MRT. **Open** 11.30am-10.45pm daily. **Main courses** $10-$22. **Credit** AmEx, DC, JCB, MC, V. **Map** p249 L6 **❸** Pan-Asian
Make believe you're Somerset Maugham (once a regular at the Raffles Hotel) strolling in for a meal at one of the hotel's best eateries. The high ceilings conspire with the old-world furniture to create a casually nostalgic vibe – just right for the menu of Asian classics such as nasi goreng, rojak salads, huge

Summer Pavilion. *See p112.*

bowls of laksa noodles, and chicken rice. Though pricier than the hawker stall version, the experience is nevertheless captivating.

Makansutra Gluttons Bay

#01-15 Esplanade Mall, Marina (6336 7025/www.makansutra.com). City Hall MRT then 10mins walk/bus 36, 106, 133, 171, 195. **Open** 6pm-3am daily. **Main courses** $3-$10. **No credit cards.** **Map** p251 L8 **❹** Hawker centre
The original Gluttons Bay was on Orchard Road, but it closed in the 1990s. In 2005, hawker food bible Makansutra handpicked a dozen of Singapore's best stalls and set up this open-air mini hawker centre bang next to Esplanade theatre complex. It's touristy (the stalls are retro-style push carts) and pricier than other centres, but the food, from oyster omelettes to char kwey teow, is great. And the waterfront location is a bonus on a balmy night.

No Signboard Esplanade

#01-14 Esplanade Mall, 8 Raffles Avenue, Marina (6336 9959/www.nosignboardseafood.com). City Hall MRT then 10mins walk//bus 36, 106, 133, 171, 195. **Open** 11am-11pm daily. **Main courses** $8-$40. **Credit** MC, V. **Map** p251 L8 **❺** Chinese seafood

A late arrival may earn you a stern rebuke from the harried maître d', but you will forgive him when the food arrives: perfectly steamed fish, tangles of kang kong fried with dried prawns or astonishing sambal But the restaurant (one of four in town) makes its name with crabs, including the iconic black pepper and chilli varieties.

Other locations: #03-02 VivoCity, 1 HarbourFront Walk, HarbourFront (6376 9959); #01-02 Block 1202, East Coast Seafood Centre, East Coast (6448 9959); Kallang Oasis, 50 Stadium Boulevard, Kallang (6344 9959); 414 Geylang, Geylang (6842 3415).

Rakuzen

#01-14-19 Time2@Millenia Walk, 9 Raffles Boulevard, Marina (6333 1171). City Hall MRT then 10mins walk. **Open** 11.30am-3pm, 6-10pm Mon-Fri; 11.30am-10pm Sat, Sun. **Main courses** $8-$20. **Credit** AmEx, DC, JCB, MC, V. **Map** p251 M7 ❻ Japanese

The private dining booths at the rear of Rakuzen are appealing, but the best seats in the house are at the long counter. Here, chefs dish out seasonal specials such as delicately grilled Pacific sardines marinated in saké, rare forest mushrooms, firm, fleshy toro, sea-eel tempura, and incredible loops of snowy udon dipped in a soy jus thickened with onions and ginger. The house special is the nutty, fragrant Japanese rice, milled fresh each morning.

Rang Mahal

3/F Pan Pacific Singapore, 7 Raffles Boulevard, Marina (6333 1788/www.rangmahal.com.sg). City Hall MRT then 10mins walk. **Open** noon-2.30pm Mon-Fri, Sun; 6.30-10.30pm daily. **Credit** AmEx, DC, MC, V. **Map** p251 M7 ❼ Indian

With slick stonework and glass, mood lighting and luxury finishings, this does not feel like your typical Indian restaurant. But the scent of lingering spices – not to mention the tables laden with curries and lassis – gives the game away. The food is delicious, whether it's fat prawns crimson from the tandoor oven; minced lamb kebabs perfumed with cloves; or piles of garlicky and buttery naans. A new menu and renovations were under way at the time of writing.

Summer Pavilion

3/F Ritz-Carlton Millenia, 7 Raffles Avenue, Marina (6434 5286/www.ritzcarlton.com/hotels/singapore). City Hall MRT then 10mins walk. **Open** 11.30am-2.30pm, 6.30-11pm daily. **Main courses** $12-$50. **Credit** AmEx, DC, JCB, MC, V. **Map** p251 M8 ❽ Cantonese

As befits a restaurant wrapped in the glamorous folds of the ritzy Ritz-Carlton hotel, the Summer Pavilion is a slice of the good life complete with a haute Cantonese menu and interiors by Hirsch Bedner. Reliable favourites include the fragrant fried lobster noodles, Black Angus tenderloin stir-fried with vibrant peppers, and the dim sum. Every so often, the kitchen surprises with a few unexpected touches like fried courgette flowers and foie gras. Service is superb. **Photo** *p111*.

European

Morton's

4/F The Oriental, 5 Raffles Avenue, Marina (6339 3740/www.mortons.com). City Hall MRT then 10mins walk. **Open** 5.30-11pm Mon-Sat; 5.30-10pm Sun. **Main courses** $73-$172. **Credit** AmEx, DC, MC, V. **Map** p251 M8 ❾ Steakhouse

Among steakhouses, clubby Morton's reigns supreme. The cheerful *Stepford Wives*-style servers are entertaining – and flawless. And from the baked Idaho potatoes and onion loaf to the porterhouse and shrimp cocktail, the huge servings are legendary (but brace yourself for huge prices). Leave room for the gigantic Grand Marnier soufflé – a fluffy confection that could feed a village.

Poppi

2/F The Legends, 11 Canning Walk, Fort Canning Park, Colonial District (6339 8977/www.poppi.com.sg). Dhoby Ghaut MRT. **Open** noon-2pm, 7-10pm Mon-Fri; 7-10pm Sat. **Main courses** $36-$48. **Credit** AmEx, MC, V. **Map** p250 I7 ❿ Modern European

Leave it to an Aussie chef to come up with such imaginative combinations as fig, mozzarella and basil tart or asparagus wrapped in juniper-cured ocean trout. Perched high in the bucolic setting of Fort Canning Park, Christopher Millar's restaurant is a warm cocoon of timber and comfortable food. The Sunday brunch is especially fun, featuring dim-sum-sized portions of scrambled eggs topped with caviar, shellfish bisque, and little cones of newspapers filled with tiny tiles of fish and fries. *See also p128* **Taste makers**.

Chinatown & the CBD

Asian

Ikukan Japanese Restaurant

23 Mohamed Ali Lane, off Club Street, Chinatown (6325 3362/www.ikukan.com.sg). Chinatown MRT then 10mins walk. **Open** noon-2.15pm, 6-10.15pm Mon-Sat; 6-10.15pm Sun. **Main courses** $15-$29. **Credit** AmEx, DC, JCB, MC, V. **Map** p250 I11 ⓬ Japanese

This tiny restaurant makes up for its size with a power-packed menu. Chef Hideto Setomoto specialises in flavourful, colourful dishes. The sashimi is a safe bet, as are giant prawns studded with shredded potatoes and then deep-fried. Gather your courage and try the grilled salmon head, a meaty treat bathed in a reduction of shoyu and balsamico.

Jade

1/F The Fullerton Hotel, 1 Fullerton Square, CBD (6877 8188/www.tunglok.com). Raffles Place MRT. **Open** 11.30am-2.30pm, 6.30-10.30pm daily. **Main courses** $10-$60. **Credit** AmEx, DC, JCB, MC, V. **Map** p251 K10 ⓭ Cantonese

Set in the sumptuous Fullerton Hotel, Jade – part of the ever-growing Tung Lok restaurant group – is a

Eat, Drink, Shop

magnet for expense account types, suits and ladies who lunch. The modern Canto classics are served in individual portions, all exquisitely prepared. Choose from ribs braised in honey and mocha, tofu drizzled with truffle oil, lobster bathed in citrus cream, and sautéed beef shot through with black pepper. The dim sum is superb.

Ka Soh
96 Amoy Street, Chinatown (6224 9920/www. ka-soh.com.sg). Tanjong Pagar MRT. **Open** noon-2.30pm, 5.30pm-2am daily. **Main courses** $7-$18. **Credit** MC, V. **Map** p250 H12  **14** Cantonese
Everything about Ka Soh – Cantonese for mother-in-law – shrieks 1950s kitsch. But the daily crowds don't come to this Chinatown eatery for the decor. The bustling, motherly staff dish out stern love and terrifically homely Canto classics in equal measure. Bestsellers include deep-fried chicken marinated in prawn paste, deep-fried cubes of salted tofu and a milky, fish-head beehoon noodle soup.
Other locations: 2 College Road, Outram Park, Chinatown (6473 6686); 726 Upper Changi Road East, Changi (6214 0425).

Lau Pa Sat
Corner of Boon Tat Street & Robinson Road, CBD. Raffles Place MRT. **Open** around noon-10pm daily. **Main courses** $3-$10. **No credit cards. Map** p251 K11 **15** Hawker centre
Packed at lunchtime with suits from neighbouring offices, this hawker centre in the heart of the CBD is set in a lovely, cast-iron Victorian structure, with delicate columns and an octagonal floorplan. It was shipped over from Glasgow in 1894 (by the same company that made the iron for the 1868 Cavenagh Bridge). Try the grilled skate and seafood at stall 43, and a multicoloured ice kachang at one of the many dessert stalls. Alfresco satay stalls appear at night.

Majestic
1/F New Majestic Hotel, 31-37 Bukit Pasoh Road (6511 4718/www.newmajestichotel.com). Outram Park MRT. **Open** 11.45am-2.30pm, 6.30-11pm daily. **Main courses** $14-$48. **Credit** AmEx, MC, V. **Map** p250 G11 **16** Cantonese
The small dining room in this stylish boutique hotel is austerely furnished and the acoustics are terrible, but the food is sensational. Expect to see families and society big-wigs tucking into fat, flash-fried prawns in wasabi sauce, lobsters baked in Carnation milk and shards of fragrant Peking duck nestling on slabs of pan-fried foie gras.

Maxwell Food Centre
Corner of South Bridge Road & Maxwell Road, Chinatown. Tanjong Pagar or Chinatown MRT. **Open** approx 7am-10pm daily. **Main courses** $3-$10. **No credit cards. Map** p250 H11 **17** Hawker centre
Eating at this crowded, frantic hawker food centre in the heart of Chinatown is like pushing a kid into a sweet shop: there's a real danger of sensory overload. Where to start? Rule of thumb: take your cue from the queue. For great pan-fried radish cakes, make a beeline for Jin Ji Mei Shi (stall 96); China Street Fritters (stall 61) has crisply fragrant ngoh hiang (Asian spring rolls); while the congee at Zhen Zhen (stall 54) is superb. And the chicken rice at Tian Tian (stall 10) is deservedly legendary.

Eat, Drink, Shop

Noodle soup just like (you wish) your mother used to make at **Ka Soh.**

Grub hubbub

For a uniquely Singaporean experience, head to a hawker centre. The food is fantastic and made to order, prices are rock-bottom (a dish plus drink costs about $5), and they're noisy, vibrant and bustling warrens of local life – an antidote to the sanitised, manicured side of Singapore.

Hawker centres have been around since the late 1950s, often attached to a wet market selling fresh produce. But it wasn't until the government clamped down on street food (mainly for hygiene reasons) in the early 1980s that they became so ubiquitous, each neighbourhood having its own designated centre – all owned and managed by the government. There are around 120 hawker centres in Singapore, each sheltering anywhere from 50 to 100-plus food stalls, often family-run and each specialising in a few dishes (chicken rice, say, or fish porridge or roti prata), drinks (soy bean milk, teh tarik or freshly squeezed fruit juices) or desserts (grass jelly or chendol). The centres are roofed over, but otherwise open to the air, with ceiling fans, not air-con. So much food, so little time! But which one to visit?

As a general rule, the best hawker centres are outside the CBD, including the ones we've listed: **Chomp Chomp Food Centre** (*see p125*), **Lau Pa Sat** (*see p113*), **Newton Hawker Centre** (*see p121*), **Makansutra Gluttons Bay** (*see p111*), **Maxwell Food Market** (*see p113*), **Tiong Bahru Market** (*see p127*) and **Zion Riverside Food Centre** (*see p122*).

The annually updated *Makansutra* guide, available from any bookshop, is an invaluable and comprehensive aid; there's also a website (www.makansutra.com) and a TV series. The guide is divided by dish rather than location (which means it's not so useful if you're at a hawker centre and want to know

Eat, Drink, Shop

Chomp Chomp Food Centre

Spring Court

52-56 Upper Cross Street, Chinatown (6449 5030/ www.springcourt.com.sg). Chinatown MRT. **Open** 11.30am-2.30pm, 6-10.30pm daily. **Main courses** $8-$30. **Credit** AmEx, JCB, MC, V. **Map** p250 H10 ⑱ Cantonese

This family-run restaurant has been rattling around since 1929 and is still going strong. Classical and comfortingly familiar, it takes few wrong turns: the suckling pig, peking duck, chilli Sri Lankan crabs and crisp roast chicken all fly from the kitchen at a dizzying rate. A must-try are the golden cereal prawns: huge crustaceans encrusted with oatmeal flakes and sweetly salty.

European

Buko Nero

126 Tanjong Pagar Road, Chinatown (6324 6225). Tanjong Pagar MRT. **Open** 6.30-9.30pm Tue, Wed; noon-2pm, 6.30-9.30pm Thur-Sat. **Main courses** $25-$30. **Credit** AmEx, MC, V. **Map** p250 H12 ⑲ Modern Italian

You often have to book two weeks ahead to get into Buko Nero but, in this case, patience is a virtue. The restaurant is small, seating just over 20. Tucking into Oscar Pasinato's exquisite mushroom timbale and superb penne with bolognaise ragout, the entire room bonds with a feeling of smugness.

which stalls are good), with chopstick ratings for the best: three chopsticks wins the ultimate accolade: 'die, die, must try!'

In recent years, many of the major hawker centres have undergone face-lifts, though not always for the better. Most Singaporeans care little that their favourite spots sport grimy floors or stained table tops; what matters is the quality of the food and the price. All stalls get a cleanliness rating (A to D – posted on the front of the stall) and many claim that the lower-rated stalls produce the best food. As you'd expect, the busiest times are around lunch (noon-2pm) and dinner (6-8pm). Stalls generally close at around 9pm, though Newtown Hawker Centre and Makansutra Gluttons Bay stay open until the small hours.

Communal sharing of tables is the norm. To reserve, or 'chope', a space, some people place a packet of tissues on the seat – but this practice is generally frowned upon. To order, join the queue at the stall (tip: a long, snaking line of customers is a good sign), wait for the cook's assistant to bark at you – courtesy is not a strong point – then tell him what you want and the number of your table. Pay when your food arrives: usually it will be brought to you, but some stalls are self-service (Makansutra Gluttons Bay is completely self service).

Food courts are similar to hawker centres, but are enclosed, air-conditioned and found inside shopping malls; they're usually self-service. Many are privately owned, by chains. Eating at a food court is a rather bland experience compared to the noisy chaos of the average hawker centre, though there are some excellent stalls in the older ones and the food is reliably standardised.

Maxwell Food Market

Crêperie Ar-men

37 Duxton Road, Chinatown (6227 3389/www. creperie armen com). Tanjong Pagar MRT. **Open** noon-2.30pm, 6.45-10.30pm Mon-Sat. **Main courses** $17-$25. **Credit** AmEx, MC, V. **Map** p250 H12 ❷⓪ French

Not even the prostitutes along Duxton Hill can keep the foodies away from this temple to Breton crêpes. Each delicate buckwheat pancake – made to order on cast-iron griddles – enfolds a host of fab fillings, including grilled seafood, hams and curries. In season, oysters are flown in from Brittany every Thursday. For pud, don't miss the buttered, caramel crêpe sprinkled with toasted almond flakes.

Ember

Hotel 1929, 50 Keong Saik Road, Chinatown (6347 1928). Outram Park MRT. **Open** 11.30am-2pm, 6.30-10pm Mon-Fri; 6.30-10pm Sat. **Main courses** $23-$40. **Credit** AmEx, MC, V. **Map** p250 H11 ❶⓪ Modern European

Located in fashionable boutique Hotel 1929 (*see p42*), Ember is a serene spot, with an eclectic Mod Euro menu from the talented Sebastian Ng. The food is consistently good and imaginative, including pan-seared scallops with parma ham and orange and tarragon vinaigrette; and sea bass with smoked bacon ragout and truffle-yuzu butter sauce. Like the food, the decor is neither fussy nor pretentious.

Le Papillon

*#01-02 Red Dot Traffic Building, 28 Maxwell Road,
Chinatown (6327 4177/www.le-papillon.com.sg).
Tanjong Pagar MRT.* **Open** noon-2.30pm, 6.30-
10.30pm Mon-Fri; 6.30-11.30pm Sat. **Main courses**
$26-$38. **Credit** AmEx, DC, JCB, MC, V. **Map** p250
I12 ② Modern European

After leaving the great Fig Leaf (now closed),
Anderson Ho went to work at Singapore Airlines, of
all places. He recently roared back on to the dining
scene with Le Papillon. The minimalist decor is clean
and bright, and Ho's touch bold and assured. The
seasonal menu includes blocks of chilled watermelon topped with dollops of creamy Meredith goat's
cheese, pesto and pine nuts; and a divine pan-fried
filo parcel of braised oxtail and sautéed mushrooms.
See also p128 **Taste makers.**

My Dining Room

*L/2 81 Club Street, Chinatown (6327 4991/
www.mydiningroom.com.sg). Chinatown MRT then
10mins walk.* **Open** noon-4pm, 6.30-11pm Mon-Fri;
6.30-11pm Sat. **Main courses** $34-$48. **Credit**
AmEx, MC, V. **Map** p250 I11 ② Modern European

After an aperitif in the slick Union bar downstairs,
head up to Vincent Teng's criminally underrated
restaurant. Everything here buzzes with quiet con-
fidence, from the oyster bar to the old-fashioned
comfort food. Notable dishes include braised pork
shoulder with garlic mash; home-made gravadlax;
lobster lasagne; and baked smoked duck round.

Oso Ristorante

*27 Tanjong Pagar Road, Chinatown (6327 8378).
Tanjong Pagar MRT.* **Open** noon-2.30pm, 6.30-
10.30pm Mon-Sat. **Main courses** $22-$34. **Credit**
AmEx, JCB, DC, MC, V. **Map** p250 I11 ② Italian

Diego Chiarini's short menu changes monthly. Its
strengths lie in its variety and authenticity, with soft
accents from the Tuscan and Piedmonte regions.
There is much that delights, not least the attentive
service. The pasta dishes are a triumph; standouts
include robust rigatoni bathed in a deep red sauce
of thyme, black olives and tender rabbit. Loosen
your belt and keep the prosecco flowing.
Other locations: Papi 5 Mohamed Sultan Road,
River Valley (6732 6269).

Pierside Kitchen & Bar

*#01-01 One Fullerton, 1 Fullerton Road, CBD (6438
0400/www.piersidekitchen.com). Raffles Place MRT.*
Open 11.30am-3pm, 6-11pm Mon-Thur; 11.30am-
3pm Fri; 6pm-midnight Sat, Sun. **Main courses**
$21-$55. **Credit** AmEx, DC, JCB, MC, V. **Map** p250
H11 ② International

Thanks to Aussie designer Albano Daminato, the
interiors of Pierside have been wrapped in Sydney
chic: think blond timber with huge mirrors along one
wall (perfect for people-watching). From the kitchen
come towering stacks of seafood platters, aromatic
fish pies and fried soft-shelled crabs. House faves
are oven-roasted miso cod and a glistening teriyaki-
glazed pork rack. In the evening, have your dessert
outside by the bay.

Ricciotti

*#B1-49/50 The Riverwalk, 20 Upper Circular Road,
Boat Quay (6533 9060/www.garibaldi.com.sg/r.htm).
Clarke Quay MRT.* **Open** 10am-11pm Mon-Fri; 8am-
11pm Sat, Sun. **Main courses** $14-$20. **Credit**
AmEx, DC, JCB, MC, V. **Map** p250 J8 ② Italian

Fresh from a rather chic makeover, Ricciotti remains
a draw for the sweet of tooth. Concentrate on its delicious range of rum babas, sfogliatelles, tiramisus
and fruit gelatos. Chef Stefano Deiuri and his ancestors have been making pastries since 1580, and it
shows in every single mouthful. For a relaxing, post-
dinner treat, sit outside facing the river.
Other locations: #01-36/37 China Square
Central Nankin Row, 3 Pickering Street, Chinatown
(6438 8040).

Saint Pierre

*#01-01 Central Mall, 3 Magazine Road, Chinatown
(6438 0887/www.saintpierre.com.sg). Clarke Quay
MRT/Chinatown MRT then bus 51, 143, 174, 186.*
Open noon-2pm, 7-9.30pm Mon-Fri; 7-10pm Sat.
Main courses $38-$80. **Credit** AmEx, DC, MC, V.
Map p250 H9 ② Modern French

The platinum blond and ever-smiling Belgian chef
Emmanuel Stroobant is the closest thing Singapore
has to a celebrity chef (*see p128* **Taste makers**).
The restaurant made its name with its astonishing
foie gras menu, but these days its aggressively
French tastes are tempered with Asian inflections,
such as lobster with yuzu-green tarts, scallops and
seaweed oil, wild kiniko mushroom soup, or a sail-
boat of filo and wasabi-scented wild barramundi
served with grilled aubergines and pine nuts.

Toast

*#01-09 OUB Centre, 1 Raffles Place, CBD (6438
5015/www.marmaladegroup.com). Raffles Place
MRT.* **Open** 8am-6pm Mon-Fri; 8am-3pm Sat.
Main courses $6-$11. **Credit** AmEx, DC, MC, V.
Map p250 J10 ② Café

After a CD-buying spree at Gramophone next door,
pop to Toast for sustenance: chicken and avocado
wraps, Moroccan salads, thick sandwiches and
imported juices. The cupcakes are sinfully good; try
the lemon frosting version (though, for sheer decadence, the Nutella-smothered ones are pretty hard
to beat). Tip: for a more relaxing experience, avoid
the crushing lunch crowd.
Other locations: #02-11 Ngee Ann City, 391
Orchard Road (6733 8489).

Whatever

*20 Keong Saik Road, Chinatown (6224 0300/
www.whatever.com.sg). Outram Park MRT.*
Open 9am-10.30pm daily. **Main courses** $4-$13.
Credit AmEx, DC, MC, V **Map** p250 G11 ②
Organic vegetarian

Shirley MacLaine would feel at home in the lower
half of this split-level restaurant: it is filled with crystals, spiritual guides, tarot cards and yoga pam-
phlets. Upstairs is a cute, sun-bathed space serving
wholesome, delicious vegetarian fare. Offerings
include protein shakes; eggs with slow-roasted

Eat, Drink, Shop

tomatoes; kapiti blue cheese salads studded with apples and walnuts; roasted vegetable lasagne; and a swathe of wheat/gluten/dairy-free cakes.

Wiener Kaffeehaus

148 Neil Road, Chinatown (6226 3148/www. wienerkaffeehaus.com.sg). Outram Park MRT. **Open** 10am-10pm daily. **Main courses** $7-$18. **Credit** AmEx, DC, MC, V. **Map** p250 G12 ❸ Viennese
Lined with art nouveau timber panelling, romantic wall lamps, marble tables and sparkling Klimt-style artworks, this shophouse is old-world Vienna transplanted to the tropics. The fiaker gulasch – a large serving of tender beef, fried egg, sausage and a bread dumpling – is terrific, as are the house-ground coffee and rich, dense sachertorte.

Little India & the Arab Quarter

Asian

Banana Leaf Apolo

54-58 Race Course Road, Little India (6293 8682/ www.bananaleafapolo.com). Little India MRT. **Open** 10.30am-10.30pm daily. **Main courses** $18-$25. **Credit** AmEx, DC, MC, JCB, V **Map** p248 K2 ❸ Indian
A fish-head curry institution, this place hums with activity and locals – a good sign. Banana leaves are used instead of plates, topped with mounds of rice, curried vegetables and tasty pickles. Go native and eat the curried red snapper heads with your fingers

(though knives and forks are also supplied). The curries can be spicy to neophytes; take the edge off with popadoms and chutneys.
Other locations: #01-32 Little India Arcade, 48 Serangoon Road, Little India (6297 1595).

HJH Maimunah

11&15 Jalan Pisang, Arab Quarter (6291 3132/ www.hjhmaimunah.com). Bugis MRT then 10mins walk. **Open** 7am-9pm Mon-Sat. **Main courses** $3-$12. **No credit cards. Map** p249 M4 ❸ Indonesian/Malay
The façade may be unimposing, but this place has a loyal following, as demonstrated by the traffic through the shophouse doors. The Indonesian fare recalls a time of rustic villages, hand-pounded herbs and recipes passed from mother to daughter. Choose from tender chunks of beef braised in a creamy coconut sauce, chicken curries, grilled meats and a technicolour spread of puddings and cakes.
Other locations: #01-02 20 Joo Chiat Road, Katong (6348 5457).

Jaggi's

34/36 Race Course Road, Little India (6296 6141/ www.jaggis.com). Little India MRT. **Open** 11.30am-3pm, 6.30-10.30pm Mon-Sat; 11.30am 3pm Sun. **Main courses** $3-$6. **Credit** AmEx, DC, JCB, MC, V. **Map** p248 K3 ❸ Indian
Don't be put off by the school canteen vibe. The nosh is excellent and good value. Just about everything deserves a second helping: sambal fish, densely flavoured chicken curry, creamy dahl, and wonderfully aromatic butter chicken. Wash it down with masala tea or lime juice.

Eat, Drink, Shop

Finger food: fish heads to the fore at **Banana Leaf Apolo**.

Muthu's Curry

138 Race Course Road, Little India (6392 1722/ www.muthuscurry.com). Farrer Park MRT. **Open** 10am-10pm daily. **Main courses** $4-$30. **Credit** AmEx, DC, JCB, MC, V. **Map** p248 K2 ❸ Indian

The setting may have been jazzed up with fountains and onyx, but the pride of place remains the fragrant cooking: creamy chicken korma, barbecued butter chicken, mutton done every which way – curried, fried with dried chillies and sprinkled with cashews or sautéed with peppers. According to legend, this is where fish-head curry originated – and it's a pot of flavourful gold, dotted with pineapple slices and tamarind and laced with cinnamon and cardamom.

P&P Thai

#01-101 Block 638 Veerasamy Road, Little India (8157 1245). Farrer Park MRT. **Open** 11am-3pm, 5-10pm Mon-Sat. **Main courses** $3-$25. **No credit cards. Map** p249 L3 ❸ Thai

It's not quite Bangkok standard, but this breezy café serves some of the best Thai food in Singapore, at astonishingly cheap prices. The small menu features delicious green curries; tart tom yam made with fresh herbs and seafood stock; crisp pork chops; mango salad; and a superb belachan fried rice.

European

Yogi Hub

16 Madras Street, Little India (6298 8198/www. yogihub.com.sg). Little India MRT. **Open** 11.30pm-2.30pm, 6-10pm Tue-Sat; 11.30am-5pm Sun. **Main courses** $8. **Credit** MC, V. **Map** p248 K3 ❸ Vegetarian

Chef and owner Lily Ko crafts a wonderful menu filled with organic, homespun food. Don't miss the pumpkin salad: a sweet mix of pumpkin wedges, alfalfa sprouts, plump raisins and plum sauce. Another favourite is the faux tuna sandwich, its earthy warmth of shredded mushroom stems bound by an almond sauce tasting, miraculously, like tuna. If it's on the menu, the avocado cheesecake is a must.

Other

Alaturka

16 Bussorah Street, Arab Quarter (6294 0304/ www.alaturka.com.sg). Bugis MRT then 10mins walk. **Open** noon-11pm daily. **Main courses** $13-$15. **Credit** AmEx, DC, JCB, MC, V. **Map** p249 M4 ❸ Turkish/Mediterranean

The Arab Quarter is a peek into another world, jammed with crumbling architecture, carpet sellers and little eateries like Alaturka where the exotic vibe suggests you're not in Singapore any more. Highlights include the karisik kebab: a large copper platter of combination kebabs (including charcoal-grilled lamb chops), served with tender chunks of grilled chilli, pilaf and rich buttery vegetables. For a post-prandial treat, sit outside and puff a strawberry-scented shisha.

Baladi

709 North Bridge Road, Arab Quarter (6396 6451). Bugis MRT then 10mins walk. **Open** 11.30am-11.30pm daily. **Main courses** $20-$28. **Credit** AmEx, DC, MC, V. **Map** p249 M4 ❸ Lebanese

With the shophouse windows thrown open to a view of palm trees and the Sultan Mosque, upstairs at Baladi feels like another world. Its spread of food is homely, consisting of puffed-up Lebanese bread, vine leaves stuffed with rice, salads spiked with pomegranate and olive oil, beef and chicken sharwarma, earthy grilled aubergine dips, piquant pickles, smoked meats and vegetarian classics. After dinner, puff on a scented shisha.

Café Le Caire

39 Arab Street, Arab Quarter (6292 0979). Bugis MRT then 10mins walk. **Open** 11.30am-5.30am daily. **Main courses** $9-$15. **Credit** AmEx, JCB, MC, V. **Map** p249 M4 ❸ Middle Eastern

Dr Ameen Ali Talib, a third-generation Arab Singaporean, runs this Middle Eastern café, which serves kebabs with an exquisite selection of shishas. Flavours include vanilla, caramel, rose and apple.

Chatterbox. See p119.

Sofra

#02-42/44 Shaw Tower, 100 Beach Road, Bras Busah & Bugis (6291 1433/http://sofra.com.sg). *Bugis MRT.* **Open** noon-11pm daily. **Main courses** $9-$19. **Credit** AmEx, MC, V. **Map** p249 M5 ④⓪
Turkish

Though service can be erratic and the food varies in quality, low-key Sofra is still one of the few places near Marina Bay where you can get a cheap, decent meal in a comfortable (read: air-conditioned) setting. The menu, featuring photos of seemingly identikit dishes, is stuffed with reliable favourites including doner kebabs, platters of houmous and aubergine dips served with puffed-up crispbreads, and sweet apple tea.

Orchard Road & Around

Asian

Bon Goût

#01-01 The Quayside, 60 Robertson Quay (6732 5234). Bus 51, 64, 123, 186, 811. **Open** noon-10pm daily. **Main courses** $9-$16. **Credit** DC, JCB, MC, V. **Map** p250 G8 ④① Japanese

With a name like this, it's strange to walk into a space so distinctly mod-Japanese. There are comfy couches, and walls lined with floor-to-ceiling anime books and Japanese magazines. But it's the little café to the side that holds the attention. There are curries (Japanese style, which is to say not a hint of heat), tonkatsu sets and lovely bricks of tofu and soya sauce. The Japanese regulars say it all.

Chatterbox

1/F South Tower, Meritus Mandarin Hotel, 333 Orchard Road (6831 6291/www.mandarin-singapore.com). Somerset MRT. **Open** 5.30am-12.30am Mon-Thur, Sun; 24hrs Fri, Sat. **Main courses** $19-$29. **Credit** AmEx, DC, JCB, MC, V. **Map** p247 F4 ④② Pan-Asian

A local institution, the Chatterbox has recently emerged from a makeover. It's a bit bright and pla-sticky, but the food still passes muster. The menu – a broad church that covers Malay, Peranakan and Indian – includes local favourites like rojak and nasi goreng, but the marquee attraction is the chicken rice: soft, plump chunks of tender chicken, a mound of wonderfully oiled rice and a trio of lovely dipping sauces. Though it's fairly pricey at $20, it's a guilty pleasure. **Photo** *p118.*

Din Tai Fung

#B1-03/06 Paragon, 290 Orchard Road (6836 8336). Orchard MRT. **Open** 11am-10pm Mon-Fri; 10am-10pm Sat, Sun. **Main courses** $8.50-$13.50. **Credit** MC, V. **Map** p247 F4 ④③ Shanghainese

Purists insist that the original Taipei location is superior to the Singaporean outpost. But it is hard to find fault with the fab xiao long bao: tiny rounds of pleated pastry filled with sweet minced pork and fragrant soup. Each silken mouthful is an explo-sion of flavours – sweet, salty and sour, gingery

and vinegary. Before you know it, a whole basket has been consumed. The braised beef noodles are also superb.
Other locations: throughout the city.

Hua Ting

2/F Orchard Hotel, 442 Orchard Road (6734 3880). Orchard MRT. **Open** 11.30am-2.30pm, 6.30-10.30pm Mon-Fri; 11am-2.30pm, 6.30-10.30pm Sat, Sun. **Main courses** $18-$90. **Credit** AmEx, DC, JCB, MC, V. **Map** p247 D3 ④④ Cantonese

The hotel foyer has seen better days, but second-floor Hua Ting exudes a luxurious vibe that lures a crowd of suits, high society types and long-time fans. The service glides along effortlessly, and the Canto menu is irresistible. If you're on an expense account, indulge in the thick, milky and politically incorrect shark's cartilage soup. The slivers of roast goose are a treat, and the steamed fish and delicate dim sum spread are perfect.

Imperial Treasure Nan Bei

#05 12/13 Ngee Ann City, 391 Orchard Road (6738 1238). Orchard MRT. **Open** 11am-11pm daily. **Main courses** $12-$138. **Credit** AmEx, DC, JCB, MC, V. **Map** p247 F4 ④⑤ Chinese

If you don't have a reservation at the weekend, for-get about getting a table here after noon. The menu can be intimidating, so let the staff guide you. Scrumptious dim sum includes deep-fried yam pas-tries, sautéed snake beans and rice-flour rolls stuffed with prawns. From the à la carte menu, the steamed fish is excellent. Ask for a booth seat. the other tables are exposed to heavy traffic.
Other locations: throughout the city.

Kazu Sumiyaki

#04-05 Cuppage Plaza, 5 Koek Road (6734 2492). Somerset MRT. **Open** 6-10pm daily. **Main courses** sashimi from $25; set meal $23-$32. **Credit** AmEx, DC, JCB, MC, V. **Map** p247 H4 ④⑥ Japanese

This small dining room is hard to find, claustro-phobic and uncomfortable. But on most nights, you can't get a table for love nor money. The draw here is yakitori, made with deliciously fresh ingredients barbecued on bamboo spears. Try the lightly salted foie gras, chicken meatballs matched with chunks of black mushrooms, moist chicken wings dipped in salt and marbled wagyu beef. Reservations are essential at the weekend.

Lao Beijing

#03-01 Plaza Singapura, 68 Orchard Road (6738 7207/www.tunglok.com). Dhoby Ghaut MRT. **Open** 11.30am-3pm, 6-10pm Mon-Fri; 11.30am-5pm, 6-10pm Sat, Sun. **Main courses** $10-$48. **Credit** AmEx, JCB, MC, V. **Map** p248 I5 ④⑦ Northern Chinese

The decor at Lao Beijing (complete with wooden stools and mood lighting) is a little kitsch, prompt-ing flashbacks to *Crouching Tiger, Hidden Dragon*, but the menu is absolutely faultless. The roast peking duck is a standout, the skin crisp and the doughy wraps just-so. It's also hard to pass up the onion-flecked pancakes, fried noodles and luminous cubes of tofu braised in a black bean sauce and finely minced pork.

Other locations: #02-12/12 Novena Square, 238 Upper Thomson Road, Novena (6358 4466).

The Line

1/F The Shangri-La, Orange Grove Road (6213 4275/www.shangri-la.com). Orchard MRT then 15mins walk/bus 190. **Open** 24hrs daily. **Main courses** $23-$35. **Credit** AmEx, DC, JCB, MC, V. **Map** p246 C2 ⑳ International buffet

Not to be outdone by the Grand Hyatt's Straits Kitchen, the Shangri-La hotel has its own snappy (and expensive) take on the food court. Located right next to the lovely green swimming pool area, it's an ultra-modern space in a Stanley Kubrick-esque palette of white-on-white, with bright orange panels, put together by celebrated designer Adam Tihany. There's a wealth of international flavours to choose from on the menu, including dim sum, sushi, hawker fare, vegetarian options and marvellous bread puddings.

Min Jiang

G/F Goodwood Park Hotel, 22 Scotts Road (6730 1704). Orchard or Newton MRT then 10mins walk. **Open** 11am-2.15pm, 6-10pm daily. **Main courses** $22-$68. **Credit** AmEx, DC, JCB, MC, V. **Map** p247 F2 ⑳ Sichuan

Deeply dishy

Chicago's signature dish is the deep-pan pizza; in Bangkok it's tom yam; and in Russia, borscht. But pint-sized Singapore outshines the rest with a lengthy list of culinary trademarks – below are some must-try examples. The best versions are usually found in the island's cheap-as-chips hawker centres, though many are also served in more upmarket (and expensive) settings.

Bah kut teh

The dish literally means 'pork-rib tea', but it's actually a clear soup punched with herbs, garlic cloves, pepper, pieces of fritter and tender chunks of pork ribs. Served with steamed rice and dark soy sauce flecked with red chillies, this is a favourite late-night supper.

Char kway teow

Thin loops of local fettucine are piled into a sizzling wok with a shower of cockles and bean sprouts, a spray of dark soy sauce, cubes of fried lard, garlic and perhaps slices of Chinese sausage. The hot wok imparts a fragrant smokiness to the dish. Essential.

Chicken rice

It originated on China's Hainan island, but Singapore has claimed this dish as its own. Whole chickens are poached in alternating pots of hot and cold water; the firm and succulent flesh is paired with ruby red chilli sauce and rice steamed with ginger, garlic and chicken stock.

Chilli crab/black pepper crab

When it comes to comfort food, few locals can resist a steaming platter of fried crabs. The crustacean of choice is the Sri Lankan crab, famed for its sweet flesh. It's a perfect foil for the thick, tangy gravy (infused with ginger, chilli and turmeric, or, in the black pepper version, flecked with crushed peppercorns). Best eaten in a restaurant; try **Long Beach** (*see p126*) on the East Coast.

Fish-head curry

An Indian speciality (*pictured*) that is unique to Singapore. Huge fish heads are steeped in a spicy golden gravy made from okra, tomatoes and aubergine; some versions include pineapple chunks. Unexpectedly, the head is very fleshy: devotees savour the cheeks and eyes. Usually eaten in a restaurant; try **Muthu's Curry** (*see p118*) or **Banana Leaf Apolo** (*see p117*) in Little India.

Grilled stingray

Who knew that stingray (skate) could be so delicious? Basted with hot sambal – a paste of chilli and garlic – the thin slab of fish is lightly grilled over a hot flame. The snowy-white strips of flesh are firm, moist and moreish.

Recently made over, Min Jiang is lovely to look at. There are long corridors sheathed in iron and wood, dramatic silk-wrapped lamps and flattering lighting; french doors open on to poolside tables. Sichuan classics include the famous hot and sour soup, thinly sliced garlic pork, deep-fried prawns coated in oats and chilli, and fragrant seared noodles tossed with venison. If you're feeling brave, try the best-selling but pungent durian pudding.

Newton Hawker Centre

Corner of Clemenceau Avenue North & Newton Circus. Newton MRT. **Open** approx 6pm-4am daily. **Main courses** $3-$10. **No credit cards.** **Map** p247 H1 **60** Hawker centre

Laksa

The Singaporean version of laksa – a luxurious coconut curry soup laced with fish cake, cockles and the perfume of daun kesum leaves – inspires passionate debate over which hawker stall serves the best. The consensus? The stalls on East Coast Road are the ones to beat.

Popiah

A traditional Chinese snack done with a local twist. A circular spring roll skin made of flour or eggs is the starting point. On to the bare canvas is lashed hoisin sauce, chilli and garlic paste, followed by a lettuce leaf and a dollop of braised radish. With a deft flick of the chef's wrist the popiah is wrapped and served with more chilli sauce (a Singaporean variation).

Rojak

Literally meaning 'wild mix' in Malay, rojak is a crunchy salad of cucumbers, turnips, bean sprouts, pineapple, crisp shards of fritters and assorted fruits, tossed with a dressing of lime juice, sugar, tamarind, prawn paste and chilli. Thoroughly addictive.

Roti prata

Part of the thrill of eating roti prata – a Malaysian dish that's ubiquitous in Singapore – is watching the Indian chef make it. A glob of oily dough is smacked on to a steel surface and, by sleight of hand, transformed into a translucent sheet and folded. Fried on a griddle, the crisp, fragrant pancake is served with curry sauce.

Singapore's most famous hawker centre recently emerged from a makeover – and it's not a good look. While the original opened on to the roads, attracting people with its bustle and bright lights, mark II is enclosed and uninviting. You can eat well enough here, but it's touristy and pricey compared to other hawker centres. Hong Kong movie star Chow Yun-Fat comes here whenever he's in town.

Pondok Jawa Timur

#02-66/67 Far East Plaza, 14 Scotts Road (6333 8785). Orchard MRT. **Open** 11.30am-9.30pm daily. **Main courses** $3.50-$7. **No credit cards.** **Map** p247 F3 **61** East Javanese
Ignore the drab setting: the bowels of a shopping centre, surrounded by hair salons and reflexologists. What appeals is the decent, cheap food. The Javanese street food menu is, for such a small restaurant, surprisingly comprehensive. There's sunny curry chicken, fried fish in tart assam sauce, and mounds of gado-gado blanketed by crisp prawn crackers and a mild Surabayan peanut gravy. Service can be absent-minded, but at these prices, who cares?

Princess Terrace

1/F Copthorne King's Hotel, 403 Havelock Road, River Valley (6318 3168). Tiong Bahru MRT then 15mins walk/bus 51, 64, 186. **Open** 6am-1am daily. **Main courses** $18-$28. **Credit** AmEx, DC, JCB, MC, V. Peranakan
The hardy Peranakans have a cuisine that's justly famed for its splendid blend of sweet, spicy and sour flavours. Since the 1970s, the Princess Terrace's Peranakan buffet has been booked solid, especially at weekends, luring gourmands with its irresistible spread of Penang-styled laksa, char kway teow, rust-red prawn noodles and colourful, coconut-infused desserts. Skip breakfast and tuck in.

Rice Table

#02-09 International Building, 360 Orchard Road (6835 3783/www.ricetable.com.sg). Orchard MRT. **Open** noon-2.30pm, 6-9.30pm daily. **Set lunch/dinner** $14/$20. **Credit** AmEx, DC, MC, V. **Map** p247 E3 **62** Indonesian
If there's a cheaper, more filling meal in town, we've not seen it. At the prix-fixe lunch, diners are served 14 dishes within moments of sitting down. Each plate is filled with terrific Indonesian comfort food: tahu telor, creamy beef rendang, grilled chicken, coconut curried vegetables and satay. Empty plates are instantly replenished. At dinner, expect around 30 dishes for $6 more. Bookings are essential. **Other locations:** Cuppage Terrace, 43-45 Cuppage Road, Orchard Road & Around (6735 9117).

Samy's Curry Restaurant

Block 25A Dempsey Road (6472 2080/www.samys curry.com). Orchard MRT then bus 7, 105, 106, 111, 123, 174. **Open** 11am-3pm, 6-10pm daily. **Main courses** $6-$20. **Credit** AmEx, MC, V. Indian
A dyed-in-the-wool local institution, Samy's is as low maintenance as they come. It's more mess hall than restaurant, with its high ceilings, shuttered

windows and ceiling fans. In place of plates are banana leaves on to which servers slop mounds of aromatic, richly flavoured and blisteringly hot curries. Cool down with some fresh lime juice.
Other locations: Katong Village, 86 East Coast Road, Katong (6345 1726).

Song of India

33 Scotts Road (6836 0055/www.thesongofindia. com). Newton MRT. **Open** noon-2.30pm, 6-10.30pm daily. **Credit** AmEx, DC, JCB, MC, V. **Map** p247 F2 ❸ Modern Indian
Veteran chef Milind Sovani, one of Singapore's finest (*see p128* **Taste makers**), has created a show-stopping pan-Indian restaurant in a charming black and white bungalow off Orchard Road. The carefully crafted menu deftly crisscrosses the subcontinent's colourful regional cuisines, ranging from melt-in-the-mouth Keralan-spiced lamb shanks and tandoori prawns in pomegranate marinade to astonishing Gilawat kebabs – a Lucknavi classic of pan-seared ground lamb patties perfumed with cardamom, ground rose petals and raw papaya.

Soup Restaurant

#02-01 DFS Galleria Scottswalk, 25 Scotts Road (6333 8033). Orchard MRT. **Open** 11.30am-2.30pm, 6-10pm daily. **Main courses** $7-$35. **Credit** AmEx, DC, JCB, MC, V. **Map** p247 E3 ❸ Chinese
There are several branches around town, but it's hard to beat this one for its kitsch interiors, complete with pond and frangipani-lined courtyard. The menu is stuffed with good comfort food. The herbal ginseng soups soothe, the mapo tofu is richly fragrant and the pièce de resistance is the huge plate of gently steamed, velvety chicken wrapped in lettuce leaves, served with a ginger/garlic sauce.
Other locations: throughout the city.

Straits Kitchen

G/F Grand Hyatt Singapore, 10 Scotts Road (6732 1234/http://restaurants.singapore.hyatt.com). Orchard MRT. **Open** 6.30am-midnight daily. **Main courses** $20-$32; buffet $35-$38. **Credit** AmEx, DC, JCB, MC, V. **Map** p247 E3 ❸ International buffet
The traditional hawker centre concept is given a dramatic face-lift at the Grand Hyatt. Designed for $6 million by Tokyo restaurant mavens Super Potato, the dramatic space is kitted out in steel, timber and marble. Meanwhile, the various open kitchens serve the gamut of the island's varied cuisines, from laksa, satay and char-grilled stingray to chicken rice, puffs of naan, tandooried meats and a bevy of Peranakan desserts. Pricey, but good.

Sun with Moon

#03-15 Wheelock Place, 501 Orchard Road (6733 6636/www.sfbi.com.sg). Orchard MRT. **Open** 11.30am-11pm Mon-Thur, Sun; 11.30am-midnight Fri, Sat. **Main courses** $12-$25. **Credit** AmEx, DC, JCB, MC, V. **Map** p247 E3 ❸ Japanese
You have to love a restaurant where your order lands on the table almost as soon as you've handed the menu back to the waiter. The lunch menu offers

great value: a set course of fried chicken, braised salmon, rice, salad and miso for about $14. The quality of the cooking is flawless: no wonder the place is packed with hurried locals and Japanese expats.
Other locations: **Japanese Dining Sun @ Chijmes** #02-01 Chijmes, 30 Victoria Street, Colonial District (6336 3166).

Zion Riverside Food Centre

Corner of Zion Road & Ganges Avenue, River Valley. Tiong Bahru MRT then 10mins walk. **Open** approx 7am-11pm daily. Hawker centre
Slurp down sweet Asian desserts at Mohammed Sultan Road Cheng Tng (stall 32) or a lushly smooth soy bean curd at House of Soya Beans (stall 14), before attacking terrific rojak – the spicy Malay version of mixed vegetable and fruit salad – at Clementi Brothers Rojak (stall 21). Finish with a serving of wok-seared char kway teow at stall 18.

European

Big O

#02-04/05 Wheelock Place, 501 Orchard Road (6737 8472). Orchard MRT. **Open** 11.30am-10.30pm daily. **Main courses** $14-$20. **Credit** AmEx, MC, V. **Map** p247 E3 ❸ Café
There are two big draws to the Big O. One is its friendly and knowledgeable service (a novelty in Singapore); the other is its simple, well-executed, all-day menu of cakes and fuss-free meals. Think fish and chips, juicy baby ribs, fried calamari, crabmeat linguine and sides of sautéed field mushrooms. The upside-down pineapple cake is a treat.

Iggy's

3/F The Regent Singapore, 1 Cuscaden Road (6732 2234). Orchard MRT then bus 36, 105, 111 or 15mins walk. **Open** noon-1.30pm, 7-9.30pm Mon-Fri; 7-9.30pm Sat, Sun. **Set lunch/dinner** $45-$95/ $150-$175. **Credit** AmEx, MC, V. **Map** p246 C4 ❸ Modern European
Iggy's is fast becoming one of Singapore's most famous (and best) restaurants, under owner Ignatius Chan (*see p128* **Taste makers**) and chef Dorin Schuster. Its bold, counter-dining, set-menu-only experience shifts with the seasons, but recent meals have included char-grilled sea bass with truffle gnocchi and rosemary oil, a piña colada soufflé and a champagne jelly and sorbet with elderberry foam and lemon zest. **Photo** *p123*.

La Strada

#02-10 Shaw Centre, 1 Scotts Road (6737 2622/ www.lesamis.com.sg). Orchard MRT. **Open** noon-2pm, 7-9.30pm Mon-Sat. **Main courses** $30-$54. **Credit** AmEx, DC, MC, V. **Map** p247 E3 ❸ Modern Italian
La Strada hits all the right notes with flawless service and a classic menu created by Aussie chef Leandro Panza. The menu changes regularly, but past triumphs have included succulent baby calamari stuffed with a tart tomato salsa, and a wild mop of home-made tagliatelle tangled with red

mullet pieces, black Ligurian olives and a tomato saffron sauce shredded with celery. It's a pity the adjoining pizzeria falls so short of the mark.

Les Amis

#02-16 Shaw Centre, 1 Scotts Road (6733 2225/ www.lesamis.com.sg). Orchard MRT. **Open** noon-2pm, 7-9.30pm Mon-Sat. **Main courses** $55-$90. **Credit** AmEx, DC, MC, V. **Map** p247 E3 ⑥⓪ Modern French

For a long time, Les Amis has been a byword for fine French dining. The wine cellar and service remain impressive, though the worn carpeting, glassware, cutlery and faded silver-trimmed show plates could do with a makeover. The menu is still top-notch, though it's a little more modern (with a splash of Asian) these days. The foie gras is always good, as is the suckling pig with beer sauce. If you happen to be in town during truffle season, splash out here.

Marmalade Pantry

#B1-08/11 Palais Renaissance, 390 Orchard Road (6734 2700/www.marmaladegroup.com). Orchard MRT. **Open** 11.30am-9.30pm Mon-Fri; 10am-9.30pm

Iggy's. See p122.

Sat; 10am-4.30pm Sun. **Main courses** $15-$30. **Credit** AmEx, DC, MC, V. **Map** p246 D3 ⑥⓵ Modern European

The carpet is in need of replacing and the quality of the food can be uneven, but this circular basement venue is a great place for people-watching. The lunch crowd brings bling-bling chicks and their beaus, and the Sunday brunch is very popular. Check out the perennial favourites: a huge steak burger and irresistible cupcakes.
Other locations: #01-04 Hitachi Tower, 16 Collyer Quay, CBD (6438 5015).

Mezza9

2/F Grand Hyatt Singapore, 10 Scotts Road (6732 1234/http://restaurants.singapore.hyatt.com). Orchard MRT. **Open** noon-11pm Mon-Sat; 11.30am-11pm Sun. **Main courses** $25-$45. **Credit** AmEx, DC, MC, V. **Map** p247 E3 ⑥⓶ International buffet

It's hard to go wrong with flattering lighting and a sprawling steel, stone and wood space designed by Tokyo-based hotshots Super Potato. The numerous open kitchens dish out everything from Japanese teriyaki and Thai curries to Western barbecue and stir-fries. The Sunday champagne brunch is popular: counters are laden with mounds of oysters, king prawns, roasts, yakitori, sashimi, molten chocolate fountains and everything in between.

PS Café

28B Harding Road (9070 8782/www.pscafe.sg) Orchard MRT then bus 7, 75, 77, 106, 123, 147. **Open** 6.30pm-midnight Tue-Thur; 6.30pm-2am Fri; 9.30am-5pm, 6.30pm-2am Sat; 9.30am-5pm, 6.30pm-midnight Sun. **Main courses** $18-$38. **Credit** AmEx, MC, V. Café

Building on the success of the packed café cum-fashion boutique at Paragon, this beautiful sequel – in the midst of Dempsey Road's bucolic greenery – is a winner. Crowds brave the sniffy front desk to enjoy Aussie chef Roland Graham's breezy café menu. Memorable offerings include English roast beef with tarragon sour cream, and beef ragout studded with mushrooms and spatzle dumplings. **Photo** *p124* **Other locations:** Projectshop Café #02-02 Paragon Shopping Centre, 29 Orchard Road (6735 0071).

Sage, the Restaurant

#03-13 Robertson Walk, 11 Unity Street (6333 8726/www.sagerestaurants.com.sg). Clarke Quay MRT. **Open** 6.30-10.30pm Tue-Sun. **Main courses** $28-$33. **Credit** AmEx, DC, JCB, MC, V, **Map** p250 H8 ⑥⓷ Modern European

After a relatively low-key opening, Sage is hitting its stride with a carefully wrought menu. The kitchen's chefs trained at Les Amis, which explains why the seared foie gras is so good and the frothy, wild mushroom cappuccino so familiar. Elsewhere, the menu skates smoothly between perfectly done baked lamb loins and smoky duck, here paired with sweet caramelised pear and the salty undertow of bacon lurking beneath braised savoy cabbage.

PS Café. *See p123.*

Sentosa

European

The Cliff

Sentosa Resort & Spa, 2 Bukit Manis Road (6371 1425/www.thesentosa.com). HarbourFront MRT then Sentosa Express. **Open** 6.30-10pm daily. **Main courses** $40-$80. **Credit** AmEx, DC, JCB, MC, V. **Map** p252 D3 ⓬ Seafood

Against the stunning backdrop of Yasuhiro Koichi's interiors, chef Shawn Armstrong turns out an equally gorgeous seafood menu. Look for caramelised Hokkaido scallops served with Indian spiced aubergine salsa or and pan-roasted barramundi with mussel emulsion and chorizo. Mood lighting and a pretty crowd create a sexy vibe.

Il Lido

Sentosa Golf Club, 27 Bukit Manis Road, Sentosa (6866 1977/www.il-lido.com). HarbourFront MRT then Sentosa Express. **Open** 11am-midnight Mon-Thur, Sun; 11am-late Fri, Sat. **Main courses** $30-$45. **Credit** AmEx, DC, JCB, MC, V. **Map** p252 D3 ⓭ Italian

After some teething problems, Il Lido has come into its own. The sea views are gorgeous and the curved balcony offers prime sunset-watching. Beneath the restaurant's centrepiece – a Marc Wanders chandelier – guests dine on chef Michele Pavanello's superb home-made pasta with creamy sea urchins, squid ink tortelli stuffed with Atlantic cod, and crab meat blanketed with a lurid saffron and tarragon sauce. For pudding, the tiramisu is superb. The lounge bar (*see p137*) is worth a visit too.

Eastern Singapore

Asian

Bombay Café
332-334 Tanjong Katong Road, Katong (6345 0070/www.bombaycafe.com.sg). Paya Lebar MRT then bus 43, 76, 135. **Open** 11am-3pm, 6-11pm Mon-Fri; 11am-11pm Sat, Sun. **Main courses** $6-$10. **Credit** AmEx, MC, V. Indian

With pink walls and plasma screens showing energetic Bollywood numbers, this is a cheerful little haven. Friendly servers plonk down plate after plate of Bombay street food. Try the gol gappa – golden semolina puffs served with a potato-pea mix and mint and tamarind sauce – and the huge, golden dosai filled with everything from spinach to grated cheese, accompanied by flavourful mint, tomato and coconut relishes.

Other locations: #B1-020 Suntec City Mall, 3 Temasek Boulevard, Marina (6238 8239), Indian Wok 699 East Coast Road, Siglap (6448 2003).

Canton Wok
382 Joo Chiat Road, Joo Chiat (6285 6919). Eunos MRT then bus 13. **Open** 11.30am-3pm, 5.30-10.30pm daily. **Main courses** $12-$68. **Credit** AmEx, MC, V. Cantonese

You know a restaurant is good when the prime minister's wife has been spotted tucking into the food – cosily nostalgic Cantonese fare by Hong Kong-trained owner and chef Ang Song Kang. Double-boiled soups include apple and pea, and abalone with chicken. Regulars swear by the mounds of glutinous rice that are paired with fresh steamed garlic crab, and the silky tofu served in a sauce of dried scallops and shiitake mushrooms.

Changi Airport Terminal 2 Food Centre
Carpark C, 3M floor, Terminal 2, Changi Airport. Changi Airport MRT. **Open** approx 5am-9pm daily. **Main courses** $3-$5. **No credit cards.** Hawker centre

If you've become addicted to hawker centres while in Singapore, or are ravenous when you arrive, the airport's food centre is open to the public. The quality of the stalls pales in comparison to those in the suburbs, but good bets are the crunchy vegetables and chilli heat of Aishah Indian Muslim, and the smoky flavours of Rex Satay. There's a (recently renovated) food centre in Terminal 1 too.

Chat Masala
158 Upper East Coast Road, Siglap (6876 0570). Eunos MRT then bus 13. **Open** 6pm-11pm Mon; noon-2.30pm, 6-11pm Tue-Sun. **Main courses** $13-$17. **Credit** AmEx, DC, MC, V. Indian

Tucked away in a row of shophouses by a small car park, this tiny spot is the last place you'd expect to find top-notch Indian fare. But the deliciously named Dhershini Winodan works magic with her spices, infused with the pungent flavours and colours of India. The fish biryani is studded with crushed cashews, raisins and rings of fried onions, and finished with exuberant splashes of saffron.

Other locations: Hillcrest Park, 18 Greenwood Avenue, Bukit Timah (6762 2133).

Chef Heng's Teochew Porridge
Crescendo Building, 27 Upper East Coast Road, Siglap (6442 0910). Bedok MRT then bus 14. **Open** 11.30am-2.30pm, 6.30-9.30pm Mon, Wed-Sun. **Main courses** $6-$25. **Credit** MC, V. Teochew

The house special is the Teochew congee – grainier and thicker in consistency than its watery Cantonese cousin. Other Teochew classics include pork-belly 'tiles' or golden omelettes filled with a choice of Chinese sausages, anchovies or oysters. Steamed fish is served with a concoction of heady Chinese wine, sour assam, salted beans and baby tomatoes and topped with spring onion and coriander.

Chin Mee Chin
204 East Coast Road, Katong (6345 0419). Paya Lebar MRT then bus 43, 76, 135. **Open** 8.30am-5pm Tue-Sun. **Main courses** $3-$6. **No credit cards.** Peranakan

A Singaporean breakfast doesn't get more authentic than this. For 60 years, generations of loyal, local residents have been turning up at Chin Mee Chin for their morning kick-start of black coffee (served in traditional porcelain cups) and soft-boiled eggs. Don't miss the thick slabs of buttered toast with a side slathering of kaya, an addictively rich Peranakan jam made from pandan leaves, sugar, eggs and coconut cream.

Chomp Chomp Food Centre
20 Kensington Park Road, Serangoon Gardens. Serangoon MRT then bus 317. **Open** approx 6pm-midnight daily. **Main courses** $3-$10. **No credit cards.** Hawker centre

With such a posh-sounding English address, it's a shock to experience Chomp Chomp's bright lights, bustling vibe and high noise level (from countless clashing woks). In the evening, try to snag a seat on the timber deck facing the road – it's cooler there. Recommendations include Chomp Chomp Barbecue Food's grilled stingray (stall 1) and luscious barbecued chicken wings from Daily Fresh (stall 3).

Kim Choo Kueh Chang
109/111 East Coast Road, Katong (6741 2125/ www.kimchoo.com). Eunos MRT then bus 13. **Open** 8am-9pm daily. **Main courses** $6-$30. **Credit** DC, MC, V. Peranakan

Lee Kim Choo's grandmother taught her the secrets of making great bak zhang, a savoury pyramid-shaped dumpling made of rice, pork and nuts. She sold her first in 1945, and six decades later the business is still going strong in the ground-floor café. Upstairs, the restaurant's bestsellers include warm Eurasian beef stews, gently braised vegetables, fish-head curries steeped in tart assam, and rich chicken stews dotted with Indonesian nuts. *See also p90* **Peranakan pleasures**.

Eat, Drink, Shop

Long Beach

#01-04 East Coast Seafood Centre, 1202 East Coast Parkway, East Coast (6448 3636/www. longbeachseafood.com.sg). Orchard MRT then bus 14. **Open** 1.30pm-midnight daily. **Main courses** $6-$34. **Credit** AmEx, DC, JCB, MC, V.
Chinese seafood

Long Beach has been around for as long as anyone can remember and, judging from the weekend crowds of multi-generational families, it will remain for a long time to come. Don't be distracted by the goodies piled high on surrounding tables. Just concentrate on the huge Sri Lankan crabs bathed in an eggy, tangy gravy, or the famous black pepper crab doused with jet-black sauce. Mop it all up with crispy, fried mantou dumplings.
Other locations: 1018 East Coast Parkway, East Coast (6445 8833); #01-02 Planet Marina, Carpark A, Marina Park, Marina South (6323 2222); #01-80 IMM Building, Jurong East Street 21, Jurong (6566 9933).

Mango Tree

Unit B23, 1000 East Coast Parkway, East Coast (6442 8655/www.themangotree.com.sg). Orchard MRT then bus 14. **Open** 11.30am-2.30pm, 6.30-10.30pm Mon-Fri; 11.30am-10.30pm Sat, Sun. **Main courses** $14-$30. **Credit** AmEx, DC, JCB, MC, V.
Indian

Sitting on the timber deck, under the shade of a mango tree that lends the restaurant its name, it's easy to feel like you're on a beach in Kerala. The coastal Indian seafood, done simply and well, adds to the illusion. Under the watchful eye of a Cochin chef, the kitchen sends out memorable classics including superb garlic crabs, thick vegetable stews punched with spices, fish curries and irresistible piles of hot naans.

Sticky Rice

5 Kensington Park Road, Serangoon Gardens (6284 6266). Ang Mo Kio MRT then bus 73, 136. **Open** 11am-3pm, 6-9.30pm Mon-Thur, Sun; 11am-3pm, 6-10.30pm Fri, Sat. **Main courses** $7-$15. **Credit** AmEx, DC, MC, V. Thai

Sticky Rice has raised the glamour quotient of the staid suburb of Serangoon Gardens. The restaurant has been designed to within an inch of its life, complete with smoky mirrors and dramatic, blood-red lacquered panels. On weekends, the place buzzes as fashionistas tuck into crispy soft-shelled crabs with pomelo pearls and chopped garlic. Don't miss the sweet mango desserts.

True Blue

117 East Coast Road, Katong (6440 0449). Eunos MRT then bus 13. **Open** 11.30am-3pm, 6-10pm Tue-Sat. **Main courses** from $10. **Credit** AmEx, DC, JCB, MC, V. Peranakan

A two-storey shophouse, with Peranakan jewellery and clothing for sale on the ground floor, and this cosy little restaurant upstairs. The food is quietly triumphant: fried spring rolls scented with five-spices; dense chicken stews studded with tropical nuts; and deliciously tart salads of baby pink prawns and banana flowers. Other favourites include wok-charred okra and creamy beef rendang. *See also p90* **Peranakan pleasures**.

Western Singapore

Asian

Cheah Sun Kee Eating House

#01-72 Block 57 Eng Hoon Street, Tiong Bahru (9696 9921/9848 9938). Tiong Bahru MRT. **Open** 11.30am-3pm, 5.30-9.30pm daily. Closed alt Tue. **Main courses** $3-$10. **No credit cards**.
Cantonese café

Cheah Sun Kee serves some of the best sweet and sour pork in town. The location is appealing too. Set in a row of beautiful art deco apartments, the coffeeshop spills out on to the alley, where an artsy crowd dines alongside chattering families. Other culinary highlights include Cantonese porridge (breakfast only), braised tofu, fried beef noodles and to-die-for deep-fried chicken marinated with prawn paste. Be warned: there's no air-con, so come in the evenings, when the temperature has dropped.

Crystal Jade La Mian Xiao Long Bao

241/241A Holland Avenue, Holland Village (6463 0968). Buona Vista MRT then 15mins walk/bus 7, 61, 75, 106, 970. **Open** 11am-10.45pm Mon-Thur, Sun; 11am-11pm Fri, Sat. **Main courses** $6-$18. **Credit** AmEx, DC, JCB, MC, V. Shanghainese

One of the best things about eating at a Crystal Jade restaurant (there are branches across the island) is the consistent quality of the food – and this Holland Village outpost is no exception. Nutty, al dente noodles are the perfect foil for assorted dressings of chilli oil, minced pork and tender slabs of braised beef. Best are the xiao long bao, little steamed dumplings filled with pork, hot jus and goodness. **Other locations**: throughout the city.

Dulukala

#04-04 Beauty World Centre, 144 Upper Bukit Timah Road, Bukit Timah (6465 2036/www.sbest food.com/dulukala). Bus 61, 75, 170, 171, 184. **Open** noon-3pm, 6-9.30pm Mon, Tue, Thur-Sun. **Main courses** $4-$20. **No credit cards**.
Peranakan

Set in Beauty World, a 1970s shopping centre that is practically a byword for retro kitsch, Dulukala will induce a giggle. But the Peranakan classics – delicious fish-head curries and pork stews cooked in home-made style – are nothing to joke about. Don't come on Sunday as the place will be packed with the après-church crowd.

Shiro

Hillcrest Park, 24 Greenwood Avenue, Bukit Timah (6462 2774/www.imaginings.com.sg). Bus 66, 74, 157, 171, 174. **Open** noon-2pm, 6.30-10pm Mon-Sat. **Main courses** $18-$55. **Credit** AmEx, DC, JCB, MC, V. Japanese

Laze over lunch at **Long Beach**'s seafood bonanza. See p126.

Shiro is like Fort Knox: the door is always locked and you must ring a bell to enter (and then wait for someone to emerge from the depths). The dramatic interiors – cocoon-like, with draped curtains and mood lighting – are worth the effort. The wagyu and kaiseki sets are always a treat, with seasonal, often daily, specials of fresh fish, seafood and vegetables. Bookings are encouraged, children discouraged.

Tiong Bahru Market
Corner of Lim Liak Street & Seng Poh Road, Tiong Bahru. **Open** approx 7am-11pm daily. **Main courses** $3-$10. **No credit cards.** Hawker centre It's worth spending quality time sniffing around the produce section of this market, which also sells poultry, seafood and the like. Then dive into its other famous attraction: the hawker centre. Highlights include roast pork from Tiong Bahru Roasted Pig Specialist (stall 02-38) and fluffy pancakes from Mian Jian Kueh, a few stalls down at No.34. It's also worth investigating the food stalls in the neighbouring blocks.

European

Choupinette
#01-01 607 Bukit Timah Road, Bukit Timah (6466 0613). Bus 66, 74, 157, 171, 174. **Open** 8am-8pm Tue-Sun. **Main courses** $16-$23. **Credit** AmEx, MC, V. French
There's a whiff of French nostalgia about this bakery and confectionery, filled with aged wooden furniture and the aroma of freshly baked brioches and

baguettes. Go early for their famous macaroons: available in rose, chocolate, lemon, hazelnut and other scrumptious flavours. Choupinette also does a mean croque monsieur and other sandwiches.

Corduroy & Finch
779 Bukit Timah Road, Bukit Timah (6762 0131/ www.corduroyandfinch.com). Bus 66, 74, 157, 171, 174. **Open** 8am-11pm Mon-Thur; 8am-midnight Fri-Sun. **Main courses** $18-$36. **Credit** AmEx, DC, MC, V. Café
There's a touch of New York glamour about this café. Its two levels are anchored by a glazed kitchen, and shelves are lined with fancy oils, kitchen utensils, gourmet drinks, granolas and chocolates. There's a good selection of pasta, antipastos, sandwiches and roasts. The burger is a towering stack of ground sirloin, grilled just so and served between thick buns.
Other locations: Corduroy Café #01-106 VivoCity, 1 HarbourFront Walk, HarbourFront (6376 9895).

Da Paolo Il Giardino
#01-03 Cluny Court, 501 Bukit Timah Road, Bukit Timah (6463 9628/www.dapaolo.com.sg). Newton MRT then bus 66, 67, 170. **Open** 11.30am-2.30pm, 6.30-10.30pm Tue-Sat; 11am-2.30pm, 6.30-10.30pm Sun. **Main courses** $18-$26. **Credit** AmEx, MC, V. Italian
The entrance is lovely: a corridor of bamboo stands and stone walls opening on to a bijou courtyard. The latter leads to a pretty dining room, dominated by a long concrete bar, more stonework and a glass

Taste makers

Singapore's chefs are breaking new culinary ground with their take on local and global cuisines, attracting top talent from around the world in the process. Here is small sample of the chefs who are making the island's taste buds tingle.

Samia Ahad

Pakistan-born Ahad trained and worked as a chef and caterer in London and New York before relocating to Singapore to open the much-loved **Coriander Leaf** (*see p111*). Her inventive menu incorporates Thai, Indian, Persian and South-east Asian ingredients.

Ignatius Chan

One of the driving forces behind the success of **Les Amis** (*see p123*), Chan channelled his formidable talent for fusing European flavours with Asian subtlety into the eponymous **Iggy's** (*see p122*).

Chan Chen Hei

In a remarkable career, Guangzhou-born Chan worked his way up from Hong Kong restaurants frequented by Triad thugs to the position of top gun at the fabled Hai Tian Lo in Singapore's Pan Pacific hotel. His restaurant, Chef Chan's, currently closed, should re-open in a new location come autumn 2007.

Anderson Ho

Ho was one of Singapore's brightest culinary stars in the late 1990s. So his decision to trade it all in for a job with Singapore Airlines (consulting on their in-flight meals) was perplexing, to say the least. Happily, he's back with **Le Papillon** (*see p116*) and a reassuringly confident and mature menu.

Sam Leong

Malaysian Sam Leong jump-started his career with the Tung Lok group of restaurants as executive chef at **Jade** (*see p112*), where he wowed the crowd with a modern take on trad Cantonese classics. Now the group's director of kitchens, he brings the same bold imprint to 19 restaurants around town.

Christopher Millar

After graduating with a degree in advertising and marketing from Melbourne, the Aussie high-tailed it to London where he worked with Antony Worrall Thompson for seven years, followed by stints as executive chef at Melbourne's Windsor Hotel and Sydney's Pavilion on the Park. The experience shows up on his imaginative menu at **Poppi** (*see p112*).

Milland Sovani

After putting a slick fusion spin on Indian cuisine at Vansh, Sovani was lured to the **Song of India** (*see p122*), where he emphasises intense flavours while staying true to the culinary heritage of various regions of India.

Emmanuel Stroobant

Author and local celeb chef, Belgium-born Stroobant earned his stripes at the three-Michelin-starred Maison de Bouche in Brussels. This was followed by stints in the US and Australia before he seduced Singapore with his foie gras menu at **Saint Pierre** (*see p116*).

Helen Sugiono Sim

The glamorous and flamboyant owner of **Eva's** (*see p129*) turns out sumptuously flavoured Peranakan dishes based on secret recipes handed down from her Indonesian family.

Valentino Valtulina

After making his mark at Cantina, the Milanese Valtulina struck out on his own with **Ristorante Da Valentino's** (*see p129*). His experience working in Tuscany shows up in the sunny, earthy flavours, and he knows a thing or two about pasta.

---

curtain shielding diners from the kitchen. The culinary stars are the home-made pastas and garden salads sprinkled with oranges and duck foie gras. Round off the meal with a prosecco in the courtyard.

Da Paolo Pizza Bar

#01-46 Chip Bee Gardens, 44 Jalan Merah Saga, Holland Village (6479 6059/www.dapaolo.com.sg). Buona Vista MRT then 15mins walk/bus 7, 61, 75, 106, 970. **Open** 11.30am-2.30pm, 6.30-10.30pm Tue-Fri; 9am-2.30pm, 6.30-10.30pm Sat, Sun. **Main courses** $15-$24. **Credit** AmEx, MC, V. Italian Decorated with brown cowhide, brown leather banquettes, blond wood counters and mirrors, this is a lovely, luxurious space. The imaginative pizza dough – made with rocket leaves, or coloured purple with squid ink, or threaded with chilli and tomatoes – emerges from the oven topped with anything from gorgonzola and arugula to tiny forest mushrooms and white streaks of feta.

Ristorante Da Valentino's

11 Jalan Bingka, off Rifle Range Road, Bukit Timah (6462 0555/www.valentino.sg) Bus 74, 75, 77, 151, 154, 171. **Open** noon-2.30pm, 6pm-midnight Tue-Sun. **Main courses** from $30. **Credit** AmEx, MC, V.
Italian

Deep in the suburbs, this family-run trattoria is worth seeking out. Milan-born Valentino Valtulina spent many years cooking in Tuscany, hence his penchant for sunny, coloured foods, dense flavours and simply prepared vegetables. The squid ink pasta, golden carbonara and paper-thin slices of pork loin (braised in white wine, garlic and bay leaves) are served with brio. Though the dessert trolley looks spectacular, the puddings are often disappointing. *See also p128* **Taste makers.**

La Braceria

Ban Guan Park, 70 Greenleaf Road, off Sixth Avenue, Bukit Timah (6165 5918). Buona Vista MRT then taxi/bus 77, 156. **Open** noon-2.30pm, 6-10.30pm Mon, Wed-Sun. **Main courses** $18-$32. **Credit** AmEx, MC, V. Italian

Hearty, rustic Italian cooking is the draw at La Braceria. Wonderful, thin-crust pizzas with dense, flavourful toppings emerge from the blackened dome of the oven, but best of all are the home-made sausages – fat tubes stuffed with fresh meat, marinated for days in a secret blend of seasonings and spices. It's very popular and can get pretty squashed on weekends.

Turquoise Room

7 Lock Road, Gillman Village (6473 3655). Bus 97, 970. **Open** noon-11pm Mon-Thur; noon-midnight Fri, Sat; 10am-10pm Sun. **Main courses** $25-$32. **Credit** AmEx, DC, JCB, MC, V.
Modern European

Once an army barracks, Gillman Village now pulls a more peaceful crowd with its collection of galleries and eateries, set in lush tropical rainforest. The funky Turquoise Room is painted, er, turquoise, and framed by French windows. The best seats in the house are actually outside, on the timber deck overlooking the jungle. Try grilled portobello, juicy lamb racks or pork tenderloin with apple and prosciutto. Thin-crust pizzas are also served.

Other

Brazil Churrascaria

14/16 Sixth Avenue, Bukit Timah (6463 1923). Bus 66, 71, 157, 171, 174. **Open** 6-10.30pm daily. **Buffet** $26-$38. **Credit** AmEx, DC, MC, V. Brazilian

The exuberant mood here is matched by the sheer amount of food. The salad bar – a large island filled with potatoes, rice, beans and every imaginable green – is a meal unto itself. But the marquee attractions are the passadors, who emerge from the kitchen with metal spikes carrying chicken, beef, pork, sausages, ham and roasted pineapple. Portions are limited only by your appetite.

Island Creamery

#01-03 Serene Centre, 10 Jalan Serene, Bukit Timah (6468 8859). Bus 66, 67, 157, 170, 171. **Open** 11am-10pm daily. **Ice-cream** $2.50-$8. **No credit cards.** Ice-cream parlour

On an island where the weather varies between hot and hotter, it's a wonder there aren't more ice-cream parlours. Forget about vanilla: Stanley Kwok's melange of ice-creams is dominated by local flavours with clever twists, such as Kopi-O (a local coffee beverage) and teh tarik (hawker-style tea).

Central & Northern Singapore

Asian

Eva's

12 Jalan Leban, Upper Thomson Road, Bishan (6556 1538). Ang Mo Kio MRT then bus 169/ Bishan MRT then bus 163. **Open** 11.30am-3pm, 6-9.30pm daily. **Main courses** $5-$10. **Credit** AmEx, MC, V. Peranakan

The decor is spartan, but the food is fantastic. Glamorous Peranakan owner/chef Helen Sugiono Sim (*see p128* **Taste makers**) hails from Indonesia and her menu is overlaid with an additional layer of intense flavour. Everything from the buah keluak to the sambal kangkong and golden, coconut-infused chicken curry is worthy of multiple helpings. Don't miss the layered kueh lapis, which is flown in from Sim's aunt's kitchen in Indonesia. It's sinfully good.

House of Hunan

#03-09/10 Velocity at Novena Square, 238 Thomson Road, Novena (6733 7667/www.tunglok.com). Novena MRT. **Open** 11.30am-2.30pm, 6-10.30pm Mon-Fri; 11.30am-4.45pm, 6-10.30pm Sat, Sun. **Main courses** $9-$42. **Credit** AmEx, JCB, MC, V. Hunanese

For a couple of years, the Tung Lok group lay low in Singapore, concentrating on opening restaurants in China. The experience inspired them to recruit a cabal of chefs from Hunan province. Robust, fiery flavours dominate with a patina of well-water salt (rural China's equivalent of sea salt). Try the prawns flash-fried with ginger and pretty lantern chillis; garlicky, spicy cuttle-fish rings; and crisp bean curd skins sandwiched between paper thin pancakes.

Peach Garden

#01-06 Novena Gardens, 273 Thomson Road, Novena (6254 3383). Novena MRT. **Open** 11.30am-2.30pm, 6.30-10.30pm daily. **Main courses** $18-$55. **Credit** AmEx, DC, JCD, MC, V. Cantonese

It's easy to understand why this understated, suburban Cantonese restaurant remains such a favourite. The muted interiors are offset by a menu of fab classics including cold crab and Hong Kong-style beef noodles. The kitchen is justly famed for its roast meats: the thick-cut roast pork has crackling skin and sweet flesh. Service can be distracted.

Eat, Drink, Shop

Bars

Liquid lounges and tropical tipples.

Singapore's watering holes are a mixed bag: chillout lounges, Irish theme pubs, glam hotel bars, alfresco spots and ethnic enclaves. Though the scene draws its fair share of barflies (expats, students and high-flying businessmen are the biggest bingers), on the whole this is not a particularly hard-drinking town. If this means there is sometimes a lack of buzz, the relaxed vibe – complemented by lush outdoor settings – makes up for it.

The scene is spread out, but there are a few key areas for bar-hopping. Along the Singapore River, the busy Quays (touristy Boat, retro-flavoured Clarke and dynamic Robertson) feature a concentration of bars in waterfront settings. The Orchard Road area is dominated by upmarket hotel bars, but Emerald Hill Road is a charming enclave off the main drag. Further afield, there's green and secluded Dempsey Road and the colonial bungalows of Rochester Park.

In recent years, a trend for alfresco bars and chillout lounges (or a hybrid of both) has swept Singapore as locals embrace their inner islander. These lounges follow the same formula – hip furniture, verdant greenery and downtempo DJs – but their popularity shows no sign of waning. Martinis are also currently very fashionable: try **Morton's**, the **Martini Bar** or **One Rochester**. Another distinctive Singaporean drinking trend is happy hour: most bars offer one, and this is when most locals come out to play. You won't find many locals at the Long Bar of the Raffles Hotel, drinking Singapore Slings – do it if you must, but, frankly, it's an overrated and expensive experience.

Maybe one of the reasons Singaporeans tend to be moderate drinkers is the cost of booze. Outside happy hour, brace yourself for shocking prices: $10 for a pint of local Tiger beer, more for imports; $12 for a shot of house spirits; $15-$20 for premium brands; and $100 for a bottle of champagne. All bills include a ten per cent service charge and eight per cent in taxes, so tipping is uncommon.

---

❶ Pink numbers given in this chapter correspond to the location of each bar or pub as marked on the street maps. *See pp246-252.*

Colonial District

Balaclava
#01-01B Suntec City, 1 Raffles Boulevard, Marina (6339 1600/www.imaginings.com.sg). City Hall MRT then 10mins walk. **Open** 3pm-1am Mon-Thur; 3pm-2am Fri; 6pm-2am Sat. **Credit** AmEx, DC, JCB, MC, V. **Map** p251 M7 **❶**
This large buzzy bar is filled to the brim with a post-work crowd. Happy hour (3-8pm) brings great deals on beer and house pours, while acoustic sets (*see p187*) take place most nights. Somewhere to watch the corporate crowd let loose.

Barfly
#02-02 The Cannery, Block C, River Valley Road, Clarke Quay (6887 3733/www.barfly.com.sg). Clarke Quay MRT. **Open** 6.30pm-2am daily. **Credit** AmEx, DC, JCB, MC, V. **Map** p250 I8 **❷**
Created by Raymond Visan, the man behind Paris' famous Buddha Bar, Barfly features some of the same dark and velvety touches. Named after the 1980s film written by Charles Bukowski, it's a sexy space with plush banquettes lining the long bar. It's part supper club, part bar, so you can start with dinner (chic Asian fusion) and stay late.

Brewerkz Restaurant & Micro Brewery
#01-05 Riverside Point, 30 Merchant Road, Clarke Quay (6438 7438/www.brewerkz.com). Clarke Quay MRT. **Open** noon-midnight Mon-Thur; noon-1am Fri, Sat; 11am-midnight Sun. **Credit** AmEx, DC, JCB, MC, V. **Map** p250 I9 **❸**
One of Singapore's few microbreweries, Brewerkz offers beers concocted on site by a Canadian brewmaster. Sit outside along the river or in the airy atrium, done up like a factory with exposed copper pipes. Choose from 12 handcrafted ales, lagers and stouts. The American-slanted food isn't bad either.

China One & Baize
#02-01 Block 3E, River Valley Road, Clarke Quay (6339 0280/www.baize.com.sg). Clarke Quay MRT. **Open** 6pm-2am Mon-Thur, Sun; 7pm-4am Fri, Sat. **Credit** AmEx, MC, V. **Map** p250 I8 **❹**
This laid-back bar and pool hall is a cool mix of old and new: Chinese antiques mixed with slick leather furniture, old lanterns versus dim, arty lighting. Local bands throughout the week. Service is friendly.

Fashion Bar
#01-02A The Cannery, Block C, River Valley Road, Clarke Quay (6887 3733/www.fbar.com.sg). Clarke Quay MRT. **Open** 5.30pm-3am daily. **Credit** AmEx, DC, JCB, MC, V. **Map** p250 I8 **❺**

Dedicated to all things fashionable and fabulous, this slick bar is bling central. Brace yourself for black chandeliers, silver booth seating and a 4,000-piece crystal curtain. There's even a runway. Big plasma screens play fashion shows on a loop; champagne cocktails pack a punch. Dress for attention.

Loof

#03-07 Odeon Towers, 331 North Bridge Road, Colonial District (6338 8035/www.loof.com.sg). City Hall MRT. **Open** 5.30pm-1.30am Mon-Thur, Sun; 5.30pm-3am Fri, Sat. **Credit** AmEx, MC, V. **Map** p251 K6 ❻

Billed as a 'sanctuary for fools' and a 'canvas for the budding artist', Loof is an eccentric outdoor rooftop bar. A playful contrast to its neighbour, the Raffles Hotel, it attracts an easy-going, eclectic crowd (especially media types). Punters relax on leather loungers and the deck is lit by a huge electric billboard. Pray for rain: when the heavens open, drinks are two for the price of one. **Photo** *below.*

Morton's Atrium Bar

4F The Oriental, 5 Raffles Avenue, Marina (6339 3740/www.mandarinoriental.com/singapore). City Hall MRT then 10mins walk. **Open** 5-11pm Mon-Sat; 5-10pm Sun. **Credit** AmEx, DC, MC, V. **Map** p251 M8 ❼

Situated in the Oriental hotel, Morton's is elegant but unpretentious. Topped by a pagoda roof and opening on to the hotel's atrium, the setting is striking.

Its Martinis are the biggest and best in town (though also the priciest), and free steak sandwiches are served during happy hour (5-7pm). The friendly crowd (regulars, hotel guests and business types) and staff keep the place down to earth.

New Asia Bar

71/F Swissôtel The Stamford, 2 Stamford Road, Colonial District (6837 3322/www.equinoxcomplex. com). City Hall MRT. **Open** 3pm-1am Mon-Wed, Sun; 3pm-2am Thur; 3pm-3am Fri, Sat. **Admission** $22. **Credit** AmEx, DC, JCB, MC, V. **Map** p251 K7 ❽

If you want the city at your feet, board the express lift at Swissôtel The Stamford, disembark at the New Asia Bar on the 71st floor and gasp. Drawing a mixed crowd of locals, expats and tourists, the bar offers a winning combination of staggering views and happy hour prices. The weekday crowd thins out at about 9pm; at the weekend the mood gets clubby with action on a small dancefloor. **Photo** *p132.*

Q Bar

The Annex @ The Old Parliament House, #01-04 1 Old Parliament Lane, Colonial District (6336 3386/ www.qbar.com.sg). City Hall or Raffles Place MRT. **Open** 6pm-2am Mon-Tue, Sun; 6pm-3am Wed-Fri; 6pm-4am Sat. **Credit** AmEx, MC, V. **Map** p251 K9 ❾

Inspired by the famous Q Bars in Ho Chi Minh and Bangkok, this outpost is set beside the river in the annex of Singapore's former parliament house. In

Enjoy a spot of star-gazing with your tipple, at the rooftop **Loof.**

New Asia Bar. *See p131.*

contrast to the colonial exterior, the bar is decorated in a slick and modern style. Plush sofas dot the bar; there's also an outdoor lounge and intimate dance club. But its biggest claim to fame is the extensive premium vodka list.

Suba

#01-75A Millenia Walk, 9 Raffles Boulevard, Marina (6333 0822). City Hall MRT then 10mins walk. **Open** 4pm-1am Mon-Thur, Sun; 4pm-2am Fri, Sat. **Credit** AmEx, MC, V. **Map** p251 M7 **①**
Chocolate walls and black chandeliers set the sumptuous mood at this sliver of a bar, tucked in the back of Millenia Walk. Outside, an after-work crowd sprawls on loungers and daybeds facing a waterfall. Victoria Bitter on tap is a popular choice, but on Wednesday nights (6-9pm) free Cosmopolitans (with chocolate-dipped strawberries) flow for the ladies. R&B, funk and soul tunes reign.

Chinatown & the CBD

Archipelago Craft Beer Hub
79 Circular Road, Boat Quay (6327 8408/ www.archipelagobrewery.com). Clarke Quay MRT. **Open** 3pm-1am Mon-Thur, Sun; 3pm-3am Fri, Sat. **Credit** Amex, DC, MC, V. **Map** p250 J9 **①**
The new kid on Circular Road (just behind tacky Boat Quay), Archipelago was the island's first commercial brewery circa 1931. It's back with a 21st-century venture: a beer bar, where brick walls and open, colonial-inspired verandas lure drinkers to hand-crafted Trader's Ale, Traveller's Wheat and Straits Pale, each concocted with Asian flavours such as ginger, gula melaka (palm sugar mixed with coconut milk) assam (tamarind) and lemongrass. You can sample the beers before you decide; a good idea if you're unfamiliar with strong flavours.

Bacchus BoatHouse Wine Bar

#03-01 Fullerton Waterboat House, 3 Fullerton Road, CBD (6538 9038/www.bacchusboathouse. com). Raffles Place MRT. **Open** 4pm-midnight Mon-Thur; 4pm-2am Fri, Sat. **Credit** AmEx, DC, JCB, MC, V. **Map** p251 K9 ⓬
The Bacchus Wine Bar sits on the rooftop of a former lighthouse, to one side of the Fullerton Hotel and just opposite the harbour. Run by a wine expert whose retail shops are the haunts of enthusiasts, it offers a comprehensive list of old and new world wines, plus a stunning view from the open-air deck.

Breeze

The Scarlet, 33 Erskine Road, Chinatown (6511 3326/www.thescarlet.com). Tanjong Pagar MRT. **Open** 7pm-1am Mon-Thur; 7pm-2am Fri, Sat. **Credit** AmEx, MC, V. **Map** p250 I11 ⓭
Set atop the Scarlet, the flamboyant and popular boutique hotel, this open-air terrace bar has a natural feel, from the timber decking and tented seating areas to the lush greenery. It also offers good views of surrounding Chinatown. Tapas, seafood platters, salads and barbecue fare are washed down by exotic cocktails and an extensive wine selection. Staff can be brusque, but the mellow, magic location makes up for it.

Kazbar

#01-03 Capital Square, 25 Church Street, CBD (6438 2975/www.kazbar.com). Raffles Place MRT. **Open** noon-midnight Mon, Tue; noon-1am Wed-Fri; 5.30pm-1am Sat. **Credit** AmEx, DC, MC, V. **Map** p250 J10 ⓮
A stylish, after-work lounge, Kazbar is a chillout favourite with big-spending oil traders and advertising types. Decked out in chic Middle Eastern style, it has cosy alcoves for hiding or a tented divan for decadent drinking (try sipping a cardamom Martini and smoking a shisha pipe). The dinner menu is extensive and authentic.

Molly Malone's

56 Circular Road, Boat Quay (6536 2029/www. molly-malone.com). Raffles Place MRT. **Open** 11am-midnight Mon, Sun; 11am-1am Tue-Thur; 11am-2am Fri, Sat. **Credit** AmEx, MC, V. **Map** p250 J9 ⓯
Singapore's first Irish pub is an expat institution. Housed in a three-storey green building, it is perpetually filled with drinkers, who quaff copious amounts of ale and Guinness and scoff excellent pub grub (fish and chips, Irish stew). Diversions include sports on TV and live Irish music (*see p189*).

Post Bar

The Fullerton Hotel, 1 Fullerton Square, CBD (6733 8388/www.fullertonhotel.com). Raffles Place MRT. **Open** 3pm-2am Mon-Fri, Sun; 5pm-2am Sat. **Credit** AmEx, DC, JCB, MC, V. **Map** p251 K9 ⓰
Despite patchy service, a somewhat snooty crowd and pricey drinks, the Post Bar in the historic Fullerton Hotel building has its merits. The tasteful beige decor, high ceilings and flattering lighting ooze sophistication. Uniformed staff serve the city's best Caipirinha; and the Great Sunday Post (seafood and unlimited vodka cocktails, 3-6pm Sunday) is very popular. Dress elegantly and bring cash – it takes forever to pay by credit card.

Little India & the Arab Quarter

Café Samar

60 Kandahar Street, Arab Quarter (6398 0530). Bus MRT then 10mins walk. **Open** 24hrs daily. **Credit** MC, V. **Map** p249 N4 ⓱
The Arab Street area oozes old school charm. City planning hasn't messed with its natural sprawl, thankfully, allowing Café Samar to spill over on to the pavement. It's strictly alcohol-free, but Arabic charms – reclining chairs, low-slung lamps and exotic carpets – make for a moody vibe. Try the fresh apricot smoothies and teas, best enjoyed on the upper outdoor terrace or in the corridor out front.

Divine Wine Extraordinaire

Parkview Square, 600 North Bridge Road, Bras Basah & Bugis (6396 4466/www.parkviewsquare. com). Bugis MRT. **Open** 11am-midnight daily. **Credit** AmEx, DC, JCB, MC, V. **Map** p249 M5 ⓲
Parkview Square always causes visitors to stop and stare at its outlandish, copper-clad, art deco-style façade. Inside, on the ground floor, is an equally dramatic bar with a 12m/40ft floor-to-ceiling wine cooler. If you order one of the 3,000 bottles within, a server dons a tutu and gets hoisted up a steel cable to find it. It's usually a members-only bar, but if a wine tasting or corporate do isn't on, non-members can visit (with an advance reservation).

Prince of Wales

101 Dunlop Street, Little India (6299 0130/ www.pow.com.sg). Little India MRT. **Open** 9am-midnight daily. **Credit** MC, V. **Map** p248 K3 ⓳
Next door to the hostel of the same name, this unpretentious, yellow-painted pub is a slice of Down Under. The sunny decor features touches of red gum timber; Aussie draught beers include Gippsland Gold and Brewers Pilsener. Outside, expect wooden benches, barbecues and revelry; sandals and shorts are de rigueur. Bands play nightly (*see p189*). **Photo** *p137*.

Orchard Road & Around

Balcony Bar

#01-K5 The Heeren Shops, 260 Orchard Road (6736 2326/www.balconybar.com). Somerset MRT. **Open** 24hrs daily. **Credit** AmEx, MC, V. **Map** p247 G4 ⓴
Inside the trendy Heeren shopping arcade, Balcony Bar is a souk-like respite from retail mania, day o night (it's open 24 hours). Basket chairs, swings an billowing sheets hang downstairs; on the uppe deck, you can lounge on sunken seats and cushion get wet in the Jacuzzi or take in the view of Orchar Road. A dinner and snack menu is also available.

Let us shed some light on great beer.

If you like beer, you'll love one of the handcrafted brews we create right here at Riverside Point. They go great with our American-style menu and relaxed atmosphere. Visit our illuminating website at: www.brewerkz.com

Restaurant & Microbrewery
·BREWERKZ·
SINGAPORE

We do what Werkz

Brewerkz Restaurant & Microbrewery, 30 Merchant Road, #01-05/06, Riverside Point, Singapore, 058282 Tel: (+65) 6438 7438

Coffee Bar K

#01-76 UE Square, 205 River Valley Road, Robertson Quay (6720 5040/www.coffeebark.co.jp). Bus 32, 54, 143, 195. **Open** 6pm-3am Mon-Fri, Sun; 6pm-4am Sat. **Credit** AmEx, DC, JCB, MC, V. **Map** p250 H7 **㉑**

This quirky Japanese bar has won rave reviews since opening in 1992. Its decor (chocolate brown and black, leather and marble, arty lighting) is sophisticated; its Japanese bartenders exceptionally well trained and its drinks large and artfully presented (if steeply priced). The whisky list is a forte.

DayBed Bar

15 Mohamed Sultan Road, River Valley (6733 6695/www.daybedlounge.com). Bus 32, 54, 143, 195. **Open** 7pm-3am Mon-Fri, Sun; 7pm-4am Sat. **Credit** AmEx, MC, V. **Map** p250 H7 **㉒**

Previously known for its cheesy bars, Mohamed Sultan Road is slowly getting smarter. DayBed Bar, for instance, provides a classy contrast to its tacky predecessor, Coyote Ugly. The all-white interior, lounge-worthy daybeds and Martini-heavy menu are the draws. Tucked away and equipped with a soothing soul soundtrack, it's a welcome respite from the noisy crowds of nearby Robertson Quay.

eM by the River

#01-05 The Gallery Hotel, 1 Nanson Road, Robertson Quay (6836 9691). Bus 51, 64, 123, 186, 811. **Open** 11am-2am Mon-Thur, Sun; 11am-3am Fri, Sat. **Credit** AmEx, JCB, MC, V. **Map** p250 G8 **㉓**

A chilled café by day, chic bar by night. The tasteful decor reflects the natural setting: a mix of earth tones and natural woods, complemented by ponds and trickling water features. The emphasis is on sharing: beers, shooters and cocktails arrive by the bottle, accompanied by small glasses. The menu is small but hearty (sandwiches, kebabs, salads and satays), and is available late into the evening.

Hacienda

13A Dempsey Road, Orchard Road & Around (6836 2922/www.hacienda.com.sg). Bus 7, 105, 123, 174. **Open** 5pm-1am Mon-Thur; 5pm-2am Fri, Sat; noon-midnight Sun. **Credit** AmEx, MC, V.

Far from the city centre crowds, this hipster hideout was originally designed as a stylish weekend villa, replete with a chic white colour scheme, green lawns, open-air decks and courtyards. Grab yourself a communal table and while the night away, fresh watermelon Martini in hand, listening to groovy, chilled-out tunes.

K Box Karaoke

#08-01 Orchard Cineleisure, 8 Grange Road, Orchard Road & Around (6756 3113/www.kbox. com.sg). Orchard MRT. **Open** 11am-6am daily. **Admission** (incl 2 drinks) $16 Mon-Thur, Sun; $21 Fri, Sat. **Credit** AmEx, JCB, MC, V. **Map** p247 G5 **㉔**

The convenience store of the karaoke world, K Box has 12 locations. This one's the most convenient, with a long list of English songs, 100 rooms, a dial-your-food service and an assortment of pool tables

Bargain booze

Alcohol is expensive in Singapore, but cheap deals are possible if you know where to look – and when to drink. Most bars operate a happy hour period (often between 6pm and 9pm) where deep discounts even extend to premium spirits and quality champagnes. Notable destinations include **Morton's Atrium Bar** (*see p131*), where, between 5pm and 7pm, Martinis cost $9.95 and complimentary filet mignon sandwiches are handed out; and the **Introbar** on the ground floor of the Swissôtel The Stamford, where drinks are half price between 3pm and 9pm (promotions change, so call before setting out). Other drinking deals, such as two-for-one offers and special cocktail nights, are widespread and often tied to drinks companies' promotions. On 'ladies nights', usually held on a Wednesday, bars practically give booze away – but only to women.

If cheap beer is your tipple of choice, head to a *kopitiam* (basic coffee shop) or hawker centre (where you can drink local and imported brews until midnight). Try the **Maxwell Food Centre** in Chinatown, **Newton Hawker Centre** north of Orchard Road or the **East Coast Lagoon Food Village** on East Coast Parkway. At the latter, you can drink with views of the ocean and sand beneath your feet.

Cocktails at **No.5**: one of a trio of popular bars, including **Que Pasa**, on Emerald Hill.

should you get bored of warbling badly. Cheap rates and deals tempt a young (largely teenage) crowd. **Other locations**: throughout the city.

The Living Room
Singapore Marriot Hotel, 320 Orchard Road (6831 4506/www.barnoneasia.com). Orchard MRT. **Open** 4pm-1am Mon-Tue, Sun; 4pm-6am Wed-Sat. **Credit** AmEx, DC, MC, V. **Map** p247 E3 ㉕
Though hidden in the back of the Marriot Hotel, the Living Room is a hotspot because it stays open until 6am, Wednesday through Saturday. Despite being known as a chic lounge, complete with fireplace and smart sofas, it feels like a house party after hours, helped along by a DJ, dancefloor and drink promos (always ask at the bar). Packed at the weekends.

Martini Bar
Grand Hyatt Singapore, 10 Scotts Road, Orchard Road & Around (6416 7189/http://singapore.grand. hyatt.com). Orchard MRT. **Open** 11am-2am daily. **Credit** AmEx, DC, JCB, MC, V. **Map** p247 E3 ㉖
Long before the Martini became trendy, there was the Grand Hyatt's Martini Bar. Housed inside the hotel's showy Mezza 9 restaurant, this glass-walled space is a nice spot for a pre-dinner Martini. If you can't choose from the 30 on offer ($19-$38), try the lychee version. Sit at the bar overlooking busy Scotts Road, or sink into a sofa.

Oosh
22 Dempsey Road, Orchard Road & Around (6475 0002/www.oosh.com.sg). Bus 7, 105, 123, 174. **Open** noon-2.30am, 6pm-1am Mon-Thur, Sun; noon-2.30am, 6pm-2am Fri, Sat. **Credit** AmEx, MC, V.

Singapore's largest alfresco bar and restaurant, this massive venue houses nine areas in which to drink, lounge and eat (mainly Japanesey cuisine). Despite its size, the place feels surprisingly cosy – and well heeled. Quality is the watchword, from the premium booze and cigars to the designer furniture and landscaped greenery.

Que Pasa
7 Emerald Hill Road, Orchard Road & Around (6235 6626/www.emeraldhillgroup.com). Somerset MRT. **Open** 6pm-2am Mon-Thur, Sun; 6pm-3am Fri, Sat. **Credit** AmEx, JCB, MC, V. **Map** p247 G4 ㉗
One of the oldest, best-loved wine and tapas bars in Singapore, Que Pasa has a devoted following. The rustic, Spanish-style interior is charming, the vibe is casual, and the wine list features extensive offerings from old and new worlds. It's located on one of Singapore's most atmospheric and charming bar alleys, in the exclusive Emerald Hill residential nook just off busy Orchard Road. It's flanked by two other bars (all under the same ownership): No 5 (**photo** *above*), set in a converted shophouse, entices a party-friendly crowd with its cocktail- and spirits-driven menu, while Ice Cold Beer is just that: a kick-back, beers-after-work joint with sport on the plasma TVs, and a menu of stomach fillers (hot dogs, chicken wings). All three bars have open-air seating amid tropical trees, and are connected by a narrow corridor.

The Wine Company @ Dempsey
Block 14-2/3 Dempsey Road, Orchard Road & Around (6479 9341/www.thewinecompany.com.sg).

Bus 7, 105, 123, 174. **Open** 3pm-midnight Mon-Thur; 3pm-1am Fri; noon-1am Sat; noon-11pm Sun. **Credit** AmEx, MC, V.

Though Dempsey Road is rapidly becoming hipster central, it still has the feel of a well-kept secret. The Wine Company is a case in point. Tucked away in an old army barracks surrounded by tropical vegetation, it has ambience by the bucketload. The interior is homely, but the open-air courtyard is the best spot. The emphasis is on South African tipple at low, by-the-bottle rates (the bar grew out of a small wine import shop). Offerings on the small changing menu range from cheese platters to steak dinners.
Other locations: The Wine Company @ Evans, #01-05 26 Evans Road, Orchard Road & Around (6732 1229).

Sentosa & Around

Il Lido Lounge Bar

Sentosa Golf Club, 27 Bukit Manis Road, Sentosa (6866 1977/www.il-lido.com). HarbourFront MRT then Sentosa Express. **Open** 11.30am-2.30pm, 6.30-11pm daily. **Credit** AmEx, DC, JCB, MC, V. **Map** p252 D4 ㉘
Part of a renowned Italian restaurant, this chic lounge attracts an after-dinner crowd as well as sophisticated barflies. Set on Sentosa island, it comes with an outdoor deck – a prime spot for watching sunsets over the golf course (with a glass of bubbly from the superior champagne list). A DJ spins nu-soul and Balearic beats from 9pm till late every Friday and Saturday.

The Jewel Box

109 Mount Faber Road, HarbourFront (6377 9688/ www.mountfaber.com.sg). HarbourFront MRT then bus 409. **Open** 11am-1am Mon-Tue, Sun; 11am-3am Wed-Sat. **Credit** AmEx, MC, V. **Map** p252 B1 ㉙
Literally a sparkler, this brightly lit glass box atop Mount Faber is best approached via cable car. It houses two bars – the open-air Altivo and appropriately named glass-walled Glass Bar – both with amazing views of the harbour and city. The former features plush lounge chairs and a Chinese/international menu; the latter has floor-to-ceiling windows and a flashy, futuristic interior.

Villa Bali

9A Lock Road, Gillman Village, Bukit Merah (6473 6763/www.littlebali.com). Bus 57, 195, 274. **Open** 4pm-1am Mon-Thur, Sun; 4pm-2am Fri, Sat. **Credit** AmEx, DC, JCB, MC, V.
For a taste of the magic isle, cross a wooden bridge that leads into a luxuriant garden. Filled with daybeds and divans and surrounded by wild plants and ponds, it's an idyllic drinking spot. Service is efficient but unobtrusive, allowing you to kick back undisturbed. The usual bar stock dominates, but there are also Balinese wines that go very well with the Indian tapas.

Western Singapore

One Rochester

1 Rochester Park, off North Buona Vista Road, Queenstown (7633 0070/www.onerochester.com). Buona Vista MRT. **Open** 5pm-1am Mon-Fri; 5pm-2am Sat; 10am-3pm (brunch), 5pm-1am Sun. **Credit** AmEx, MC, V.
Part of the Rochester Park dining enclave, where each historic black-and-white 'bungalow' houses a different restaurant. The decor may be grand, but One Rochester is packing in the hipsters. Each of the four rooms has a theme: living room, library, play room and bar. But the best is outside: the deck with its low-slung sofas, tropical greenery and water features, plus the balcony bar. The wine list – 200 well-priced bottles – is impressive, as are the sakés, Martinis and fancy bar food.

Wala Wala

31 Lorong Mambong, Holland Village (6462 4288/ www.imaginings.com.sg). Bus 7, 61, 75, 106, 970. **Open** 4pm-1am Mon-Thur, Sun; 4pm-2am Fri, Sat. **Credit** AmEx, DC, JCB, MC, V.
Put on your shorts and T-shirt, grab six friends and a sidewalk table and knock back some cheap beers. Music (*see p189*) features nightly in the upstairs bar: the early evening features acoustic sets; a revolving roster of great local bands follows. Saturday nights rock, Sunday evenings are chilled.

Prince of Wales. See p133.

Shops & Services

You've died and gone to retail heaven.

Eating and shopping are often described as Singapore's national obsessions – and with good reason. Visitors will be astonished by the wealth of retail opportunities on this tiny island, particularly the number of massive shopping centres, some containing over 800 outlets in shiny, air-conditioned settings.

Orchard Road is Singapore's major shopping zone. The key stretch, with towering malls on either side of the street, lies between the Meridien Hotel and the Hilton Hotel – about a mile in length – with more on adjoining **Scotts Road** and **Tanglin Road**. Many visitors on a brief stopover only make it as far as the Orchard Road nexus, but there are charecterful shopping areas elsewhere, in Chinatown, the Arab Quarter and Holland Village (*see p146* **Beyond the mall**). HDB estates offer heavily discounted shopping; though the quality of the merchandise (from miniskirts to Chinese herbal tea) can be poor, there's more local flavour.

Well-travelled, affluent locals used to grumble about the lack of variety, imagination and individuality in Singapore's shopping scene. But things are looking up. In recent years, most of the major players in fashion and design have staked a claim here. From Marks & Spencer to Mothercare, Mango to Massimo Dutti, Singapore is full of well-known Western brands and chain stores.

City shops and malls are open from 10am or 11am until 9pm or 10pm daily. During the year-end festive season, the main malls stay open until almost midnight. Independent boutiques close at about 7pm or 8pm, and are sometimes shut on Sundays. Suburban estate shops and malls tend to keep hours as late as their downtown counterparts. Much of the city centre is connected by a network of air-conditioned underground tunnels, so you can shop comfortably in all weathers. If you're in town between May and July, look for big discounts during the **Great Singapore Sale** (*see p162*).

AIRPORT SHOPPING

Changi Airport deserves its reputation as one of the best (and biggest) airports in the world. Alongside the orchid garden, transit hotels, swimming pool, internet centres, cafés and restaurants, there are, of course, lots of shops – over 100, in fact. You can buy goods on arrival, as well as when you leave. The advantage of the former is that if you find the same item for less in any fixed-priced store in town within 30 days, the Changi Airport Shopping Guarantee will refund double the price difference.

You'll find souvenirs aplenty, as you would expect, plus the usual luggage and clothing outlets. Duty-free discounts are good on alcohol and cigarettes – claimed to be 40-60 per cent lower than in the city – and perfumes and cosmetics, but don't assume everything is a bargain. If you're after a digital camera or electronic goods, you'll find more choice and lower prices at city centre specialists.

TAX REFUNDS

A five per cent Goods & Services Tax (GST) is charged on most items. Foreign visitors can claim back the GST (minus an administration fee) when leaving Singapore at Changi Airport (land or cruise departures aren't valid). To qualify, you need to spend $100 or more at a participating shop; ask for a GST refund form at the time of purchase – you'll need your passport. Take the forms, receipts and goods in question (so don't pack them in your hold luggage) to the customs counters located before and after immigration.

One-stop shopping

Department stores

Singapore has a plethora of department stores. Apart from those reviewed below, the following are the major players (with the address of a city-centre branch): **Robinsons** (Centrepoint, 176 Orchard Road, 6733 0888, www.robinsons.com.sg), **Isetan** (Shaw House, 350 Orchard Road, 6733 1111, www.isetan.com.sg), **Seiyu** (Bugis Junction, 200 Victoria Street, Bras Basah & Bugis, 6223 2222, www.bhgsingapore.com.sg), **John Little** (Specialists' Centre, 277 Orchard Road (6737 2222, www.johnlittle.com.sg – Singapore's oldest department store), and **Metro** (#02-28 Paragon, 290 Orchard Road, 6835 3322, www.metro.com.sg).

Carrefour

#01-199 Suntec City Mall, 3 Temasek Boulevart, Marina (6333 6868/www.carrefour.com.sg). City Hall MRT then 10mins walk. **Open** 10am-10.30pm Mon-Thur, Sun; 10am-11pm Fri, Sat. **Credit** AmEx, DC, JCB, MC, V. **Map** 249 M6.

This French-owned hypermarket runs the gamut from budget clothing and underwear to garden furniture, books, CDs, electronics and wine – all at unbeatable prices. The mammoth food supermarket (everything from imported cheeses to local produce) sits on a separate level. Don't miss the speciality: freshly baked tarte tartin.
Other locations: #B1-09 Plaza Singapura, 68 Orchard Road (6836 6868).

Mustafa Centre
145 Syed Alwi Road, Little India (6295 5855/ www.mustafa.com.sg). Farrer Park MRT. **Open** 24hrs daily. **Credit** AmEx, DC, JCB, MC, V. **Map** p249 L2.
A Singapore institution, Mustafas is open round the clock, offering 75,000sq ft of bargains, not to mention a hotel, café and supermarket. It's a treasure trove of discount shopping, carrying everything from skincare and electronics to sportswear and luggage. Sumptuous sari fabrics can be found in basement 1, and beauty products and appliances at ground level.

Takashimaya
Tower A, Ngee Ann City, 391 Orchard Road (6738 1111/www.takashimaya-sin.com). Orchard MRT. **Open** 10am-9.30pm daily. **Credit** AmEx, DC, JCB, MC, V. **Map** p327 F4.
This mammoth, Japanese-owned department store inside the huge Ngee Ann City mall carries all the chi-chi fashion labels that appeal to the rich tourists who frequent the place. Big fashion names – Cartier, Gucci, Georg Jensen, Bulgari, Fendi and so on – dot the shop with mini replicas of their larger flagship stores. Expect jostling for the latest Dior bag or Hermès scarf.

Tangs Orchard
310 Orchard Road (6737 5500/www.cktang.com). Orchard MRT. **Open** 10.30am-9.30pm Mon-Sat; 11am-8.30pm Sun. **Credit** AmEx, DC, JCB, MC, V. **Map** p247 E4.
Singapore's most fashionable – and prettiest – department store. The Beauty Hall on the ground floor is a veritable temple to narcissism. Head upstairs to the plushly decorated Dressing Room and Wardrobe for lingerie and designer labels. On the third level, a DJ can often be found spinning thumping techno while metrosexual men and street-savvy girls shop for streetwear from Adidas, Pony, G-Star and FCUK.
Other locations: Tangs VivoCity #01-187 & #02-189 VivoCity, 1 HarbourFront Walk, HarbourFront (6303 8688).

Yue Hwa
70 Eu Tong Sen Street, Chinatown (6538 4222/ www.yuehwa.com.sg). Chinatown MRT. **Open** 11am-9pm daily. **Credit** DC, JCB, MC, V. **Map** p250 H10.
Housed in the former Nan Tin Hotel, a landmark building in the heart of Chinatown, this traditional Chinese department store is a treasure trove of all things from the Far East. Come here to stock up on embroidered Chinese slippers, silk pouches, cheongsam fabrics, oriental handicrafts, curious herbs and health tonics. Live hairy crabs and mooncakes are available in season.

Malls

Singapore has hundreds of malls; many are multi-faceted venues that blur the lines between food, shopping and entertainment. Below are

Ngee Ann City. *See p141.*

Eat, Drink, Shop

the main ones. Opening times are for the mall in general; hours for individual shops can vary, as can the credit cards accepted.

Bugis Junction
200 Victoria Street, Bras Basah & Bugis (6557 6557/www.bugisjunction-mall.com.sg). Bugis MRT. **Open** 10am-10pm daily. **Map** p249 L5.
Formerly Singapore's red-light district, Bugis has been cleaned up and redeveloped. Straits-Chinese shophouses were glassed in to form part of this mall (also called Parco Bugis Junction), which contains Japanese department store Seiyu and plenty of teen-friendly shops. Of particular interest is the Edge, a collection of Japanese-inspired streetwear boutiques; purists dismiss it as a poor imitation of popular youth fashion destinations the Heeren Shops or Far East Plaza, but there are bargains.

Causeway Point
1 Woodlands Square, Woodlands (6894 2237/ www.causewaypoint.com.sg). Woodlands MRT. **Open** 10am-10.30pm daily.
So named because of its proximity to the bridge that links Singapore to Malaysia, Causeway Point is a typical suburban shopping mall. Expect the usual formula: cineplex, gaming arcade and a sprinkling of clothes and knick-knack shops that drive the heartlanders wild. Local department stores Metro and John Little, and supermarket chain Cold Storage, are anchor tenants.

Far East Plaza
14 Scotts Road, Orchard Road & Around (6734 6837/www.fareast-plaza.com). Orchard MRT. **Open** 10am-10pm daily. **Map** p247 F2.
When it comes to street fashion, this grubby five-level mall just off Orchard Road is the spot, offering everything from common Korean imports to rare cult items such as $2,000 sneakers. Basically, the more decrepit the shop, the cooler it is. Sub-culture types flock here to stock up on clothes, scoff cheap but delicious food and get tattooed and pierced – Far East Plaza has the largest concentration of tattoo parlours in Singapore.

The Heeren Shops
260 Orchard Road (6733 4725/www.heeren. com.sg). Somerset MRT. **Open** 10am-11pm daily. **Map** p247 G4.
A hangout for the young, trendy and impressionable, this cluster of boutiques was designed to mimic the frenetic youth mall of Tokyo's Harajuku. It hawks affordable streetwear (Instant Karma, Daytripper, Ed Hardy) and local independent fashion labels (Benno La Mode, Garçon, RE-, i.e.). Music shop HMV adds to the MTV vibe.

IMM
IMM Building, 2 Jurong East Street 21, Jurong (6665 8268/www.imm.sg). Jurong East MRT. **Open** 9am-11.30pm daily.
A bit far out in the west, but popular for dirt-cheap necessities and gizmos from Daiso and Giant Hypermart. A choice venue for bridal shows, it lures brides-to-be with its budget packages.

Marina Square
6 Raffles Boulevard, Marina (6339 8787/www. marinasquare.com.sg). City Hall MRT then 10mins walk. **Open** 11am-10pm daily. **Map** p251 M8.
Not too long ago, Marina Square was a dowdy mall, favoured by errant teenagers for its game arcades and middle-aged shoppers for its middle-aged offerings. After a makeover, it's practically unrecognisable, with hip new boutiques, an array of eateries and a plush new cineplex.

Ngee Ann City
391 Orchard Road (6739 9323/www.ngeeanncity. com.sg). Orchard MRT. **Open** 10am-9.30pm daily. **Map** p247 F4.
The choice venue for fashion shows and roadshows, this massive red granite building with two towers (A and B) is the lifeblood of Orchard Road, drawing throngs of locals and tourists. It's also known as Takashimaya Shopping Centre (aka Taka) after anchor tenant Takashimaya department store. It contains more than 130 shops, including Japanese giants Kinokuniya (books) and Best Denki (electronics), and over 30 food and drink outlets (from Indonesian to Korean). A branch of the National Library offers tomes for browsing, and a quiet café for rejuvenation. **Photo** *p139.*

Paragon
290 Orchard Road (6738 5535/www.paragonsc. com.sg). Orchard MRT. **Open** 10.30am-9pm daily. **Map** p247 F4.
Upmarket Paragon is Singapore's sleek epicentre of fashion. The new wing houses Gucci, Prada and Yves Saint Laurent boutiques, among others, while fine watch shops dot the old wing alongside younger fashion labels such as G-Star and Miss Sixty. There's also a large Marks & Spencer, spas and beauty parlours, a gourmet supermarket (in the basement) and a couple of famous restaurants.

Parkway Parade
80 Marine Parade Road, East Coast (6344 1242/ www.parkwayparade.com.sg). Bus 31, 36, 76, 135, 197. **Open** 9.30am-10pm daily. **Credit** AmEx, DC, JCB, MC, V.
An East Coast institution for more than 20 years, Parkway Parade contains 250 shops spread over six levels. The boutiques are varied, charming and surprisingly urban. Rent a Kiddy Cab to appease the tots while you check out Katong Cuty, a quirky, old-school lingerie shop.

Raffles Hotel Shopping Arcade
Raffles Hotel, 328 North Bridge Road, Colonial District (6337 1886/www.raffleshotel.com). City Hall MRT. **Open** 10.30am-7pm daily. **Map** p249 L6.
Surrounded by babbling birdbaths and pristine courtyards, well-heeled shoppers drop thousands at this semi-outdoor arcade at the iconic Raffles Hotel

Spend, spend, spend: shoppers of the world unite on **Orchard Road**.

(see p38). Bespoke tailors, art galleries, rare antiques and luxury labels (Louis Vuitton, Tiffany) match the grandeur of the setting.

Suntec City Mall

3 Temasek Boulevard, Marina (6825 2667/8/9/70/ www.sunteccity.com.sg). City Hall MRT then 10mins walk. **Open** 10am-9.30pm daily. **Map** p251 M7.
Though recently dethroned by VivoCity as the largest mall in Singapore, Suntec City is still so massive that shoppers are given pencil and paper to record the number of their parking space. Divided into four themed zones (Galleria, Tropics, Entertainment Centre and Fountain Terrace), it has over 350 shops and a barrage of eateries.

VivoCity

1 HarbourFront Walk, HarbourFront (6377 6860/ 70/www.vivocity.com.sg). HarbourFront MRT. **Open** 10am-10pm daily. **Map** p252 C1.
Opened in October 2006, VivoCity is practically the size of a town – a futuristic one complete with amphitheatre, rooftop pool and cinema complex. It's unlikely you'll cover all one million square feet of retail, leisure and entertainment space in a day, so conserve your energy. The shops are picture-pretty and varied; it also contains Singapore's first Gap.

Wisma Atria

435 Orchard Road (6235 2103/www.wismaonline. com). Orchard MRT. **Open** 7.30am-11pm daily. **Map** p247 E3.
Located next to Takashimaya SC, Wisma Atria commands quite a bit of human traffic, mainly for the Topshop flagship, local jewellery boutiques Aspial and Lee Hwa, and a lively food court on the top level called Food Republic.

Antiques

Antiques enclaves are scattered throughout the island. Within easy reach are **Pagoda Street** in Chinatown, and **Tanglin Shopping Centre** and **Tudor Court**, both on Tanglin Road. Further afield is leafy **Dempsey Road**, with its South-east Asian artefact shops.

Antiques Of The Orient

#2-40 Tanglin Shopping Centre, 19 Tanglin Road, Orchard Road & Around (6734 9351/www.aoto. com.sg). Orchard MRT then bus 7, 106, 111, 123, 174. **Open** 10.30am-6pm Mon-Sat; 11am-4pm Sun. **Map** p246 C3.
This quaint hole in the wall is an international authority and specialist purveyor of antiquarian maps, books, photographs and prints. Many pieces document early voyages and South-east Asia.

Galerie Cho Lon

#01-73 Chip Bee Gardens, 43 Jalan Merah Saga, Holland Village (6473 7922/www.cho-lon.com). Bus 7, 61, 75, 106, 970. **Open** 11am-7.30pm Mon-Fri; 11am-8.30pm Sat; noon-7pm Sun. **Credit** AmEx, MC, V.
A sprawling shop filled with an expertly curated collection of new and old furniture (Rajasthani bookshelves, Vietnamese beds) plus pretty accessories and knick-knacks. Cho Lon also has hundreds of literary travel books.

Books & magazines

Affectionately known as 'mama shops', newsstands are often owned and run by Indian stall owners. The selection of magazines – both local and imported – is astounding. Mass-market fashion glossies and niche hobby publications are fanned out on makeshift racks on street corners, or squeezed into a sliver of a shop in a mall. For the best selections, go to **Thambi Magazine Store** (2 Lorong Mambong, Holland Village, 6462 5031) and **Saranya Link** (#B1-15 Siglap Centre, 55 Siglap Road, East Coast, 6242 3454). **Bras Basah Complex** (231 Bain Street, Bras Basah & Bugis) is chock-a-block with stationery, printing, engraving and art supply shops. For couch potatoes, **www.bookcraves.com** rents books at a minimal fee, with delivery and pick-up thrown into the deal.

Borders Books, Music & Café

1F Wheelock Place, 501 Orchard Road (6235 7146/ www.borders.com.sg). Orchard MRT. **Open** 9am-11pm Mon-Thur, Sun; 9am-midnight Fri, Sat. **Credit** AmEx, DC, JCB, MC, V. **Map** p247 E3.
Said to be the most profitable branch of Borders in the world, this is also a popular meeting spot thanks to its browser-friendly approach. You can't miss it: the conical glass entrance of Wheelock Place is a landmark on Orchard Road. **Photo** *p140*.

Kinokuniya

#3-10/15 Takashimaya Shopping Centre, Tower B, Ngee Ann City, 391 Orchard Road (6737 5021/ www.kinokuniya.com.sg). Orchard MRT. **Open** 10am-9.30pm Sun; 10am-10pm Sat.
Credit AmEx, DC, JCB, MC, V. **Map** p247 F4.
With so many titles across so many genres (in English, Japanese, Chinese, German and French), this Japanese book giant's computerised search stations are a blessing. This is also where locals and Japanese expats come for their dose of manga. **Other locations:** #3-9 Bugis Junction, 200 Victoria Street, Brash Basah & Bugis (6339 1790); #3-50 Liang Court Shopping Centre, 177C River Valley Road, River Valley (6337 1300).

Sunny Bookshop

#3-58/59 Far East Plaza, 14 Scotts Road, Orchard Road & Around (6733 1583). Orchard MRT. **Open** 10.30am-8pm Mon-Thur; 10.30am-9pm Fri, Sat; 11.30am-7pm Sun. **Credit** MC, V. **Map** p247 F3.
Crammed with thousands of books, this tiny shop may seem daunting, but the well-read staff seem to have every title at their fingertips. Books – from bestsellers to classics to romance – come new or second-hand, and customers can rent or buy. The fantasy selection is hard to beat.

Specialist

Basheer

#4-19 Bras Basah Complex, 231 Bain Street, Bras Basah & Bugis (6336 0810/www.basheer graphic.com). City Hall MRT. **Open** 10am-8.30pm daily. **Credit** AmEx, MC, V. **Map** p249 L5.

Advertising types and creative souls make regular pilgrimages for the latest art books and design magazines. Owner Basheer possesses an encyclopaedic knowledge of advertising, animation, photography, fashion and design publications.

Books Actually

125A Telok Ayer Street, Chinatown (6221 1170/ www.booksactually.com). Tanjong Pagar MRT. **Open** 11am-9pm Mon-Sat. **No credit cards.** **Map** p250 J11.
Tucked away on the second floor of an old shophouse, this indie bookshop offers titles from small foreign presses and lesser-known works by renowned writers. Poetry readings are held every Saturday. Charming touches – hand-made poetry books, decorative vintage typewriters, jazz music – encourage lingering.

Earshot

1F The Arts House, Old Parliament House, 1 Old Parliament Lane, Colonial District (6334 0130/www.earshot.com.sg). City Hall or Raffles Place MRT. **Open** 11am-10pm daily. **Credit** AmEx, MC, V. **Map** p251 K9.
Two parts bookshop, one part music store, one part café, this cosy hideout has a lot covered. It's nestled in the Arts House (*see p202*), a multipurpose arts venue, so the promotion of local works – music, art and literature – is a priority. **Other locations:** #01-01/03 Esplanade Mall, 8 Raffles Avenue, Colonial District (6884 5658)

Select Books

#3-15 Tanglin Shopping Centre, 19 Tanglin Road, Orchard Road & Around (6732 1515/www.select books.com.sg). Orchard MRT then bus 7, 106, 111, 123, 174. **Open** 9.30am-6.30pm Mon-Sat; 10am-4pm Sun. **Credit** AmEx, JCB, MC, V. **Map** p246 C3.
A longtime specialist in books about South-east Asia or by authors from the region. Local politics is a forte. There's also a broader range of art, literature, business, design, history, religion and travel titles.

Children

Family-friendly malls such as **Forum The Shopping Mall** (583 Orchard Road, 6732 2469, www.forumtheshoppingmall.com), **United Square Shopping Mall** (101 Thomson Road, Thomson, 6251 5885, www.unitedsquare.com.sg) and **Tanglin Mall** (163 Tanglin Road, Orchard Road & Around, 6736 4922) are brimming with kids' boutiques, babycare shops and toy stores. Chainstore **Toys 'R' Us** (www.toysrus.com.sg), every child's fantasy, has seven branches around the island.

The Better Toy Store

#4-20F Takashimaya Shopping Centre, Tower B, Ngee Ann City, 391 Orchard Road (6836 4645). Orchard MRT. **Open** 10am-9.30pm daily. **Credit** AmEx, JCB, MC, V. **Map** p247 F4.

Time Out
Travel Guides

Far East

Time Out
Bangkok
& Beach Escapes

Time Out
Beijing

Time Out
Hong Kong

Time Out
Shanghai

Time Out
Singapore

Time Out
Tokyo 東京

A classy shop where mothers and children have been known to go gaga over the quality toys from brands like Haba. Screaming kids are conspicuous by their absence.
Other locations: #01-11/12 Tanglin Mall, 163 Tanglin Road, Orchard Road & Around (6836 2450).

Bookaburra
#02-03/04 Forum The Shopping Mall, 583 Orchard Road (6235 9232/www.bookaburra.com). Orchard MRT. **Open** 9.30am-8pm daily. **Credit** AmEx, MC, V. **Map** p246 D3.
A specialist children's bookshop, run by two Australians. Storytelling sessions ($5) are held at 4pm on Wednesday and Friday; call two days in advance to book a place.

Kids Mall
#3-121 IMM Building, 2 Jurong East Street 21, Jurong (6563 7677/www.kidsmall.com.sg). Jurong East MRT. **Open** 11am-9.30pm Mon-Fri, Sun; 11am-10pm Sat. **Credit** MC, V.
Clothes, cribs, strollers, toys and nursing accessories jostle for space in this family-themed mini-mall.

LIFEbaby
#2-78 VivoCity, 1 HarbourFront Walk HarbourFront (6376 9441/www.lifebaby.com). HarbourFront MRT. **Open** 10.30am-9.30pm daily. **Credit** AmEx, MC, V. **Map** p252 C1.
On a spin-off fashion label from homeware store LIFEShop, these hip Eastern-style clothes are adorned with Asian icons or motifs, and worn by fashionably precocious kids.
Other locations: #3-34 Raffles City Shopping Centre, 252 North Bridge Road, Colonial District (6338 3552).

Tai Sing
754 North Bridge Road, Arab Quarter (6291 2633/www.taising.com). Lavender MRT then bus 7, 32, 63, 80, 197. **Open** 9am-5.30pm Mon-Sat; 11am-7pm Sun. **Credit** AmEx, MC, V. **Map** p249 M4.
Flying cows, drumming chimpanzees and other cheap, kitsch toys are displayed from floor to ceiling. Hobbyists can choose from the plentiful range of miniature model cars, tanks and planes.

Cleaning & repair

The best cobblers and key cutters – the old men who set up shop on the pavement – are an endangered species nowadays. The few that remain are positioned outside the **Holland Village Market & Food Centre** (Holland Village), outside **Republic Plaza** (Raffles Place, CBD) and on the walkway between **Somerset MRT station** and **Specialists' Centre** (Orchard Road).

Presto Drycleaners
#4-00 Takashimaya Shopping Centre, Tower B, Ngee Ann City, 391 Orchard Road (6735 7477/www.prestodrycleaners.com.sg). Orchard MRT.

Open 10am-9pm Mon-Sat; 10am-5.30pm Sun. **Credit** MC, V. **Map** p247 F4
One of the largest dry-cleaning and laundry specialists in Singapore, Presto is recommended for leather and suede cleaning, as well as mending and garment alterations.
Other locations: throughout the city.

Shukey Services
#B1-004 Tower 5, Suntec City Mall, 3 Temasek Boulevard, Marina (6339 8833). City Hall MRT then 10mins walk. **Open** 11am-9pm Mon-Sat; noon-8pm Sun. **No credit cards. Map** p249 M6.
A reliable chain of repair shops, Shukey Services is the place to come when you need to get keys cut, holes punched in belts, or any leather goods (shoes, bags, jackets and boots) mended.
Other locations: throughout the city.

Electronics & cameras

Singapore has long been synonymous with bargains on electronic goods. These days, however, prices are cheaper in Hong Kong - but you can still find bargains in Singapore. To make sure you're getting a good deal, check market prices before you go, and make sure you get a worldwide guarantee. The big stores **Best Denki** (www.bestdenki.com.sg), **Courts** (www.courts.com.sg) and **Harvey Norman** have branches throughout the city and offer everything from headphones to electric shavers under one roof. **Mustafa Centre** (*see p138*) also has good prices, and there are plenty of electronics shops in the basements or first floors of older malls along Orchard Road (Lucky Plaza, *see p151*; Far East Plaza, *see p141*). A word of warning: the basement shops are notorious for persuading tourists to buy expensive bundles of needless accessories.

Funan DigitaLife Mall
109 North Bridge Road, Colonial District (6336 8327/www.funan.com.sg). City Hall MRT. **Open** 11am-8.30pm daily. **Map** p250 J8.
With its central location and orderly atmosphere, this huge mall offers the most relaxed electronics shopping experience. It has two specialist Apple outlets, including the Mac Shop (#04 11, 6334 1633), and plenty of shops selling digital cameras, MP3 players and games. The Challenger Superstore (6339 9000, www.challenger.com.sg) on the sixth floor sells digital goods of every model, gigabyte and price, while John 3:16 (#5-46, 63372877) is a reliable camera specialist. Staff are friendly and sometimes willing to negotiate. If you visit during one of the frequent shows held in the atrium, there are great deals.

iShop by Club 21
#3-04/05/06 Orchard Cineleisure, 8 Grange Road, Orchard Road & Around (6622 8988/http://ishop.club21.bz). Somerset MRT. **Open** 11am-9pm daily. **Credit** MC, V. **Map** p247 G4.

Beyond the mall

Shiny, sanitised shopping centres full of chainstores may predominate in Singapore, but there are alternatives. One-off boutiques and quirky specialists can be found, notably in various shopping pockets across town.

The brightly coloured conservation shophouses in the enclave formed by **Ann Siang Road, Erskine Road** and **Club Street** in Chinatown are home to an increasing number of hip-to-the-beat boutiques, offering expertly curated ranges of cult fashion, chic furniture and homeware, and quirky gifts. The baroque **Scarlet** hotel (*see p43*) forms an imposing landmark here, setting the tone for shops like **Egg3** (33 Erskine Road, 6536 6977), with its glossy homeware and graphic T-shirts, and **Asylum** (22 Ann Siang Road, 6324 2289, www.theasylum.com.sg, *pictured above*). The latter is one of Singapore's top design companies, with an office in the basement and a concept shop on ground level filled with vintage Enid Blyton books, art publications and clothing by too-cool-for-school local and international designers. Also here are **Front Row** (*see p147*), **Style:Nordic** (*see p159*), and **Venue Asia** (*see p147*).

Budget bohemia thrives in **Haji Lane**, a sliver of an alley sandwiched between Arab Street and Bali Lane in the Arab Quarter.

Mini boutiques mix with Middle Eastern shisha cafés and design houses. Hotspots include **Pluck** (No.31/33, 6396 4048) for kitschy cushions, jewellery, clothing, vintage fabrics and wallpaper, and a tiny ice-cream parlour; and **Salad** (No.25/27, 6299 5808), which specialises in black and white goods – from T-shirts to home accessories. Fashionistas flock to **Hoity Toity** (No.53A, 6396 6902, www.hoitytoity.com.sg) for pretty dresses from Australian designers; **House of Japan** (No.55, 6396 6657) for second-hand and vintage clothing from, er, Japan; and **White Room** (*see p148*). Indie music shop **Straits Records** (*see p159*) has recently moved one block over to Bali Lane.

While you're in the neighbourhood, browse the proliferation of ethnic shops along nearby **Bussorah Street**, the pedestrianised strip in front of the Sultan Mosque. **Zara Vintage Home Accents** (No.66, 6341 5901, http://zaravintage.com), **Zan's Loft** (No.34, 6392 1480, www.zansloft.com), **Grandfather's Collections** (No.42, 6299 4530) and **Merlor's Curios** (*see p154*) are crammed with retro goodies from Southeast Asia and the Middle East. **Arab Street**, which houses fabric emporium **Maruti Textiles** (*see p152*), is also worth a stroll. Opening times can be erratic, and most shops close around 6pm (earlier on Fridays, as this is a Muslim area).

Further afield, the **Dempsey Road** area, occupying the former British army barracks, is a great place for lovers of antiques, notably objets d'art from Indo-China. It's across from the Botanic Gardens, but you'll need a cab to get into the densely forested enclave. **Shang Antique & Craft** (#01-04/05 16 Dempsey Road, 6388 8838, www. shangantique.com.sg) sells antiques dating from the seventh century as well

---

Cutting-edge computer firm Apple and fashion empire Club 21 have produced this loungey, über-stylish offshoot. A fun way to buy Mac products.

Parisilk Electronics
15A Lorong Liput, Holland Village (6466 6002/ www.parisilk.com). Bus 7, 61, 75, 106, 165. **Open** 11am-8pm Mon-Sat; 11am-4pm Sun. **Credit** MC, V.

Discounted prices on electronics, home appliances and computers are the order of the day here, plus an impressive range of home and car audio equipment. Popular with expats.

Sim Lim Square
1 Rochor Canal Road, Bras Basah & Bugis (6338 3859/www.simlim.net). Bugis MRT. **Open** 11am-9pm daily. **Map** p249 L4.

as fine reproductions, while **Eastern Discoveries Antiques** (#01-04 26 Dempsey Road, 6475 1814, www. eastern-discoveries.com) has Buddha statuettes, wood carvings, jewellery, paintings and opium pipes. Restaurants and bars dot this verdant patch.

Holland Village is a much-loved shopping enclave, especially with expats, but the tight-knit community of **Chip Bee Gardens**, across from Holland Village proper, is way hipper. **Jalan Merah Saga** is the main drag. Food is a theme: in addition to cafés, restaurants and gourmet butchers, you'll find organic foodstore **Bunalun** (see p152), baked goods specialist **Phoon Huat** (#01-48 Block 44, 6471 5250, www. phoonhuat.com) and **Shermay's Cooking School** (#03-64 Block 43, 6479 8442, www.shermay.com). Antiques specialist **Galerie Cho Lon** (pictured below, see p142) is also here, as is **Work Loft @ Chip Bee**, which houses a number of funky art galleries (see p179).

Though rough around the edges, and full of sour-faced, hard-nosed shopkeepers, this old mall offers some of the best deals in town. Crammed with hundreds of tiny shops, it's a good bet for hard-to-find computer and electronic parts, but also crowded and frustrating. The higher you go, the lower the prices are for accessories and blank DVDs and CDs. Haggling is compulsory, but be warned: the great deals are matched by tremendous rip-offs.

Fashion

Westerners often have problems with Singapore's Asian sizing. Small equals US2/ UK8, medium is the equivalent of US4/UK10, large is a US6/UK12 and extra-large is US8/ UK14 – and that's often as big as it gets.

Boutiques

Local boutique chains **gg<5** and **m)phosis** are also worth a look: you won't find too much personality and quirkiness in the designs, but the togs are trendy and affordable.

Antipodean

27A Lorong Mambong, Holland Village (6463 7336/www.antipodeanshop.com). Bus 7, 61, 75, 106, 970. **Open** 11am-9pm daily. **Credit** AmEx, MC, V.
This sunny space is filled with top designerwear from Australia and New Zealand. The list includes Akira Isogawa, Body, Arabella Ramsey, Morrison, Nicola Finetti and One Teaspoon. Little-known but incredibly talented Aussie jewellery designer Elke Kramer sells her cool, crazy pieces here. Look for the shop above Harry's jazz bar.

Felt

#01-18 Capitol Building, 11 Stamford Road, Colonial District (6837 3393/www.felt.com.sg). City Hall MRT. **Open** 11am-8.30pm Mon-Sat, noon-6pm Sun. **Credit** AmEx, MC, V. **Map** p251 L8.
A haven for fashionistas, Felt makes you feel like a star with its in-store runway, cutting-edge threads and cult labels such as Tina Kalivas, Jayson Brunsdon and Lisa Ho from Australia. The boutique also carries Zambesi from New Zealand and the quirky designs of Hansel (see p149 **Home-grown talents**), Singapore's answer to Anna Sui.

Front Row

5 Ann Siang Road, Chinatown (6224 5502/ www.frontrowsingapore.com). Tanjong Pagar MRT. **Open** noon-8pm Mon-Sat. **Credit** MC, V. **Map** p250 I11.
From polished ready-to-wear by the likes of APC and United Bamboo to Dean & Deluca delicacies in the tea parlour, this three-storey shop packs in a bit of everything. Local fashion heroes such as Woods & Woods (see p149 **Home-grown talents**) and Twinkle by Wenlan are stocked, together with Umbro by Kim Jones, Carry Simone, Fab & Jo, and in-house label Crux for Front Row. The wearable art is complemented by a gallery space on the top floor.

Venue Asia

44-46 Club Street, Chinatown (6323 0640/ www.venue.com.sg). Chinatown MRT then 10mins walk. **Open** 11am-9pm daily. **Credit** AmEx, MC, V. **Map** p250 I10.
When the first Venue shop opened on Club Street a few years ago, the fashion set were in a tizzy about its cult labels such as Raf Simons, Nuala and Puma.

Now branches have sprouted around the island, bringing their Alexander McQueen-Puma hybrid sneakers to the masses.
Other locations: Venue Berlin #1-07 Palais Renaissance, 390 Orchard Road (6732 6140); **Venue Lab** #1-05 The Heeren Shops, 260 Orchard Road (6235 4655); **Venue VivoCity** #1-187 Tangs VivoCity, VivoCity, 1 HarbourFront Walk, HarbourFront (6303 8688).

White Room
37 Haji Lane, Arab Quarter (6297 1280/www.at whiteroom.com). Bugis MRT then 10mins walk. **Open** 1-8pm Mon-Sat. **Credit** MC, V. **Map** p249 M5.
The irreverent interior was inspired by the film *Eternal Sunshine of the Spotless Mind*: merchandise is displayed under a giant table, and smaller tables are turned on their head. Maverick local labels (Fru Fru & Tigerlily, Fantastik Antik and Stray) are stocked here. Holy Grail, the shop's accessories collection, includes funky cut-acrylic necklaces that spell out 'Drama Queen'.

Budget & mid-range

Budget shopping in Singapore means very, very cheap. Suburban neighbourhoods are a rich source of bargains, especially if you're looking for throwaway styles rather than quality – dresses and co-ordinates can be found for $20, often less. Some of the best shopping neighbourhoods are **Toa Payoh**, **Clementi**, **Whampoh** and **Ang Mo Kio**. As a rule of thumb, the heart of these shopping villages is around the MRT station. **City Plaza** in Geylang (810 Geylang Road), with its raft of fashion wholesalers, is dirt cheap.

Closet Affair
#03-96 Far East Plaza, 14 Scotts Road, Orchard Road & Around (6733 0396). Orchard MRT. **Open** 1.30-9.30pm daily. **Credit** AmEx, MC, V. **Map** p247 F3.
Closet Affair is like the well-edited wardrobe of a stylish bohemian girl. Vintage-inspired dresses, catwalk-current prints and frothy skirts hang in mock closets. Make your way to the glass case at the back: it's a glitter-fest of accessories, hand-made from vintage parts by local jewellery designers.

CYC Shanghai Shirt Co
#02-21 Raffles Hotel Shopping Arcade, Raffles Hotel, 328 North Bridge Road, Colonial District (6336 3556/www.cyccustomshop.com). City Hall MRT. **Open** 10.30am-7.30pm Mon-Sat; 11am-7pm Sun. **Credit** AmEx, MC, V. **Map** p249 L6.
Although this bespoke tailor is in the swanky Raffles Hotel Shopping Arcade, it's good value. Its claim to fame is that Senior Minister Lee Kwan Yew is partial to its finely crafted shirts. Designed for men and women, these are customised according to colour, fabric, cut, even down to the buttons, cuffs, collars and monograms.

Other locations: #01-21 Republic Plaza, 9 Raffles Place, CBD (6538 0522).

Feng
120 Sophia Road, Orchard Road & Around (6334 9752). Dhoby Ghaut MRT then 10mins walk. **Open** 10am-6pm Mon-Fri. **No credit cards.** **Map** p248 J4.
Advanced appointments are vital to secure a sitting with this fine Chinese tailor. Feng is Mandarin for 'sew', and the seamstresses at this shophouse can bring to life almost any pattern you dream up. Their specialities are cheongsams and evening dresses.

Flowers In The Attic
#04-35 The Heeren Shops, 260 Orchard Road (6737 9665). Somerset MRT. **Open** 11am-9.30pm daily. **Credit** AmEx, MC, V. **Map** p247 G4.
Local singing star Kit Chan co-owns this girlie boutique tucked away in the Heeren Shops. Cute, perky and feminine are the operative words: floral blouses and ruched dresses fly off the shelves, as do the whimsical, hand-made accessories.

Forever 21
#B1-21 Wisma Atria, 435 Orchard Road (6238 6656). Orchard MRT. **Open** 10.30am-10pm Mon-Thur, Sun; 10am-10pm Fri, Sat. **Credit** AmEx, MC, V. **Map** p247 E3.
Whatever you're looking for, from fancy denims to party frocks, casual wear to sensible work clothes, chances are you'll find it under a pile at this American chain. And it won't cost much. The accessories racks are brimming with ethnic earrings, enamel bangles and other knick-knacks, while gorgeous knickers come at flimsy prices.
Other locations: #1-71 VivoCity, 1 HarbourFront Walk, HarbourFront (6376 9091).

This Fashion
MacDonald House, 26-36 Orchard Road (6336 9594/www.thisfashion.com.sg). Dhoby Ghaut MRT. **Open** 10am-10pm daily. **Credit** AmEx, DC, MC, V. **Map** p248 I5.
This chain of boutiques, the largest in the country, is synonymous with (sometimes cheesy) catwalk knock-offs and low prices. A good place at which to fill up a suitcase with trendy but disposable gear.
Other locations: throughout the city.

Designer

There's no shortage of international high-fashion brands in Singapore. Many are concentrated at designer enclaves on Orchard Road, including sleek **Paragon** (*see p141*), **Palais Renaissance** (390 Orchard Road, 6737 1520), **Hilton Shopping Gallery** (Hilton Hotel, 581 Orchard Road, 6734 5250, www.hilton.com) and **DFS Galleria Scottswalk** (25 Scotts Road, 6229 8100, www.dfsgalleria.com). Also try the **Raffles Hotel Shopping Arcade** (*see p141*).

Home-grown talents

Singapore's local fashion scene is tiny compared to the giants of Milan and Paris, but there's a healthy number of world-class talents here. Most designers have to go abroad to achieve success and recognition, but their creations are available at home too. Here are a few names to look out for.

Baylene
www.baylene.com.
Baylene's eponymous fashion label is a toddler in fashion terms at only three years old, but her use of charcoal, jet black and stark white, graphic shapes and fine pleats is very grown-up. She recently launched a men's collection – Baylene's Boyfriend – in the hope of changing the drab face of the local menswear scene.
Baylene is available at #01-04 Stamford House, 39 Stamford Road, Colonial District (6336 9619); #03-27 Mandarin Gallery, 333 Orchard Road (6333 8132). Baylene's Boyfriend is available at **Bulb** *(see p158).*

Benno La Mode
The Victorian-inspired, crazed creations of Medan-born Benno Asmoro are found on the Benno La Mode label. His dresses, blouses and skirts are sexy and flouncy, but they fall surprisingly well on the body. The man himself often functions as sales assistant at his own boutique.
Available at #04-06A & #04-07 The Heeren Shops, 260 Orchard Road (6732 2886).

Fling
www.fling-undress.com.
Central St Martin-trained lingerie designer Goh Ling Ling has an industry advantage: her family owns an undergarment manufacturing business. Her cheeky, stylish bra-and-knicker sets have caught the attention of Beams in Japan, Fenwick and Koh Samui in London, D-Mob in Hong Kong and Follie Follie in Italy. Her Fling boutique is a girlie wonderland, complete with heavy-curtained, ornately wallpapered dressing rooms and a manicure corner.
Available at Fling, #04-05A The Heeren Shops, 260 Orchard Road (6732 0067).

Hansel
www.ilovehansel.com.
Former fashion stylist Jo Soh is possibly the freshest, most fun and unpredictable designer in Singapore. Her label Hansel (named after her Jack Russell terrier) is a big hit in the Western world, especially Australia. Her designs are quirky, vibrant and varied, often inspired by trivial topics – candies, for instance, or pet camels.
Available at Felt (see p147).

Nicholas
www.nicholasnic.com.
Nic Wong's label Nicholas has recently had fashion critics sitting up and taking notice. His trinity of collections – Gold, Black and Pink – shrewdly captures several corners of the fashion market. Gold features romantic, flowy, feminine dresses in touch-me fabrics like silk and cotton voile; Black offers edgy, androgynous pieces; while Pink (the youngest of the three) is casual and cutesy, with corsages and ribbons.
Available at #02-04 Stamford House, 39 Stamford Road, Colonial District (6339 0223).

Woods & Woods
www.woods-woods.com.
Jonathan Seow has won numerous accolades for his Woods & Woods label, and regularly shows his Femme and Homme collections at Berlin and Paris Fashion Weeks, among others. The look is understated, the colours neutral. But genius is in the details: look closer and discover the fine stitching and his commitment to quality fabrics.
Available at Front Row (see p147).

Club 21 Ladies
#01-02 Four Seasons Hotel, 190 Orchard Boulevard (6235 0753/www.clubtwentyone.com). Orchard MRT. **Open** *10am-7pm Mon-Sat; 11am-6pm Sun.* **Credit** *AmEx, DC, JCB, MC, V.* **Map** *p246 D4.*
The largest high-fashion chain, Club 21 runs a string of mono-brand boutiques for the likes of Armani, Balenciaga, Calvin Klein, Dolce & Gabbana and Paul Smith (to name a few). Its flagship multi-label store carries the best of the prêt-à-porter collections from Dries Van Noten; Viktor & Rolf; Alexander McQueen; Martin Margiela and more. The shop directly opposite, Club 21 Men, is a three-storey, sleek temple of metrosexual style .

The Link
#02-02 Mandarin Gallery, Meritus Mandarin Hotel, 333 Orchard Road (6733 7185/www.thelink.com.sg). Somerset MRT. **Open** *10.30am-8pm Mon-Sat; 1-7pm Sun.* **Credit** *AmEx, DC, JCB, MC, V.* **Map** *p247 G4.*

Eat, Drink, Shop

This chi-chi boutique has been dressing the city's fashion elite for decades. The refined collection – including pieces by Alessandro Dell'Acqua, Roberto Cavalli and Vera Wang – is curated by local fashion icon and socialite Tina Tan-Leo.
Other locations: The Link Home #01-10 Palais Renaissance, 390 Orchard Road (6737 7503); **The Link Bagbar** #01-31 Paragon, 290 Orchard Road (6235 5965); **The Link Wedding** Shangri-La Hotel Singapore, Orange Grove Road, Orchard Road & Around (6235 4648).

Mumbai Se

#02-03 Palais Renaissance, 390 Orchard Road (6733 7188/www.mumbaise.com). Orchard MRT. **Open** 10.30am-8pm Mon-Sat; 11am-7pm Sun. **Credit** AmEx, DC, JCB, MC, V. **Map** p246 D3.
Singapore's first high-end Indian fashion store, luxurious Mumbai Se showcases a revolving array of avant-garde fashion designers. Baroque-style mirrors and ornate chaise longues are juxtaposed with modern Ganesha statues and Zen-style paintings. The clothes are unmistakeably Indian – vibrant colours, heavy prints and lashings of crystals and beads. Bollywood, here we come.

Streetwear

There's streetwear, and then there's streetwear. To the uninitiated, the shops at the **Edge** in **Bugis Junction** (*see p140*) are acceptable for a casual day out; further up the fashion chain, the **Heeren Shops** (*see p141*) is an enclave for local labels; and **Far East Plaza** (*see p141*) is absolutely the epicentre of street fashion.

Ambush/Surrender

119 Devonshire Road, Orchard Road & Around (6733 2130/www.ambushstore.com/ www.surrenderous.com). Somerset MRT. **Open** 1-9pm daily. **Credit** AmEx, DC, JCB, MC, V. **Map** p247 F5.
Surrender, a collaboration by local designer Earn Chen and DJ extraordinaire James Lavelle, is a sought-after label on the streets of New York, Tokyo and LA. It represents the highest spectrum of the streetwear rainbow (labels include Neighbourhood, Visvim, Headporter Plus) with sometimes astronomical prices. It shares accommodation with Ambush, whose men's labels include Original Fake, NYthing and Good Enough UK, in a two-storey conservation shophouse on Devonshire Road.

BlackJack

#01-10 Forum The Shopping Mall, 583 Orchard Road (6735 0975). Orchard MRT. **Open** 10.30am-7.30pm Mon-Sat; 11am-6pm Sun. **Credit** AmEx, DC, JCB, MC, V. **Map** p246 D3.
Designer streetwear – a contradiction in terms if ever there was one – often means spending an obscene amount of dough to look sloppy. Cult international labels such as Edwin, Sass & Bide, Dsquared2 and

Trovata are good examples. Also look for Edun: an eco-friendly, poetic collection by U2's Bono, his wife Ali Hewson and New York designer Rogan Gregory.

Flesh Imp

#03-27 Wisma Atria, 435 Orchard Road (6238 6738/www.fleshimp.com). Orchard MRT. **Open** 10.30am-9.30pm daily. **Credit** AmEx, DC, JCB, MC, V. **Map** p247 E3.
This mid-priced local street label is hot in both the fashion and club scenes. Several DJs are walking models for the brand, as are a few local party animals. Occasional collaborations with American graffiti artists, such as the San Francisco-based Sam Flores, gives Flesh Imp added street cred.
Other locations: #B1-32B Plaza Singapura, 68 Orchard Road (6238 8678); #04-17 The Heeren Shops, 260 Orchard Road (6235 2258).

77th Street

#01-33/35 Far East Plaza, 14 Scotts Road, Orchard Road & Around (6734 7767/www.77th street.com). **Open** 11am-9.30pm daily. **Credit** AmEx, DC, JCB, MC, V. **Map** p247 E3.
This chain was a streetwear pioneer in Singapore. Expect affordable singlets, tops, low-slung jeans, backpacks, bandanas and studded belts. The range of accessories is dazzling: sterling silver ear studs and hoops of every size, metal dog-tags, and all the bling a rapper could ever want.
Other locations: throughout the city.

S.O.U.L.S.

#01-14 The Riverwalk, 20 Upper Circular Road, Boat Quay (6557 0121). Clarke Quay MRT. **Open** noon-9pm Mon-Sat; 1-7pm Sun. **No credit cards.** **Map** p250 J8.
This new shop is where to come to for cult labels like Hellz Bellz, Haze and Crooks & Castles. Hard-to-get items (limited-edition Haze watches, for instance) are reasonably priced. Bern, the owner, supports local talent with a passion, and uses local sneaker artists to customise Nikes.

Vintage & second-hand

Bordello Princess (www.bordelloprincess.com), considered a vintage prêt-à-porter label, carries pieces that are lush, rare and European in style. You'll find a small selection at **Pluck** (31/33 Haji Lane, Arab Quarter, 6396 4048).

The Attic Lifestyle Store

#04-146A Far East Plaza, 14 Scotts Road, Orchard Road & Around (6732 3459). Orchard MRT. **Open** 2.30-9.30pm daily. **No credit cards.** **Map** p247 F3.
There's hardly any space to move in this tiny, dimly lit shop, crammed as it is with treasures. Expect vintage clothing and costume jewellery, 1970s lamps and nostalgic knick-knacks.

Oppt Shop

#04-36 The Heeren Shops, 260 Orchard Road (6733 9406/www.opptshop.com). Somerset MRT.

Open 11am-9.30pm daily. **Credit** AmEx, DC, JCB, MC, V. **Map** p247 G4.
Not the best-looking shop in town, but the good range of vintage threads – from the US, Canada and Japan – makes up for it. The in-house jewellery designs are pretty, well made and reasonably priced.

Salvation Army Family Store
309 Upper Serangoon Road, Little India (6288 5438/www.salvationarmy.org.sg). Woodleigh MRT. **Open** 10am-5.45pm Mon-Sat. **No credit cards.**
While one-off pieces make good finds, you might be lucky enough to stumble upon whole batches of dead stock – new but discontinued shoes and clothes – donated by corporations. Prices are low, as you'd expect, but leafing through rack upon rack of dusty clothes can be hard work. **Other locations:** throughout the city.

Swirl
#02-05 Stamford House, 39 Stamford Road, Colonial District (6338 5020/www.ilovetoswirl.com). City Hall MRT. **Open** noon-8.30pm Mon-Sat. **Credit** AmEx, DC, JCB, MC, V. **Map** p251 K8.
This girlie shop is decked out with chandeliers and pink walls. Swirl around in exclusive frocks made from rare vintage fabrics, designed by owners Evelyn Foo and Suzanne Sng. You'll also find classic vintage apparel and accessories, as well as quaint notebooks and lampshades.

Fashion accessories

Jewellery

Popular chains, selling reasonably priced jewellery to the masses and with branches everywhere, include **Lee Hwa** (www.leehwa.com.sg), **Gold Heart** (www.goldheart.com.sg), **Soo Kee** (www.sookee.com.sg) and **Poh Heng** (www.pohheng.com.sg). You'll find **Cartier** and **Tiffany** at **Ngee Ann City** (*see p140*) and **Van Cleef & Arpels** at DFS Galleria Scottswalk (25 Scotts Road, Orchard Road & Around, 6229 8173, www.vancleef-arpels.com). Serangoon Road in Little India is home to many goldsmith shops, often Chinese-run. Many have abolished the archaic price-by-weight structure, though the **Mustafa Centre** (*see p139*) has a huge jewellery department that still sells gold pieces by weight.

De Stijl Collection
#B1-05 Palais Renaissance, 390 Orchard Road (6536 4906/www.destijl.com.sg). Orchard MRT. **Open** 11.30am-7.30pm Mon-Sat; noon-5pm Sun. **Credit** AmEx, DC, JCB, MC, V. **Map** p246 D3.
One of the best (yet underrated) Singaporean jewellery designers, De Stijl fashions pieces with imagination and whimsy, without going over-the-top. Refined finish and workmanship, along with reasonable prices, add to the appeal.

Pomellato
#01-17 Hilton Shopping Gallery, Hilton Hotel, 581 Orchard Road (6235 3152/www.pomellato.com). Orchard MRT. **Open** 10am-7pm Mon-Sat; 11am-6pm Sun. **Credit** AmEx, DC, JCB, MC, V. **Map** p246 D3.
Brushed gold, molten shapes and coloured precious stones are the mainstays of Pomellato. This Italian outfit walks the line between fashion and jewellery better than any other.

Lingerie

The second-floor lingerie department at **Tangs** (*see p138*) has some of the best underwear labels and plush, private dressing rooms.

Blush! Lingerie Boutique
#03-09 Scotts Shopping Centre, 6 Scotts Road, Orchard Road & Around (6733 4830). Orchard MRT. **Open** 11am-9pm Mon-Fri, Sun; 11am 9.30pm Sat. **Credit** AmEx, DC, JCB, MC, V. **Map** p247 E3.
A good range of mid-priced underwear – more functional than decorative. Ideal if you're looking for push-up bras, second-skin thongs and see-through camisoles from Chantal Thomas, Princesse Tam Tam, Dim, Wonderbra and Vanity Fair. **Other locations:** #03-20 Paragon, 290 Orchard Road (6235 2009); #02-13 OUB Centre, 1 Raffles Place, CBD; #02-49 Centrepoint, 176 Orchard Road (6836 9781); #02-24 Tampines Mall, 4 Tampines Central 5, Tampines (6781 0190).

Chalone
#02-16 Wisma Atria, 435 Orchard Road (6735 9463/www.chalone.com.sg). Orchard MRT. **Open** 11am-9pm daily. **Credit** AmEx, DC, MC, V. **Map** p247 E3.
Indulge your senses with premium French lingerie from the likes of Lejaby, Simone Perèle and Billet Doux. There's also functional seamless lingerie by Nuage Lejaby in basic shades. **Other locations:** #1-76 Millenia Walk, 9 Raffles Boulevard, Colonial District (6337 2647); #1-119 VivoCity, 1 Harbour Front Walk, HarbourFront (6376 9787).

Luggage & bags

Aside from the liberal smattering of luggage shops at **Lucky Plaza** (304 Orchard Road, 6235 3294, www.luckyplaza.com.sg), two of the best places for suitcases and bags are the very affordable **Mustafa Centre** (*see p139*) and department stores such as **Tangs** (*see p138*).

Colette
#03-13 Forum The Shopping Mall, 583 Orchard Road (6333 8589). Orchard MRT. **Open** 10.30am-8pm daily. **Credit** AmEx, MC, V. **Map** p247 F4.
This characterful shop stocks quirky bags and the odd piece of jewellery. Indie handbag and accessory labels like My Apartment In London, little odd for est, Exquisite J and Comfort Station are stocked.

Planet Traveller

*#03-113 Marina Square, 6 Raffles Boulevard,
Marina (6337 0291/www.planettraveller.com).
City Hall MRT then 10mins walk.* **Open** 11am-9pm
daily. **Credit** AmEx, DC, MC, V. **Map** p251 M8.
A one-stop travel shop. Labels include Victorinox,
Samsonite and Mandarina Duck.
Other locations: #04-15/16 Paragon, 290 Orchard
Road (6732 5172).

Scarves & textiles

You'll find bale after bale of vibrant fabric in
Singapore's ethnic shopping zones. Try the
Golden Landmark Complex (390 Victoria
Street) and **Textile Centre** (200 Jalan Sultan)
in the Arab Quarter; **People's Park Centre**
(101 Upper Cross Street) in Chinatown; and
shops in Little India. Prices vary wildly, and
bargaining is recommended: prices are often
marked up by as much as 50 per cent.

Bin House

*#02-12F Tower B, Ngee Ann City, 391 Orchard
Road (6733 6789/www.binhouse.com). Orchard
MRT.* **Open** 11am-8pm Mon-Sat; 11am-7pm Sun.
Credit AmEx, DC, JCB, MC, V. **Map** p247 F4.
The traditional Indonesian art of cloth making – ikat
weaving, batik dyeing and tie-dyeing – takes centre
stage here. You can find cheaper options elsewhere,
but these hand-woven, artisan-made pieces will
stand the test of time.

Maruti Textiles

*93 Arab Street, Arab Quarter (6392 0253). Bugis
MRT then 10mins walk.* **Open** 9am-6pm Mon-Sat.
Credit AmEx, DC, JCB, MC, V. **Map** p249 M5.
If you're browsing on Arab Street, you won't (and
shouldn't) miss this garish, charming shop. The
stock, from linens and tablecloths to fabulously
detailed sari fabrics, is from India, and the quality
is a cut above the rest. As are the prices.

Shoes

LeftFoot

*#02-07A Orchard Cineleisure, 8 Grange Road,
Orchard Road & Around (6736 3227/www.left
foot.com.sg). Somerset MRT.* **Open** 12.30-10pm
Mon-Thur, Sun; 12.30-11.30pm Fri, Sat. **Credit**
AmEx, DC, JCB, MC, V. **Map** p247 F5.
Among the racks of streetwear trainers, you'll find
limited editions from Bathing Ape, Nike, Adidas,
Converse, Vans and Vis Vims – sold at prices that
are close to retail.
Other locations: #03-94 (6734 3227) & #03-16
(6735 3227) Far East Plaza, 14 Scotts Road, Orchard
Road & Around.

M.A.D. Shoes

*#01-274, 183 Toa Payoh Central, Toa Payoh
(6356 8978/www.mad-shoes.com). Toa Payoh MRT.*
Open 10am-10pm daily. **Credit** AmEx, MC, V.

When caught with blisters from an unwise shoe
choice, you'll be thankful for the nearest MAD store.
OK, the shoes aren't exactly Manolos, but they
interpret the latest trends at rock-bottom prices.
Other locations: throughout the city.

On Pedder

*#02-12P/Q Tower B, Ngee Ann City, 391 Orchard
Road (6835 1307). Orchard MRT.* **Open** 11am-
8pm daily. **Credit** AmEx, DC, JCB, MC, V.
Map p247 F4.
The designer shoes and tiny designer bags are
almost too pretty to use. This large, multi-label shop
also stocks pricey but irresistible jewellery from
obscure designers. In-house label Pedder Red is
cheaper, and available in a boutique one level down.

Tangs + Co

*#2F Tangs Orchard, 310 Orchard Road (6737
5500/www.cktang.com). Orchard MRT.* **Open**
10.30am-9.30pm Mon-Sat; 11am-8.30pm Sun.
Credit AmEx, DC, JCB, MC, V. **Map** p247 E3.
Middle-of-the-range designer shoes are the order of
the day, along with finely crafted satin Mary Janes,
grosgrain-beribboned spike heels and beaded
sandals. Complete the look with tasteful designer
clothing, dainty bags and accessories, plus decadent
scented treats at Tangs + Co Beauty.
Other locations: #B1-05 Tower A, Ngee Ann City,
391 Orchard Road (6732 7003); #01-187 Tangs
VivoCity, VivoCity, 1 HarbourFront Walk,
HarbourFront (6303 8688).

Food & drink

Wet markets such as **Tekka Market** (665
Buffalo Road, Little India, **photo** *p153*) offer
fresh meat, fruit and vegetables, seafood, spices,
dried foods and, of course, deliciously cooked
local fare. Two of the best food halls are at
Takashimaya (*see p139*), where you'll find
Japanese savouries, Chinese desserts, meat-
filled rice dumplings and quirky items like
prata-wrapped sausages, plus a cluster of fine
food shops. **Tangs** (*see p138*) has a gelato
stand, sushi takeaway counter, Peranakan
snack bar, bean-curd stand and a fresh fruit
and veg section.

Aussimart

*70 Race Course Road, Little India (6291 6534).
Little India MRT.* **Open** 11.30am-6pm, 7-10pm
Mon-Fri; 11.30am-3pm, 7-10pm Sat; 11.30am-3pm
Sun. **No credit cards. Map** p248 K2.
This hole-in-the-wall specialist is stocked with the
best of Australian food and drink. Expect lollies,
breakfast cereals, canned and bottled drinks, house-
hold items and fresh foods. Excellent prices.

Bunalun

*#01-70 Chip Bee Gardens, 43 Jalan Merah Saga,
Holland Village (6472 0870/www.bunalun.com.sg).
Bus 7, 61, 75, 106, 970.* **Open** 9am-9pm daily.
Credit AmEx, MC, V.

This organic store stands apart from the crowd by producing its own jams, spices, condiments and teas. It also does a range of organic skincare and home toiletries, though it's pricey by local standards. This location serves breakfasts and lunches, and there's a branch in Takashimaya.

Candy Empire

#B2-32 VivoCity, 1 HarbourFront Walk, HarbourFront (6376 9610). HarbourFront MRT. **Open** 11am-10pm daily. **Credit** AmEx, DC, JCB, MC, V. **Map** p252 C1.

Those who lack self-discipline should stay away from the biggest sweet shop in Singapore. Candy-sprinkled chocolates, biscuits, potato crisps and other treats fill the shelves.

Other locations: #01-95/98 Millenia Walk, 9 Raffles Boulevard, Colonial District (6336 2968).

German Market Place

609 Bukit Timah Road, Bukit Timah (6466 4044). Bus 74, 151, 170, 171, 174 **Open** 10am-7pm Mon-Sat. **Credit** AmEx, MC, V. **Map** p248 J2.

Aside from the usual Bavarian suspects like beer and bratwurst, German sweets are also sold

Hédiard

Tudor Court, 125 Tanglin Road, Orchard Road & Around (6333 6683/www.hediard.com.sg), Orchard MRT then bus 7, 106, 111, 123, 174. **Open** 10.30am-8.30pm daily. **Credit** AmEx, DC, JCB, MC, V. **Map** p246 C3.

A slice of Paris in Singapore, this fine French deli is the place to go to for caviar, wines, liqueurs, cordials, fruit jellies, olive oils and condiments.

Lana Cakes

36 Greenwood Avenue, Bukit Timah (6466 5315/ 8940). Bus 74, 151, 170, 171, 174 then 5mins walk. **Open** 10.30am-5.30pm Wed-Fri; 10.30am-4.30pm Sat. **No credit cards.**

This Singapore legend looks more like an aunt's cosy house than a bustling cake business. Violet Kwan, aged 78, has been selling rich, home-baked chocolate fudge cakes (500g or 1kg) for over 40 years. They don't look fancy, but they taste like heaven.

Layers Lapis

52 Burnfoot Terrace, East Coast (6876 1108/ www.layerslapis.com). Bus 10, 12, 14, 40, 155. **Open** 4-8pm Tue-Sun. **No credit cards.**

Kueh lapis is a traditional, rich layer cake made from eggs and butter; some of the best recipes are said to come from Peranakan grannies. Owner Bruce Ngam offers four permutations of his family recipe: classic, prune, liqueur and the works (prune and liqueur). Advance orders are essential.

L'Organic Market

Block 18 Dempsey Road, Orchard Road & Around (6836 1091/www.lorganic.sg). Orchard MRT then bus 7, 105, 106, 111, 123, 174. **Open** 9am-3pm Wed; 8am-2pm Sat. **No credit cards.**

Tekka Market. *See p152.*

Eat, Drink, Shop

Amble among displays of beurre bosc pears, pink lady apples, baby spinach, mesclun and pumpkins at this outdoor organic market – Singapore's first. Over 60 items are sold, including fresh herbs, veggies, fruit, dried fruit, oils, coffees, teas, syrups, pastas, vinegars and freshly baked breads.

Meidi-Ya
#B1-50 Liang Court Shopping Centre, 177 River Valley Road, River Valley (6339 1111/www.meidi-ya.com.sg). Clarke Quay MRT. **Open** 10am-10pm daily. **Credit** AmEx, JCB, MC, V. **Map** p250 I8.
The Japanese expat community could never get by without Meidi-Ya. It consists of a fully fledged Japanese supermarket, as well as sweet shops, a pharmacy, gelato stand, several food stands and a restaurant – all Japanese.

Sins Choc Shoppe Boutique
#01-85 Millenia Walk, 9 Raffles Boulevard, Colonial District (6337 0755/www.sinschoc.com). **Open** 10.30am-9pm daily. **Credit** AmEx, DC, JCB, MC, V. **Map** p251 M8.
This popular chain deserves kudos for its Valentine-worthy packaging and pretty candy. See if you can stomach exotic creations like durian truffles.
Other locations: 1F Atrium, Centrepoint, 176 Orchard Road (6734 3469); #01-17 Republic Plaza 3, 9 Raffles Place, CBD (6557 0023); #01-K1 HarbourFront Centre, 1 Maritime Square, HarbourFront (6276 7567).

Yixing Xuan Teahouse
30 Tanjong Pagar Road, Chinatown (6224 6961/ 6324 4780/www.yixingxuan-teahouse.com). Outram MRT then 10mins walk. **Open** 11am-10pm Mon-Sat; 11am-7pm Sun. **Credit** AmEx, DC, JCB, MC, V. **Map** p250 H12.
A shop, teahouse and Chinese restaurant rolled into one. Buy leaves (green, black, white, oolong, pu-erh) and tea-making equipment, or pop by for a tea appreciation workshop.

Gifts & speciality shops

Explore **Little India Arcade** (48 Serangoon Road, Little India) for garish but great jewellery; **Bussorah Street** in the Arab Quarter for hand-woven baskets, tie-dye fabrics and retro knick-knacks; **Holland Road Shopping Centre** (211 Holland Avenue, Holland Village) for South-east Asian gifts and homeware; and **Peace Centre** (1 Sophia Road, Orchard Road & Around) for an assortment of oriental curiosities.

DFS Galleria Scottswalk (25 Scotts Road, Orchard Road & Around, 6229 8100, www.dfsgalleria.com) sells Merlion-shaped chocolates, sarong kebayas for kids and assorted Singapore memorabilia that you could haul home in bulk. Bring your passport and plane tickets along: your purchases are delivered to you at the airport when you depart.

Museum Shop by Banyan Tree (www.museumshop.com.sg) sells quality replicas, museum-inspired furnishings, stationery, apparel and accessories, as well as Asian crafts and books. It has outlets at the **Asian Civilisations Museum** (*see p58*), **National Museum of Singapore** (*see p60*) and **Singapore Art Museum** (*see p76*). The gift shop at the **Chinatown Heritage Centre** (*see p66*) is good for nostalgic reminders of old Singapore.

Jothi Store & Flower Shop
1 Campbell Lane, Little India (6338 7008/ www.jothi.com.sg). Little India MRT. **Open** 9am-9pm daily. **No credit cards. Map** p248 K3.
The heady scent of jasmine garlands hangs in the air at this crammed Indian mart. The flowers are sold specifically for Hindu offerings, as are other prayer items like incense sticks and statues of gods. A multitude of general items can also be found: garish crafts, glass bangles, human-hair buns and braids, toiletries and food.

JR Texas
#03-33 Peninsula Shopping Complex, 3 Coleman Street, Colonial District (6334 3534). City Hall MRT. **Open** noon-8pm Mon-Sat; 1-6pm Sun. **Credit** DC, JCB, MC, V. **Map** p250 J8.
From cowboy hats to boots, this quirky shop specialises in all things from the Wild West. There are kitsch badges, stylish belts and enough paraphernalia to kit out a spaghetti western.

Lim's Arts & Living
#02-01 Holland Road Shopping Centre, 211 Holland Avenue, Holland Village (6467 1300). Bus 7, 61, 75, 106, 970. **Open** 10am-8.30pm daily. **Credit** AmEx, DC, JCB, MC, V.
This large, family-owned emporium is bursting with reasonably priced furniture and furnishings, crafts, artworks, table linen, cutlery and regional artefacts. Typical treasures include Peranakan lace doilies, wooden wind chimes and Chinese silk slippers.

MAAD
Red Dot Traffic, 28 Maxwell Road, Chinatown (6534 7209/www.maad.sg). Tanjong Pagar MRT. **Open** 11am-6pm Sun. **Credit** MC, V. **Map** p250 H12.
This weekly flea market feels more like a special exhibition: only original works are sold. Custom-printed T-shirts, hand-crafted jewellery, framed pieces made of intricate Peranakan cutlery and self-published art books share the space with installation art. The Red Dot Traffic building is bright red – you can't miss it.

Merlor's Curios
39 Bussorah Street, Arab Quarter (6292 3934). Bugis MRT then 15mins walk/bus 100, 107, 961, 980. **Open** 10am-6pm daily. **Credit** AmEx, DC, JCB, MC, V. **Map** p249 M4.
The rest of the world has yet to discover this quaint, hole in the wall, so make the most of it. You never

know what you'll find: framed vintage Peranakan tiles, old teak dining tables, retro lamps, wrought-iron furniture, batik or metal evening bags.

No. 1 Costume

32 Aliwal Street, Arab Quarter (6333 9440).
Bus 100, 107, 961, 980. **Open** 10.30am-8pm Mon-Fri; 10am-5pm Sat. **Credit** AmEx, DC, JCB, MC, V.
Map p249 N4.

The biggest costume rental place in town. You name it, they've got it: nuns and bishops, gingerbread men and ketchup bottles, police and crooks, doctors and nurses, fairies and demons. And if they don't stock it, they'll make it for you.

Oohtique

50A Circular Road, Boat Quay (6557 0469/
www.oohtique.com). Raffles Place MRT. **Open** noon-8.30pm Mon, Sun; noon 11.30pm Tue Sat.
Credit AmEx, DC, JCB, MC, V. **Map** p250 J9.

Discreet on the outside (Asians are bashful about sex toys), this adult shop makes up for it inside, selling erotic massage oils, dildos, penis extenders and S&M toys, plus kinky outfits for the ladies.

Primitive Art Piercing & Tattoo

#04-101 Far East Plaza, 14 Scotts Road,
Orchard Road & Around (6735 3710). Orchard
MRT **Open** 10am-8.30pm daily. **Credit** MC, V.
Map p247 F3.

This buzzing, fluorescent-lit joint is one of Singapore's first piercing salons – and still one of the best. Tattooing is done too, and piercing accessories and jewellery are sold.

Other locations: #02-49 Far East Plaza, 14 Scotts Road, Orchard Road & Around (6735 6889); #02-36 Queensway Shopping Centre, 1 Queensway, Alexandra (6475 8057).

Sia Huat

7, 9 & 11 Temple Street, Chinatown (6223 1732/
www.siahuat.com). Chinatown MRT then 10mins
walk. **Open** 8.30am-6.30pm Mon-Fri; 8.30am-5.30pm Sat. **Credit** MC, V. **Map** p250 H10.

Restaurateurs, chefs and homemakers come to this large, cluttered Chinatown shop to load up on all manner of kitchenware, from cookers and cutlery to quality knives, sieves and dim sum steamers. Hauling it back home is another story.

Health & beauty

Beauty treatments

Singaporeans spend a lot of time and money to look good, so beauty shops, salons, nail bars and hairdressers abound. There's also a trend for slimming salons (offering debatable diet-and exercise-free weight-loss methods) and cosmetic surgery. The 'medi-spa' is on the rise, a phenomenon that combines beauty and medical treatments. For Singapore's top spas, *see p156* **Super spas**.

Mask Skincare

#02-11 The Cathay, 2 Handy Road, Orchard Road
& Around (6836 4456/www.maskskincare.com).
Dhoby Ghaut MRT. **Open** 10am-9pm Mon-Sat;
10am-7pm Sun. **Credit** AmEx, DC, JCB, MC, V.
Map p248 I5.

The Bayzone section does quick pick-me-ups (head, eye, neck and scalp massages) for the time-starved. The Backroom offers customised facial sessions and a range of aesthetic treatments (such as diamond microdermabrasion and botanical stem cell-infused facials. The Retail Bar dispenses New York apothecary skincare brand Malin+Goetz.
Other locations: #03-05 Wheelock Place, 501 Orchard Road (6238 7737).

Norhaidah Traditional Malay Massage Services

#04-42 Far East Plaza, 14 Scotts Road, Orchard
Road & Around (6235 1041) Orchard MRT.
Open 11am-10pm Mon-Sat; 11am-6pm Sun.
No credit cards. Map p247 F3.

Post-partum mothers swear by the tummy-flattening miracles of traditional Malay or Indonesian massage. And this is the place to come for body treatments, body scrubs, baths and a neck and shoulder cream bath (combining a shampoo with a firm neck and shoulder massage).

Rupini's Bridal & Beauty Salon

24 & 26 Buffalo Road, Little India (6291 6789/
www.rupinis.com.sg). Little India MRT. **Open** 11am-8pm Mon-Fri, 11am 6pm Sat. **Credit** MC, V.
Map p248 K3.

This Indian beauty parlour is always packed to the gills, thanks to the popularity of its eyebrow threading and henna painting. There are some bizarre beauty services too – skin bleaching, for example. They can often accommodate walk-ins.
Other locations: #02-11C Midpoint Orchard, 22 Orchard Road (6738 6261); #01 168, 927 Yishun Central 1, Yishun (6754 6706).

Serendipity The Nail Spa

10A Lorong Mambong, Holland Village (6468 6826/
www.serendipity.com.sg). Bus 7, 61, 75, 106, 970.
Open 10am 8pm Tue Sat; 11am 6pm Sun. **Credit** AmEx, MC, V.

Innovative pedicure and manicure spa treatments are the forte at this sophisticated salon. Natural ingredients like clay, lemon, milk and honey are used. Prices are reasonable – so don't be tempted to penny-pinch and go to a cheap salon. The latter are known for hiring young, inexperienced girls and providing minimal training.

STRIP in the Village

34C Lorong Mambong, Holland Village (6467
7219/www.strip.com.sg). Bus 7, 61, 75, 106, 970.
Open 10am-9pm Mon Sat; 10am-7pm Sun. **Credit** AmEx, DC, JCB, MC, V.

Haircare for the nether regions is the thing at this beauty parlour, where the extremity of the job is determined by the number of Xs. One X keeps

Escentials Fragrance Boutique

#01-24 Raffles Hotel Shopping Arcade, Raffles Hotel, 328 North Bridge Road, Colonial District (6339 7727). City Hall MRT. **Open** 10.30am-8pm Mon-Sat; 10.30am-7pm Sun. **Credit** AmEx, MC, V. **Map** p249 L6.

An exquisite perfumery for fragrance fanatics. Call in advance for a consultation with the fragrance analyst to get a personalised blend. Or go for a bottle of luxurious Annick Goutal fragrance or a chic Diptyque candle. There are also counters in Tangs department stores.

Sasa

#01-14/15 Wisma Atria, 435 Orchard Road (6738 8232/www.sasa.com). Orchard MRT. **Open** 11am-10pm daily. **Credit** AmEx, DC, JCB, MC, V. **Map** p247 E4.

This chain store sells imported big-name brands in skincare, make-up and fragrances (SK-II, Elizabeth Arden, Estée Lauder, Lancôme). You won't find the latest lines, but prices are reduced by 10-30%. **Other locations**: throughout the city.

Hairdressers

Most suburbs have a resident Indian barber who will give a quick, no-frills snip for a few dollars; try Little India and oldish malls such as **Queensway Shopping Centre** (1 Queensway, Alexandra) and **Siglap Centre** (55 Siglap Road, East Coast). Neighbourhoods like Ang Mo Kio and Toa Payoh also have a proliferation of 'aunty salons' that will dispense anything from a quick hairwash to perms.

Mahogany

#01-04 Winsland House, 3 Killiney Road, Orchard Road & Around (6737 5956). **Open** 10.15am-8pm daily. **Credit** AmEx, DC, JCB, MC, V. **Map** p247 H5.

A hair salon-cum-spa. After your haircut, you can get a manicure or a total body exfoliation. The Kerastase hair spa is a lengthy affair that treats hair problems with scalp massages and colour therapy.

Passion Hair Salon

#02-01/02 Palais Renaissance, 390 Orchard Road (6733 5638). Orchard MRT. **Open** 11am-8pm Mon-Fri; 10am-7pm Sun. **Credit** AmEx, MC, V. **Map** p246 D3.

Local celebrities trust only hairstylist-to-the-stars David Gan with their crowning glory. He's a genius with the scissors, and his gallery-like salon is perpetually filled with ladies who lunch and anyone who can afford the exorbitant prices.

Opticians

Specialist Eyecare Centre

#01-38 Great World City, 1 Kim Seng Promenade, River Valley (6733 5665). Bus 16, 75, 195, 970. **Open** 11am-9pm daily. **Credit** AmEx, DC, JCB, MC, V.

This sprawling shop sells a wide range of designer frames from the likes of Gucci, Prada and Alexander McQueen. Sales assistants can be pushy.

Yes! Your Eyewear & Hearing Aid Specialists

#01-037 Suntec City Mall, 3 Temasek Boulevard, Marina (6332 5332). City Hall MRT then 10mins walk. **Open** 11am-9pm Mon-Fri; 11am-9.30pm Sat, Sun. **Credit** AmEx, DC, MC, V. **Map** p249 M6.

An extensive range of frames, sunglasses, contact lenses and optical paraphernalia. The open layout allows for easy browsing.

Pharmacies

You'll find branches of **Guardian Pharmacy**, **Apex Pharmacy** and **Unity Pharmacy** everywhere. There aren't any 24-hour chemists, however; outside shopping hours, your best bet is to consult the doctor at a hospital's outpatient clinic. If you run out of aspirin or toothpaste, 24-hour convenience stores, such as **Cheers** and **7-Eleven**, carry the basics. You can also order non-prescription medicine, health supplements, organic foodstuffs and medical accessories from **Changi General Hospital**'s online pharmacy (www.mypharmacy.com.sg). Allow one to two days for delivery.

Homewares

Though best known for its watering holes and restaurants, **Club Street** in Chinatown also contains stylish design boutiques; and there's a host of upmarket lighting, kitchen and furniture shops in **Park Mall** (9 Penang Road, 6339 4031), next to Dhoby Ghaut MRT station. Swedish giant **IKEA** (www.ikea.com.sg) has two superstores in Singapore, in Alexandra (317 Alexandra Road, 6474 0122) and Tampines (60 Tampines North Drive 2, 6786 6868).

Bulb

8 Gemmill Lane, Chinatown (6225 0158/www.bulb.com.sg). Chinatown MRT. **Open** 11am-7pm Mon-Sat. **Credit** MC, V. **Map** p250 H10.

A proponent of the baroque resurgence. Prices are astronomical, but the chandeliers, vintage reproduction furniture and design paraphernalia are top-notch. Baylene's Boyfriend, the menswear line by local designer Baylene (*see p149* **Home-grown talents**), is also stocked.

Lorgan's

#1-3 Century Warehouse, 100E Pasir Panjang Road, Pasir Panjang (6272 4988/www.lorgans.com). Bus 10, 30, 51, 143, 176, 188. **Open** 10.30am-7pm daily. **Credit** AmEx, MC, V.

A blast from the past, this retro favourite stocks a greatest hits medley of furniture from the 1950s, '60s and '70s. Choice picks include authentic Eero Aarnio

Lorgan's

Ball chairs and Arne Jacobsen Swan chairs, complemented by vintage curtain fabrics, lamps and other groovy accessories.

Recaptured
110 Upper East Coast Road, East Coast (6449 8003/www.fidelityresources.com.sg). Tanah Merah MRT then bus 12, 14 . **Open** 11.30am-8pm daily. **Credit** MC, V.
Recaptured is worth the trek to the East Coast for its stylishly fussy homeware and carved picture frames The window displays – full of baroque-style beds and chandeliers – are eye-catching.

Style:Nordic
39 Ann Siang Road, Chinatown (6423 9114/ www.stylenordic.com). Tanjong Pagar MRT. **Open** noon-8pm Mon-Sat; noon-5pm Sun. **Credit** MC, V. **Map** p250 I11.
This Scandinavian lifestyle boutique, housed in a conservation shophouse in the hippest street on the island, is filled with cool Nordic furniture from the likes of Offecct, David Design and Nola, plus wine glasses, vases and accessories from Iittala and Design House Stockholm. Fashion labels Nudie Jeans and Filippa K round out the offerings.

Music

Though the three-storey **HMV** (#01-13 The Heeren Shops, 260 Orchard Road, 6733 1822) has been shaved down, it's still the biggest music shop in the country.

Earz
#03-280 Marina Square, 6 Raffles Boulevard, Marina (6339 3280/www.earzmusic.com). City Hall MRT then 10mins walk. **Open** 11am-10pm Mon-Thur, Sun, 11am-midnight Fri, Sat. **Credit** AmEx, MC, V. **Map** p251 M8.
A nondescript shop that sells new and used mainstream CDs for low prices. A good option if you're a chart fanatic and don't want to pay too much for the latest Robbie Williams.

Rhapsody Records
#03-10A Holland Road Shopping Centre, 211 Holland Avenue, Holland Village (6875 1154). Bus 7, 61, 75, 106, 970. **Open** 1-8pm daily. **Credit** MC, V.
Bypassing the usual Top 40 fare, Rhapsody Records has a carefully curated collection of world music and dance grooves, including house, funk, garage, classic bossa nova and rare electronica.

Straits Records
22 Bali Lane, Arab Quarter (9385 3211/9341 1572). Bugis MRT then 10mins walk. **Open** 2-11pm daily. **No credit cards. Map** p249 M4.
Rastafarians and musical slackers hang out in this indie shop along shabby-chic Haji Lane. The owners are passionate about supporting the burgeoning local music industry. Expect hard-core, indie, hip-hop and other alternative music selections.

Eat, Drink, Shop

That CD Shop

#01-01 Pacific Plaza, 9 Scotts Road, Orchard Road & Around (6238 7254). Orchard MRT. **Open** 10am-midnight daily. **Credit** AmEx, MC, V. **Map** p247 F3.
With its ornate framed portraits and majestic chandeliers, That CD shop is the prettiest music store in town. In contrast to the grandeur, the music selection leans towards lounge, jazz and chill-out.
Other locations: #B1-87/88 Raffles City, 252 North Bridge Road, Colonial District (6336 5885); #01-20 Tanglin Mall, 19 Tanglin Road, Orchard Road & Around (6732 2568); #B1-01 Great World City, 1 Kim Seng Promenade, River Valley (6738 0894).

Sport

Sports Connection

#06-18 Plaza Singapura, 68 Orchard Road (6339 6218). Dhoby Ghaut MRT. **Open** 11am-10pm daily. **Credit** MC, V. **Map** p248 I5.
A decent selection of tents, heavy-duty rucksacks, footwear (for every height and size) and other camping equipment.
Other locations: throughout the city.

Sports Link

#02-03 Causeway Point, 1 Woodlands Square, Woodlands (6767 9488/www.sportslink.com.sg). **Open** 11am-9.30pm daily. **Credit** AmEx, DC, MC, V.
The sportswear, shoes and equipment at this large chain are not the latest models, but you'll often find good discounts. Brands include Yonex, Nike, Adidas, Diadora and Lotto.
Other locations: throughout the city.

Stadium

#B2-15/23 Tower B, Ngee Ann City, 391 Orchard Road (6538 8888/www.rshlimited.com). Orchard MRT. **Open** 11am-9.30pm Mon-Thur, Sun; 11am-10pm Fri, Sat. **Credit** AmEx, DC, JCB, MC, V. **Map** p247 F4.
If you like to sweat in style, get your trendy torso down to Stadium. The sporting empire is filled with labels, labels, labels on items like shoes, clothes, rackets, balls and other sporting gear (including apparel for basketball, aerobics and jogging).

Travel

Eureka Travel

619B Bukit Timah Road, Bukit Timah (6469 4766/www.eurekatravel.com). Bus 74, 151, 170, 171, 174. **Open** 9am-6pm Mon-Fri; 9am-2pm Sat. **Credit** AmEx, DC, JCB, MC, V.
Eureka's forte lies in regional excursions to Cambodia, Malaysia, Vietnam, Laos, Indonesia and Thailand. Packages border on the adventurous and the educational, though you can always count on a luxurious beachfront holiday in Bali.

Misa Travel

#03-106 Hong Lim Complex, 531A Upper Cross Street, Chinatown (6538 0318/www.airfares.com.sg). Chinatown MRT. **Open** 9am-6pm Mon-Fri; 9am-1pm Sat. **Credit** MC, V. **Map** p250 H10.
Good deals on air tickets, hotels, short breaks, cruises and packages. Misa works more efficiently via website and phone bookings – a trip to the shoddy premises might burst your bubble.

Hitting the right note: **That CD Shop** has cool decor and music.

Arts & Entertainment

Festivals & Events

Parties, parades, processions and a plethora of new years.

Singapore's religious and ethnic diversity is reflected in the sheer number and variety of festivals and celebrations held during the year. The major religious and ethnic events – and public holidays – are **Chinese New Year**, **Mid-Autumn Festival**, **Hari Raya** (which has two parts) and **Deepavali**. Cultural highlights include the **Singapore Arts Festival**, **Singapore International Film Festival** and **Singapore Food Festival**, while **National Day** – the anniversary of the country's independence – is a big affair.

Because of the perpetually sunny climate (give or take unpredictable tropical downpours), events are often held outdoors. Many festivals are based on the lunar calendar, so dates change from year to year. For the latest information, check the daily papers or the STB's website (www.visitsingapore.com) or hotline (1-800 736 2000, toll-free in Singapore only). For dates of public holidays, *see chapter* **Resources A-Z**.

Spring

World Gourmet Summit
Various venues (6270 1254/www.worldgourmet summit.com). **Date** Apr.
Gourmands have a ball during this three-week fine food festival, spread across town at some of the city's best eating and drinking venues. World-renowned celebrity and Michelin-starred chefs, as well as vintners, fly in to preside over a gastronomic orgy, including wine masterclasses, gourmet BBQs and charity dinners. Book tickets in advance.

Singapore International Film Festival
Various venues (www.filmfest.org.sg). **Date** Apr.
For over two decades, SIFF – Singapore's longest-running independent cultural event – has pretty much single-handedly championed foreign, regional and local films (with a competition section for new Asian cinema), and set the agenda for film appreciation outside the multiplex. Expect a serious and provocative mix of up to 300 international documentaries, features, animation, shorts and retrospectives over three weeks.

Singapore Airlines International Cup
Singapore Turf Club, 1 Turf Club Avenue, Kranji (6879 1000/www.turfclub.com.sg). Kranji MRT. **Tickets** $3-$7. **Credit** AmEx, DC, JCB, MC, V. **Date** May.

Singapore Airlines sponsors this leg of the prestigious World Series Racing Championship. With a $3 million prize, it's one of Asia's richest racing events, attracting hordes to the Turf Club.

Vesak Day
Various venues (Singapore Buddhist Federation 6744 4635/www.vesakcelebrations.sg). **Date** May.
A sizeable proportion of Singapore's population commemorates the birth, enlightenment and nirvana of the Buddha on Vesak Day (the first full moon day of the fourth lunar month). Vegetarian food is served at Buddhist temples, where devotees flock to make offerings of flowers, incense, oil lamps or lighted candles. Some even release captive animals like turtles and birds as offerings.

Summer

Great Singapore Sale
Various venues (www.greatsingaporesale.com.sg). **Date** May-July.
The national obsession for shopping becomes even more frenzied during the biggest sale of the year. Department stores, malls and individual boutiques offer discounts that range from cursory to crazy, and late-night shopping events are organised at weekends. Stock up like there's no tomorrow.

Singapore Arts Festival
Various venues (www.singaporeartsfest.com). **Date** late May-June.
Celebrating its 30th anniversary in 2007, this month-long arts extravaganza brings a mind-boggling array of mainstream and experimental music, dance, theatre and visual arts to venues all over town. It's organised by the National Arts Council, and international and regional acts tend to dominate – UK theatre group Station House Opera, Belgian dance outfit Rosas, and the Oslo Philharmonic Orchestra appeared in 2006 – but there's local fare too, as well as a slew of free street performances and workshops.

Singapore Dragon Boat Festival
Bedok Reservoir Park, Bedok Reservoir Road, Bedok (Singapore Dragon Boat Association 6440 9763/www.sdba.org.sg). Bus 18, 21, 65, 67, 228. **Date** June.
A 2,000-year old festival held on the fifth day of the fifth lunar month to commemorate the death of Qu Yuan, a Chinese poet who drowned himself in protest at political corruption. Fishermen raced their boats to rescue him, but to no avail. To distract the fish from feasting on his body, people threw bah chang (glutinous rice and meat dumplings wrapped

Arts & Entertainment

Colourful, noisy, everywhere: it must be **Chinese New Year**. *See p165.*

in bamboo leaves) into the water. Today, local, regional and international teams race beautifully decorated boats on Bedok Reservoir, while *bah chang* are sold widely throughout the island.

Singapore Food Festival

Various venues (www.singaporefoodfestival.com.sg).
Date July.

Another national obsession – eating, and talking about eating – comes to the fore with this month-long string of food events across town. From chilli crab buffets and street stalls selling heritage dishes to chef competitions, cookery workshops and demonstrations, it's a great opportunity to experience the best of the island's gastronomic offerings.

Festival of the Hungry Ghosts

Various venues. **Date** July-Sept.
The Chinese believe that during the seventh lunar month, the gates of hell open to allow its spirit inhabitants to roam the earth – so they ritually offer food and burn 'hell money' for their deceased loved ones, ancestors and deities. There's a host of activities, especially in Chinatown and Chinese neighbourhoods, including celebration dinners, loud auctions and outdoor street performances (known as *getai*) of Chinese opera, puppetry, singing and comedy.

National Day Parade

www.ndp.org.sg. **Date** 9 Aug.
The anniversary of Singapore's independence (a public holiday) is greeted with much pomp and hullaballoo. The official Parade involves patriotic Singaporeans dressed in red and white (the national colours) watching a series of decorated floats, military marches and painstakingly synchronised dances, culminating with fireworks. Formerly held at the Padang or the National Stadium (currently being rebuilt), the event has moved temporarily to Marina Bay. Tickets are free, but only citizens and permanent residents (not tourists) can attend – though the whole shebang is televised live.

Singapore Fireworks Festival

Marina Bay. City Hall MRT then 10mins walk.
Map p251. **Date** early/mid Aug.
Visitors can, however, enjoy the visual extravaganza that is the Singapore Fireworks Festival, also held at Marina Bay and lasting four days. Some 300,000 visitors watched the 2006 displays, with pyrotechnic expertise from Europe and beyond.

WOMAD Singapore

Fort Canning Park, Colonial District (Womad Projects Singapore 6220 2676/www.womad.org). Dhoby Ghaut, Clarke Quay or City Hall MRT. **Tickets** (available from Sistic, 6348 5555, www. sistic.com.sg) approx $40 1 day, $70 2 days, $90 3 days; $30 concessions; $95 family; free under-7s. **Credit** AmEx, DC, JCB, MC, V. **Map** p250 I7. **Date** end Aug.
Founded by rock legend Peter Gabriel, WOMAD (World Of Music, Arts & Dance) has been entertaining audiences in more than 20 countries for over 20 years. Usually held on the last weekend of August in the lovely leafy setting of Fort Canning Park, the Singapore version draws expat families with kids in tow, clubbers looking to party and all kinds of music-lovers who have been starved of exciting live music all year. Expect bands, DJs, dancers, arts and crafts, and food from Peru to Korea, Australia to Africa.

Arts & Entertainment

Autumn

Mid-Autumn Festival

Various venues. **Date** Sept-Oct.
This Buddhist festival in honour of the full moon is celebrated during the eighth lunar month (especially on the 15th day), and is also known as the Mooncake Festival, Lantern Festival or August Moon Festival. Colourful paper lanterns, elaborate decorations, spectacular street lights, and markets selling traditional goodies abound in Chinatown and elsewhere. Mooncakes – round pastries filled with

Devotees wear body-piercing kavadis for the Hindu festival of **Thaipusam**. *See p165.*

lotus seed paste, preserved duck egg and other sweet fillings – are sold throughout the island.

Hari Raya Puasa
Geylang Serai. Paya Lebar MRT. Kampong Glam. Bugis MRT. **Date** Sept-Oct.
Starting on the first day of the tenth lunar month, Hari Raya Puasa (the Malay name for Eid Al Fitr) celebrates the end of the month-long fasting period of Ramadan. Geylang Serai and Kampong Glam – the Muslim areas of town – come alive with festive decorations, street lighting, bustling roadside bazaars and a mouth-watering array of traditional Malay foodstuffs. Hari Raya Haji, which marks the conclusion of the Haj pilgrimage to Mecca, is also a public holiday, but is less of a public event; it usually falls around December.

Singapore Biennale
Various venues (www.singaporebiennale.org). **Date** Sept-Nov.
Singapore joined the biennale club in 2006, hosting a blockbuster showcase of work – on the theme 'Belief' – by 95 artists from over 38 countries. With an internationally renowned curator (Nanjo Fumio, from Tokyo's Mori Art Museum) and most of the work exhibited in public spaces, including churches, temples, mosques and City Hall, it carefully mixed the cerebral and the cryptic with plenty of playful, accessible art. Expect similar things for the next edition in 2008.

Deepavali
Around Little India. Little India or Farrer Park MRT. **Date** usually Oct.
Diwali – known in Singapore under its Tamil name, Deepavali – also called the Festival of Lights, is a major Hindu festival for Hindus, Jains and Sikhs throughout the world, symbolising the triumph of good over evil and light over darkness. Hindu families offer prayers at local temples, which are illuminated with a profusion of oil lamps, candles and fairy lights. For most of October, Serangoon Road, the heart of Little India, is abuzz with spectacular street decorations and lighting, and evening roadside bazaars sell garish jewellery, saris, spices, crafts, jasmine garlands and foodstuffs.

Theemidhi Festival
Sri Mariamman Temple, 244 South Bridge Road, Chinatown (6223 4064). Chinatown MRT. **Map** p250 I11. *Sri Srinivasa Perumal Temple, 397 Serangoon Road, Little India (6298 5771). Farrer Park MRT.* **Map** p249 L1. **Date** Oct.
Barefoot Hindus walk across a 4m/13ft bed of red-hot coals to show their devotion to the Goddess Draupadi, who was said to have done the same to prove her innocence. Unstinting concentration is needed by the fire-walkers, and pure faith leaves them unscathed. The ceremony begins about 3am at Sri Mariamman Temple in Chinatown; respectful attire is required. Look out for the Silver Chariot procession around the same date, when a statue of

the goddess is carried from Sri Mariamman Temple to Sri Perumal Temple in Little India (Campbell Lane is a good spot from which to see the action).

Kusu Island Pilgrimage

Ferry from Marina South Pier, 31 Marina Coastal Drive, Marina Bay (6275 0388). Marina Bay MRT then bus 402. **Date** Oct-Nov.

Legend says that a magical giant turtle turned itself into Kusu Island, off Singapore's southern coast, to save two shipwrecked sailors. Grateful, the sailors visited the island regularly to give thanks. Taoists in Singapore and the region make an annual pilgrimage during the ninth lunar month to Tua Pekong Temple on the island, praying for luck, prosperity and fertility. It gets incredibly busy, so non-pilgrims might want to visit at another time.

Singapore Fashion Week

Various venues (6735 8390/www.singaporefashionweek.com.sg). **Date** Oct-Nov.

The Singapore fashion scene is always striving to keep up with the major fashion capitals, as can be seen at this week-long event, which pulls in players from all over South-east Asia. It includes contests for fledgling designers from Singapore's top four design schools, and culminates in an expensive gala dinner. Paid tickets are needed for most shows, but some events are free.

Swissotel Vertical Marathon

Swissotel The Stamford, 2 Stamford Road, Colonial District (6438 1715/www.swissotelvertical marathon.com). City Hall MRT. **Map** p251 K7. **Date** mid Nov.

The original vertical marathon began in 1987. About 1,000 participants race up 1,336 steps to the top of the 73-storey Swissotel The Stamford, South-east Asia's tallest hotel; Bavinder Singh set the fastest time of six minutes 55 seconds in 1989.

Winter

ZoukOut

Sentosa (6738 2988/www.zoukout.com). HarbourFront MRT then Sentosa Express. **Tickets** (available from Sistic, 6348 5555, www.sistic.com.sg) $28-$48. **Credit** AmEx, DC, JCB, MC, V. **Map** p252. **Date** early Dec.

Mega-club Zouk organises this gigantic, weekend-long beach party on Sentosa, usually on Siloso or Tanjong Beaches. First held in 2000, it has grown every year: 20,000 revellers turned up in 2006. Local and overseas music acts and big-name DJs play in tents and outdoor arenas; expect everything from rock to hip hop, lounge to house.

Christmas celebrations

Date late Oct-25 Dec.

All of Orchard Road is dressed in Yuletide finery from late October, marking the beginning of the Christmas shopping and dining rush. Hotels and shopping malls also get in on the act, ensuring that

the city's decorations are pretty splendid. There's a parade on Orchard Road on Christmas Day itself (which is a public holiday), but the city doesn't completely shut down – many Singaporeans don't celebrate Christmas, after all – and it's back to normal straight afterwards.

Singapore Marathon

6416 3949/www.singaporemarathon.com. **Date** early Dec.

Currently sponsored by Standard Chartered Bank, the Singapore Marathon draws up to 13,000 runners (elite and amateur) from all over the world. Starting at Esplanade Bridge, the route loops through the CBD and beachfront East Coast Park, finishing at the Padang. It's a tough marathon, owing to the island's humid weather, but a spectacular one – during which the city grinds to a momentary halt.

New Year's Eve

Various venues. **Date** 31 Dec.

New Year's Eve is celebrated in a big way. The Nation's Countdown is a televised event that includes performances by local celebrities, followed by several big public parties, in varying venues. Bars and restaurants across town throw their own bashes, as do popular entertainment hubs like Clarke Quay and Esplanade. The morning after, streamers and other debris litter the streets – the only day you'll find Singapore less than spotless.

Chinese New Year

Various venues. **Date** Jan-Feb.

Thanks to Singapore's largely Chinese population, this is the biggest festival/holiday period of the year. In the weeks leading up to New Year, celebrations erupt all over the island, but are centred on Chinatown, with street lighting, music, performances and a massive street market hawking traditional Chinese goodies, decorative items and food. Associated events include the wonderfully kitsch Chingay Parade of Dreams (www.chingay.org.sg) on Orchard Road, an outdoor variety show, float parade and carnival rolled into one; and the River Hong Bao fair next to Esplanade. **Photo** *p163.*

Thaipusam

Procession starts from Sri Srinivasa Perumal Temple, 397 Serangoon Road, Little India. Farrer Park MRT. **Map** p249 L1. *Finishes at Sri Thendayuthapani Temple, 15 Tank Road, River Valley. Bus 32, 54, 139, 195.* **Map** p250 H7. **Date** Jan/Feb.

One of the most colourful and ritual-heavy festivals in Singapore, held in honour of the Hindu deity Subramaniam (Lord Murugan). Penitents carrying kavadis – elaborately decorated semi-circular structures with skewers and hooks piercing the body – walk the 3km/2-mile route from Little India's Sri Perumal Temple, via Serangoon Road, Selegie Road, Penang Road and Clemenceau Avenue, to Sri Thendayuthapani Temple. Friends and family chant in support as they go. **Photo** *p164.*

Children

Indoor and outdoor amusements for toddlers and teens.

Singaporean families used to be big enough to play five-a-side by themselves, but these days most consist of working parents and one child. It's not surprising, therefore, to find that children are often treated like little princes and princesses.

Indeed, 'family' is a topical buzzword in this child-starved nation, and the government metes out incentives – commonly known as the 'baby bonus' – to parents. Goods and services for children continue to increase and improve. Baby and kid gyms are burgeoning island-wide; nursing and family rooms are de rigueur for major malls – Japanese department store Isetan even took out a full-page ad in the *Straits Times* to publicise its nursing room's extra touches, including two qualified childcare staff. Almost every big attraction boasts a children's entertainment section, and several have water-based playgrounds that are a hit with all ages.

Even luxury hotels have wised up to the potential of the kiddie dollar: the **Four Seasons** (*see p47*) and **Swissôtel The Stamford** (*see p39*) have fully furnished rooms for children that are equipped with mini bathrobes, slippers, cutlery, plush toys and other kid-friendly accessories. Designer labels are muscling in on the action too, so if you're looking for a Gucci baby carrier or want to dress your child in head-to-toe Burberry, you're in luck.

Not your style? Take heart. There are many other (cheaper) ways to spend quality time with your children without subjecting them to another shopping mall. Singapore is full of places – parks, nature reserves, museums, wildlife attractions and more – where kids can just be, well, kids.

Museums

Mint Museum of Toys
26 Seah Street, Colonial District (6339 0660/ www.emint.com). City Hall MRT. **Open** 9.30am-6.30pm daily. **Admission** $10; $5 concessions; $24-$28 family; free under-2s. **Credit** MC, V. **Map** p249 L6.
More than 50,000 items from over 25 countries: from Mickey Mouse to Astroboy, Batman, Steiff bears, and pre-war Japanese toys. There are five floors to explore, but alas, it's a 'see but don't touch' place. Thankfully, there's a nice café on the premises to adjourn to if the kids start to fuss.

Museum of Shanghai Toys
83 Rowell Road, Little India (6294 7747/ www.most.com.sg). Farrer Park MRT. **Open** 10am-8pm daily. **Admission** $8; $5 3-11s; free under-3s. **No credit cards. Map** p249 L2.
This private museum displays vintage oriental toys made in Shanghai between the 1910s and the '70s. Owner Marvin Chan will gladly oblige a young visitor's desire for a private tour. Don't miss the shop – it's a great source of souvenirs, including old-fashioned tin toys.

Open House at Central Fire Station
62 Hill Street, Colonial District (6848 1519). City Hall or Clarke Quay MRT. **Open** 9am-11am Sat. **Admission** free. **Map** p250 J7.
The red and white Central Fire Station, completed in 1908 (and still in use), has a watchtower and living quarters for firemen. On Saturday mornings kids can ride on an engine and take pictures with the Red Rhinos (a smaller version of the fire truck) and the firemen. Then head next door to the Civil Defence Heritage Gallery (open 10am-5pm Tue-Sun), a mini fire-fighting museum housing old trucks and equipment, plus interactive games and activities on the second level.

Singapore Discovery Centre
510 Upper Jurong Road, Jurong (6792 6188/ www.sdc.com.sg). Boon Lay MRT then bus 182, 193. **Open** 9am-6pm Tue-Fri, Sun; 9am-8pm Sat. **Admission** $10; $6 3-11s; $28 family; free under-3s. **Credit** AmEx, DC, JCB, MC, V.
Out in the west, this centre contains plenty of high-tech and interactive exhibits on what it means to be a Singaporean. It's patriotic almost to a fault, right up to the tacky singing and rapping Merlion, but the place is worth a visit to find out what makes the Singaporean mind tick. Kids can boogie at the multicultural dance zone, try a stint as a broadcast journalist, create an ideal neighbourhood and even figure out how to become good entrepreneurs. The most thrilling section for older boys (and girls) is probably the computerised shooting range simulator, complete with modified SAR 21 rifles. For an insight into the importance Singapore attaches to defence, take a bus tour of the SAFTI Military Institute. **Photo** *p167.*

Singapore Science Centre
15 Science Centre Road, Jurong (6425 2500/ www.science.edu.sg). Jurong East MRT then bus 66, 335. **Open** 10am-6pm Tue-Sun. **Admission** $6; $3.60 concessions; $3 3-16s; free under-3s. **Credit** AmEx, MC, V.

Lots of noise, flashing lights and interactive exhibits make this a great destination for kids. Since it is educational as well as fun, local parents (who will do almost anything to help further their child's knowledge) love it. The Omni-Theatre (*see p176*) screens 3D planetarium shows and Omnimax movies – even blockbusters like *Harry Potter* – on a huge, hemispherical screen. Outside, the Kinetic Garden blends science and art with interactive sculptures, displays and exhibits. When information-gathering has reached a plateau, little ones will enjoy cooling off at the large outdoor water play area.

Parks & reserves

Run around the wide, open spaces or feed the swans at the **Singapore Botanic Gardens** (*see p80*). Mid 2007 sees the opening of the Jacob Ballas Children's Garden opens, where kids can find out more about plants and conservation, or simply have fun at playgrounds and other facilities. The **Chinese Garden** (*see p100*) is worth a visit, especially during the **Mid-Autumn Festival** (*see p163*), when oversized lanterns in traditional and modern designs, imported from China and elsewhere, are on display – an arresting sight when lit at night. Prefer beaches? Make your way to **East Coast Park** (*see p91*), where bicycle and in-line skating trails abound. You can rent bikes and rollerblades near the McDonald's restaurant.

For a wilder time, head to the hiking trails at **Bukit Timah Nature Reserve** (*see p98*), **MacRitchie Reservoir** (*see p104*) or **Sungei Buloh Wetland Reserve** (*see p101*). And for a taste of old-fashioned village life, take a bumboat to **Pulau Ubin** (*see p94*) and rent bikes from the shops near the jetty. Pedal upon rustic roads under swaying palms, and explore old rubber plantations, secluded beaches, disused quarries and kampong houses.

Pasir Ris Park
Pasir Ris MRT station, then 10mins walk.
Next door to the Pasir Ris theme parks (*see p168*), this seaside park is perfect for cycling and rollerblading (bikes and skates can be rented), kite-flying or simply digging for mud crabs in the mangrove swamps. Ponies (near car park C) are the latest attraction, sweet and mild enough for toddlers to ride on. And everyone loves the massive Children's Adventure Land playground, with its maze garden, jungle gym, cableways and play stations. After all that activity, have dinner with the waves lapping your feet at Fisherman Village, a cluster of alfresco restaurants serving decent barbecued seafood.

Find out what it means to be Singaporean, at the **Singapore Discovery Centre**. *See p166*.

Sentosa

Getting to Sentosa is half the fun. Forget land transport; take the cable car instead. The ride is slower, but it brings an amazing view of the surrounding islands, as well as the thrill of dangling precariously in the air.

There's probably too much to see and do, from trapeze-flying and luge-riding to swimming with dolphins and messing about on the beaches. But don't miss the aquarium **Underwater World**; small kids love the 'touch pool' for hands-on experiences with rays, starfish and baby sharks, while over-12s can try out the 90-minute Discover Scuba programme. Near the **Merlion**, specially designed fountains 'dance' to music nightly, accompanied by synchronised lights, lasers, computer graphics and a slightly scary cast of hyperactive characters including a singing, dancing octopus and jellyfish. Somehow, children are mesmerised by it. The **Carlsberg Sky Tower** offers more views, this time from an air-conditioned cabin that rotates as it slowly ascends. At the top, you can see as far as Malaysia and the Indonesian islands – and it's safe for small children. Boys can pretend to be men at **Fort Siloso**, perched on the western tip of the island. Almost every Singaporean has a childhood photo taken atop one of the 17th-century cannons.

For more information on all these, and the rest of Sentosa, *see pp82-87*.

Theatre

Act 3 International (6735 9986, www.act 3international.com.sg) was the first to bring kid-friendly theatricals to Singapore, in 1984. It produces four shows a year for children aged two to 12, and also organises the city's biggest kids' festival, Prudential Children First! (March), and KidsFest (June). Also look out for **I Theatre** (6344 4840, www. itheatre.org), which stages about five sell-out productions annually, mixing mime, physical theatre, puppetry, musical theatre and more traditional plays, always with a strong educational slant.

Theme parks

Although the parks are adjacent to each other, there is no combined admission fee.

Escape Theme Park

1 Pasir Ris Close, Pasir Ris (6581 9112/www. escapethemepark.com.sg). Pasir Ris MRT then free shuttle bus. **Open** 10am-8pm daily. **Admission** $16.50; $8.30 3-12s; $40 family; free under-3s. **Credit** AmEx, MC, V.

A ferris wheel, a haunted house, dodgem cars, kiddie bumper boats, a miniature train and rides for tots, scary 'flying' rides, go-karts – pretty much every imaginable element of a great children's carnival can be found here. Strollers are available for hire, and there are also lockers, picnic tables and benches and food kiosks.

Wild Wild Wet

1 Pasir Ris Close, Pasir Ris (6581 9128/www. wildwildwet.com). Pasir Ris MRT then free shuttle bus. **Open** 1-7pm Mon, Wed-Fri; 10am-7pm Sat, Sun. **Admission** $12.90; $8.80 3-12s; free under-3s. **Credit** AmEx, MC, V.

From high-speed flume rides to four-storey slides and wave pools, there's plenty to do at this water park. Small children can take it easy in the meandering river or splash around in Yippie!, a shallow sloshing area. The Yakult Professor's Playground, with its slides, ladders, water cannons and fountains, will entertain older kids for hours. More adventurous ones will prefer the exhilarating trip down the Ular-Lah raft slide, with its high, banked corners and 360° spins.

Wildlife

Most children love zoos, and **Singapore Zoo** (*see p104*) is a particularly fine one. Start with a Jungle Breakfast, where kids can get close to an orang utan or pose with a snake. Budding animal conservationists can watch vets at work from the glass-panelled viewing gallery at the Wildlife Healthcare & Research Centre, while Children's World with its playground, miniature train, petting zoo, sheep round-up show and water play area is ideal for younger kids. At the Animal Friends Show (12.30pm and 4.30pm daily), friendly trainers, using simple language and funny antics to keep things lively, explain how ducks, dogs, rats and even chickens are trained.

The adjacent **Night Safari** (*see p104*) might be too late for smaller children (it doesn't open until 7.30pm), though the tram ride is a relaxing way to see the animals. It's worth catching the Creatures of the Night show with its all-star cast of binturongs, otters, raccoons, owls, wolves and servals.

You can also have breakfast – with feathered friends, this time – at **Jurong BirdPark** (*see p100*). The air-conditioned Panorail provides a panoramic view of the park. Revive flagging spirits at the large children's playground or the Splash N Slide Station, a combined wet and dry playground. Its jet sprays, geysers, water cannons and fire hydrants are perfect for cooling down on hot, sticky days, and disabled kids can also join in the fun without having to get out of their wheelchairs.

Clubs

Get your dancing shoes on.

Watch out, Asia. Singapore is in the middle of a nightlife revival. It may not yet compare with the well-marinated night-time charms of Hong Kong or the sybaritic leaps of Shanghai, but what Singapore's looser, juicier soul currently does offer is a savvy, cosmopolitan vibe with a bit of the unusual and underground thrown in – and it's become an essential stop-off for big-name international DJs.

Site specific

The following are the best sources of up-to-date info on private parties, one-off events and the latest happenings on the clubbing scene.

www.b-yond.com.sg
A private party launch pad that's grown to include a selection of other bespoke lifestyle services: dining, art and, oddly, personal training.

www.e-clubbing.com
News, reviews, forums, clubbing FAQs and 'best of' lists come together in an easy-to-navigate space.

www.elegantly-wasted.com
For the well-heeled clubber who prefers being at the right place at the right time, without having to think about it too much.

www.exitmusik.com
Listings, playlists, reviews, parties, resources and anything else to do with the underground music cultures (mainly drum n bass and future jazz) of Singapore, Bangkok, Hong Kong and Kuala Lumpur.

www.mumtazz.com
The sister Singapore portal to the Dubai original. Reigning top site for up-to-date local commercial nightlife information, with weekly alerts (sign up online) to keep you clued in.

www.trancerepublic.sg
An extensive, all-things-trance site, featuring DJs, events, forums, blogs and also fresh trance samples.

The bulk of the sound, light and music show takes place along the quays of the Singapore River, where waterfront promenades and pedestrianised malls allow for easy club-hopping. For the glitz, head for Clarke Quay, which has gone from outdated riverside cliché to buzzing nightlife central, housing UK super-club **Ministry of Sound** and a slew of chic, smaller establishments such as **Kandi Bar**, experimental the **Clinic** and always bursting at the seams **Attica**. Along Riverwalk (before you get to Boat Quay – which desperately needs a face-lift of its own) sits cultish underground club **HomeClub**, beneath a nondescript shopping centre. For a sexy, overcrowded hip hop joint, Robertson Quay houses **Butter Factory** between restaurants and bars.

If big, beautiful and schizophrenic is your thing, a disused coal powerhouse facing Sentosa offers nine new reasons to stay out late every day of the week. **St James Power Station** is a cleverly conceived multi-club destination that caters to the Singaporean fascination with Latin and world music, as well as Mandarin pop, karaoke, big band sounds, and more – all yours for a tasty single admission price. At the other end of the spectrum, the beaches of Sentosa offer sand-between-your-toes parties with lounge clubs like **Km8** and newly arrived **CafeDelMar**.

For commercial dance music and a roster of big DJ names, old faithfuls like **Zouk** never fail to come up with the goods. Search a little and you'll find independent clubs such as **Bar Baa Black Chic**, which occupies a shophouse on a backstreet in Little India, or music parties like Heineken's highly anticipated **Green Room** series (www.heinekenmusic.com.sg). Zouk's annual beach party in December, **ZoukOut** (see p165), also pulls in critically acclaimed local and international DJs.

The distinction between bar, music venue and club is often blurred, with many places, including **Bar None**, **China Black** and **Devils Bar**, offering bands and dancefloors as well as drinks – see pp130-137 **Bars** and pp185-192 **Music** for more possibilities.

ETIQUETTE AND INFORMATION
A few things to remember. Don't consume drugs, don't bring them into the country and don't try to buy them here: Singapore has (and uses) severe laws for consumption, and the

Butter Factory. *See p171.*

death penalty for possession and distribution. Double check that the person you're thinking of hooking up with is really available: Singaporean women are pretty forward, and Singaporean men extremely territorial. Dress well; all clubs have strict dress codes, so forget the flip-flops, shorts and singlets. Check your bill and credit card slip (scams have surfaced recently). Have the numbers for a couple of taxi firms: the MRT system stops running at 12.30am and regular bus services around 1am.

For up-to-date information, try magazines *Juice*, *Time Out Singapore* and *I-S*, as well as nightlife websites (*see p169* **Site specific**).

Colonial District

Attica/Attica Too

#01-03 3A River Valley Road, Clarke Quay (6333 9973/www.attica.com.sg). Clarke Quay MRT. **Open** *Attica* 5pm-2am Mon, Tue, Sun; 5pm-3am Thur; 5pm-6am Wed, Fri, Sat. *Attica Too* 11pm-6am Fri, Sat. **Admission** $12-$20 after 11pm. **Credit** AmEx, DC, JCB, MC, V. **Map** p250 I8.
The cheeky upstart that revved the trend for small clubs. An indoor-outdoor vibe (dancefloor and bar inside, wooden-decked courtyard outside) makes it one hell of a pick-up joint. The bold, beautiful, desperate, weird and, ahem, 'working' converge, sprawl and titillate from Thursday to Saturday nights. Hip hop grinds at ground-floor Attica; upstairs, at Attica Two, a wild, Euro-trashy sound and crowd reigns.

Clinic

The Cannery, Block 3C, River Valley Road, Clarke Quay (6887 3733/www.theclinic.sg). Clarke Quay MRT. **Open** *Bar* 6pm-late daily. *Club* 6pm-late Wed-Sat. **Credit** AmEx, DC, JCB, MC, V. **Map** p250 I8.
Singapore's first supper club writes a new party prescription, mixing medical themes with dramatic experimentation and wild art. Thirteen party rooms, two bars, 'molecular food' from Michelin-starred chefs and two dancefloors (one open from midnight to sunrise) where you can suck on frozen passion fruit-flavoured whisky sour pastilles, give new meaning to playing doctor and nurse.

DXO

#01-13F 8 Raffles Avenue, Esplanade Mall, Marina (6582 4896/www.dxo.com.sg). City Hall MRT then 10mins walk. **Open** 3pm-3am Wed, Thur; 3pm-4am Fri, Sat. **Admission** $18 after 10pm. **Credit** AmEx, DC, JCB, MC, V. **Map** p251 L8.
A cavernous, empty dance club next door to the Esplanade, run, bizarrely, by Singapore's national trade union. It tends to remain empty unless a fashion academy show or visiting foreign DJ attracts a late teens to early twenties crowd. Special mention goes to the novel 'towers' that grace tables in the patio space outside, which you can fill with beer or a mixed house pour (a steal at just $19.80).

Kandi Bar

The Cannery, Block 3C, River Valley Road, Clarke Quay (6887 3733/www.hedkandi.com.sg). Clarke Quay MRT. **Open** early afternoon-late daily.

Admission free. **Credit** AmEx, DC, JCB, MC, V. **Map** p250 I8.

Launched by the people behind the roving Hed Kandi music label/clubbing movement, and MOS, Kandi Bar opened in December 2006. Designed to be the sexier, grown-up groove pad alternative to MOS, it combines mirrored, fibre-optic floors, female cartoon portraits on the walls and a chill brand of house music. Come for drinks and schmoozing, with dancing thrown in.

MOS

The Cannery, Block C, River Valley Road, Clarke Quay (6235 2292/www.ministryofsound.com.sg). Clarke Quay MRT. **Open** 9pm-4am Wed-Sat. **Admission** $15-$25. **Credit** AmEx, DC, JCB, MC, V. **Map** p250 I8.

The Ministry of Sound label may be something of a 1990s leftover these days, but club-parched Singaporeans lined up by the hundreds when MOS first hit town in late 2005, with traffic jams on the main street. It's still fairly popular, mainly with a young expat crowd and an assortment of thirty-somethings. There's a multitude of themed spaces, including the all-white, house-playing Pure, disco-fantastic Studio 54, and R&B-flavoured Smoove, where the likes of local wunderkind DJ Kinetic have played. The UK's Paolo Mojo recently appeared in the Arena, the main room. The bouncers can come across confused and rude trying to handle the odd mix of age groups.

Chinatown

Club Momo

#01-02/03 Central Mall, 6 Magazine Road, Chinatown (6536 3030/www.clubmomo.net). Clarke Quay MRT/Chinatown MRT then bus 51, 143, 174, 186. **Open** 9pm 5am Wed; 9pm-6am Fri, Sat. **Admission** free women, $18 men Wed; $15 women, $18 men Fri, Sat. **Credit** AmEx, DC, JCB, MC, V. **Map** p250 H9.

Club Momo heaves with a horny, nubile, up-for-any-thing crowd. Private dance platforms in the Boudoir, live bands in Momo Live, and pool tables and games consoles in the Sports Bar all compete for your attention. The look is Moroccan – all colourful cushions, subdued lighting and draped tents – and the place is packed to the rafters on ladies', retro and R&B nights. It's a notorious hang-out for Chinese working-class party-goers, known as Ah Lians (girls) and Ah Bengs (boys).

HomeClub

#B1-01/06, 20 Upper Circular Road, Riverwalk, Chinatown (9665 8697/www.homeclub.com.sg). Clarke Quay MRT. **Open** 8pm-6am daily. **Admission** $15-$20. **Credit** AmEx, DC, JCB, MC, V. **Map** p250 J8/9.

Voted 'Best Small Club' when in opened in 2005 by Singapore's dance/lifestyle mag *Poptart*, Home has held ground as much for its mismatched interiors, filled with velvet granny sofas and Salvation Army

kitsch, as for its alternative sounds and crowd. It's basically a large room with a bar, a raised DJ booth and a small basement party space down curving stairs. Pulling in a healthy list of international acts such as Goldie and Storm, this is where the art, fashion and music set comes home to roost.

Little India

Bar Baa Black Chic

10 Perak Road, Little India (6297 9397/www.barbaablackchic.com). Little India MRT. **Open** 6pm-midnight Wed, Sun; 6pm-3am Thur, Fri; 6pm-4am Sat. **Admission** free. **Credit** MC, V. **Map** p249 L3.

Corny name and obscure address (along a back street in Little India) aside, Baa Bar Black Chic has gained a name for its seriously cutting-edge tech-house and electronica, for attracting critically acclaimed DJs (both local and international) and for its cheap booze. There's exposed brickwork and kaleidoscopic lighting on the lower floor; daybeds offer respite upstairs. It attracts locals seeking a good time well off the trodden path, and travellers from nearby backpacker lodges. There's not much room, so it's often packed.

Orchard Road & Around

Butter Factory

#01-03 Riverside 48, 48 Robertson Quay (6333 8243/www.thebutterfactory.com). Bus 51, 64, 123, 186, 811. **Open** 5pm-1am Tue; 5pm-3am Wed-Fri; 5pm-4am Sat. **Admission** (after 10pm) $20 women, $25 men. **Credit** AmEx, DC, JCB, MC, V. **Map** p250 G8.

Red, gaping lips at the entrance draw you in to the Factory (opened March 2006), which combines street styling, hip hop and artistic licence. The dancefloor is a swimming pool complete with life buoys and ladders, while graffiti-covered walls, commercial hip hop and R&B on the decks, and lots of cheek, keep the queues snaking round the corner. Drem and Mylk are the resident DJs, while guest DJs from Asia and beyond turn up regularly. Celebs, stylists, models and creatives drop by, as does the nattily dressed ordinary joe. **Photo** *p170*.

dbl O

#01-24 Robertson Walk, 11 Unity Street, River Valley (6735 2008/www.emeraldhillgroup. com). Bus 32, 54, 143, 195. **Open** 8pm-3am Tue-Fri; 8pm-4am Sat. **Admission** $15 women, $20 men. **Credit** AmEx, DC, JCB, MC, V. **Map** p250 H8.

A loud, crowded dance venue that received a much-needed face-lift in 2006. It's the only real club on the 'so over it could come back' Mohamed Sultan stretch next to Robertson Quay, and continues to do outrageously well with the salaryman and his girl. Commercial dance music and cheap drinks – $3 for premium house pours – are the draws, bringing thirsty queues Thursday through Saturday nights.

Multi-purpose **St James Power Station**.

Thumper

Goodwood Park Hotel, 22 Scotts Road, Orchard Road & Around (6735 0827/www.thumper.com.sg). Orchard MRT then 10mins walk. **Open** 6pm-2am Mon, Tue; 6pm-3am Wed, Thur; 6pm-4am Fri, Sat. **Credit** AmEx, DC, JCB, MC, V. **Map** p247 F2.
A loud and friendly crowd, jumping band and danceable tunes, all tucked into a former restaurant space in the basement of historic Goodwood Park Hotel, at the top of Scotts Road. A tiny dancefloor is surrounded by low tables and banquette seats; when the resident band isn't playing, top 40 and commercial house hits reign. An outdoor deck provides breathing space, and the house Cosmopolitans give the right kick. The owners run a modelling agency next door, so expect more than a few gazelle-like creatures slipping through the cracks between the regular-sized patrons.

Zouk

17 Jiak Kim Street, River Valley (6738 2988/ www.zoukclub.com.sg). Bus 16, 195. **Open** 6pm-3am daily. **Admission** $12-$28. **Credit** AmEx, DC, JCB, MC, V.
Singapore's pioneer multi-venue dance club has started to feel the heat of competition – especially from MOS – after enjoying more than a decade of faithful followers. Its motto 'One World, One Music, One Tribe, One Dance' could well be the motto of most of Singapore's newer clubs. Still, the place is packed almost every night of the week, from the main dancefloor to the chill-out Wine Bar, experimental Phuture, and intimate dance club Velvet. Despite the obvious charms of Singapore's newly revamped nightlife scene, Zouk, like all unexplainable love brands, remains a bit of a phenomenon.

CaféDelMar

40 Siloso Beach Walk, Siloso Beach, Sentosa (6235 1296/www.cafedelmar.com.sg). HarbourFront MRT then Sentosa Express. **Open** 11am-1am Mon-Thur; 24hrs Fri; 11am-late Sat, Sun. **Admission** free. **Credit** AmEx, DC, JCB, MC, V. **Map** p252 B2.
After the success of Km8, it was only a matter of time before another beachside venue appeared. CaféDel Mar set up this glam shack on Siloso Beach in early 2007. It's sister to the original Ibiza Sunset Bar, where the music genre 'chill-out lounge' was invented. Expect beach fluff (girls in designer swimwear and large sunnies), languid tunes, daytime preening on the outdoor lounge beds, and nighttime romping in the sunken pools, Jacuzzis and cabanas. There's also a tiny dance club and a deck for viewing perfect sunsets and sunrises.

Km8

120 Tanjong Beach Walk, Tanjong Beach, Sentosa (6274 2288/www.km8.com.sg). HarbourFront MRT then Sentosa Express. **Open** 11am-11pm Mon-Thur; 11am-1am Fri-Sun. **Admission** free. **Credit** AmEx, DC, JCB, MC, V. **Map** p252 D4.
Well before glam shacks laid tracks, there was Km8, located on Tanjong Beach (exactly eight kilometres from Orchard Road). It used to be all about the salacious crowd, splash pool and hot sounds, but the hip quotient seems to have dropped off the radar recently. Still, it's a great spot from which to watch the sun sink while lying in a pastel-hued, sand-embedded deckchair, guzzling champagne and watching pert bottoms laze by. Look out for news of sister club Liquid Room, a key player on the nightlife scene for ten years: it closed in 2006, but should be re-opening in new premises in 2007.

St James Power Station

3 Sentosa Gateway, HarbourFront (6270 7676/ www.stjamespowerstation.com). HarbourFront MRT. **Open** varies at different venues. **Admission** $20. **Credit** AmEx, DC, JCB, MC, V. **Map** p252 C1.
The biggest new kid on the block, this multi-purpose nightlife venue opened in late 2006 and offers nine different clubs and bars under one roof – for a single admission charge. It's housed in a huge former power station next to the new VivoCity mega-mall. The main space is the Powerhouse, a dance club that's aiming to steal some of Zouk's thunder; Movida (*see p189*) features a Paraguayan band playing Afro-Cuban sounds; the Bellini Room (*see p190*) boasts Martinis, and a house band playing lounge and swing tunes; Dragonfly (*see p186*) has Mandarin pop, back-up dancers and acrobatic aerialists; the Boiler Room focuses on live R&B, rock or pop; and black-and-white Mono offers public karaoke as well as ten private rooms. There's also the chic second-floor Gallery Bar, for a bird's eye view of all the other outlets; alfresco Peppermint Park for beers and unwinding; and the Lobby Bar, a casual lounge bar with sports on TV. **Photo** *above.*

Arts & Entertainment

Film

Home-grown movies are few, but cinemas are plentiful.

Singapore is not known for its cinematic output. Even at home, only a handful of Singaporean films is released each year; of these, very few make a ripple at the box office. For one thing, they are surrounded by a glut of Hollywood product. And more importantly, unlike its larger neighbours such as Malaysia, Indonesia and Thailand, Singapore doesn't have a film industry to speak of. There are merely a few ambitious filmmakers who have scraped the resources together, and one dedicated film outfit – Raintree Pictures, a subsidiary of the big government-linked broadcast firm Mediacorp.

In this light, it's amazing to think that Singapore was once home to two powerhouse movie studios. Between World War II and the late 1960s, Cathay and the Shaw Brothers studios pumped out feature films at an amazing rate. Run by immigrant Chinese businessmen (Loke Wan Tho at Cathay; Run Run and Runme at Shaw Brothers), they made films on studio backlots and locations in Singapore. Dialogue was scripted in the Bahasa language and the actors were Malay. Films were exported all the way up Malaya (as it then was) and to Indonesia, where there was a vast market for Malay comedies, musicals, melodramas and horror flicks. The stars of this era are still fondly remembered, especially the Shaw Bros' leading man, P Ramlee, whose legacy as a director, singer and actor endures even today.

Not long after Singapore and Malaysia were separated in 1965, the filmmaking scene moved to Kuala Lumpur and it was a wrap for the Malay film industry in Singapore – though Cathay and Shaw Brothers continued in the exhibition business. Without the studios' infrastructure, subsequent Singaporean film efforts were largely isolated. One notable success was the cheesy action thriller *They Call Her… Cleopatra Wong* (1978), a Philippines/ Singapore co-production partly shot around the Island (and on Sentosa); it has since been gushed over by Quentin Tarantino.

Foreign film and TV crews, which had been using Singapore as an 'exotic' location since the 1920s, continued to fly in and shoot European James Bond rip-offs, and also a few higher-profile adaptations of novels set in Singapore, including Noel Coward's *Pretty Polly* (1967) and Paul Theroux's *Saint Jack* (1979). But as the country modernised, it

became harder for foreigners to find 'old' Singapore. Meanwhile, domestic production dropped off to zero during the 1980s.

In the following decade, there was a revival in Singapore's cinematic fortunes. Jack Neo, an immensely popular TV comic, drew the masses to a series of crudely effective, satirical comedies. Eric Khoo, son of the late hotel tycoon Khoo Teck Puat, scored 'art-house' hits with *Mee Pok Man* (1995), *12 Storeys* (1997) and *Be With Me* (2005), films that explored the loneliness of ordinary Singaporeans and were rewarded with slots at major international film festivals. Nowadays, more than half a dozen features are made each year. Although clichés and stiff acting abound, some do capture the public imagination, such as Kelvin Tong's horror film *The Maid* (2005) and Tan Pin Pin's wry documentary about music and public expression, *Singapore GaGa* (2005).

WATCHING MOVIES

Film-going has been a major leisure activity for Singaporeans since large cinemas first opened in the 1930s. The old family companies – Shaw, Cathay, Eng Wah – dominated the sector right up to the '90s, managing enormous 1,000-seat halls in cherished locations. As the population expanded and the demand for choice grew, these ageing, single-screen caverns were no

Cathay.
See p175.

NOW OPEN · THE CATHAY CINEPLEX

longer viable. Many of the old movie houses shut down. Then the multiplexes came, most aggressively in the form of Golden Village, a Hong Kong/Australian venture that created garishly designed, spanking new multi-screen cinemas on the top floors of shopping centres. They were an immediate hit.

Like the rest of the world, Singapore has been colonised by Hollywood. All the usual action flicks, special effects extravaganzas and lowbrow comedies arrive at the same time as, or shortly after, their US releases. But Singaporeans also have a taste for fare from other Asian countries, particularly star-heavy Chinese blockbusters, and there is a steady supply of supernatural horrors and cutesy rom-coms from South Korea and Japan.

Censorship of imported films is more relaxed than it used to be before reforms in the early 1990s. A stratified series of classifications (G, PG, NC16, M18, R21) ensures that most content is passed these days, except for explicit sexual imagery (particularly if it has a gay theme). However, distributors still regularly 'snip' commercial films in order to get a lower rating and increase their potential market. The last banned film was Taiwanese gay comedy *Formula 17* in 2004; but some long-banned titles have been quietly released in recent years.

Sadly, there are no full-time art-house or independent cinemas, but a few venues try to offer a more mature alternative to the multiplex. **The Substation**, the **Arts House** and the **Gallery Theatre** all run part-time programmes of local films, short films and other special seasons. In the past five years independent distributors have become more successful, bringing in film festival favourites from Europe and beyond. Cinema chains **Cathay** and **Golden Village** have responded to this trend by devoting one 'exclusive' screen in certain multiplexes to alternative films.

Lion City films

For a fast introduction into the cinematic world of Singapore, watch the following. All are available on DVD or VCD.

Penarik Becha
P Ramlee, 1955, Malay.
Aka *The Trishaw Puller*. An early classic directed by and starring legendary Malay movie icon P Ramlee. It's a routine melodrama of young lovers from different sides of the class divide, but essential viewing for Ramlee's melancholy performance and some stunning location shots of post-war Singapore.

Saint Jack
Peter Bogdanovich, 1979, English.
Shot entirely on location, in parts of the island that have since changed beyond recognition (Bugis Street Market, Boat Quay), this tale of an American pimp (Ben Gazzara) adrift among gangsters, prostitutes and the CIA captures the last gasps of an 'exotic', sleazy city, before it got its squeaky-clean rep. Bogdanovich shot in secret, and the film was banned in Singapore until 2006.

12 Storeys
Eric Khoo, 1997, Mandarin, Hokkien and English.
With more than a nod to the moral complexity and coolly observational style of Krzyzstof Kieslowski's *Decalogue*, this breakthrough film charts the unfulfilled and tragic lives of residents in a government housing block. Selected for the Un Certain Regard section at Cannes, the only Singaporean film to receive that honour.

Money No Enough
TL Tay, 1998, Mandarin, Hokkien and Singlish.
Written by and starring popular TV comic Jack Neo, this post-economic crisis comedy is no cinematic gem, but audiences lapped it up. It's about *kiasu* ('afraid to lose') working-class Chinese Singaporeans striving to make a quick buck, and is daring in its outspoken satire of a ruthless, grasping society. Neo then turned director, and has taken on other big social issues including the education system, but none of his recent films has as much bite.

15
Royston Tan, 2003, Mandarin and Hokkien.
Young, award-winning director Tan reworked his successful short film into a 90-minute cause célèbre: a bewilderingly stylish and harrowing docu-drama about restless Chinese teens turning to petty crime, drugs and suicide as an escape from dead-end lives. Heavily censored upon release in Singapore (all references to gangs were considered dangerous), it's only available (uncut) on DVD in the UK and US.

Arts & Entertainment

INFORMATION & TICKETS

The only definitive commercial cinema listings are found daily in the *Straits Times*, although information about all films, including indie fare, is available at www.sgfilm.com, a forum run by film fans (go to the 'News and Hype' section), which also says when a film's been trimmed.

For the commercial cinemas, ticket prices start at $7 for a daytime weekday screening and go up to $9.50 for a peak-time weekend show. Booking in advance for weekends is a must, and buying online is simpler than being trapped in a recorded phone system. English language films usually have Chinese subtitles. Tip: bring a coat or a sweater, as the air-conditioning can hit Antarctic levels.

Cinemas

Major commercial chains

Cathay

Cathay Cineleisure Orchard, 8 Grange Road (tickets 6235 1155/www.cathay.com.sg). Orchard or Somerset MRT. **Screens** 12. **Credit** MC, V. **Map** p247 G4.

Unlike Shaw, Cathay has moved with the times. Its Orchard Road flagship is extremely busy most evenings and weekends: be prepared to brave a crowd of noisy teenagers. The latest addition is the Cathay (www.thecathay.com.sg), a shopping-cinema complex that replaced the beloved old Cathay

(closed in 2000). The chain's main innovation is the Picturehouse (www.thepicturehouse.com.sg), an 82-seat cinema with luxury seats that specialises in foreign art-house films and festivals. Two new Cathay cinemas outside the city centre (Ang Mo Kio and Pasir Ris) are due to open by late 2007. **Photo** *p173*.

Eng Wah

EW Suntec, Suntec City Mall, 3 Temasek Boulevard, Marina (6836 9074/www.ewcinemas.com.sg). City Hall MRT then 10mins walk. **Screens** 5. **Credit** AmEx, MC, V. **Map** p249 M6

Eng Wah specialises in smaller cinemas in the 'heartlands' outside the town centre, although it does have one central site, in mega-mall Suntec City. Without the high number of screens of its competitors, Eng Wah differentiates itself by leading the way in high end digital projection.

Golden Village

GV VivoCity, Levels 2/3, VivoCity, 1 HarbourFront Precinct, HarbourFront (tickets 1900 912 1234/ www.gv.com.sg). HarbourFront MRT. **Screens** 15. **Credit** MC, V. **Map** p252 C1.

GV has set the standard for modern cinema-going on the island. Its cinemas may be characterless, but they are clean and well run, and its online booking service is fast and easy to use. Although the GV Plaza on Orchard Road is popular, the flagships are GV Grand (Great World City, Kim Seng Road) – the first to introduce pricey, luxury screens (Gold Class, costing $25-$30) – and, most recently, GV VivoCity, at the enormous waterfront mall of the same name. The latter is now Singapore's biggest multiplex, with 15 screens including Cinema Europa, supposedly dedicated to more art-house titles. Hindi and Tamil films are shown at GV Yishun.

Shaw

Lido 8 Cineplex, Shaw House, 350 Orchard Road (tickets 6738 0555/www.shaw.com.sg). Orchard MRT. **Screens** 8. **Credit** AmEx, MC, V. **Map** p247 E3.
With its dwindling number of screens, the Shaw chain has seen better days. The Lido 8 Cineplex and Shaw Cineplex Bugis (at Parco Bugis Junction) still do furious business at weekends, but the buildings are tatty. The once-magnificent Prince & Jade on Beach Road, which contains Singapore's largest cinema auditorium (Prince 1, with 1,200 seats) is rarely busy, and is one place where you can always get tickets. In an effort to pull a new crowd, it's started showing Hindi and Tamil movies.

Other cinemas & screens

Alliance Française

1 Sarkies Road, Orchard Road & Around (6737 8422/tickets 6734 4906/www.alliancefrancaise. org.sg). Newton MRT. **Credit** AmEx, DC, JCB, MC, V. **Map** p247 G1.
This French cultural centre has a 230-seat auditorium and equipment to show 16mm and 35mm films. It hosts the annual French Film Festival, and screens French films every Tuesday evening (tickets $8).

The Arts House

Old Parliament House, 1 Old Parliament Lane, Colonial District (6332 6900/tickets 6332 6919/ www.theartshouse.com.sg). City Hall or Raffles Place MRT. **Credit** AmEx, DC, MC, V. **Map** p251 K9.
A former parliament building, now an arts centre. On the first level is the 70-seat Screening Room. Programming is inconsistent, but has included local films, foreign embassy sponsored seasons (Swiss, Polish and Spanish movies), and classic Hong Kong martial arts epics. *See p202.*

Gallery Theatre

National Museum of Singapore, 93 Stamford Road, Colonial District (6332 3659/5642/tickets 6332 3659/www.nationalmuseum.sg). City Hall or Dhoby Ghaut MRT. **Credit** MC, V. **Map** p248 J6.
A 247-seat, multi-purpose auditorium in the newly revamped National Museum that just happens to have 35mm and digital projection facilities. Look out for its Singapore Cinémathèque programme.

Golden Theatre & Yangtze

Golden Theatre *Golden Mile Tower, 6001 Beach Road, Arab Quarter (6298 5466). City Hall MRT then bus 100, 961.* **No credit cards. Map** p249 O4.
Yangtze *Pearl's Centre, 100 Eu Tong Sen Street, Chinatown (6223 7529). Outram Park MRT.* **No credit cards. Map** p250 G11.
Although they are run by different companies, these two elderly cinemas are synonymous with steamy Filipino sex melodramas, Japanese rape-revenge flicks, American 'erotic thrillers' and the occasional

art film (with nudity). The Yangtze is edgier: the box office area is run-down, and it's the last cinema to commission wonderfully lurid painted signboards to promote its films. Refurbishment is planned for 2007, but let's hope it retains its character.

iWerks & Omni-Theatre

iWerks *Singapore Discovery Centre, 510 Upper Jurong Road, Jurong (6792 6188/tickets 6668 0352/www.sdc.com.sg/iwerks). Boon Lay MRT then bus 182, 193.* **Credit** AmEx, MC, V.
Omni-Theatre *Singapore Science Centre, 15 Science Centre Road, Jurong (6425 2500/ www.science.edu.sg). Jurong East MRT then bus 66, 335.* **Credit** AmEx, MC, V.
For two spectacular cinema experiences – think multistorey, super-surround sound, hi-tech 2D and 3D technology – you need to go west. iWerks, in the souped-up Discovery Centre, is the newest variation on the iMax 70mm theme, but claims to be bigger, sharper and louder. It shows full-length animated films and documentaries (tickets $7-$10). The older Omni-Theatre, at the more humble Science Centre, has a circular screen and specialises in nature and science films ($10-$15).

The Substation

45 Armenian Street, Colonial District (6337 7535/ tickets 6337 7800/www.substation.org). City Hall MRT. **Credit** MC, V. **Map** p250 J7.
The first venue to regularly promote local films and filmmakers, especially short films. It hosts monthly screenings and various annual and biennial festivals such as Women in Film, Young Guns (international student films), the Singapore Short Film Festival and the Asian Film Symposium. The hub of Singapore's young, independent film scene, and also a theatre and dance venue (*see p204*).

Festivals

The big one as far as cinephiles are concerned is the **Singapore International Film Festival** (*see p162*) in April, best known for showing documentaries and feature films from all over Asia. Various embassies and foreign cultural institutes also organise festivals, showcasing new films from Japan, Thailand, Spain, Italy, Australia, New Zealand and the EU; the most established are the **French Film Festival** (in October) and the **German Film Festival** (November). Outdoor screenings of summer blockbusters, usually at the Padang or Fort Canning, are a yearly fixture in September/ October, thanks to **Starlight Cinema** (www.starlightcinema.com/sg). Newer events include **Asian Festival of First Films** (www.asianfirstfilms.com) in November/ December, and **Animation Nation** in November. The latter is organised by the **Singapore Film Society** (www.sfs.org.sg), an active bunch with an informative website.

Arts & Entertainment

Galleries

Singapore's contemporary art scene is starting to push boundaries.

Singapore's visual arts scene can trace its roots to colonial days, when European painters recorded their experiences and local craftsmen practised traditional arts like ink painting and calligraphy. The first arts institution dates from before World War II, when migrant artists from China founded the Society of Chinese Artists in 1935. The country's first arts college, the Nanyang Fine Arts Academy, followed three years later.

After the war, the Society regrouped in 1949 as the multicultural Singapore Art Society, and by the 1950s a new-found patriotism had flourished into the unique Nanyang ('South Seas') style of painting, reflecting Singapore's role as a tropical paradise. This style wasn't universal, though: during the lead up to independence and after, left-wing Chinese artists created gritty social realist prints and paintings of working-class life on the streets, at work and in the kampongs. Further impetus was created with the founding of the National Museum's Art Gallery in 1976, which became an exhibition hub. In 1996 the **Singapore Art Museum** (*see p76*) opened; this now houses the national art collection of Singapore – the largest array of 20th-century South-east Asian art in public hands.

Most galleries concentrate on 2-D works, favouring paintings, photography, prints and mixed media. Nostalgic, romantic images of Asia are available everywhere, but works are becoming increasingly avant-garde, abstract and introspective, often with a noticeable Asian sensibility. But by international standards, they rarely challenge or confront: the majority of galleries – and artists – still prefer to play it safe.

While all the galleries listed below focus on contemporary Asian works, **Art Seasons, Utterly Art, Plastique Kinetic Worms** and **Taksu** are acclaimed for their support of hot, new local talent. Local artists also put on their own shows at the galleries of the **Arts House** (*see p202*), the **Substation** (*see p204*) and **Alliance Française** (*see p176*). For some of the best prints in the region, visit the **Singapore Tyler Print Institute** (41 Robertson Quay, 6336 3663, www.stpi.com.sg), while **Sculpture Square** (155 Middle Road, Bras Basah & Bugis, 6333 1055, www.sculpturesq.com.sg) is the only space dedicated to 3-D work from South-east Asia.

REGULAR EVENTS
Contemporary art got a boost in 2006 with the first **Singapore Biennale** (*see p164*), organised by the National Arts Council (NAC).

Singapore Biennale: bringing art to the masses, in public venues like City Hall.

Held in an assortment of public spaces all over town, it involved 95 artists from over 38 countries, including big names like Mark Wallinger, Jenny Holzer, Mariko Mori and Barbara Kruger – and 12 Singaporean artists. The Biennale is supposed to alternate with the **Singapore Art Show**, launched in 2005 and also run by the NAC. Also look out for **ARTSingapore** (www.artsingapore.net), the only major contemporary art fair in South-east Asia, held over five days in October.

Regional auctions are held biannually by **Sotheby's** (6732 8239, www.sothebys.com) and **Larasati** (6737 2130, www.larasati.com). Both focus on artworks and artefacts from Asia, as does **Christie's**, which has an office in the city (6235 3828, www.christies.com), but no auctions.

INFORMATION

For the latest information on what's on where, check the daily papers, magazines *Time Out Singapore, I-S* and *Arts Xplosion* (distributed free with *Today* newspaper). The **Art Galleries Association Singapore** (www.agas.org.sg, 6235 4113) also publishes an exhibition guide, available from member galleries. Admission is free to all galleries, most of which are closed on public holidays.

Colonial District

A cluster of galleries is housed within the Ministry of Information, Communication & the Arts (MICA) Building at the foot of Fort Canning Park. Formerly a police station and barracks, it's hard to miss thanks to its rainbow-coloured shutters.

Art-2 Gallery

#01-03 MICA Building, 140 Hill Street (6338 8713/ www.art2.com.sg). City Hall or Clark Quay MRT. **Open** 11am-7pm Mon-Sat. **Credit** AmEx, DC, JCB, MC, V. **Map** p250 J8.
Since 1991 Vera Ong and Seah Tzi-Yan have represented some of South-east Asia's best artists. They focus on contemporary sculpture, ceramics and paintings, and are one of the few galleries to specialise in public sculpture. Artists include Malaysian Soh Chee Hui, Burmese Min Wae Aung, and locals Hong Zhu An, Iskandar Jalil, Han Sai Por and the late Anthony Poon.

Artfolio

#02-25 Raffles Hotel Shopping Arcade, Raffles Hotel, 328 North Bridge Road (6334 4677/4866/ www.artfolio.com.sg). City Hall MRT. **Open** 11am-7pm Mon-Sat; noon-5pm Sun. **Credit** AmEx, DC, JCB, MC, V. **Map** p251 K6.
This gallery within Raffles Hotel has reduced its space by half, but continues to feature contemporary art and sculpture by notable Asian artists. You can find elegant works in watercolour and oil, plus col-

lages, etchings, cast bronze sculptures and ceramics by Malaysian Eng Tay, locals Thomas Yeo and Oh Chai Hoo, Dutch-Indonesian Arie Smit, Indonesian Hanafi, Filipina Pacita Abad and others.

Gajah Gallery

#01-08 MICA Building, 140 Hill Street (6737 4202/ www.gajahgallery.com). City Hall or Clark Quay MRT. **Open** 11am-7pm Mon-Fri; noon-6pm Sat, Sun. **Credit** AmEx, DC, JCB, MC, V. **Map** p250 J8.
This handsome red space shows large-scale artworks by well-known Singaporean, Vietnamese, Indian and Indonesian artists. Rising talents appear, as well as established names such as Singaporean Jason Lim, Indonesians Affandi, Nasirun and Heri Dono, Vietnamese Bui Xuan Phai and Nguyen Trung, and Indians Sunil Das and Jogen Chowdury.

Orchard Gallery

#01-05 MICA Building, 140 Hill Street (6334 4661/ www.orchardgallery.com.sg). City Hall or Clark Quay MRT. **Open** 11am-6pm daily. **Credit** AmEx, DC, JCB, MC, V. **Map** p250 J8.
Founded in 1984, this gallery has gone from strength to strength; a recent expansion has allowed it to further develop its collection. It is renowned for contemporary Chinese and Singaporean art, including oil paintings, watercolours and Chinese ink paintings by artists from distinguished Chinese art academies and institutes; as such, the work tends to be overtly classical. Look out for the magnificent watercolours by Singapore's Ong Kim Seng.

SooBin Art International

#01-10/11/12 MICA Building, 140 Hill Street (6837 2777/www.soobinart.com). City Hall or Clark Quay MRT. **Open** 11am-7pm Mon-Sat. **Credit** AmEx, DC, JCB, MC, V. **Map** p250 J8.
SooBin has organised more than 100 exhibitions in the region since its inception in 1990. It supports both international masters and exciting new talents from Singapore and China. In fact, it was one of the first local galleries to show China's new wave art of the 1990s. It aims to hold five master-class shows each year, featuring the likes of American-Chinese Walasse Ting, China's Wang Guangyi, Yue Minjun and Zhang Xiaogang and Singaporean Chen Wen Hsi. Work by Picasso and Miró also appears.

Chinatown & the CBD

Art Seasons

The Box, 5 Gemmill Lane, Chinatown (6221 1800/ www.artseasons.com.sg). Chinatown MRT. **Open** 11am-8pm Mon-Fri; noon-7pm Sat. **Credit** AmEx, DC, JCB, MC, V. **Map** p250 I11.
Thanks to its branch in Beijing and close ties to the Myanmar Gallery of Contemporary Art (in Yangon), Art Seasons has work by some of the most renowned Chinese and Burmese artists, and a reputation for showcasing the best new local talent. **Photo** *p179.*
Other locations: Art Seasons Warehouse #02-11/12 Eunos Technolink, 7 Kaki Bukit Road 1, Bedok (6741 6366).

iPreciation

#01-10 The Fullerton Hotel, 1 Fullerton Square, CBD (6339 0678/www.ipreciation.com). Raffles Place MRT. **Open** 10am-7pm Mon-Fri; 11am-3pm Sat; by appointment Sun. **Credit** AmEx. **Map** p251 K9.

Although a small space within the massive Fullerton Hotel, iPreciation has built up some clout over the years with its prominent exhibitions, including large-scale outdoor shows. Its stable of prominent artists from around Asia includes China's Nobel prize winner Gao Xingjian.

Utterly Art

2F 229A South Bridge Road, Chinatown (6226 2605). Chinatown MRT. **Open** 11.30am-8pm Mon-Sat; noon-5.30pm Sun. **Credit** AmEx, DC, JCB, MC, V. **Map** p250 I11.

Utterly Art differentiates itself from other galleries by actively supporting rising local and regional artists – although it has also exhibited established international names such as Ansel Adams, Robert Freeman, Russell Wong and Zulkifli Yusoff. Expect some of the most interesting work in town: painting, print, sculpture, ceramics, installation and performance art. Exhibitions change every two weeks.

Yisulang Art Gallery

60A Pagoda Street (6227 6288/www.yisulang.com). Chinatown MRT. **Open** 11am-7pm Mon-Sat; 1-6pm Sun. **Credit** AmEx, DC, JCB, MC, V. **Map** p250 H10.

Set up in 2002 and housed in a beautiful Peranakan building, Yisulang is dedicated to contemporary and traditional Chinese art. It hopes to dispel myths and stereotypes about Chinese art and the differences

Hot local talent at **Art Seasons**. See p178.

between traditionalism and modernism. Its vast network covers artists from all over China, including Shi Jianguo, Li Jin, Zhu Xinjian and Jimei Chilei.

Little India

Plastique Kinetic Worms

61 Kerbau Road (6292 7783/www.pkworms.org.sg). Little India MRT. **Open** 11am-6pm Tue-Sat. **No credit cards. Map** p248 K3.

What began as something of a social experiment in an empty shop has developed into an important space for contemporary artists. Through its programme of exhibitions, workshops, international exchanges and residencies, this artists' collective has become a vital space for emerging young talents and artistic experimentation.

p-10

10 Perumal Road (6294 0041/www.p-10.org). Farrer Park MRT. **Open** by appointment daily. **No credit cards. Map** p249 L1.

This new contemporary art space, run by a collective of artists and curators, has been coming up with consistently inventive exhibitions, education and residency programmes since it opened in 2004.

Orchard Road & Around

Art Forum

82 Cairnhill Road (6737 3448/www.artforum.com.sg). Newton MRT. **Open** 10am-6pm Mon-Sat; by appointment Sun. **Credit** AmEx, DC, JCB, MC, V. **Map** p247 G3.

Singapore's oldest gallery is run by one of the industry's most colourful characters, Marjorie Chu. She has been instrumental in the art scene's development, helping to found the Art Galleries Association of Singapore and the ARTSingapore fair. She now focuses on elegant paintings and sculptures by contemporary artists from the five founding member countries of ASEAN (Indonesia, Malaysia, the Philippines, Singapore and Thailand).

Galerie Dauphin

#03-08A Tanglin Mall, 163 Tanglin Road (6734 2137/www.galeriedauphin.com). Bus 7, 36, 77, 123, 174. **Open** 10am-9pm daily. **Credit** AmEx, DC, JCB, MC, V. **Map** p246 C3.

Recently relocated, this gallery aims to create exposure for otherwise inaccessible art and new art forms and talents. Drawing from a stable of international names, it features paintings, photography, digital art and sculptures. There's a strong representation of contemporary Indian, Indonesian and African artists, as well as folk and tribal art.

HaKaren Art Gallery

#02-43 Tanglin Shopping Centre, 19 Tanglin Road (6733 3382/www.hakaren.com). Orchard MRT then bus 7, 106, 111, 123, 174. **Open** 10.30am-6.30pm Mon-Sat; noon-6pm Sun. **Credit** AmEx, DC, JCB, MC, V. **Map** p246 C3.

Arts & Entertainment

For ten years, HaKaren has specialised in contemporary Chinese paintings and sculptures. Created by some of China's most outstanding young artists – including Yue Minjun, Xue Dai, He Chun Ye and Hu Yongkai – the works are typically steeped in classical Asian values and themes, but portrayed with distinctly western touches in composition and colour.

Jasmine Fine Arts

#05-29 Paragon, 290 Orchard Road (6734 5688). Orchard MRT. **Open** 11.30am-8pm daily. **Credit** AmEx, DC, JCB, MC, V. **Map** p247 F4.
Jasmine's collection has changed dramatically over the years. From representing Filipino and Indonesian art, it is now dedicated to bringing in the hottest work from China. Visitors can expect dynamic pieces from Yue Minjun, Wang Guangyi, Zeng Fanzhi and other big names on the international art market.

Linda Gallery

#01-03 Block 15, Dempsey Road (6476 7000/ www.lindagallery.com). Bus 7, 75, 77, 106, 174. **Open** 11am-7pm daily. **Credit** AmEx, MC, V.
From its beginnings in Jakarta, this gallery has branched out to Singapore and, in 2006, Beijing. The Dempsey Road outlet specialises in contemporary South-east Asian art, particularly by eminent Indonesian artists such as Affandi, Hendra Gunawan, Nyoman Gunarsa and Krijono, much of which is bold and loud of palette. You can also find contemporary Chinese work by Walasse Ting and Zhong Biao.

Opera Gallery

#02-12H Takashimaya Shopping Centre, Ngee Ann City, 391 Orchard Road (6735 2618/www. operagallery.com). Orchard MRT. **Open** 11am-7pm Mon-Fri; 10am-8pm Sat, Sun. **Credit** AmEx, DC, MC, V. **Map** p247 F4.

From humble beginnings – two guys selling posters on the streets of Paris – Opera Gallery has grown into an international network of galleries in Paris, London, Venice, Singapore, Hong Kong, New York and Miami. Need a Picasso, Chagall, Gaugin or Dali for the bedroom? No problem. It also stocks paintings and sculptures by South American, US, Chinese and French contemporaries. Be warned: the price tags will melt your credit card.

Western Singapore

The following are a short walk from the centre of Holland Village.

Block 43 Studio Gallery

#03-80 Work Loft @ Chip Bee, 43 Jalan Merah Saga (6471 1359). Bus 48, 61, 106, 970. **Open** by appointment Mon-Sat. **No credit cards**.
This artist-run studio/gallery was founded by British artist James R Holdsworth in 2001. His Access Hanoi and Access Indonesia shows were well received, although today James specialises in contemporary Vietnamese art. Artists include Doan Hoang Lam, Nguyen Quang Huy, Nguyen Minh Thanh and Dinh Y Nhi; all grew up during the Vietnam War and are graduates of the renowned School of Fine Arts in Hanoi. There are also four-week courses in drawing, painting, photography, art history and art theory.

Ketna Patel Art Studio

33 & 35 Jalan Puteh Jerneh (6479 3736/www.ketna patel.com). Bus 48, 61, 106, 970. **Open** 9am-9pm daily. **Credit** AmEx, DC, JCB, MC, V.
There's nothing dull about the works of Ketna Patel. She excels in creating psychedelic Pop Art-inspired interpretations of Asian motifs, while her furniture (including the kitchen sink) is dazzling and highly desirable. If you're looking for pretty Asian maidens all in a row, you'll be disappointed. **Photo** *left*.

Sunjin Gallery

#03-62 Work Loft @ Chip Bee, 43 Jalan Merah Saga (6738 2317/www.sunjingalleries.com.sg). Bus 48, 61, 106, 970. **Open** 11am-7pm Tue-Fri; 11am-6pm Sat; 1-6pm Sun. **Credit** AmEx, DC, JCB, MC, V.
Sunjin exhibits a diverse mix of classical and modern art, sourced from across South-east Asia and China. Work ranges from figurative paintings to abstract sculptures, and mixed media installations to conceptual art, by established and emerging artists.

Taksu

#02-74 Work Loft @ Chip Bee, 43 Jalan Merah Saga (6476 4788/www.taksu.com). Bus 48, 61, 106, 970. **Open** 10am-7pm Mon-Sat; by appointment Sun. **Credit** DC, JCB, MC, V.
This gallery had already carved out an enviable reputation for itself in Kuala Lumpur before it opened branches in Singapore and Jakarta. The work tends to be young and edgy, yet always accessible (and affordable), making this a popular hunting ground for the new collector.

Ketna Patel Art Studio

Gay & Lesbian

Singapore's closet door is starting to swing open.

For pick-up antics by the bold and the beautiful, visit **Attica**. *See p182*

As a country where sex with a member of the same sex could land you in prison, Singapore is not exactly a queer hotspot. At the time of writing, homosexual acts are illegal, although the penal code is vaguely worded: all anal sex is against the law, so in theory straight people could also get banged up for bedroom misdemeanours. Still, Singapore is a gateway to Asia for many gay tourists, who stop here en route to Japan, Thailand or Hong Kong.

It's true that gay men and lesbians do not openly demonstrate their orientation and public displays of affection are rare. Yet most Singaporeans are comfortable with homosexuality; recent surveys conducted by local media show an increasing acceptance of gays and lesbians; those aged under 30 are particularly tolerant. And the small scene is gradually livening up. It started in the 1980s when mainstream clubs began holding gay events in order to drum up business on Sunday nights. Police tolerated same-sex disco dancing and eventually slow dancing. Now there are bona fide gay clubs, some open all night.

A few years ago, Singapore was firmly on the gay map. In 2001, it hosted its first Nation Party on Sentosa island, around the time of the country's National Day. It was a smash hit and soon mushroomed into a three-day event. The biggest gay bash in Asia, Nation attracted visitors from Hong Kong, Taiwan, Japan, Australia and the US. But its growing visibility concerned the government, and in 2005 the police withdrew the organisers' permit, claiming that same-sex kissing in public was detrimental to the public interest. And a senior minister claimed that the party had fuelled a surge in the number of AIDs cases. As a result, the party moved to Thailand.

Still, there is gay partying to be done in Singapore. Pinpointing the scene is easy – it's centred on the Tanjong Pagar area, with a good mix of chillout bars, clubs and karaoke joints. Long-time haunt **Taboo** is the current 'it' spot on weekends. Also watch for the opening of a new gay venue beneath **Mox Bar & Café** to replace the much-loved Happy Bar, which closed at the end of 2006. Other hangouts include the beaches at Sentosa and to a lesser extent, the East Coast; public swimming pools and gyms are also gay meeting spots. But be careful not to jump to conclusions: Singaporeans are discreet ('down low') and friendliness is not the same as cruising

WHERE TO STAY

While Singapore has no hotels that cater specifically to gays and lesbians, most visitors are happy to stay at international hotels in the centre of town. Boutique hotels are also gay favourites: the **Scarlet Hotel**, **New Majestic Hotel** and **Hotel 1929** (for all, *see p42*), all located in Chinatown, are close to the gay bars and clubs.

PLAYING SAFE

Crime rates are low and gay hate crimes are uncommon (though not unheard of). Although the number of cases of HIV and AIDS is low, local AIDS group **AFA** (Action For AIDS, 21 Norris Road, Little India, 6254 0212, www.afa.org.sg) has launched an ad campaign to promote awareness, and safe sex is emphasised across the scene. It also has an anonymous HIV testing and counselling clinic.

There is a small number of private men's clubs (bathhouses) in Singapore, but they keep a low profile for obvious reasons. Many are by invitation only, so get to know some friends on the scene if you want to visit.

INFORMATION

Regional gay websites **www.fridae.com** and **www.trevvy.com** are a good guide to the scene, and provide a social network for thousands of men and women. **People Like Us** (www.plu.sg) is a local gay rights group campaigning for legislative changes; the phrase, and the acronym PLU, are also the local codewords for 'gay'. A great information resource is the **Pelangi Pride Centre** (#04-01 21 Tanjong Pagar Road, Chinatown, www.pelangipridecentre.org), above Mox Bar, which also has a community space and library/archive. For lesbians, there's the **RedQueen** social mailing list (www.auntieteck.com/special/redqueen.html).

Gay

Bars & clubs

Straight club **Attica** (*see p169*; **photo** *p181*) is the current gay hotspot on Sunday night, when a queer crowd dances to pop remixes. Mega-club **Zouk** (*see p171*), on the other side of the river from Robertson Quay, is always gay-friendly; the queer crowd often congregates in front of the main bar by the dancefloor.

Backstage Bar

13A Trengganu Street, Chinatown (6227 1712/ www.backstagebar.moonfruit.com). Chinatown MRT. **Open** 7pm-2am Mon-Thur, Sun; 7pm-3am Fri, Sat. **Credit** MC, V. **Map** p250 H11.
A little rainbow marks out Backstage Bar. As at its sister Tantric, the booze is dirt-cheap, but the alfresco area is larger. In fact, several levels await exploration. You can snuggle on a sofa in the corner or park yourself at the counter and watch old movies. The posters of musicals will scare the straight crowd away.

Mox Bar & Café

#04-01 21 Tanjong Pagar Road, Chinatown (6323 9438/www.mox.com.sg). Tanjong Pagar MRT. **Open** 7pm-midnight Tue-Thur; 7pm-3am Fri; 7pm-4am Sat. **Credit** MC, V. **Map** p250 H12.
Eclectic furniture and a wide range of strong, reasonably priced drinks are the highlights of this pre-clubbing favourite. Friendly waiters add to the sexy, feel-good vibe. The place is packed to the rafters on Friday, quieter during the week. There's no smoking inside, but you can puff away on the veranda. The bar's lease is up in 2008; fingers crossed it will stick around.

Taboo

65/67 Neil Road, Chinatown (6225 6256/ www.taboo97.com). Tanjong Pagar MRT. **Open** 8pm-2am Wed-Thur; 10pm-3am Fri; 10pm-4am Sat. **Admission** $11-$25 Sat. **Credit** AmEx, DC, MC, V. **Map** p250 H12.
Be warned: this three-level club, a gay institution, has long queues. It's a veritable crowd-pleaser, with a happy hour that lasts until midnight. The first level has a long bar and a DJ spinning pop remixes; the second is more relaxed, with sofas and a gallery overlooking the dancefloor; the attic is a cosy spot where groups of friends congregate. Special events include Bodwatch (a swimsuit show) and handbag house night. If you get your hand stamped, you can leave, bar-hop and then come back. Handbag Party, with hangbag tunes and diva music, is on the second Saturday of every month.

Tantric

78 Neil Road, Chinatown (6423 9232/www.backstagebar.moonfruit.com). Tanjong Pagar MRT. **Open** 8.30pm-3am daily. **Credit** MC, V. **Map** p250 H12.
Sporting a big rainbow flag, Tantric is hard to miss. Most of its customers are here for a (stiff) drink before partying the night away at Taboo opposite. The sister venue to Backstage Bar, it offers a similar set-up: an alfresco setting and a crowd of expat men (and the men who love them). The interior is small and slightly sleazy. But sleaze and booze – look out for the two-for-one offers – is a winning combination for this bunch.

Why Not

56-58 Tras Street, Chinatown (6323 3010/www.whynot.com.sg). Tanjong Pagar MRT. **Open** varies. **Map** p250 H12.

Island queen

'When it comes to humour, I've put Singapore on the map.' So says Kumar, Singapore's first and most famous drag queen. And he's not joking. Since 1992, crowds of locals and tourists have been flocking to see Kumar's scathing stand-up comedy, provocative cabaret – and mile-high legs.

It's easy to see why he's a star. In staid, conservative Singapore, Kumar is a dash of spice. But sensitive souls be warned: his wickedly witty act – in thick Singlish – is characterised by merciless bitching and controversial, tasteless topics. Sex jokes, racial quips and all things politically incorrect come fast and furious, while hecklers are ripped to shreds. In mocking racial stereotypes he sails close to the wind, but perhaps his Indian ethnicity allows him to push the envelope; his graphic sexual material stands in stark contrast to his fierce privacy (he has never come clean about his own sexuality). A back-up troupe of dancers and the usual lip-synch numbers provide a brief respite from the bitching.

Unlike most drag queens, Kumar has managed to break out of the gay scene and into the mainstream. In 1992, he had a television hit with the *Ra Ra Show*, but his no-holds-barred schtick was too spicy for the masses (or the government), and, despite its popularity, was cancelled. For a long period, he was banished from TV but recently he ditched his drag to appear in sitcoms *Oh, Carol!* and *My Sassy Neighbour*.

Still, live drag shows remain Kumar's true love. 'I've elevated drag to an art form,' says Kumar, who got his start at the age of ten,

dressing in his mother's clothes. 'With the way the world is now, nothing makes me happier than putting a smile on people's faces.' Which is just about the sweetest thing that will ever come out of his bitchy mouth.

Catch the diva in action at **3 Monkeys Restaurant** (#01-20 Orchard Towers, 400 Orchard Road, 6735 3707), at 11pm and 1am, Thursday to Saturday – though call to check first as venues and timings can change frequently.

Also known as the 'twink bar', Why Not is frequented by young Malaysian men and their older fan club; drag performers are also a fixture. During the week, it's a karaoke lounge; at the weekend, a disco playing outdated pop. Drinks are reasonably priced, and the U-shaped room makes it easy to survey the talent as you take a tour. The blue lighting is tacky, but twink-chasers can't be choosers.

Lesbian

Singapore's lesbian community is more low key than the gay male scene. And there is a divide between the older and younger sets: the mature women, especially the closeted, power-suited ones, tend to steer clear of the louder, prouder 'baby butches'. As for nightlife, lesbians just

don't party as much as their male counterparts, let alone go cruising. There is only a handful of bars catering to gay women. Located mainly in the Tanjong Pagar/Chinatown vicinity, these attract a more mature crowd and are kept afloat by a bunch of regulars. The monthly and quarterly parties are more popular.

Bars

Dai Empire

4/F 114 Neil Road, Chinatown (6536 0456). Outram Park MRT. **Open** 8pm-1am Mon-Thur; 8pm-3am Fri, Sat; 8pm-1am Sun. **Credit** MC, V. **Map** p250 H12. No men allowed. That's the rule at this friendly lesbian hangout. Stamina is another requirement as there are three flights of stairs to this rooftop bar.

It's worth it: the outdoor seating offers a bird's eye view of the surrounding area. There's also a pool table inside and a lengthy Martini menu. On weekends, the tables are pushed aside, the strobes appear and the girls go wild on the dancefloor.

Club 95

95 Club Street, Chinatown (9128 9595). Chinatown MRT. **Open** 6pm-2am Mon-Thur; 6pm-4am Fri, Sat. **Credit** AmEx, DC, JCB, MC, V. **Map** p250 I11.
This hole in the wall was Singapore's only dedicated lesbian bar until Bar Empire popped up in 2006. Though it's located on fashionable Club Street, don't expect scenes from *The L Word*; the lack of eye candy is matched by the uninspiring decor. But the claustrophobic confines are great for getting to know people. It's deserted on weekdays, except for (occasional) lesbian film screenings. **Photo** *below*.

Cows & Coolies

30 Mosque Street, Chinatown (6221 1239). Chinatown MRT. **Open** 6pm-1am Mon-Thur, Sun; 6pm-2am Fri, Sat. **Credit** AmEx, MC, V. **Map** p250 I10.
This back-to-basics karaoke pub in the heart of Chinatown is a favourite watering hole of the Mandarin-speaking set. The ambience is refreshingly relaxed, unpretentious and friendly. Regulars belt out Chinese pop hits or shoot some pool.

Crocodile Rock

#05-29 14 Scotts Road, Orchard Road & Around (6738 0535). Orchard MRT. **Open** 7.30pm-midnight Tue, Wed; 7.30pm-1am Thur; 7.30pm-3am Fri, Sat. **Credit** AmEx, MC, V. **Map** p247 F3.
Singapore's oldest lesbian pub has been in business for more than 15 years. Though owned by a lesbian, it isn't exclusively for women (there's a handful of

Club 95

male regulars). Expect a crowd of working professional women in their late twenties and above. Weekdays are a good bet if you love to sing (English lyrics only): it's quiet and you won't have to arm wrestle anyone for the karaoke mic.

Fuego

5 Gemmil Lane, Chinatown (6327 1098). Chinatown MRT. **Open** 6pm-1am Mon-Thur, Sun; 6pm-2am Fri, Sat. **Credit** AmEx, MC, V. **Map** p250 I11.
The dancefloor at Fuego is the real deal: by day, the salsa bar doubles as a dance studio. At night, regulars from nearby offices come to chill out. The drinks are good (happy hour 6-9.30pm daily), the DJ plays Latin music from 9.30pm, and there are free salsa classes on Sunday (7-9pm). Not strictly gay, but very gay-friendly, it hosts the occasional pink party.

Greyzone Bar

2/F 44A Tras Street, Tanjong Pagar (6220 5271). Tanjong Pagar MRT. **Open** 7pm-2am Mon-Thur; 7pm-3am Fri, Sat. **Credit** MC, V. **Map** p250 H12.
Greyzone is not as queer as it used to be. Formerly known as the Alternative Bar, it underwent a name change in 2006 as the owners tried to lure a straight crowd. However, lesbians still monopolise the 50-seater, second-storey bar. They don't seem deterred by the spartan interior, equipped with a pool table (free games on Monday), a TV and… not much else. The owner is a football fanatic, so English Premier League matches are shown every Saturday.

Parties

Both websites are also good forums for getting to know people, with news, advice, chatrooms and personal ads.

Herstory

www.herstory.ws.
Singapore's best-known girl parties have been running since 1998. Herstory bashes tend to attract a young crowd that enjoys boozing and being seen. Gimmicks include the popular Butch Hunt and Femme Quest – quasi-beauty contests to crown the most charming butches and femmes – and Herstory Idol, a *Pop Idol*-style singing competition. Each winner is decided by lesbian voters. The parties usually take place on the second Thursday of March, June, July, September and December, at Zouk (*see p171*).

Two Queens

www.twoqueensparty.com.
Hosted by a well-known local actress/comedienne, the Two Queens' girl parties have garnered such a strong following with their mix of stage games and performances that a sister party has been launched at a separate location. The main event, held on the first Thursday of the month, attracts 21s and above. The new Thirst Thurs Nites (18s and above) held on all other Thursdays, feature a mix of aspiring and established singers and bands. The current venue for both is Club Momo (*see p170*).

Music

Sound advice.

Rock & pop

Singapore might be at the cutting edge of global capitalism, but it's a backwater when it comes to rock and pop. The government is partly to blame. Though the country had a crop of big home-grown stars in the 1960s – the Crescendos and the Quests gave the Beatles a run for their money in the local charts – the glory days came to an end in the 1970s, when the government clamped down on the scene. Viewed as a corrupt influence on the nation's youth (sex and drugs and all that), rock became an enemy of the state. Jukeboxes were banned; Led Zeppelin was refused entry to the country in 1972 (their long hair was deemed subversive); and the number and quality of local bands declined, receiving little support from local press, TV and radio. Venue owners and promoters turned to cover bands and DJs to plug the gap. Fans had to be content with the nostalgia circuit – older acts such as the Eagles, Stones and Cliff Richard still draw massive crowds – and dreadful 'Big in Asia' groups.

Things have improved since then, although serious musicians still struggle to earn a living at home – the market is just too small – and have a hard time breaking into the English-speaking, US and UK-dominated scene in the West. And the pubs and clubs remain dominated by cover bands, with most venue owners discouraging original material. There's also a lack of decent large venues. With a capacity of 10,000, the **Indoor Stadium** is the biggest, but the acoustics (though improved) are not ideal – and it's simply not big enough for mega-stars such as Madonna or U2. Purpose-built midsized venues for smaller acts are in short supply too.

However, Bowie, Coldplay, Travis, Franz Ferdinand and other big international groups have appeared in recent years, and a new crop of critically acclaimed local indie bands has sprung up: the Observatory play spacey avant-rock; Electrico is known for melodic guitar pop and was nominated for a 2005 MTV Asia Award; and Ronin is characterised by a hard-rocking sound and energetic live shows. Cover bands are widening their horizons too, choosing jazz, folk, reggae and funk numbers.

Annual music festivals are also livening up the scene: events to look out for include **Baybeats** (www.baybeats.com.sg), an indie rock event held in July at Esplanade, and **Mosaic** (www.mosaicmusicfestival.com), a platform for jazz, world and soul in March. And there is a small but growing experimental electronic music scene, with occasional gigs at **Esplanade**, the **Substation** (see p176) and the **Arts House** (see p176). The **Gas Haus** is also a good venue to catch up-and-coming indie acts.

INFORMATION

As well as venues' own websites, check the daily papers and magazines *Time Out Singapore* and *I-S* for up-to-date concert and gig listings.

Major venues

Except for huge international acts like the Eagles or the Rolling Stones, tickets take some time to sell out – you can often get good seats on the day of the show. For ticket agents, *see* chapter **Resources A-Z**. Smoking, eating and drinking aren't allowed at any indoor venue.

Fort Canning Park is sometimes used for big rock concerts and festivals such as WOMAD (see p163). Performers have ranged from big rock acts like INXS and Deep Purple to edgier bands like Suede and Asian Dub Foundation. **Esplanade** lures smaller, edgy international bands such as Tortoise and Kings of Convenience.

D'Marquee

Downtown East, 1 Pasir Ris Close, Pasir Ris (6589 1688/www.downtowneast.com.sg). Pasir Ris MRT then bus 3, 12, 17, 354.
Designed to resemble a circus marquee, this small-ish 'heartland' venue (capacity 2,000) caters mostly to families and older fans. It has hosted easy listening acts such as Smokie (UK soft rockers that are 'big in China') and tribute shows to evergreen artistes like Taiwan's Teresa Teng.

Max Pavilion @ Singapore Expo

#01-01 1 Expo Drive, Tanah Merah (6580 8308/ www.singapore-expo.com.sg). Expo MRT.
Though mainly a place for exhibitions and fairs, this state of the art centre hosts regular gigs for a midsized crowd (capacity 7,000). Asian chanteuse Jenny Tseng, saxophonist Kenny G, pop-jazz singer Jamie Cullum and Chinese rocker Wu Bai have all performed here.

I like Chinese

Chinese pop music first swept Singapore in the 1960s, when people were agog for 'a-go-go music'. The genre – which fused Latin American flavours with funk beats – was hot in Hong Kong, and Singapore got caught up in the craze. These days, Singapore's Chinese music scene is still influenced by Hong Kong, as well as Taiwan and China. The most successful local artists record in Mandarin. And though local artists are often based overseas, when they return home to perform, their shows sell out. Big names include Kit Chan, Stefanie Sun, JJ Lin, Sun Ho, Eric Moo and Tanya Chua. Chinese music stations include YES (93.3FM), Love (97.2FM) and Capital (95.8FM).

On the live scene, the genre with the greatest local relevance is *xinyao*. From the Chinese term *xin jia po ge yao*, meaning 'Singapore songs', it features clean, harmonised singing, often accompanied by solo guitar. Usually written by the performers themselves, the songs ooze local flavour. It is a far cry from the rhythmic beats of Cantopop (Cantonese pop songs) or Mandopop (Mandarin pop songs).

There aren't many live Chinese music venues, owing to the popularity of KTV (karaoke) joints and an old stereotype that live venues were sleazy – but a few spots are worth checking out.

The Ark Café

#02-00 SAFRA Town Club, 29 Carpenter Street, Boat Quay (6538 0366/www.theark. com.sg). Clarke Quay MRT. **Open** 6.30-11pm Mon-Sat. *Shows* 8pm Mon-Sat. **Credit** MC, V. **Map** p250 J9.

The first tea lounge to promote *xinyao* singers, often sponsoring competitions and shows. Up-and-coming singers – usually several a night – perform here. In contrast to the music, the menu is Western bistro-style.

Dragonfly

#01-01 St James Power Station, 3 Sentosa Gateway, HarbourFront (6270 7676/ www.dragonfly.sg). HarbourFront MRT. **Open** 6pm-6am daily. *Shows* 7.30pm daily. **Admission** (incl 1 drink) $10 women, $12 men Mon-Thur; $15 women, $20 men Fri-Sun. **Credit** AmEx, MC, V. **Map** p252 C1.

Plays host to some of Singapore's flashier Chinese pop-rock acts like Puzzle, William Scorpion, Skye and *Singapore Idol* runner-up Sylvester Sim. The club (part of the new multi-venue St James Power Station, *see p172*) also tries to wow the crowd with state of the art sound, video projection and dancers.

Este The Club

#02-04 Block D, Clarke Quay, 3 River Valley Road, Clarke Quay (6338 0712/ www.esteclub.com). Clarke Quay MRT. **Open** 6pm-6am daily. *Shows* 10.30pm daily. **Credit** AmEx, MC, V. **Map** pp250 I8.

An all-in-one venue, Este offers private karaoke rooms, bar areas and a dancefloor where you can ogle the pole dancers. The crowds flock here to watch pop-rock bands Fantasy and Crystal – and their attractive female singers – belt out the latest hits.

EZ50

#01-01 1 Neil Road, Chinatown (6223 0050). Outram Park MRT then 10mins walk. **Open**

Singapore Indoor Stadium

2 Stadium Walk, Kallang (6344 2660/www.sis. gov.sg). City Hall MRT then bus 16 or Kallang MRT then bus 11.

This 10,000-seat venue was built as a sports stadium, hence the poor acoustics. However, it's still the first choice for big international acts. Bands that have graced the stage include Coldplay, Franz Ferdinand and REM, plus Asian superstars like Faye Wong, Andy Lau and Sandy Lam.

Suntec City Convention Centre

1 Raffles Boulevard, Marina (6337 2888/ www.suntecsingapore.com). City Hall MRT then 10mins walk. **Map** p251 M7.

In addition to holding meetings, trade shows and special events, Suntec City (with a capacity of 5,000)

is also used as a concert venue. International acts have included Damien Rice, the Scorpions and French pop-rock singer Zazie.

Pubs & clubs

Singapore has dozens of pubs, bars and clubs where you can see bands perform. While most are packed in the main city area, there are good venues in the 'burbs too. Admission is usually free, but some impose a entrance fee or first-drink charge at weekends. In keeping with Singapore's culinary reputation, the food is often a cut above your standard pub grub. The dress code is universal (and enforced): no singlets, short shorts or sandals – unless

6pm-2am Mon-Thur, Sun; 6pm-3am Fri,
Sat. *Shows* 9pm daily. **Credit** AmEx, DC,
JCB, MC, V. **Map** p250 H11.
Decked out in deep red paint, draped
curtains and loungy sofas, EZ50 is a
striking venue. Watch bands from China
work the crowd every night. Wannabe
popstars can strut their stuff on stage at
the Sunday night jam. **Photo** *above.*

The 50s

*47/49/51 Tanjong Pagar Road, Chinatown
(6226 1118). Tanjong Pagar MRT.*
Open 7.30pm-3am daily. *Shows* 8pm
daily. **Credit** AmEx, DC, JCB, MC, V.
Map p250 H12.
Though this four-storey club has karaoke
rooms and a dance area upstairs, the
ground floor is where the action lies.
There, singers backed by a house band
perform a range of material, from Chinese
Top 40 to Chinese punk metal.

you're a hot babe. The minimum requirement is
'casual' (bermudas and sandals are acceptable
in some venues).

Other venues with live music include mega
dance club Zouk *(see p172)*, where Suede,
Bjork and, more recently, Peaches and Chicks
on Speed have performed. **Balaclava** *(see
p130)* specialises in crowd-pleasing, Top 40
bands (though you might hear the occasional
Morrissey tune).

Acid Bar

*#01-01/02 Peranakan Place Complex, 180
Orchard Road (6738 8828). Somerset MRT.*
Open 5pm-2am Mon-Thur, Sun; 5pm-3am Fri,
Sat. *Shows* 7pm daily. **Credit** AmEx, MC, V.
Map p247 H4.

Though housed in a quaint shophouse, the Acid Bar
is hip and loungey. Billed as a good place for 'dark
night conversation', the chilled-out bar also hosts
acoustic gigs, with local musicians performing folk,
jazz, pop and rock.

Bar None

*Basement, Singapore Marriott Hotel, 320 Orchard
Road (6831 4657/www.barnoneasia.com). Orchard
MRT.* **Open** 7pm-3am daily. *Shows* 10.45pm daily.
Admission (incl 1 drink) $25 women, $30 men Fri,
Sat. **Credit** AmEx, DC, JCB, MC, V. **Map** p247 E3.
This swanky hotel bar is actually one of Singapore's
best live venues – and surprisingly unpretentious.
The aptly named resident band Energy plays high-
octane rock every night except Mondays. Chill out
in the upstairs bar, the Living Room *(see p136)*.

Le Baroque

*#B1-07 Chijmes, 30 Victoria Street, Colonial District
(6339 6696/www.lebaroque.com.sg). City Hall MRT.*
Open 5pm-3am daily. *Shows* 10.30pm Mon-Sat.
Admission (incl 2 drinks) $21 women, $23 men
Fri, Sat. **Credit** AmEx, MC, V. **Map** p251 K7.
If you want to rock out in elegant surroundings,
come to Le Baroque; the lavish decor features chandeliers, gold walls and Roman columns. It's a suitably over-the-top setting for the music, ageing local
music sex symbol Douglas O, one of Singapore's
biggest rock acts, jams here with his band, Satellite.

Brix

*Basement, Grand Hyatt Singapore, 10 Scotts
Road, Orchard Road & Around (6416 7107/
http://singapore.grand.hyatt.com). Orchard MRT.*
Open 7pm-3am daily. *Shows* 9.30pm daily.
Admission (incl 1 drink) $25 Thur-Sat. **Credit**
AmEx, DC, JCB, MC, V. **Map** p247 E3.
One of Singapore's nightlife hotspots, Brix adopts a
sophisticated air with its brick and wood decor and
separate wine and whisky bar (featuring a good
selection of wine, single-malt scotch and cognac).
The music bar brings in a range of bands – playing
jazz, funk, hip hop, pop and R&B – including some
from overseas. Sunday is Latin night.

Carnaval

*#B1-05 Chijmes, 30 Victoria Street, Colonial
District (6339 3870/www.carnavalkrewe.com).
City Hall MRT.* **Open** 5pm-2am Mon-Thur, Sun;
5pm-3am Fri, Sat. *Shows* 9.30pm Wed-Fri. **Credit**
AmEx, DC, JCB, MC, V. **Map** p251 K7.
Carnaval claims to be the only Brazilian club in
town, but don't expect a raucous, Rio-style party; the
vibe is distinctly chilled. Although the acts occasionally play bossa nova and samba, blues and other
musical styles are also common.

Carriage Bar

*1F York Hotel Singapore, 21 Mount Elizabeth,
Orchard Road & Around (6235 1715). Orchard
MRT then 10mins walk.* **Open** 6pm-1am Mon-
Thur, Sun; 6pm-2am Fri, Sat. *Shows* 8.45pm
Mon-Sat. **Admission** $2 Fri, Sat. **Credit** AmEx,
MC, V. **Map** p247 F3.

Arts & Entertainment

Listen here: **Gas Haus** is the place for original sounds, from thrash to punk.

This hotel bar has attracted a steady stream of regulars for 20 years. Some come for the karaoke (every night from 6.30pm); others to hear the Thunderbirds, one of Singapore's biggest rock bands from the 1960s (from 8.45pm). Now the house band, they play an upbeat mix of golden oldies and ballads. There's no happy hour, but after the first drink all subsequent tipples are reduced by 25%.

Devil's Bar

#01-01 Orchard Parade Hotel, 1 Tanglin Road, Orchard Road & Around (6732 0819/ www.devilsbar.com.sg). Orchard MRT. **Open** 5pm-3am Mon, Tue, Thur; 5pm-6am Wed, Fri, Sat; 5pm-4am Sun. *Shows* 6pm Mon-Sat; 9.30pm Sun. **Admission** (incl 1 drink) free women, $12-$15 men Mon-Thur; $12 women, $20 men Fri, Sat. **Credit** AmEx, DC, MC, V. **Map** p246 D3.

Dedicated to English Premier League football team Manchester United, Devil's Bar is decked out in the team's colours. The entertainment is suitably laddish: expect eye candy (bar-top dancers) and rock bands RED and Puzzle, which bring the house down with their raucous shows. Sunday nights are softer, with Mandarin/Canto pop acts.

Gas Haus Music Café

#01-00 Lee Kai House, 114 Middle Road, Bras Basah & Bugis (6337 1967/www.gashaus.com). Bugis MRT. **Open** 5pm-1am Mon-Fri; 11am-2am Sat, Sun. *Shows* 7.30pm Mon-Fri; 3pm Sat, Sun. **Admission** $8-$16 Sat, Sun. **Credit** MC, V. **Map** p249 L5.

This intimate venue calls to mind the late CBGB in New York or Ronnie Scott's in London. The cosy spot encourages bands to play original material (a rarity in Singapore) and places no restrictions on musical direction. Several bands often share the bill, so don't be surprised to hear indie, thrash metal, neo-punk or grunge on the same night.

Hard Rock Café

#05-01 HPL House, 50 Cuscaden Road, Orchard Road & Around (6235 5232/www.hardrock.com.sg). Orchard MRT. **Open** 11am-3am Mon, Sat, Sun; 11am-2am Tue-Thur. *Shows* 9.30pm daily. **Admission** $12 Mon, Sun; $23 Sat. **Credit** AmEx, DC, JCB, MC, V. **Map** p246 D3.

Though known mainly as a touristy restaurant, the Hard Rock has retained its musical roots, offering bands daily (except Thursdays, when it's salsa night). Don't expect much 'hard' rock, even though guitar god Steve Vai once performed here. Tuesdays are open mic nights; Sundays feature blues. Famous rockers drop by occasionally (Blondie in late 2006).

Harry's @ Orchard

#01-05, #02-08/09 Orchard Towers, 1 Claymore Drive, Orchard Road & Around (6736 7330/ www.harrys.com.sg). Orchard MRT. **Open** 3pm-2am Mon-Thur; 3pm-3am Fri; noon-3am Sat; noon-1am Sun. *Shows* 9.45pm Mon-Thur; 10pm Fri, Sat. **Credit** AmEx, DC, JCB, MC, V. **Map** p247 E3.

Though the Harry's chain is known for good jazz music, the Orchard branch features one of Singapore's veteran pop bands, Tania, which plays old-school stuff from the 1960s to '80s and is fronted by flamboyant lead singer Alban de Souza (expect false eyelashes and glittering make-up).
Other locations: throughout the city.

House of Rock

83A Tras Street, Chinatown (6221 3353). Tanjong Pagar MRT. **Open** 6pm-3am daily. *Shows* 10.30pm daily. **Credit** AmEx, MC, V. **Map** p250 H12.

This no-nonsense joint gets your adrenaline pumping the moment you step in. Ministry of Rock, the house band, plays loud classic rock from the likes of Led Zeppelin, Deep Purple and Black Sabbath. If you're looking for conversation, you've come to the wrong place: the volume is deafening.

Insomnia Live Music

#01-21 Chijimes, 30 Victoria Street, Colonial District (6338 6883). City Hall MRT. **Open** noon-4am Mon, Tue, Sun; noon-5am Wed-Sat. *Shows* 11pm Mon, Tue; 9.30pm Wed, Sun; 9.15pm Thur-Sat. **Admission** (free drinks 9pm-midnight women, 9-11pm men) $18 Wed. **Credit** AmEx, DC, MC, V. **Map** p251 K7.

Like the name says, this is the place to come to if you can't sleep and want to rock. Though set in the historic Chijmes complex, this small, intimate venue looks unremarkable, but the musical offerings keep the crowds coming back. The house bands change regularly, but the formula is always the same: hearty rock until the wee hours.

Molly Malone's

56 Circular Road, Boat Quay (6536 2029/ www.molly-malone.com). Raffles Place MRT. **Open** 11am-midnight Mon, Sun; 11am-1am Tue-Thur; 11am-2am Fri, Sat. *Shows* 8.30pm Tue-Fri. **Credit** AmEx, MC, V. **Map** p250 J9.

Opened in 1995, Molly Malone's was Singapore's first Irish pub (*see p132*) and has spawned legions of copycats. But it's the real deal: it was built in Ireland and reassembled here. And the music is authentic too. Irish singer Gerry Cox performs acoustic sets that mix traditional Celtic folk with contemporary hits.

Momo Live

Club Momo, #01-02/03 Central Mall, 5 Magazine Road, Chinatown (6535 3030/www.clubmomo.net). Clarke Quay MRT/Chinatown MRT then bus 51, 143, 174, 186. **Open** 9pm-5am Wed; 9pm-6am Fri, Sat. *Shows* 10.30pm Fri, Sat. **Admission** (incl 1 drink) free women, $18 men Wed; $15 women, $18 men Fri, Sat. **Credit** AmEx, DC, MC, V. **Map** p250 H9.

This anteroom to Club Momo (*see p171*) provides an alternative to the dance music in the main club. The space is small and the decor spartan, but the focus is the resident band, Infinity, which performs its own sassy brand of rock at weekends.

Movida

St James Power Station, 3 Sentosa Gateway, HarbourFront (6270 7676/www.movida.sg). HarbourFront MRT. **Open** 6pm-3am daily. *Shows* 7.30pm daily. **Admission** (incl 1 drink) $12 women, $15 men Mon-Thur, Sun; $15 women, $20 men Fri, Sat. **Credit** AmEx, MC, V. **Map** p252 C1.

In a small corner of mega nightclub St James Power Station (*see p172*), this sleek, minimalist bar is worth seeking out. It's one of the few Singapore venues to offer world music – though take the term with a pinch of salt: sure, you might dance to folk songs by the Paraguayan house band, but the first half of the evening features acoustic covers of English pop.

Muddy Murphy's Irish Pub

#B1-04 Orchard Hotel Shopping Arcade, 442 Orchard Road (6735 0400/www.muddy murphys.com). Orchard MRT. **Open** 11.30am-1am Mon-Thur; 11.30am-2am Fri, Sat; 11.30am-midnight Sun. *Shows* 9.30pm Fri; 10pm Sat; 4.30pm Sun. **Credit** AmEx, DC, MC, V. **Map** p246 D3.

This cosy Irish basement bar tempts punters with Guinness, fry-ups and camaraderie. It used to offer traditional Irish music – and folk acts still make the odd appearance – but these days you're more likely to hear electric guitar than uilleann pipes. Two bands strut their stuff on Fridays; Sunday afternoons are also popular.

Prince of Wales

101 Dunlop Street, Little India (6299 0130/ www.pow.com.sg). Little India MRT. **Open** 9am-midnight daily. *Shows* 9pm daily. **Credit** MC, V. **Map** p248 K3.

There are no airs and graces at this backpacker pub (*see p133*). The nightly selection of music is eclectic in style – indie, rock, folk – and variable in quality: many of the acts are just starting out and being paid in drinks (and it shows). Sunday and Monday are open mic nights, when anyone can take the stage.

Pump Room

#01-09/10 The Foundry, 3B River Valley Road, River Valley (6338 0138/www.pumproomasia.com). Clarke Quay MRT. **Open** noon-3am Mon-Thur, Sun; noon-4am Fri, Sat. *Shows* 10.30pm Tue-Sun. **Admission** (incl 1 drink) $15 ladies, $18 men Fri, Sat. **Credit** AmEx, MC, V. **Map** p250 I8.

Comprising three sections – a microbrewery, bistro and bar – the Pump Room is a crowd-pleaser. Cherished local band Jive Talking plays its populist blend of R&B/pop every night except Monday.

Rouge Club

#02-00 Peranakan Place Complex, 180 Orchard Road (6738 1000). Somerset MRT. **Open** 6pm-3am Wed-Fri; 7pm-4am Sat. *Shows* 10.30pm Wed-Sat. **Admission** (incl 1 drink) $15 women, $18 men Wed, Thur; $18 women, $20 men Fri, Sat. **Credit** MC, V. **Map** p247 H4.

Behind a classic Peranakan façade lies a modern, loft-like venue. Decorated in warm and earthy tones, Rouge is intimate and comfortable, but this is no chillout zone. Local celebrity rocker John Molina pumps up the volume with his modern rock stylings, backed by his band Krueger.

Timbre Music Bistro

The Substation, 45 Armenian Street, Colonial District (6338 8277/www.timbre.com.sg). City Hall MRT. **Open** 6pm-1am Mon, Tue; 6pm-2am Wed, Thur; 6pm-3am Fri, Sat. *Shows* 10pm Mon-Sat. **Credit** AmEx, MC, V. **Map** p250 J7.

Located in the garden of the Substation at its centre (*see p176*), Timbre showcases a variety of musical styles and bands, which change nightly. Genres range from acoustic folk to fist-pumping rock. The alfresco setting and wooden furniture provide a relaxed, beachy atmosphere.

Wala Wala Café & Bar

31 Lorong Mambong, Holland Village (6462 4288/ www.imaginings.com.sg). Bus 7, 61, 75, 106, 970. **Open** 4pm-1am Mon-Thur, Sun; 4pm-2am Fri, Sat.

Arts & Entertainment

Shows 7.30pm solo, 9.45pm band daily. **Admission** 1 drink Thur-Sat. **Credit** AmEx, DC, JCB, MC, V.
The upstairs room at Wala Wala used to be a jazzy chill-out lounge; these days, it's a rocking live venue, favoured by a studenty crowd. Thursday and Saturday are the most popular nights, when pop-rock act the UnXpected takes to the stage. Fronted by singer Shirlyn Tan, the band plays original material plus a quirky selection of covers.

Jazz & blues

Like English pop, blues music only became popular in Singapore in the 1960s. Even then, top blues artists of the day – Siva Choy, Pest Infested and Stray Dogs – preferred the blues-rock or R&B styles of bands such as the Walker Brothers, the Yardbirds and Cream rather than traditional blues from the likes of BB King or Robert Johnson. It wasn't until the 1980s that bands like the Calcutta Blues Experiment reverted to the older American sounds of Chicago or Southern blues.

Similarly, the jazz scene was initially more influenced by the free-form or fluid improvisational styles of artists such as John Coltrane rather than 'traditional' choices such as Lionel Hampton or Glenn Miller. But these days, thanks to the efforts of the likes of Jeremy Monteiro (dubbed Singapore's 'King of Swing') and the Thomson Jazz Club, jazz music is more accessible and its fan base has grown.

Venues

Admission is free unless otherwise stated.
Tanglin Community Club Blues Jam (245 Whitley Road, Tanglin, 6251 3922) runs a blues jam, open to all, on Sundays from 2-6pm.

Bellini Room
#01-01 St James Power Station, 3 Sentosa Gateway, HarbourFront (6270 7676/www.belliniroom.sg). HarbourFront MRT. **Open** 9pm-3am Mon-Sat. *Shows* usually 9.30pm Mon-Sat. **Admission** (incl 1 drink) $10 women, $12 men Mon-Thur; $15 women, $20 men Fri, Sat. **Credit** AmEx, MC, V. **Map** p250 J7.
With its glamorous decor and dashing house band, the Bellini Room – housed in the new St James Power Station entertainment complex (*see p172*) – is a perfect way to jazz up your night. The band plays finger-snapping standards from the likes of Sinatra, Gershwin, Porter and Miller.

Crazy Elephant
#01-03 Clarke Quay, 3E River Valley Road, Clarke Quay (6337 7859/www.crazyelephant.com). Clarke Quay MRT. **Open** 5pm-2am Mon-Thur, Sun; 5pm-3am Fri, Sat. *Shows* 10pm daily. **Credit** AmEx, DC, JCB, MC, V. **Map** p250 I8.
Despite its reputation as a tourist trap, this rock-blues club attracts a steady stream of locals plus famous guests such as Deep Purple, Robbie Williams and REM's Mike Mills. Currently, the Don Victor Blues Band plays Monday and Thursday while the Blues Machine plays the rest of the week. *Photo p190.*

Harry's @ Boat Quay
28 Boat Quay, Boat Quay (6538 3029/www.harrys. com.sg). Raffles Place MRT. **Open** 11.30am-1am Mon-Thur, Sun; 11.30am-2am Fri, Sat. *Shows* 9.30pm Mon-Thur, Sun; 10pm Fri, Sat. **Credit** AmEx, DC, JCB, MC, V. **Map** p250 J10.
This popular jazz joint opened in 1992. But the building, a renovated shophouse, dates from the early 1900s (it has retained its colonial façade and features classic rattan furniture). It comes alive after work, when punters flock to hear one of Singapore's hottest jazz bands, ChromaZone. There are six other branches dotted around town.
Other locations: throughout the city.

Crazy Elephant

Harry's @ The Esplanade

#01 05/07 Esplanade Mall, 8 Raffles Avenue, Colonial District (6334 0132/www.harrys.com.sg). City Hall MRT. **Open** 5pm-1am Mon-Thur, Sun; 5pm-2am Fri, Sat. *Shows* 8.30pm Tue-Sat. **Credit** AmEx, DC, JCB, MC, V. **Map** p251 L8.

Though located in Singapore's leading arts hub, this branch of Harry's is casual and unpretentious. Jazz is the mainstay, but on weekends blues guitarist extraordinaire Paul Ponnudurai (Singapore's answer to BB King) makes his guitar gently weep. **Other locations**: throughout the city.

Jazz@South Bridge

82B Boat Quay, Boat Quay (6327 4671/2/ www.southbridgejazz.com.sg). Clarke Quay MRT. **Open** 6pm-1am Tue-Thur, Sun; 6pm-2.30am Fri, Sat. *Shows* 9.30pm daily. **Admission** 2 drinks Fri, Sat; $15-$20 international bands. **Credit** AmEx, DC, JCB, MC, V. **Map** p250 J9.

One of Singapore's main jazz venues, this intimate spot conjures up images of the smoky jazz bars of Chicago or New York. There is a rotating roster of performers (both local and international), and a range of styles from traditional to improv. The owners eschew 'pop jazz' (no Michael Bublé here).

Roomful of Blues

72 Prinsep Street, Orchard Road & Around (6837 0882). Dhoby Ghaut MRT then 10mins walk. **Open** 5pm-2am Mon-Sat. *Shows* 10pm Mon-Fri; 11.30pm Sat. **Credit** AmEx, DC, MC, V. **Map** p248 K5.

Run by guitarist and aficionado Stephen Low, this unpretentious venue provides an outlet for young blues bands. In the week, acoustic sessions provide a quieter musical backdrop, but the bands pull out all the stops at the Saturday Blues Jam (9-11pm).

Classical & opera

Despite the lack of a sizeable market, Singapore's classical music scene has managed to thrive through the years and is now one of the most vibrant in South-east Asia.

Classical music became popular in the 19th century, introduced by British colonials and traders from Europe and the US. By the 1950s Singapore had an active, albeit amateur, classical scene, influenced by the British military forces. Musical life revolved around the concerts and soirées staged by two amateur orchestras: the Singapore Chamber Ensemble and another run by the Singapore Music Society (the first ensemble to bear the name Singapore Symphony Orchestra). International artistes and orchestras – such as Italian violinist Ruggerio Ricci and Japan's NHK Symphony Orchestra – also visited. More amateur and semi-professional orchestras formed and folded in the next 20 years, until January 1979, when the **Singapore Symphony Orchestra** – the country's first

fully professional orchestra – gave its inaugural performance at the Singapore Conference Hall.

Home-grown opera is an even more recent invention. Until the mid 1980s, the only opera performances came from visiting international companies; then a group of opera aficionados, under the banner of the National University of Singapore Society, decided to stage their own productions. After four successful operas in five years, it was decided that performances should be put on a more permanent basis and in 1990 the Singapore Lyric Theatre – now called the **Singapore Lyric Opera** – was formed.

Chinese opera – or *wayang* – is, sadly, a dwindling art form. You're most likely to catch performances during the **Hungry Ghost Festival** (*see p163*) and occasionally at the **Kreta Ayer People's Theatre** in Chinatown (30A Kreta Ayer Road, 6222 3972, www.kapt. com.sg) The **Chinese Opera Institute** (6339 8168, 6339 1292, www.chineseopera institute.com.sg) also puts on events, but its main role is educational, as a training and research centre.

Venues

Esplanade – Theatres on the Bay

1 Esplanade Drive, Marina (6828 8222/ www.esplanade.com). City Hall MRT then 10mins walk/bus 36, 106, 133, 171, 195. **Box office** noon-8.30pm daily. **Tickets** varies. **Credit** AmEx, DC, JCB, MC, V. **Map** p251 L8.

With its prickly twin domes that glow at night, Esplanade is an unmissable Singapore landmark. Its two main performance spaces are the Theatre (seating 2,000) and the Concert Hall (1,600). Designed by renowned acoustician Russell Johnson, the latter can handle loud Cantopop or delicate sonatas equally well. There are also a couple of smaller multipurpose venues, and outdoor amphitheatres for pop and dance shows. *See also p203.*

Singapore Conference Hall

7 Shenton Way, Chinatown (6440 3839/6557 4030/www.sch.org.sg). Tanjong Pagar MRT. **Box office** 10am-6.45pm (until 9.30pm on concert days) Mon-Fri; 4.30-9.30pm (on concert days) Sat; 2.30-5.30pm (on concert days) Sun. **Tickets** $12-$80. **Credit** AmEx, MC, V.

Opened in 1965, this was once the prime venue for international conferences. Renovated in 1999, it now houses an improved concert hall, an expansive exhibition hall and a practice hall. It is also the main residence of the Singapore Chinese Orchestra.

Shaw Foundation Symphony Stage

Symphony Lake, Singapore Botanic Gardens, 1 Cluny Road, Orchard Road & Around (6337 1282/www.sso.org.sg/education). Orchard MRT then bus 7, 105, 106, 123, 174. **Map** p246 A2.

Arts & Entertainment

From concert halls to housing estates: **Singapore Chinese Orchestra**.

Situated on an islet in the Singapore Botanic Gardens' Symphony Lake, this amphitheatre is an idyllic venue for open-air concerts, with the audience sitting at the water's edge. Of the monthly concerts held – from jazz, Latin and classical to pop and R&B – the Singapore Symphony Orchestra's free, biannual SSO In the Park is the most popular.

University Cultural Centre

National University of Singapore, 10 Kent Ridge Crescent, Clementi (6516 7171/2492/www.nus. edu.sg/cfa/UCC). Bus 95, 96, 151, 97, 198.
Situated in the grounds of the National University of Singapore, the UCC is not famous, but it is a vibrant, innovative performing arts venue, playing host to such diverse talents as British jazz diva Carol Kidd and Japanese taiko drum troupe Wadaiko Yamato. It also hosts local musicals, and classical and pop performances.

Victoria Concert Hall

11 Empress Place, Colonial District (6338 1230/ www.vch.org.sg). City Hall or Raffles Place MRT.
Box office 10am-6.30pm Mon-Fri; 5-8.30pm (on concert days) Sat, Sun. **Tickets** $11-$52.
Credit AmEx, DC, JCB, MC, V. **Map** p251 K9.
The grand dame of local concert halls, built in 1862 as the town hall – hence the splendid clock tower. After renovations in the 1950s and '70s, it became the major venue (it seats 800) for classical music. The Singapore Symphony Orchestra called it home until moving to Esplanade in 2002.

Orchestras & groups

The **NUS Chinese Orchestra** (6516 2492) promotes Chinese music through public concerts and performances in schools, playing ditties, folk music and Chinese ensemble pieces such as *Legend of the Dragon*.

Singapore Chinese Orchestra

6440 3839/www.sco.com.sg.
Founded in 1996, the SCO is the only professional Chinese orchestra in Singapore. Though resident orchestra of the Singapore Conference Hall, the 70-strong group also performs for the community in parks and housing estates. Creative milestones include the Millennium Concert (featuring 1,400 musicians) and commissioning Michael Nyman to write a piece for them in 2005.

Singapore Lyric Opera

6336 1929/www.singaporeopera.com.sg.
Staging its first production in 1991, the Singapore Lyric Opera has gone on to present regular operas and other types of musical concerts, ranging from jazz to show tunes. Diverse productions range from *Madama Butterfly* and *The Merry Widow* to *Bunga Mawar*, written by renowned local composer Leong Yon Pin. The comapany also runs a children's choir, to nurture opera stars of the future.

Singapore Symphony Chorus

Information 6338 1230/tickets 6339 6120/ www.symphonychorus.sg.
One of the finest choirs in South-east Asia, the SSC gave its first performance in 1980, with Brahms' *A German Requiem*; today it performs regularly with the Singapore Symphony Orchestra.

Singapore Symphony Orchestra

Information 6338 1230/tickets 6339 6120/ www.sso.org.sg.
Respected around the world, the 96-member SSO is Singapore's main full-time professional orchestra, performing over 50 concerts a year. Its wide repertoire ranges from old masterpieces to avant-garde works. Popular series include the Casual Concerts, SSO in the Park, the Proms and the Masters. It has toured the US, China and Europe and often performs with famous guest musicians.

Sport & Fitness

Let the games begin.

Singaporeans are blessed with ample opportunity to savour the great outdoors. A huge range of sports is on offer – but in concentrated form, thanks to the island's small size. The colonial influence is evident in the popularity of cricket, football, horse riding, polo and racquet sports, while extreme activities like wakeboarding and triathlons have made waves in recent years. Numerous clubs cover everything from bowling to squash.

The **Singapore Sports Council** (www. ssc.gov.sg) is the governing agency for sport and is a key player in the development of a variety of sporting endeavours, from managing stadiums to bringing in world-class events. **Singapore Sport** (www.singapore sport.com.sg) provides an advisory service for locals, expats and visitors – though its (commercial) website feels very much like a work in progress.

Participation sports/fitness

Badminton, tennis & squash

Badminton holds sway as the racquet sport of choice: shuttlers play everywhere, from schools to housing estates to public courts. For accessible, well-maintained courts, try the **Toa Payoh Sports Complex** (*see p197*).

Many top hotels have all-weather tennis or squash courts, and there are plenty of private clubs. As for public courts, **Burghley Squash & Tennis Centre** (43 Burghley Drive, Serangoon, 6283 1251) has four tennis courts and four squash courts, while the **Singapore Tennis Centre** (1020 East Coast Parkway, East Coast, 6449 9034, www.sungtao.com/ stc.htm) offers ten well-lit tennis courts in a spacious beachfront location. Both centres are open 7am to 10pm daily, and rates are around $10 per hour.

Bowling

Around two dozen bowling centres are scattered about the island. Some are open 24 hours, with rates starting as low as $2 per game on weekdays, $3 at night and weekends. Try **Super Bowl Marina South** (15 Marina Grove, Marina South, 6221 1010) for a game any time of the day.

Climbing

While there are definitely no mountains (and hardly any hills) in Singapore, there's a small but enthusiastic group of sport climbers that can't resist the vertical challenge.

SAFRA Adventure Sports Centre

60 Yishun Avenue 4, Yishun (6852 8200/www. safra.sg). Yishun MRT then bus 812. **Open** 9.30am-9.30pm Tue-Sat; 9.30am 6pm Sun. **Rates** from $11.55; $5.35 equipment rental. **Credit** V.
The largest outdoor climbing centre in Singapore. Facilities include the first artificial ice-climbing wall in South-east Asia, a 25m (85ft) sport climbing wall, a free-form crack wall and an indoor bouldering wall. Various courses are available from $70.

Cycling

Be warned: without designated cycle lanes on Singapore's roads, cyclists are at the mercy of road hogs. Cycle paths within parks and beach areas are pleasant alternatives, with park connectors – green corridors of various lengths – providing links between parks, courtesy of the **National Parks Board** (1800 471 7300, www.nparks.gov.sg). Leisure cycling on **Pulau Ubin** (*see p94*), off Singapore's north coast, remains a favourite weekend pastime. Bike rentals start as low as $4 per hour.

Diving

The **Singapore Underwater Federation** (6334 5519, www.suf.org.sg) is a one-stop resource for all underwater activities. Accredited courses by the Professional Association of Diving Instructors (PADI) and National Association of Underwater Instructors (NAUI) are conducted in Singapore, with diving typically taking place nearby in Malaysian waters. Basic courses take three to four days and cost around $400. Various Malaysian islands are known for their scuba sites, see *p210* **Take a dive** for more info.

Fishing

Water, water everywhere and each drop teeming with the promise of aquatic life. While deep sea anglers head offshore in search

Arts & Entertainment

of barracuda and threadfin, recreational fishermen take a siesta in parks and beaches, hooking the occasional prawn, carp and snakehead. To join the action, try **Pasir Ris Fishing Pond** or head to the popular eastside destinations of **East Coast Park** (*see p91*) and **Changi Beach Park** (*see p94*).

Pasir Ris Fishing Pond
Pasir Ris Town Park, Pasir Ris (6583 3616/9786 7796). Paris Ris MRT. **Open** 24hrs daily. **Rates** $34-$45. Sure-catch pond $10/fish. Pro pond $25/ 1st hr; $50/3hrs. **No credit cards**.
This fishing pond offers 'sure-catch' options for lazy fishermen as well as pro fishing for serious anglers. Expect to catch mangrove jacks, golden pomfrets and groupers. An onsite restaurant, specialising in seafood (of course), is open until 11.30pm.

Golf

Private golf clubs cater mostly to the elite – with well-equipped facilities including restaurants and fitness centres – while public courses and driving ranges are increasingly available to the average Joe. Some private courses accept non-members on weekdays with proof of handicap.

Green Fairways Golf Course
60 Fairways Drive, off Eng Neo Avenue, Bukit Timah (6468 7233). Orchard MRT then taxi. **Open** *Course* 7am-5.30pm daily. *Driving range* 7am-10.30pm daily. **Rates** (for walk-ins) $42 Mon-Fri; $52.50 Sat, Sun. **No credit cards**.
This public course has nine holes and a 62-bay golf driving range in the heart of Bukit Timah, just ten minutes from Orchard Road.

Keppel Club
10 Bukit Chermin Road, Telok Blangah (6375 5570/ www.keppelclub.com.sg). HarbourFront MRT then bus 10, 100, 131, 143, 166. **Open** 7am-8pm Tue-Sun. **Rates** (for walk-ins) from $138. **Credit** MC, V. **Map** p252 A1.
A charming, highly rated private club with characteristic undulating fairways over 18 holes, city skyline views and glimpses of Sentosa island. Minimum handicap required. Members (and their guests) also have access to tennis courts, a gym, Olympic-sized pool and bowling alley.

Seletar Base Golf Club
244 Oxford Street, Seletar Base, Seletar (6481 4745/www.seletarbaseclub.org.sg). Yio Chu Kang MRT then taxi. **Open** 11am-5.30pm Mon; 7am-5.30pm Tue-Sun. **Rates** from $30. **Credit** MC, V.
On the northern tip of Singapore, this well-maintained nine-hole public course awaits nature lovers. Nostalgic types will eat up the area's colonial charm – *see p103* **Base concerns**.

Gyms

As the yuppie lifestyle kicks into high gear in Singapore, there is a proliferation of good gyms around town, Here are a few of the best.

California Fitness
Orchard Building, 1 Grange Road, Orchard Road & Around (6834 2100/www.californiafitness.com). Somerset MRT. **Open** 6am-midnight Mon-Sat; 8am-10pm Sun. **Admission** $35. **Credit** AmEx, JCB, MC, V. **Map** p247 G5.
The most prominent gym in central Orchard, with innovative offerings, numerous classes, steam and sauna facilities, and scores of cardio machines conveniently placed for people-watching. This outlet

In-line skating, East Coast Park. *See p195.*

attracts beefy men who may or may not be looking at other men. There are branches at Raffles Place, Victoria Street and Thomson Road.

Fitness First

#09-01 Capital Tower, 168 Robinson Road, Chinatown (6536 5595/www.fitnessfirst.com.sg). Tanjong Pagar MRT. **Open** 6am-10pm Mon-Fri; 7am 7pm Sat, Sun. **Admission** $40. **Credit** AmEx, MC, V. **Map** p250 J12.

This upmarket UK chain has pool facilities at some of its six outlets. It attracts the well-heeled, ladies of leisure and corporate gym rats who juggle workouts with late hours at the office.

Other locations: throughout the city.

Planet Fitness

#02-158 VivoCity, 1 HarbourFront Walk, HarbourFront (6235 9622/www.planetfitness. com.sg). HarbourFront MRT. **Open** 6am-1pm Mon-Fri; 7am-9pm Sat, Sun. **Admission** $26.25. **Credit** AmEx, JCB, MC, V. **Map** p252 C1.

Planet Fitness has the lot, from state-of-the-art gym equipment to dedicated studios for spinning, pilates and yoga. Part of the VivoCity branch resembles a chic nightclub, and there are views of Sentosa island. The male-female balance is about equal.

Other locations: throughout the city.

Hiking

For such a highly urbanised city state, Singapore has an abundance of nature reserves where you can appreciate flora and fauna via a multitude of hiking routes. Try **Bukit Timah Nature Reserve** (*see p98*) and **MacRitchie Reservoir** (*see p104*) for great walking trails through old growth rainforest, or **Labrador Park** (*see p82*) for cliffside views after visiting the World War II bunkers and tunnels. Hardcore nature lovers can head to the very far north to **Sungei Buloh Wetlands Reserve** (*see p101*) to spot native birds such as herons, bitterns and kingfishers, as well as mangrove inhabitants including mudskippers, water snakes and monitor lizards. **Chek Jawa** on Pulau Ubin (*see p94*) offers a slice of village living and rare marshland life (permits are required to visit).

For information on all the island's parks, contact **National Parks** (6542 4108, 6545 4761, www.nparks.gov.sg). *See also p81* **Green retreats**.

Horse riding

For most Singaporeans, getting on a horse may be a once-in-a-lifetime experience, as there are relatively few stables and certainly no wide open plains for long scenic rides. Registration and an annual membership fee is required at **Bukit Timah Saddle Club**

(51 Fairways Drive, off Eng Neo Avenue, 6466 2782, www.btsc.org.sg), but casual riders might try new arrival **Gallop Stables** in coastal Pasir Ris Park.

For more information on horsing around, contact the **Equestrian Federation of Singapore** (6466 5123, www.efs.org.sg). For polo lessons and games, visit the **Singapore Polo Club** (*see p199*).

Gallop Stables

61 Pasir Ris Green, Pasir Ris (6583 9665/ www.gallopstable.com). Pasir Ris MRT. **Open** 8am-noon, 2-7pm Tue-Sun. **Credit** AmEx, DC, MC, V.

Gallop Stables opened in 2006, with ten horses, to provide affordable lessons and a chance at dressage. Ten lessons cost about $400 (but you have to purchase your own gear, for around $250). Pony rides are $10 per ten-minute walk; there is a weight limit of 70kg (154lbs).

Ice skating & snow sports

In contrast to the beaches and watersports of the east, the west boasts icy activities in the form of **Snow City** and **Fuji Ice Palace**. Dress warmly for both.

Fuji Ice Palace

#03-01 Jurong Entertainment Centre, 2 Jurong East Street 13, Jurong (6565 1905/www.fujiice.com.sg). Jurong East MRT. **Open** 10am-10pm daily. **Admission** (2hrs incl skate rental) $15.90; $14.80 concessions. **No credit cards.**

A massive complex catering to leisure skaters, competitive figure skaters and hockey players (it's home to the National Ice Hockey League).

Snow City Singapore

21 Jurong Town Hall Road, Jurong (6560 2306/ www.snowcity.com.sg). Jurong East MRT then 10mins walk. **Open** 9am-6.30pm Tue-Sun. **Admission** (incl jacket, boots and snow-tube) $12/1hr; $18/2hrs; free under-3s. **Credit** DC, MC, V.

Unlikely to hold your interest if it snows in your own country, gimmicky Snow City offers snow-boarding, snow-tubing and skiing on a single three-storey snow slide. Some 150 tonnes of snow are manufactured to create this winter wonderland in the middle of the tropics. Part of the Singapore Science Centre (*see p166*), it incorporates educational displays for tots to learn snowy facts – and kids certainly enjoy it.

In-line skating

In Singapore, rollerblading does not attract the sport's usual spunky punks, being favoured by families. Recreational skating takes place at many parks and beach areas, most notably in **East Coast Park** (*see p91; photo p194*), where small kiosks charge $8-$10 per hour for basic equipment rental.

For lessons and more information, check out the **Singapore Inline Skating Training Centre** (6474 5139, lessons 9853 1239, www.singaporeinline.com.sg).

Running

Running is probably the favourite way for locals to get fit. The island's numerous green spaces attract both serious and casual joggers, and park connectors (which link up various parks), make it easy to go for a prolonged run. In recent years, there has been a boom in the number of marathons, runs and triathlons. Some major runs that are open to the public include the **Singapore Biathlon** (March), **SAFRA Sheares Bridge Run & Army Half Marathon** (August), **Terry Fox Run** (September), **OSIM Singapore Corporate Triathlon** (November) and **the Singapore Marathon** (December; *see p165*). A popular mass walk also takes place every May: organised by and named after a local tabloid, the **New Paper Big Walk** attracts thousands of participants – the 2000 event, with 77,500 participants, holds the Guinness world record for 'largest walk'.

Swimming

Swimming in the sea isn't much fun in Singapore. Despite being an island, it has a shortage of beaches – and those it does have are not the tropical paradise you might expect. The most popular are in **East Coast Park** (*see p91*) and the three small stretches (Siloso, Palawan, Tanjong) on **Sentosa** (*see p83*); all are man-made, the water's pretty unappealing, and the horizon is dominated by container ships waiting to get into port.

Alternatively, most decent hotels are equipped with outdoor swimming pools. Public pools fall under the auspices of the **Singapore Sports Council** (www.ssc.gov.sg); although they are well run, the majority are in the suburbs – the pool at the **Toa Payoh Sports & Swimming Complex** (*see p197*) is more central than most. If you want to avoid the masses, obtain a day pass to a gym like **Fitness First** (*see p195*).

Watersports

Easily the most popular watersport in Singapore, wakeboarding has inspired many novices to jump on a board and brave the waves. Man-made marinas are the scene of the action: Punggol, SAF Yacht Club Bedok Reservoir and Kallang Riverside Park alternate as hotspots. For details of venues, activities

and events, contact the **Singapore Waterski & Wakeboard Federation** (6348 9943, www.swwf.org.sg). Some recommended operators include **ProAir Watersports** (6756 8012, www.proairwatersports.com), one of four established firms at Ponggol. In East Coast Park, the **Ski 360 Cableski Park** (1260A East Coast Parkway, 6442 7318, www.ski360degree.com) is a new facility where athletes practice on a waterski 'track' pulled by cables. Rates start at $30 per hour on weekdays.

Sailing and windsurfing (aka boardsailing) are also popular sports – but challenging, owing to Singapore's murky waters and temperamental offshore winds.

Changi Sailing Club

32 Netheravon Road, Changi (6545 2876/ www.csc.org.sg). Tampines MRT then bus 29.
The only sailing club with a natural beachfront. Tailored courses are available in dinghies, catamarans and keelboats, and you do not have to be a member to sign up.

East Coast Sea Sports Club

1390 East Coast Parkway, East Coast (6444 0409/ www.seasports.org.sg). City Hall MRT then bus 36.
A great place to learn to windsurf. Level one covers the basics with two six-hour sessions. Level two, an 18-hour, four-day course, covers tacking, gybing, the beach start and theory. Sea Sports has other outlets (at Changi, Kallang and Pasir Ris) and also offers kayaking, sailing and powerboating instruction.

Yoga

Always ask if you can have a free trial.

Pure Yoga

#18-00 Tower A, Ngee Ann City, 391A Orchard Road (6733 8863/www.pure-yoga.com). Orchard MRT. **Open** 6.45am-11pm Mon-Fri; 8am-8pm Sat, Sun. **Rates** $40/class. **Credit** AmEx, DC, MC, V. **Map** p247 F4.
This Hong Kong import offers a slightly posher image for those in search of smaller classes and luxurious bathrooms. With over 180 classes a week, you'll probably hear chat about *chaturanga dandasana* (a challenging yoga push-up), and will soon become as trim as the other members.

True Yoga

#04-01/#06-01 Pacific Plaza, 9 Scotts Road, Orchard Road & Around (6733 9555/www.true yoga.com.sg). Orchard MRT. **Open** 7am-11pm Mon-Fri; 8am-10.30pm Sat, Sun. **Rates** $38/class. **Credit** AmEx, DC, MC, V. **Map** p247 E3.
A phenomenon, True Yoga heralded the commercialisation of yoga with its massive 1,100sq m (12,000sq ft) floor space for every kind of yoga under the sun: from breathtaking Hot Yoga and Yogalates to gentle pre-natal and kids' yoga.

Spectator sports

Stadiums

The venerable National Stadium in Kallang is being torn down to make room for a new, $225-million, state of the art Sports Hub complex, due to open in 2010. Birthplace of the infamous 'Kallang Roar', the old stadium (opened 1973) had a capacity of 60,000, hosting National Day parade celebrations and big-name pop concerts. At press time, the new complex promised a multi-purpose indoor arena for martial arts, volleyball and basketball, plus a 400-metre track and an aquatic centre. In the interim, the 6,000-seater **Jalan Besar Stadium** and 4,000-seater **Choa Chu Kang Stadium** will host field and ball games. For details of Singapore's 18 stadiums, visit the **Singapore Sports Council**'s website (www.ssc.gov.sg).

Singapore Indoor Stadium

2 Stadium Walk, Kallang (6344 2660/www.sis.gov.sg). City Hall MRT then bus 16/Kallang MRT then bus 11. Like many local icons, the Singapore Indoor Stadium is a futuristic landmark envisioned by a foreign architect – in this case, the late Kenzo Tange, Japan's most famous Pritzker Prize winner. Located next to the National Stadium, the SIS seats 10,000 and hosts sporting events such as the AVIVA Badminton Open and the Singapore Slingers basketball team. But the headliners are glamorous international events such as the MTV Asia Awards, Disney on Ice and big-name concerts. A classy promenade hosts fairs, restaurants and free concerts.

Toa Payoh Sports & Swimming Complex

301 Toa Payoh Lorong 6, Toa Payoh (6259 4808). Toa Payoh MRT. **Open** 6.30am-9pm daily.
Built in 1973, this suburban swimming complex is still the largest in Singapore, and hosts a range of national and international competitions. The diving and competition pools are separated by an elevated viewing stand; the public may use the three 50m pools, set aside for training and teaching, water polo and wading. Other facilities include a sports stadium for track and football, with a sheltered grandstand for 2,000.

Badminton

The third most popular sport in Singapore (after jogging and swimming), badminton had its heyday in the 1970s and '80s when Singapore's own boys captured titles at the Thomas Cup and All-England Championships. The main event these days is the **AVIVA Badminton Open** (6344 1786, www. singaporebadmintonopen.com), held in June at the **Singapore Indoor Stadium** (*see above*) with prize money of $260,000.

Basketball

The first local professional basketball team, the **Singapore Slingers** (6346 1004, www.singaporeslingers.com) has breathed new life – and hope – into Singapore's sports fans. Dominated by foreign players, complemented by the cheerleading Slingers Girls, the team

Winning by a dragon's neck at the **Singapore River Regatta**. *See p198.*

Arts & Entertainment

draws an enthusiastic crowd to home matches as part of the Australian National Basketball League Philips Championship (www.nbl.com.au). Ten Australian teams and one New Zealand team compete with the Slingers for hoop glory in a season that runs from September to March.

Matches are held in various stadiums; tickets (from $11) are available from Sistic (6348 5555, www.sistic.com.sg).

Cricket

A colonial throwback, cricket in Singapore is favoured by British expats and the Indian community. Faithfully donning whites in the midday humidity, the domestic adult league of the **Singapore Cricket Association** (6348 6566, www.cricket.org.sg) plays up to 400 matches between March and November at the historic Padang in the city centre. Watch for free from the sidelines, or gain entry to the adjoining clubhouse and grandstand (but only if you're with a member of the elitist Singapore Cricket Club). Matches typically take place at 1.30pm on Saturdays and 11am on Sundays.

Dragon boating

Singapore Dragon Boat Association

Kallang Water Sports Centre, 10 Stadium Lane, Kallang (6440 9763/www.sdba.org.sg). City Hall MRT then bus 16/Kallang MRT then bus 11. **Open** 10am-6pm Tue-Sun. **Admission** free.
The SDBA maintains a national squad to field contenders in international races, some of which take place in Singapore waters. The Singapore World Invitational Dragon Boat Races in June – part of the annual Singapore Dragon Boat Festival (*see p162*) – and Singapore River Regatta in November are two world-class events. Paddlers are a common weekend sight at Kallang. **Photo** *p197*.

Football

Football is practically a religion in Singapore, with work grinding to a halt during the World Cup, big English Premiere League matches and even for local sporting events such as the Tiger Cup, which Singapore captured triumphantly in 2004 on their home ground.

British merchants brought the beautiful game to Asia in the late 19th century, and the legacy has endured. Drop by most pubs on the day of an English Premiere League match and see scores of fans cheering on their teams. Overseas fan clubs exist, such as the Official Liverpool FC Supporters Club (www.liverpoolfanclub.org.sg) and Newcastle United Supporters Club Singapore

Horse around at the **Turf Club**. *See p199.*

(www.nufcsingapore.com), and English football is covered in detail in the newspapers.

The women's national soccer team remains obscured by the men's **S League** – a fate also suffered by indoor or street soccer, better known as futsal. However, events such as the inaugural **Ladies' Futsal Challenge** in autumn 2006 may pave the way for increased opportunities for female soccer players. For more information on women's football, check the website of the **Football Association of Singapore** (www.fas.org.sg).

S League

6348 3477/www.sleague.com.
Under the auspices of the FAS, the S League was established in 1996, when Singapore pulled out of the Malaysia Cup after a row over match-fixing. Currently, 11 clubs from around the island play off in the Singapore Cup, drawing fans to 19 suburban stadiums; each team is permitted to sign five foreign players, so expect a cosmopolitan display of talent. The season runs from March to November.

Golf

Far from an old man's game, golf is highly regarded in Singapore – as demonstrated by the large number of world-class golf courses on this tiny island.

Tournaments are held at various courses, including the award-winning **Laguna National Golf & Country Club** in Tanah Merah (6248 1777, www.lagunagolf.com.sg) and the swanky **Sentosa Golf Club** (6275 0090, www.sentosagolf.com). With $1.5 million at stake, the annual **OSIM Singapore Masters** (www.singaporemasters.com), held in March, is a great opportunity to catch international PGA players in action. Vijay Singh won the inaugural event in 2001; and, in 2006, in one of Singapore's great sporting moments, native son Mardan Mamat won his first Major over defending champion Nick Dougherty. The $4.5-million **Barclays Singapore Open** (www.barclayssingapore open.com), in September, is a major event on the Asian Tour, featuring star players such as Thaworn Wiratchant and Ernie Els.

Horse racing

The main annual event is the **Singapore Airlines International Cup** (*see p162*) in May, drawing world-class jockeys and mounts. Horse betting in Singapore, as in Hong Kong, is a huge pastime, as proved by the island's 80-plus licensed betting shops.

Singapore Turf Club

1 Turf Club Avenue, Kranji (6879 1000/www.turf club.com.sg). Kranji MRT. **Open** from 6.30pm occasional Fri; from 1.45pm Sat, Sun. **Admission** *Grandstand $3-$7. VIP rooms $15-$20.* **Credit** AmEx, DC, JCB, MC, V.

The heady scent of money and sweat forms the backdrop to the Singapore Turf Club. Local and international punters rub shoulders as thoroughbreds storm the 2,000m turf and 1,500m Fibresand flat racing tracks. Race-goers must be aged 18 or above, and the dress code is smart casual (no shorts or sandals allowed). **Photo** *p198*.

Ice hockey

An unexpected game to find in tropical Singapore, perhaps. Backed by die-hard expat players, the **Amateur Ice Hockey Association** (6238 6630, www.icehockey.org. sg), organises the annual National Ice Hockey League. Players come from far-flung hockey powerhouses such as Canada, Russia and Finland. Games are held from September to April, June and July at **Fuji Ice Palace** (*see p194*) in Jurong; admission is free.

Polo

Singapore Polo Club

80 Mount Pleasant Road, Thomson Road, Toa Payoh (6854 3999/www.singaporepoloclub.org). Orchard MRT then bus 167.

The venerable Singapore Polo Club (founded 1886) still conjures genteel images of colonial life. Non-members can watch practice chukkas (usually 5pm on Tuesday, Thursday, Saturday and Sunday – but call first to check timings); international tournaments take place mainly in May. Family-friendly equestrian activities are available, as well as polo

lessons, but these are primarily intended for club members and residents, and conditions apply.

Rugby

The well-established **Singapore Rugby Union** (6469 5955, www.sru.org.sg) has several leagues under its belt. Youth and school championships are organised alongside the annual **National Rugby Championships**, which take place in September and October at various stadiums. The highly publicised annual **Singapore Sevens** (www.singaporesevens. com) is part of the International Rugby Board (IRB) Sevens Series. Sixteen international teams and 20,000 fans filled the National Stadium for the party-packed weekend event in April 2006.

Table tennis

As one of the seven 'core sports' under competitive development by the Singapore Sports Council, table tennis is on the fast track to prominence. As a result, the national squad squeaked to fourth position at the 2004 Olympics, and has won gold at various regional events, which include the **National Table Tennis Grand Finale** in November, and the more lucrative **Volkswagen Singapore Open** in May. Matches generally take place at the **Toa Payoh Sports Complex** (*see p197*). For more information, contact the **Singapore Table Tennis Association** (6354 1014, www.stta.org.sg).

Watersports

Singapore offers ample opportunity for marine-based sports, despite its murky seas. Sailing, waterskiing and windsurfing have long been popular, but in recent years wakeboarding has pulled ahead as the sport of choice. The **Singapore Waterski & Wakeboard Federation** (SWWF, 6348 9943, www.swwf. org.sg) organises regular events including the flashy **Wakeboard World Cup** in October, inviting top competitors from around the world to compete for a $90,000 purse. Look out for Singapore's own Sasha Christian, a charismatic 13-year-old who ranked sixth in the world in the under-14 category in 2006. SWWF's summer event is the **REEF Wakefest** (incorporating the Singapore National Wakeboarding Championships), a local competition that has grown into a three-stop regional event, complete with swinging after parties and a Miss Reef Bikini contest. Another highly rated event is the year-end **Asian Wakeboard Pro Tour** (usually held in November), now into its fourth year of crowning Asia's best boarders.

Theatre & Dance

The old, the new, the local, the international: quite a mix.

TheatreWorks' *Diaspora. See p201.*

Singapore's performing arts scene is one of the most varied in Asia. You'll find original plays, localised adaptations of famous crowd-pleasers, the latest mega-musicals brought in from overseas and acclaimed international productions. Singapore has around 12 main theatre and dance companies holding regular seasons each year, and just as many smaller companies or ethnic troupes making irregular appearances. It's still a young country, of course – and a long way from Broadway and the West End – so the quality of scripts, acting and directing is often patchy and can range from good to superior amateur dramatics, though many of the most established companies have made headway in raising standards.

Some would argue Singapore theatre's heyday was back in the mid 1980s, when companies such as the **Theatre Practice**, the **Necessary Stage**, **TheatreWorks** and **Action Theatre** were formed, and began staging daring new works that laid the foundation for home-grown theatre. Until this point, the English-language theatre scene had been dominated by Western plays staged by expats for the expat community. Meanwhile, the Asian population was being entertained by traditional forms of street theatre, such as Chinese opera, wayang (shadow puppets) and bangsawan (traditional Malay opera). The new groups – and the establishment of the National Arts Council (NAC), the country's arts funding body, in 1991 – inspired a new generation to take up

the arts (previously not considered a socially acceptable career choice) and invigorate it with fresh concepts and techniques.

More recently, the scene has been boosted by the arrival of several excellent new venues – the most renowned being **Esplanade – Theatres on the Bay**, the world-class arts centre gleaming bug-eyed beside the river.

Government interference in the form of censorship is still a factor. Regardless of whether it's a local show or international extravaganza, anything deemed to 'erode the core moral values of society' or 'denigrate, debase, disparage or demean a religion, race, government bodies, public institutions or national leaders and/or the nation's security' is taboo. Only recently was the ban on funding for performance art and 'forum theatre' lifted, and even today all scripts must be vetted by the Media Development Authority. A number of plays may be censored each year, and many more are deemed adult and slapped with an RA (over-18s only) rating. Such paternalism flies in the face of the government's plans for Singapore to become a cosmopolitan and robust arts hub. Like everywhere, surviving in the arts is a constant battle.

FESTIVALS

The highlight of the arts calendar is the month-long **Singapore Arts Festival** (*see p162*). Bringing in many foreign acts and companies from the festival circuit, it does commission a handful of local and international commissions – though local groups rarely produce their best work for it. Nonetheless, with dozens of shows all over town and into the suburbs, it's a breath of fresh air each June. There are lots of smaller festivals too, many held at Esplanade.

INFORMATION AND TICKETS

For event listings, check the daily papers, *Time Out Singapore*, *I-S* or the fortnightly free listings magazine *Arts Xplosion*. Tickets are available direct from the venue or via booking agents (*see chapter* **Resources A-Z**). Prices vary enormously depending on the production, but you can expect to pay from around $15 for small-scale performances to upwards of $120 for lavish extravaganzas.

Theatre

Major companies

Action Theatre

42 Waterloo Street, Bras Basah & Bugis (6837 0842/www.action.org.sg), Bras Basah MRT
Box office ticket agents only. **Tickets** approx $35-$100; concessions $25-$90. **Map** p248 K5.
Action presents original works that address topical themes (racial identity, homosexuality, loneliness), and also well-known English and American works. It also created *Chang & Eng*, Singapore's longest running home-grown musical and the first English-language musical to be staged in China. During its 20-year tenure it has staged some of the city's most acclaimed works, and also nurtures new writing talent from its own studio theatre space.

The Necessary Stage

#B1-02 Marine Parade Community Building, 278 Marine Parade Road, Marine Parade (6440 8115/www.necessary.org). Bus 15, 31, 36, 48, 76. **Tickets** $18-$40; concessions $15-$35.
If you want to see the underbelly of Singapore – the marginalised, repressed and disenfranchised – go to a TNS show. For over two decades, artistic director Alvin Tan and resident playwright Haresh Sharma have created some of Singapore's most provocative and original theatre, which continues to push boundaries on simmering social topics. It has a small studio theatre, but stages larger productions in other spaces. TNS also runs the annual cross-disciplinary M1 Singapore Fringe Festival in February, which has a substantial theatre section featuring local and foreign companies.

Singapore Repertory Theatre

For listing, see p202 **DBS Arts Centre**.
SRT produces quality 'world theatre with an Asian spirit' featuring the best talents it can find from home and abroad. It presents classics and Broadway and West End hits, such as *Hamlet* and *Kiss of the Spiderwoman*, but is best known for two original

works, *Golden Child* and *Forbidden City: Portrait of an Empress*. It also stages children's plays through the Little Company, and has its own medium-size theatre, DBS, on Robertson Quay.

TheatreWorks

72-13 Mohamed Sultan Road, Robertson Quay (6737 7213/www.theatreworks.org.sg). Bus 32, 54, 139, 195, NR3. **Tickets** free-$50; concessions available. **Map** p250 G8.
Singapore's oldest English-language theatre company is also its most travelled, frequently touring abroad. Under the leadership of dynamic artistic director Ong Keng Sen, it produces cutting-edge productions that often reinterpret traditional performance via a dizzying juxtaposition of cultures. Its landmark works, such as *Lear and Desdemona*, form the DNA of Singapore theatre. Love 'em or hate 'em, it remains an industry leader and chief source of groundbreaking works and writers. It has its own warehouse performance space near the Singapore River. **Photo** *p200*.

The Theatre Practice

#02-08 Stamford Arts Centre, 155 Waterloo Street, Bras Basah & Bugis (6337 2525/www.ttp.org.sg). Bugis MRT. **Tickets** $20-$60; concessions $18-$54. **Map** p248 K5.
Singapore's first bilingual (English and Mandarin) theatre company was founded in 1986 by the late Kuo Pao Kun, who is often described as 'the doyen of Singapore theatre'. He was instrumental in creating a new vernacular in local theatre – original plays that explored universal issues but were grounded in a local identity, using traditional and modern theatre techniques. His daughter is now one of the co-artistic directors. TTP currently produces about three main shows and one festival a year. It has a small studio theatre on Waterloo Street.

W!ld Rice

6292 2695/www.wildrice.com.sg.
Founding artistic director Ivan Heng is something of a powerhouse – a brilliant actor, and astute director and playwright. He's won numerous international awards for his solo shows such as *Emily of Emerald Hill*, and is now taking his company to great heights through edgy yet accessible explorations of identity, migration, and gender and sexual politics, notably in *Animal Farm*. W!ld Rice's Christmas pantos are always popular, and in 2006 it presented the first Singapore Theatre Festival, a showcase for local theatre.

Other companies

Other groups worth looking out for include newcomer **Cake Theatrical Productions** (6440 6267, www.caketheatre.com); and **spell#7** (6392 1772, www.spell7.net), who are best known for creating collaborative multimedia works and eloquent scripts exploring human relationships. Visit their

Arts & Entertainment

office at 65 Kerbau Road, Little India, for a copy of *Desire Paths*, their audio tour of the area (available in English, Mandarin and Japanese) – but call first. For children's theatre companies, *see p168*.

Drama Box
6324 5434/www.dramabox.org.
This Mandarin-language company is a force to be reckoned with. Led by Kok Heng Leun, it frequently tours the suburbs in an effort to engage new audiences with social and civic issues. Its main shows usually feature English subtitles.

The Finger Players
6738 6061/www.fingerplayers.com.
Few companies in Singapore have undergone such a dramatic transformation. From its days as a traditional puppetry troupe, the Finger Players has matured into one of Singapore's most exciting theatre groups. Teaming human actors with puppets to stunning effect, it has performed at 16 festivals in 13 countries, while its most recent works have bagged the city's top awards.

Teater Ekamatra
#01-10 Telok Ayer Performing Arts Centre, 182 Cecil Street, Chinatown (6323 5443/ www.ekamatra.org.sg). Tanjong Pagar MRT. **Tickets** $18; concessions $14. **Map** p250 J12.
Dedicated to supporting new acting and writing talent, the country's leading Malay theatre company explores topical matters such as the state of the Malay language, heritage and women in Singapore, in shows that manage to be controversial and often critically acclaimed. It stages three to four Malay plays a year, often with English subtitles.

Toy Factory Productions
6222 1526/www.toyfactory.com.sg.
Originally a humble puppet theatre company, Toy Factory has grown into the city's leading bilingual (English and Mandarin) theatre company, responsible for some of the edgiest shows permissible in Singapore. It presents strikingly original works, reworked classics and contemporary sizzlers (such as *Shopping & Fucking* and *Bent*) – always with sensational set designs, for which artistic director Goh Boon Teck is renowned.

Dance

Arts Fission
6238 6469/www.artsfission.org.
Describing itself as an 'Asian dance laboratory', Arts Fission aims to 'rekindle human spirit and sensibility' through a new genre of Asian dance music. Led by dance pioneer Angela Liong, the group is best known for developing memorable, site-specific works, though it also performs in its small studio at One-Two-Six Cairnhill Arts Centre on Cairnhill Road, north of Orchard Road.

ECNAD
6226 6772/www.ecnad.org.
Founded in 1996 as Dance Dimension Project, ECNAD (that's 'dance' backwards) has made its mark as one of the country's most visual dance companies. Eye-catching costumes, imaginative sets and evocative visual effects always accompany its brand of simple dance-cum-storytelling. This collaborative and multi-disciplinary approach has made it a favourite at arts festivals abroad and with community-based projects at home.

Odyssey Dance Theatre
6221 5516/www.odysseydancetheatre.com.
ODT (founded in 1999) produces around three main shows each year as well as two biennial dance festivals for local and international dancers and choreographers. It also conducts regular shows and workshops in schools and community centres. Its performances are typically dynamic and spiritual fusions of contemporary and Chinese dance.

Singapore Dance Theatre
6338 0611/www.singaporedancetheatre.com.
Now a decade old, SDT is Singapore's de facto national dance company. Its dancers, from all over the Asia-Pacific region, are trained in both classical ballet and modern dance, but excel in contemporary works by international choreographers such as Stanton Welch, Jiri Kylian, Nacho Duato, Boi Sakti, Ohad Naharin and Marie-Claude Pietragalla. Most shows, including the popular children's Christmas classics (such as *Nutcracker* and *Giselle*), are staged at Esplanade, but Ballet Under the Stars (BUTS, for short, in July) is held outside SDT's studio on the lawn of Fort Canning.

Venues

The Arts House
Old Parliament House, 1 Old Parliament Lane, Colonial District (6332 6900/tickets 6332 6919/ www.theartshouse.com.sg). City Hall or Raffles Place MRT. **Box office** 10am-8pm Mon-Fri; 11am-8pm Sat; 1hr before performance Sun. **Credit** AmEx, DC, MC, V. **Map** p251 K9.
This building began life in 1827 as a private residence, then became Singapore's first Court House and finally Parliament House. Following renovation, it reopened in 2004 as an arts centre, featuring a monthly programme of small-scale performances at the Chamber (200 seats) and Play Den (120). It has struggled to find an identity, but is now starting to develop one, though more through its music and bookshop than its theatrical offerings, which tend to be put on by groups hiring the space.

DBS Arts Centre
20 Merbau Road, Robertson Quay (6733 8166/ www.srt.com.sg). Bus 32, 64, 123, 143, 195. **Box office** 11am-7pm Mon-Fri; 1hr before performance Sat, Sun. **Credit** AmEx, DC, JCB, MC, V. **Map** p250 H8.

Asia on show

Dance Ensemble Singapore

6334 7192/
www.des.org.sg.
DES combines Chinese folk dance and ballet to create a fusion between Eastern and Western forms. It has performed at numerous Singapore events, including the Chingay Parade, National Day Parade, Festival of Asian Performing Arts (now defunct), and festivals throughout Asia.

Singapore's multicultural make-up translates into all aspects of life, including the arts. Wander the city's ethnic districts and you can find traditional art forms still being practiced, largely unchanged from their origins. While there are dozens of ethnic arts groups across the country, the following are the most renowned professional companies, each running its own student academy.

If you can brave the crushing crowds, the annual **Chingay** street parade held during the Chinese New Year celebrations (*see p165*) is always a dazzling display. Other events showcasing different local cultures and their traditional and contemporary art forms are **Huayi** (Chinese Festival of Arts), **Kalaa Utsavam** (Indian Festival of Arts) and **Pesta Raya** (Malay Festival of Arts). They're all held at Esplanade, during Chinese New Year, Deepavali and after Hari Raya, respectively.

Bhaskar's Arts Academy

6396 4523/www.bhaskarsartsacademy.com.
At the forefront of traditional Indian dance and music performance, this highly respected group is renowned for having the only Kathakali dance group outside India, and for its unique interpretation of Asian classics such as the *Butterfly Lovers* and *Manohra*.

Singapore Indian Fine Arts Society

2A Starlight Road, Little India (6299 5929/
www.sifas.org). Farrer Park MRT. **Box office**
9am-9pm Tue-Thur; 9am-4pm Fri-Sun.
Tickets $10-$30; concessions $8-$25.
No credit cards. Map p249 L1.
Founded in 1949, SIFAS excels in a wide variety of art forms. It stages annual shows of Bharathanatyam and Kathak dance and Kuchipudi theatre, as well as free monthly student events at the society's auditorium.

Sri Warisan Som Said Performing Arts

59 Kerbau Road, Little India (6225 6070/
www.sriwarisan.com). Little India MRT.
Box office 9am-6pm Mon-Fri, 9am-1pm Sat;
1-6pm Sun. **Tickets** $10-$20. **No credit cards. Map** p248 K3.
The leading proponent of traditional Malay art forms – dance, music and theatre – which it fuses with contemporary techniques. It has performed at all of Singapore's major cultural events and at over 30 international festivals. Performances ($8) are held every Wednesday at 3.30pm and Sunday at 11.30am at the Malay Heritage Centre. **Photo** *above.*

Set in a renovated warehouse in the Robertson Quay nightlife district, this elegant theatre seats 380. It's home to Singapore Repertory Theatre (*see p201*), whose repertoire fills most of the programme, but in the gaps you can find comedy festivals and concerts.

Drama Centre

3/F National Library, 100 Victoria Street, Bras Basah & Bugis (6837 8400/www.nac.gov.sg/tbo).
Bugis MRT. **Map** p249 L6.

Once upon a time the Drama Centre was a well-loved but dilapidated old theatre behind the original National Library on Stamford Road. Then both were razed and relocated to the gleaming new National Library building across town. The reborn state-of-the-art theatre has a main space seating 615 and a black box for 120. Run by the National Arts Council (as is the Victoria Theatre – *see p204*), it's mostly hired out to various companies.

Esplanade – Theatres on the Bay

*1 Esplanade Drive, Marina (6828 8222/
www.esplanade.com). City Hall MRT then 10mins
walk/bus 36, 106, 133, 171, 195.* **Box office**
noon-8.30pm daily. **Tickets** prices vary. **Credit**
AmEx, DC, JCB, MC, V. **Map** p251 L5.

Few buildings have created such a storm as this one.
Opened in 2002, the eye-catching bayfront complex
has been dubbed 'the durians' by locals, because of
its resemblance to the spiky tropical fruit. Built at a
cost of $600 million, Esplanade is Singapore's pre-
mier performing arts centre, drawing comparisons
with the Sydney Opera House. Its crown jewels are
the 1,600-seat Concert Hall and the 2,000-seat
Theatre. Built in the form of a traditional U-shaped
European opera house with the biggest stage in
Singapore, the latter has hosted major international
musicals, full-scale ballets and Chinese opera extrav-
aganzas. There is also a black box Theatre Studio
(seating 220) and a Recital Studio (245). There is no
resident company, so the programming is an eclectic mix, veering from Western to Eastern flavours
and including hired productions.

Jubilee Hall

*3/F Raffles Hotel Arcade, 328 North Bridge Road,
Colonial District (6412 1319). City Hall MRT.*
Map p249 L6.

For a nostalgic whiff of Singapore's glory days as a
key colonial trading post, visit this grand old theatre (with seating for 400) on the third floor of the
Raffles Hotel Arcade. Surrounded by beautiful
murals of tropical life, it's resplendent with chandeliers, red velvet curtains, ceiling cornices and creak-
ing floorboards. Due to its age and small stage, it's
limited to classical theatre and small-scale musicals
and dance performances.

The Substation

*45 Armenian Street, Colonial District (6337 7535/
tickets 6337 7800/www.substation.org). City Hall
MRT.* **Box office** noon-8.30pm Mon-Fri; 1hr before
performance Sat, Sun. **Tickets** $10-$30; concessions
$8-$25. **Credit** MC, V. **Map** p250 J7.

Many of Singapore's best artists will tell you they
cut their teeth at the Substation. Its founder, the late
Kuo Pao Kun, transformed the former power station
into Singapore's first independent contemporary
arts centre in 1990. Its mission, to nurture local
artists and artistic experimentation, has encouraged
an avant-garde, bohemian atmosphere. Theatre
shows are put on in the tiny Guinness Theatre.
Bands play most days in the Timbre Music Bistro
(*see p189*) in the back garden. *See also p176*.

University Cultural Centre

*National University of Singapore, 50 Kent Ridge
Crescent, Queenstown (6516 2492/www.nus.edu.sg/
cfa). Clementi MRT then bus 96.*

Situated in the west of the island on the NUS campus, this brand-new centre has a concert hall (seating 1,700) and theatre (450). It's mainly used by the
performing arts students, but high-calibre international performers also appear.

Victoria Theatre

*9 Empress Place, Colonial District (6338 8283/
www.nac.gov.sg/tbo). City Hall or Raffles Place MRT.*
Map p251 K9.

This stately colonial building next to the river was
originally Singapore's town hall. In 1905 it was converted into a 900-seat theatre for use by amateur
English drama troupes, and for almost a century it
was the most prestigious and coveted of Singapore's
theatre venues – until the arrival of Esplanade.

Big, bold and spiky: **Esplanade**, Singapore's leading performing arts complex.

Arts & Entertainment

Trips Out of Town

Features

Angsana Resort & Spa. *See p215.*

Getting Started

Tips on leaving Singapore.

Ever since Raffles first spotted Singapore's potential as a trading post for the East India Company, the island has been a key transport hub in the Asia Pacific region. These days, it's a global hub: 35 million passengers passed through Changi Airport in 2006, flying with over 80 airlines to more than 180 destinations in 57 countries. Many are long-haul passengers, of course, taking the 'kangaroo route' between Australia, New Zealand and Europe. But an increasing number are country-hopping in South-east Asia, thanks to the rise in the past couple of years of low-cost regional carriers operating out of Changi Airport. A new budget terminal opened in 2006 in anticipation of the increase in traffic; it's currently used by only two airlines, Tiger Airways and Cebu Pacific Air – but watch this space.

Fancy a weekend in Bangkok, less than two hours' flight from Singapore? Thailand, in particular, is easy to get to, with Air Asia, Bangkok Airways, Jetstar Asia and Tiger Airways flying, between them, to Bangkok, Koh Samui, Chiang Mai, Phuket and Hat Yai. Or how about the temples of Angkor Wat? Or the beaches of Bali? Fares vary, but, for example, a one-way ticket to Thailand costs about $80.

There are too many destinations for us to do justice to here, but below is a list of the regional and budget airlines currently operating out of Singapore. The two giants are **Jetstar Asia**, with flights to Cambodia, Hong Kong, Myanmar, the Philippines, Taiwan, Thailand and Vietnam; and **Tiger Airways**, which serves Indonesia, Macau, the Philippines, Thailand and Vietnam.

But you don't have to get on a plane if you want a break for a few days. You can take a bus or train or drive to Malaysia, accessible by two causeways in the north and east of Singapore. The town of **Johor Bahru**, just over the northern causeway at Woodlands, is a popular refuelling and shopping point for Singaporeans (petrol and goods in general are much cheaper in Malaysia). A couple of hours' drive up the coast is **Melaka**, once the jewel in the Portuguese empire's crown, and a favoured destination for antiques shopping and Peranakan food; a couple of hours further north lies the urban buzz of **Kuala Lumpur**.

Alternatively, jump on a ferry. The Indonesian islands of **Bintan** and **Batam** attract boatloads of visitors from Singapore

daily, many looking to relax and recharge in a beach resort (the beaches are significantly better than those in Singapore). They're close enough for a day trip – less than an hour's boat ride away – but best to make a weekend of it.

AIRLINES: REGIONAL

Adam Air 6836 9990/www.flyadamair.com
Air India 6545 0892/www.airindia.com
Bangkok Airways 6545 8481/
www.bangkokair.com
Biman Bangladesh Airlines 6221 7155/
www.bimanair.com
Korean Air 6796 2020/www.koreanair.com
Lion Air 6225 3536/www.lionair.co.id
Myanmar Air 6235 5005/www.maiair.com
Philippine Airlines 6336 1611/
www.pal.com.ph
Royal Brunei 6235 4672/www.bruneiair.com
Sri Lankan Airlines 6223 6026/
www.srilankan.lk
Vietnam Airlines 6339 3552/
www.vietnamair.com.vn
Xiamen Airlines 6221 0770/
www.xiamenair.com.cn

AIRLINES: BUDGET

AirAsia 6733 9933/www.airasia.com
Cebu Pacific Air www.cebupacificair.com
Jetstar Asia 6822 2288/www.jetstarasia.com
Tiger Airways 1800 388 8888/
www.tigerairways.com
Valuair 6229 8338/www.valuair.com.sg

Colourful **Melaka** awaits. *See p208.*

Malaysia

At play on the peninsula.

If you need a break from the hustle and bustle of Singapore, or just a change of scenery, the Malaysian peninsula is ideal for a quick day or overnight trip. A visit to **Johor Bahru**, **Melaka** or **Kuala Lumpur** offers a profusion of sights, museums, malls and food centres – a buffet compared to Singapore's set meal. While Singapore has all these in a compact setting, the Malaysian states have the luxury of space and a more favourable exchange rate. Bahasa Malaysia is the state language, though English is widely spoken. Malaysia celebrates its 50th anniversary in 2007 and **Tourism Malaysia** (www.tourismmalaysia.gov.my) promises big events and attractions to mark the occasion – including Kuala Lumpur's new 60-metre (197-foot) high ferris wheel **Eye on Malaysia**, modelled on the London Eye.

During Ramadan, the month of holy fasting practised by Muslims (usually October), visitors may find Malay establishments close early to accommodate the dawn-to-sundown fasting hours. As an Islamic state, Malaysia's Muslim celebrations take place on a larger scale than in Singapore, with a greater abundance of decorations, sales, bazaars and festival foods. Cover your arms and legs if you intend to visit mosques, though headscarves and robes are usually provided for women. Taxis tend to overcharge in all parts of the country and mild haggling is usually acceptable in independent shops and stalls.

Tourists of most nationalities can stay in Malaysia for up to three months without a visa. The notable exception to this rule is citizens of Israel, who are barred from the country (the same works in reverse – Malaysians are not permitted to enter Israel).

Phone numbers listed below are given as called within each city. If you're phoning from outside, use the city code (07 for Johor Bahru, 06 for Melaka, 03 for Kuala Lumpur). From Singapore, just add 02 at the front – or the code for Malaysia (60) followed by the city code, but without the intial 0. In an emergency, call the police or ambulance on 999, the fire department on 994. Internet facilities are widespread, in hotels and shopping malls.

Prices are quoted in Malaysian ringgit (RM); at the time of writing, $1 Singapore was worth RM2.27. Unless otherwise noted, hotel prices are for double rooms.

Johor Bahru

Located just over the Singapore-Johor Causeway, and billed as the southern gateway to Malaysia, **Johor Bahru** (usually known as JB) is the capital city of Johor state. The second largest city in Malaysia, it is an unlovable border town – the crowded, polluted city centre is filled with itinerant workers and buoyed by Singapore tourist dollars. Yet it is refreshingly free-spirited compared to staid, orderly Singapore (though be careful – snatch thefts are common).

Seedy sex and mainstream shopping aside, Johor Bahru doesn't offer much reason for lingering: it's more of a rest and refuel stop en route to Melaka or Kuala Lumpur. Most tourists will find little of note except the fresh seafood and the **Royal Abu Bakar Museum**, also called the Muzium Diraja Abu Baka (Jalan Ibrahim, 223 0555, open 10am-6pm Thur-Sat, admission non-Malaysians US$7). Formerly the Istana (palace) of Sultan Abu Bakar, the 'father of modern Johor', in the mid 19th century, this Victorian-style museum is the height of opulence, stuffed with hunting trophies, ceremonial regalia, royal treasures and other decadent displays. The **Sultan Abu Bakar Mosque** is also located on Jalan Ibrahim, a short walk west of the museum. A prime example of late Victorian architecture, with elaborate minarets, it teems with worshippers, especially on Fridays.

For shopping, the newer malls are clean and boast international labels. **Johor Bahru City Square** (Jalan Wong Ah Fook) is a good bet. Older ones such as **Holiday Plaza** (Jalan Dato Sulaiman, Century Garden) and **Plaza Pelangi** (Jalan Tebrau) are a short taxi ride from the town centre and offer cheap Malaysian products, fake designer goods and hawker centres. Both have distinctive local atmosphere, but you may be overcharged for the cab ride it should cost about RM4. Avoid the Johor Bahru Duty Free Complex on Stulang Laut: it's a dismal tourist trap.

Where to eat & stay

Many Singaporeans make a special trip across the causeway for cheap, fresh seafood; some drive over for a late-night feast at one of the many restaurant centres. **Selera Sungei Chat** on Jalan Abu Bakar, the main waterfront to the west, and **Taman Tebrau Jaya**, on Tebrau Highway in the suburbs, are famous for grilled fish, prawns and crabs.

If staying overnight in rough and ready JB, avoid the budget options and pay the most you can afford. There's a good range of smart hotels, from the 500-room **Puteri Pacific Hotel** (The Kotaraya, Jalan Abdullah Ibrahim, 223 3333, www.luxehotels.com, RM220) to the top-end **Hyatt Regency** (Jalan Sungei Chat, 222 1234, http://johorbahru.regency.hyatt.com, RM400).

Resources

Hospital
Hospital Besar Tun Aminah *Jalan Sultan Abu Bakar (223 1666).*

Police station
Jalan Meldrum (223 2222).

Post office
KOMTAR, Tingkat 2, 25-27 Kompleks Tun Abdul Razak (223 1555).

Tourist information
Tourist Information Centre *2 Jalan Air Molek (223 4935/224 1432).* **Open** 8am-5pm Mon-Fri. A small office, located a fair way from the city centre.

Melaka

Formerly known as Malacca, this coastal city-state has changed along with its moniker. Along with Penang and Singapore, it's one of the birthplaces of Peranakan culture. Thriving businessmen in the early 1900s, the Peranakans – a unique blend of Chinese and Malay clans – were cultural chameleons, adapting Western culture and dress to create a style of their own. Since then, Melaka has experienced a decline in the number of Babas and Nyonyas (male and female descendants, respectively).

The capital of the Malacca Sultanate in the 15th century, Melaka fell to the Portuguese in 1511; the Dutch and British followed, and their legacy is evident in the town's architecture. Most of the historic sights are clustered around the town square (also called Dutch Square), while Peranakan culture is centred on the main thoroughfare, Jonker Street (also called Jalan Hang Jebat). For all the beautiful shopfronts, the city is losing its heritage; original shophouses are being replaced by kitsch replicas. Soaring rents have forced out local shop owners from the main bazaar, to be replaced by chains or non-native retailers. Helpless to turn the tide, most of the old-timers

The ruins of historic **St Paul's Church**.

are fading from view. *Malacca: Voices from the Streets*, by Lim Huck Chin and Fernando Jorge, sold in many shops, chronicles the changes.

The best way to get about is on foot, or by pedal-powered trishaw. You can't miss the red-coloured **Stadthuys** in the middle of the town square; built in the mid 17th century and formerly the town hall, it's the oldest Dutch building in the East. Also in the square, the **Porta de Santiago** is the last remaining edifice of the celebrated A'Famosa Portuguese fort, built in 1511 and bulldozed by the British in early 1800. More ruins can be found in the form of **St Paul's Church**, a small chapel on the hill overlooking the A'Famosa site. A sound and light show takes place nightly at 8.30pm in the square, lighting up the ruins with a re-enactment of Melaka's past.

If you have time for only one museum, make it the **Baba & Nyonya Heritage Museum** (48-50 Jalan Tun Tan Cheng Lock, 283 1273, open 10am-4.30pm daily, admission RM8). It brings to life Peranakan culture, from vibrant ceramic ware to intricate beading on fabrics.

As for shopping, a resident orang utan (Malay for 'forest people') is Melaka's best-known landmark. A colourful mural of a grinning monkey marks the **Orangutan House** (59 Lorong Hang Jebat, 282 6872), a showcase for the controversial Melakan artist Charles Cham. He creates abstract art and T-shirts that touch on everything from human rights to endangered orang utans. There are also two other outlets, at 12 Jonker Street and 96 Heeren Street.

You can explore Melaka by rickshaw.

Simple souvenirs in the form of linen apparel, handcrafted wooden trinkets and bags are sold at the **Jonker Gallery** (29B & 66 Jalan Hang Jebat, 286 9863, 286 9861). Antiques such as dining sets with inlaid mother of pearl can still be found at **Malaqa House Museum** (70 Jalan Tan Cheng Lock, 281 4770) On weekends between 6pm and midnight, Jonker Street turns into a street-long night market with craft stalls and food vendors.

Where to eat & drink

An astounding variety of Peranakan food is dished out in Melaka, along with traditional street fare such as chicken rice balls. **Famosa Chicken Rice Ball** (Jalang Hang Kasturi, off Jonker Street, 286 0121, plus branches) is a good place at which to try the dish (you can tell by the busloads of tourist who frequently descend upon the place). Ice chendol, a dessert made with gula Melaka (thick brown coconut molasses) is another local speciality: for maximum authenticity, it is best eaten on a rickety stool at the dilapidated **Low Kong Jong Ice Cafe** (85 Jalan Hang Jebat).

For pure Nyonya cuisine in an antiquated Chinese hall, try **Jonkers** (17 Jalan Hang Jebat, 283 5578), which serves a lovingly home-cooked menu of curries and vegetarian dishes; try the set meal (RM20) for a small taste of everything. **Nancy's Kitchen** (15 Jalan Hang Lekir) is another gem. Mouth-watering sambal and otak otak (steamed fish cake) are highlights.

If your stomach is delicate, Western meals in contemporary settings are easily obtained. **Limau-Limau Café** (49 Jalan Hang Jebat, 012 698 4917) is pleasantly outfitted for lazy afternoons, while **Geographer Café** (83 Jalan Hang Jebat, 281 6813) is hard to miss - it occupies a yellow-painted shophouse on a corner – and hard to leave. The food is good, the service fun and it's open late.

For nightlife with peace of mind, the **Utan Fun Pub** at Renaissance Melaka hotel (*see below*) is respectable and offers live bands daily except Sunday. The rest of Melaka is dominated by dodgy karaoke bars.

Where to stay

Hotel Puri (118 Jalan Tun Tan Cheng Lock, 282 5588, www.hotelpuri.com, RM110) is a swish boutique hotel in a restored Peranakan house, with a garden café, glam marble lobby and adjoining spa. Standard rooms face other walls, so it's worth RM150 to get a superior with inner courtyard views. Alternatively, at No.125, **Baba House** (281 1216, 284 8911, RM59-RM95) offers a spartan though authentic Baba experience in a beautiful shophouse space. Basic rooms have air-conditioning but no windows; upgrade if you want natural light.

Renaissance Melaka (Jalan Bendahara, 284 8888, www.renaissancehotels.com, RM400) provides the only five star bed in town – and the only 24th-storey view.

Resources

Hospital
Straits Hospital *37 Jalan Parameswara (283 5336/282 2344).*

Police station
Jalan Kota (270 3238/282 2222)

Post office
Jalan Laksamana (284 8440/283 3846).

Tourist information
Tourist Information Centre *Jalan Kota (281 4803/www.melaka.gov.my).* **Open** 8.45am-5pm Mon-Thur, Sun; 8.45am-12.15pm, 2.45-5pm Fri. Opposite the main square; buy a map for RM2.

Kuala Lumpur

Boasting a gleaming new airport, awe-inspiring skyscrapers, the grandiose 'Multimedia Super Corridor' and billion-ringgit projects galore, Malaysia's capital is going through a dynamic phase. It's a striking blend of old and new, rich and poor, chaos and calm, Malay and Chinese.

Getting around the sprawling, and congested, city can be problematic. In the spirit of free enterprise, Kuala Lumpur's local transport system is highly competitive – and confusing. Options include RapidKL buses; a Light-Rail Transit system combining four separate monorail lines; and the KTM Kommuter fast train service, using a different set of stations. The most useful interchange is KL Sentral, where you can connect to all the lines. Major destinations are accessible, but factor in at least one switch of lines. Cabbies often bargain for a flat fare, drive in circles or use a doctored meter – to get a metered cab, queue in a taxi rank.

A new tourist service is the **KL Hop-On-Hop-Off City Tour** (www.myhoponhopoff. com), taking in over 40 sights and attractions in a glass-topped, double-decker bus (RM38 for 24 hours).

Sightseeing

Formerly the tallest building in the world (until the arrival of Taipei 101 in Taiwan in 2004), the 88-storey **Petronas Twin Towers** (2051 1320, 2051 1744; **photo** *p210*), designed by American architect César Pelli, is an emblem of Kuala Lumpur's modern aspirations. Though popularly described as *jagung* ('ears of corn'), the two towers also resemble rockets, with a 'skybridge' connecting the towers at the 41st and 42nd floors. The first 1,400 visitors each day are given a free pass to ascend to the skybridge (open 9am-7pm Tue-Sun); otherwise you'll have to settle for ground views – so get there early. Situated next to the Twin Towers, **Dewan Filharmonik Petronas** is Malaysia's premier concert hall, the place at which to catch the Malaysian Philharmonic Orchestra.

Muzium Negara (National Museum, Jalan Damansara, 2282 6255, open 9am-6pm daily, admission $2) is situated near **Lake Gardens**, a tranquil park. Not only does it encompass a large lake, but the park is home to two of the country's Muslim landmarks: the 1960s' **Masjid Negara** (National Mosque, closed 12.30-2pm, 3.30-5pm daily) and the **Museum of Islamic Arts Malaysia** (2274 2020, open 10am-6pm Tue-Sun, RM8).

Take a dive

Singapore's waters have little to offer scuba fans, but Malaysia boasts several islands with fantastic diving sites, most of which are easily accessible from the peninsular states. The exception is **Pulau Sipadan**, off the east coast of Sabah on Borneo. Serious divers should make the effort, though – made famous by Jacques Cousteau, who dubbed it 'an untouched piece of art', it's arguably the best dive site in the world. Singapore outfit **White Manta** (9677 8894, www.whitemanta.com) runs courses to some of the islands below, with beautiful boats and enthusiastic instructors. Check website **www.myoutdoor.com** for details, plus accommodation deals and holiday packages.

Pulau Aur

Closest to Singapore, off the coast of Johor, Pulau Aur and its surrounding islands of Dayang, Sibu, Besar, Rawa and Tinggi are rustic but popular dive sites. The further out the island, the better the visibility and the chance of parrotfish and turtle sightings.

Pulau Tioman

Arguably the most commercialised island, Tioman, off the east coast (and where they filmed some scenes for the movie *South Pacific*), nevertheless boasts dazzling deep sea dive sites. Expect a sunken hull, hard coral and manta sightings.

Pulau Redang

The supermodel of Malaysian islands, Redang (off the east coast) is a shimmering tropical paradise – above and below the shoreline. Corals and marine life are abundant at any of the nine diving spots, the most famous being Big Mount.

Pulau Perhentian

The twin marine destination of Perhentian Kecil and Perhentian Besar ('small' and 'big', respectively) are the northernmost of the dive islands off the east coast. The former has fallen prey to a busy tourist scene, while the latter retains a sedate pace of life. From snorkelling to night diving, options are plentiful.

Pulau Langkawi

Langkawi is a tourist hotspot off the west coast, with numerous resorts, duty-free shopping and cultural sightseeing. The day-trip dive site, Pulau Payar, is sheltered from the monsoons that hit the east coast. You can expect to see groupers and anemones.

Shopping

The city's flashiest malls, **Suria KLCC** (at
the base of the Petronas Towers) and **Starhill
Gallery** (181 Jalan Bukit Bintang) are loaded
with designer shops, niche boutiques and
department stores. On the same street as
Starhill, **Bukit Bintang Plaza** (No.111) and
Sungei Wang Plaza (No.138) are dizzying
mazes full of quirky shops and throngs of
locals. Mammoth mall **Berjaya Times
Square** (1 Jalan Imbi) opened with a bang in
2005, since abated to a whimper (its 1,000 shops
change hands frequently).

Pasar Seni, aka Central Market (Jalan
Hang Kasturi, 2031 0399; **photo** *p212*) is a
rustic collection of craft shops and galleries
near Chinatown. Most stall owners don't
haggle, but the Malaysian art and antiques
are well priced. **Petaling Street** in Chinatown
does a roaring trade; between 7pm and 11pm,
a night market springs to life, offering pirated
goods (clothes, DVDs). Grab a snack at the food
stalls, but beware of pickpockets.

Nightlife

Kuala Lumpur's raw nightlife scene offers a
refreshing change from polished Singapore.
Liberty comes at a price, however, and
arbitrary police raids – to stamp out drugs –
are not uncommon. The high energy zones
of Asian Heritage Row, Jalan Ampang and
Bintang Walk are good for a lively night out.
Further out (take a taxi) is hip Bangsar, a
local favourite with happening bars and
restaurants side by side.

Futuristic **Zouk** (113 Jalan Ampang, 2171
1997) is rave central, with regular appearances
by international star DJs. There's also sexy,
baroque **Maison** (8 Jalan Yap Ah Shak,
Asian Heritage Row, 2381 2088). The setting
is a smallish shophouse dotted with masks
and mirrors; the soundtrack deep house,
dance and funk. Overseas DJs play at gay bar
and disco **Liquid** (Central Market Annexe A,
Jalan Hang Kasturi, 2026 1430). The boys
(and girls) can also be found at French bar-
restaurant **Frangipani** (25 Cangkat Bukit
Bintang, 2144 3001).

For live acoustic music, newcomer **Laundry
Bar** in outlying Petaling Jaya (The Curve, 6
Jalan PJU 7/3, Mutiara Damansara, 7728 1715)
draws plenty of local acts and an easy-going
college crowd. Closer to the centre, **Alexis
Ampang** (Lot 10-11, Great Eastern Mall, 303
Jalan Ampang, 4260 2288, www.alexis.com.my)
offers wood-fired pizza and, on weekend nights,
some of KL's best jazz talents.

High life: **Petronas Twin Towers.** *See p210.*

Trips Out of Town

Central Market. *See p210.*

Where to eat

Fine dining has arrived in KL. **Third Floor** (JW Marriott Hotel, Jalan Bukit Bintang, 2141 3363) is the city's most revered restaurant thanks to local celebrity chef Ken Hoh. Combining French and Pacific Rim flavours, his cutting-edge, inspired cuisine is served in an immaculate dining room. Another standout is **Cilantro** (MiCasa Hotel Apartments, 368B Jalan Tun Razak, 2161 8833), a dynamic French eatery with Japanese touches, noted for its pan-fried eel and foie gras dishes.

For local Malay food on top of the city, **Seri Angkasa** (KL Tower, Jalan Puncak, off Jalan P Ramlee, 2020 5055) defies at least one cliché of revolving restaurants. Yes, it's touristy and you pay for the 360-degree views. But the international buffet – a medley of the best Malaysian heritage foods – is excellent. Sister restaurant **Seri Melayu** (1 Jalan Conlay, 2145 1833) is equally touristy, but the regional Malay buffet is good and the Malaysian dance show a cultural treat.

Another fine array of restaurants – both Asian and European – is available on the 'Feast Floor' of **Starhill Gallery** mall (*see p210*). While the Asian cuisine (including Indian, Chinese, Thai and Korean) is pricey by local standards, quality is good and the ornate decor offers photo opportunities galore. The most extravagant eaterie is **Shook!** (2719 8535), a theatrical space boasting Japanese, Chinese, Italian and Western Grill show kitchens. A jazz band lets you eat to the beat.

Busy street stalls serve the best of Malaysian cuisine for pocket money. Hawkers at **Jalan Alor** (behind Bukit Bintang) sell just about everything from 7pm to past midnight; try the Chinese stalls for stir-fries and the Muslim ones for fantastic grilled fish and squid. Frog-leg porridge may sound gruesome, but it tastes heavenly.

Where to stay

The two hotel hubs of Kuala Lumpur are both downtown. Most hotels call themselves 'boutique', but they are a motley collection. If you can dig deeper into your pockets, a five-star hotel starting at RM350 will guarantee luxury; anything between RM150-RM290 may be dowdy; RM50-RM150 gets you a basic bed and basin. Budget backpacker accommodation (under RM50), is best avoided.

Five-star hotels abound, the newest being **Westin Kuala Lumpur** (199 Jalan Bukit Bintang, 2731 8333, www.starwoodhotels.com, from RM300). It's a beauty, with lavish furnishings and sumptuous beds (plus a handy location next to the shopping strip). The 207-room **Hotel Maya** (138 Jalan Ampang, 2711 8866, www.hotelmaya.com.my, from RM325) is serene and modern. The simple yet luxurious rooms feature rattan touches and natural fibres;

floor-to-ceiling glass panels overlook the Petronas Towers. A gym, hydrotherapy pool and butler service add to the smart vibe.

In the heart of Chinatown, the towering **Swiss-Garden Hotel** (62 Jalan Sultan, 2072-3333, www.swissgarden.com, from RM150) offers value for money. It's air-conditioned, though some rooms have no windows.

For cheaper options, look at the butt-end of Bukit Bintang, where run-down shophouses double as cheap hostels. An exception is the lovely and contemporary **Number Eight Guesthouse** (8-10 Tengkat Tong Shin, 2144 2050, www.numbereight.com.my, dorm RM30, double RM85), which offers a soulful ambience in a renovated shophouse.

Resources

Hospital
Hospital Kuala Lumpur *Jalan Pahang (2615 5555/www.hkl.gov.my).*

Police station
Jalan Hang Tuah (2146 0522).

Post office
Jalan Tan Cheng Lock (2274 1122).

Tourist information
Malaysia Tourism Centre *109 Jalan Ampang (2163 3667/www.mtc.gov.my).* **Open** 7am-10pm daily.

Getting there

By air
Various companies fly from Changi Airport to Kuala Lumpur, including **Malaysian Airlines** (6336 6777, www.malaysiaairlines.com.my), but it's expensive (about $300 return). The flight takes 40mins; the airport is 30mins outside the centre.

By bus
Johor Bahru
Be prepared for bedlam. Though services to JB are frequent (every 15mins), there are crowds at peak hours in afternoon and evening. At the immigration checkpoints, passengers vacate the bus, then reboard the next one – so hang on to your ticket stub.

For a fuss-free ride, **SBS bus 170** (1 800 2255 663, www.sbstransit.com.sg) leaves from the Queen Street terminal in Singapore. The first bus for JB departs at 5.20am, the last one at 12.10am daily; single tickets cost $1.80. Or you can catch **SMRT bus 950** (1800 3368 900, www.smrt.com.sg), from Woodlands bus interchange (accessible via Woodlands MRT station). The service operates from 5.30am to 11.30pm daily; single tickets cost $1.30.
Melaka/Kuala Lumpur
Numerous bus companies operate between Singapore (most leaving from the Golden Mile Complex, the informal bus depot at Beach Road) and Malaysia. Go 'first-class' with the likes of **Aeroline** (6258 8800,

6341 9338, www.aeroline.com.sg) or **Plusliner** (6256 5755, www.plusliner.com), though you'll pay triple the usual $22 one-way fare to KL; more companies are listed on www.myexpressbus.com. The journey takes 3hrs to Melaka, 5-7hrs to KL. It's a less hectic experience than catching the bus to JB. To save money, buy the return fare in ringgits in Malaysia.

By car
Johor Bahru
Specially licensed Singaporean cabs – leaving from the parking lot of Queen Street in Bugis – take you to the Malaysian border checkpoint, but no further. You then have to hail a Malaysian cab. Illegal but usually safe 'private cars' also take you to the border.
Melaka/Kuala Lumpur
Car rental companies in Singapore charge a premium for driving into Malaysia, and usually require additional insurance too – check before you book.

The **North-South Expressway** from Singapore to Thailand is a fast, well-paved highway. Expect to take about 2.5hrs to Melaka (225km/140 miles) and 4hrs to Kuala Lumpur (370km/230 miles). Tolls are hefty – a one-way trip to KL costs RM50 – and you can't change currency at the toll booths, so bring a supply of ringgit (in small change). The speed limit is 110kmh/68mph on most stretches. Regular speed traps by the Malaysian police nab unwary motorists; if you're in a Singaporean car, you will be pressured to pay *duit kopi* ('coffee money') on the spot (RM50-RM100, depending on your bargaining skills). Look out for the following road signs: Perhentian Rehat means 'rest stop'; Pusat Bandar or Bandaraya means 'city centre'; Jalan Sehala indicates a one-way street. Malaysia drives on the left, as in Singapore.

By train
A reliable but slow way to travel between Singapore and towns including Johor Bahru and Kuala Lumpur. The service run by Malaysia's railway, **Keretapi Tanah Melayu** (KTM, 6222 5165, www.ktmb.com. my), is comfortable and efficient. Single fares to JB start at $2.90, with daily departures from Singapore's station on Keppel Road at 10.05am and 6.20pm; the journey takes an hour. Trains to KL leave at 8.20am, 1pm and 10.15pm daily; single fares from $34 daytime (8hrs), $21 overnight (10hrs). Buy your return ticket in Malaysia – it's half the Singaporean price – or enjoy unlimited rail travel with the **KTM Rail Pass** (from $53 for five days). It's not worth taking the train to Melaka, though: the rail station is about 45mins outside the city

Big spenders can take the luxurious **Eastern & Oriental Express** (E&O, 1 800 737 9955, 6392 3500, www.orient-express.com), which runs once a week between Singapore and Bangkok, stopping at Kuala Lumpur. Trains usually depart Singapore at 11am Wed, arriving in Bangkok at 2.45pm Fri; one-way fares start at $2,660.

On foot
Crossing the **Woodlands Causeway** on foot to Johor Bahru is an option if traffic is bad and your luggage is light. From the Singapore immigration building, it's a 20mins walk across the bridge to Malaysian customs, with a lane for hot-footers.

Bintan & Batam

Jump on a ferry for Indonesian island getaways.

A proper tropical beach: the main reason Singaporeans flock to Bintan.

Bintan and Batam are the two largest of the 3,200 islands that make up Indonesia's Riau archipelago. Located less than an hour's ferry ride from Singapore, they're popular weekend destinations for Singaporeans – largely because their sandy, palm-fringed beaches, although by no means the best that South-east Asia has to offer, are much bigger and better than the paltry man-made affairs on Singapore.

Bintan, in particular, is almost a colony of Singapore; at least, that's certainly true of the Bintan Resorts area (also known as Lagoi), a stretch of purpose-built holiday resorts on the north coast, the result of a special trade agreement between the Singaporean and Indonesian governments. Neighbouring Batam (ferries run between the two islands) also benefits from close ties with Singapore, and is a major industrial, manufacturing and investment hub; its resorts tend to be more downmarket than the ritzy affairs on Batam.

'Visa-on-arrival' arrangements apply for most nationals (unless you're visiting on business); current rates are US$10 for seven days, US$25 for seven to 30 days, payable on arrival before passport control (US dollars preferred). Bahasa Indonesia is the local language, which is similar to Bahasa Malaysia or Malay, but most people can speak some English, especially in the hotels and resorts. Bintan has a strong Chinese population, so you'll also hear Chinese dialects there. The Indonesian rupiah (Rp) is the main currency, although Singapore dollars are also widely accepted (and insisted upon at Bintan Resorts); there are money changers at the ferry terminals and the major banks have ATMs. At the time of writing, $1 Singapore was worth Rp5,900.

You'll find the sunniest weather between May and September; expect showers during the monsoon season from October to March. Weekends are much busier than weekdays. Outside the resorts, it's wise to drink bottled water, or to boil tap water before drinking. Phone numbers below are given as phoned from within each island. If you're phoning from Singapore, the country code for Indonesia is 62, followed by the respective island code (771 for Bintan, 770 for Bintan Resorts only, 778 for Batam), followed by the phone number. Both

islands are one hour behind Singapore.
For good package deals, try **Holiday Bagus**
(#03-09 Peninsula Plaza, 111 North Bridge
Road, 6339 9032, www.holidaybagus.com).

Bintan

Bintan is the largest island in the Riau
archipelago, almost three times the size of
Singapore. The capital of the Sultanate of Johor
in the early 18th century, it flourished as a
powerful trading port, attracting traders and
migrants. The island fell to the Dutch at the
end of that century and, as the political climate
changed, the island's economic success was
soon overshadowed by its neighbours.

Nowadays, most tourists flock to the **Bintan
Resorts** area in the north: it's clean, safe and
reeks of the Singaporean way of doing things;
you even have to pay in Singapore dollars (and
prices are high). Promoted as a family-oriented
resort area, it's the perfect weekend retreat –
if you're happy to just laze by the beach, play
golf and dabble in watersports. There's no
need to leave your chosen resort, in fact, this
northern section is separated from the rest of
Bintan by barbed wire, checkpoints and armed
guards, though organised tours are offered
to various sights in other parts of the island.

In 'real' Bintan, the standard of living is
much lower, and the capital, **Tanjung Pinang**,
in the south-west, is grubby and chaotic,
with wooden stilt houses and traditional
Indonesian markets. Tourists are advised not
to carry large quantities of cash, and to avoid
taking unfamiliar taxis. Prostitution is rife.

The beaches at **Trikora** on the east coast
also attract visitors looking for fun in the sun.
Stretching for about 30 kilometres (18 miles),
they're pretty idyllic, with white sand, palm
trees and cool, clear blue waters. Elsewhere
on the island are small fishing villages and
some low-key beaches.

The best way to get around is by taxi, but
unscrupulous touts abound, so book through
your hotel if possible. There are also bemos
(minivans that carry ten to 15 people, usually
within city limits), and the more adventurous
can try an ojek (motorcycle taxi, where you
ride pillion). The Batu Tujuh bus terminal is on
the outskirts of Tanjung Pinang; public buses
serve Kijang (one hour), Trikora (one to two
hours) and Tanjung Uban (two hours) during
daylight hours, but they're infrequent.

Where to stay

Bintan Resorts (www.bintan-resorts.com)
operates a direct ferry service from Singapore
and offers a comprehensive list of resorts and

their respective contacts, both in Singapore and
on Bintan. The pleasant beach chalets (from
$220) of **Mayang Sari** are ideal for couples
looking to chill out. Livelier **Nirwana Beach
Club** offers no-frills chalets (from $145) and
specialises in watersports, while family friendly
Nirwana Resort Hotel has rooms from $220.
The private villas at **Indra Maya** are pricier
(from $900), but come with their own pool. All
are run by Nirwana Gardens (692505, Singapore
6213 5830, www.nirwanagardens.com).

The most luxurious option is **Banyan
Tree Resorts** (693100, Singapore 6849 5800,
www.banyantree.com), with its standalone
seafront villas, spa facilities and championship
golf course; rates start at around $500 per
villa per night. Sister outfit **Angsana Resort
& Spa** (693111, Singapore 6849 5788,
www.angsana.com) is less expensive.

Cheaper alternatives can be found in
Tanjung Pinang, but they're basic at best.
The **Bintan Harmoni** (28742) and **Hotel
Gunung Bintan Jaya** (29288) have en suite
rooms with air con and a TV for under $30. On
Trikora, the **Shady Shack** (mobile 813 645 15
223, www.lobo.kinemotion.de, $20) offers rustic
(read: spartan) huts, with Indonesian breakfast,
for $20. **Yasin's Guest House** (26770) has
three types of thatched wooden chalets for
US$5-$10. The most upmarket spot on this
stretch of coast is the **Trikora Beach Resort**
(24454), with comfortable, well-equipped
bungalows (US$25-$40) and attractive gardens.

Where to eat & drink

All the resorts in the Bintan Resorts area
have their own bars, cafés and restaurants
(open to non-guests too), and this is where
you'll find the widest choice of cuisines, from
traditional Indonesian dishes to pizza. Expect
relatively high prices too.

In Tanjung Pinang, local food is available
at the **night markets**, such as those found
on Jalan Hang Tuah and Kedai Harapan Jaya.
Bintan's clubbing scene currently consists of
Silk (691691, www.silk-bintan.com), located
at Bintan Lagoon Resort; it's the island's first
fully fledged nightclub, with a live band, DJ,
cocktails and designated party nights. Nightlife
options in Tanjung Pinang are predominantly
dive bars, or pick up joints for prostitutes.

Resources

Hospital

Rumah Sakit Umum *Jalan Sudirman 795,
Tanjung Pinang (21733).*
Rumah Sakit Angkatan Laut *Jalan Ciptadi,
Tanjung Pinang (25805).*

Trips Out of Town

If you're staying in the Bintan Resorts area, contact your hotel if you need medical help.

Tourist information

Tanjung Pinang Tourist Office *Jalan H Agus Salim (25373)*. **Open** 8am-1.30pm Mon-Thur; 9-11am Fri; 9-12.30pm Sat.

Batam

Looking at Batam now, it's hard to imagine that it was once home to a mere 6,000 residents living in coastal fishing villages. Now it sees around 1.3 million visitors a year, making it Indonesia's second most visited destination after Bali. About two-thirds the size of Singapore, it has become a successful centre for business, manufacturing and investment, generating about 14 per cent of Indonesia's export income (other than oil or gas). Signs of Batam's ambitions can be seen in the modernistic administrative and shopping hub of **Batam Centre**. As on Bintan, most tourists flock to the beaches and golf resorts; the main town of **Nagoya** is seen more as a business district, though it has a colourful – some say sleazy – nightlife. The **Nagoya Entertainment District** (NED), an infamous cluster of bars, pubs, nightclubs, massage parlours and spas, has been touted as an area to 'relax your senses' – in more ways than one. The massage parlours are often thinly veiled fronts for brothels. Gambling (currently restricted in Singapore and in other parts of Indonesia) is another key attraction.

Where to stay

Beach resorts at Nongsa to the north and Waterfront City to the west offer the smartest accommodation and facilities. Try **Holiday Inn Resort Batam** (381333, www.ichotels group.com) and **Harris Resort** (381888, www.harris-batam.com) at Waterfront City; and **Turi Beach Resort** (761080, www.turi beach.com) and **Batam View Resort** (761740, www.batamview.com) at Nongsa. Double rooms cost $100-$150. Pristine golf courses are another attraction too, with resorts like South Link, Palm Springs and Indah Puri offering attractive golfing packages.

In Nagoya, hotels such as **Novotel** (425555, www.novotel.com) and **Panorama Regency** (452888, www.panoramaregency.com) offer reasonable accommodation for around $90.

Getting there

Ferries to Bintan and Batam depart daily from either **Tanah Merah Ferry Terminal** (6513 2100), located to the south of Changi Airport, or **HarbourFront Passenger Terminal** 6513 2200); times vary according to the operator and day of the week.

Bintan Resort Ferries (6542 4369, www.brf.com.sg) has 5-7 departures daily from Tanah Merah direct to Bandar Bentan Telani ferry terminal. For Batam, try **Batam Fast** (6270 0311, www.batamfast.com) and **Penguin** (6271 4866, www.penguin.com.sg – which also serves Tanjung Pinang on Bintan). For other operators, contact the **Singapore Cruise Centre** (6513 2222, www.singaporecruise.com).

Fares vary depending on the ferry company, but hover around $52 return to Bintan ($38 single) and $33 return to Batam ($27 single), including surcharges. It's a good idea to confirm your return booking on arrival, as the ferries can fill up.

Angsana Resort, Bintan. *See p215.*

Liquid or G...

Fine $500

o Durians

Directory

Features

Directory

Getting Around

Arriving & leaving

By air

Changi Airport
6542 1122/www.changiairport.com.
Award-winning Changi Airport,
located 20km (12 miles) north-east of
the city centre, is widely recognised
as one of the best airports in the
world. A key hub in the Asia-Pacific
region, it is served by more than 80
airlines flying to over 180 cities in
57 countries. Thirty-five million
passengers passed through in 2006.

There are two main terminals for
international and regional carriers:
Terminals 1 and **2** (T1 and T2),
connected by the free Skytrain
service, operating from 6am to
1.30am. A brand-new **Terminal 3**,
currently under construction, is due
to open in 2008. The **Budget
Terminal** (opened in 2006) caters
to budget airlines, though only Tiger
Airways and Cebu Pacific currently
operate there. Also opened in 2006 is
the **JetQuay CIP Terminal** (6262
2220, http://jetquay.com.sg) for
'commercially important persons',
touted as Asia's first standalone
luxury terminal.

In the Transit Hall between the
two main terminals, there are 50
food and drink outlets and more
than 100 shops, ranging from a 24hr
supermarket to designer boutiques,
souvenir shops and duty-free outlets.
Selected products can be pre-ordered
at www.changiairportshopping.com.
Other facilities include business
centres, wireless internet access, a
gym, 24hr luggage storage, a 24hr
medical centre (in T2), massage
services, indoor orchid gardens and
a rooftop swimming pool (in T1).
There are also two Ambassador
Transit Hotels, in T1 and T2, where
you can book a room in 6hr blocks,
for $40-$87. Make a reservation on
6541 9106, or visit the website
www.airport-hotel.com.sg.

If you have more than six hours
to spare before your connecting
flight, take a **free Singapore tour**.
There are six tours a day (10am,
1pm, 3pm, 4pm, 5pm and 6pm),
available on a first come, first served
basis. To book a tour, visit one
of the Singapore Tourist Board
visitor centres, located in T1 and T2.

GETTING TO AND FROM THE AIRPORT
The **MRT** is a convenient and cheap
way of getting to and from the
airport. The Changi Airport
Extension (located in T2) runs to
Tanah Merah station on the East
West Line; here you switch trains
to get to the city and the rest of
Singapore. The journey between the
airport and the city centre takes
about 27 minutes. Trains run from
around 5.30am to midnight Mon-Sat,
6am to midnight Sun and public
holidays. A single ticket costs under
$2 (plus $1 refundable deposit).

The six-seater **Airport Shuttle
Service** (6553 3880) goes to
anywhere within the CBD, and any
hotel except those at Changi and on
Sentosa. Book a seat for $7 ($5 child,
$42 if you want to book the entire
cab) at the counters in the Arrival
Hall. When returning to the airport,
there are four designated pick-up
points – Concorde Hotel, Mandarin
Hotel, Excelsior Hotel and Marina
Mandarin; book with the respective
hotel concierges. Return trips run
9am to 10.40pm. For groups of four
or fewer, **limousine taxis** are a
comfortable way to travel, and cost
$36 (from the airport) and $39 (to
the airport). Book a trip back to the
airport with City Cab (6545 8051)
or Comfort (6552 2828). For both
the Airport Shuttle Service and
limousine taxis, an additional $10
is payable for each extra stop
made between the initial pick-up
and final destination, plus an
additional flat fee of $12 for rides
between midnight and 6am.

Regular **taxis** are available for
hire outside the Arrival Hall, with
an airport surcharge of $3 ($5 5pm-
midnight Fri-Sun). An additional
surcharge of 50% of the metered
fare is payable between midnight
and 6am. Expect to pay $15-$20 to
the Orchard Road area; good value
if you're in a party of four.

Bus 36 operates a loop service
from Terminal 2 to Orchard Road
and back, from 6am to 11pm. The
one-hour trip costs under $2.

AIRLINES: INTERNATIONAL
For regional and budget airlines,
see p206.
Air France 6737 6355/
www.airfrance.com.sg

All Nippon Airlines 6323 4333/
www.ana.com.sg
British Airways 6589 7000/
www.ba.com
Cathay Pacific 6533 1333/
www.cathaypacific.com
China Airlines 6737 2144/
www.china-airlines.com
China Eastern Airlines
6323 2632/www.ce-air.com
Emirates 6735 3535/
www.emirates.com
EVA Airways 6226 1533/
www.evaair.com
Finnair 6733 3377/www.finnair.com
Garuda Indonesia 6250 2888/
www.garuda-indonesia.com
Japan Airlines 6221 0522/
www.jal.com
KLM 6737 7622/www.klm.com
Lufthansa 6245 5600/
www.lufthansa.com
Malaysia Airlines 6336 6777/
www.malaysiaairlines.com.my
Northwest Airlines 6336 3371/
www.nwa.com/sg
Qantas Airways 6589 7000/
www.qantas.com
Scandinavian Airlines 6235 2488/
www.scandinavianairlines.com
SilkAir 6225 4488/www.silkair.com
Singapore Airlines 6223 8888/
www.singaporeair.com
Swiss International Airlines
6823 2010/www.swiss.com
Thai Airways 6210 5000/
www.thaiairways.com.sg
Turkish Airlines 6732 4556/
www.thy.com.sg
United Airlines 6873 3533/
www.unitedairlines.com.sg

By bus
Many bus companies operate
between Singapore and
Malaysia; for details, *see p213.*

By car
Singapore is connected to
Malaysia via two land links,
at Woodlands in the north
and Tuas in the west. When
driving to Malaysia, you must
pay a series of tolls (*see p221*)
and also have at least three-
quarters of a tank of petrol.
This unpopular law was

passed to stop people from driving to Malaysia to fill up with petrol (it costs half as much there as in Singapore).

By rail

You can travel to Malaysia (and beyond) by train; for details, *see p213*.

By sea

A popular port of call, Singapore is also a gateway to regional and international destinations via luxury cruise ships run by **Superstar Virgo** (6223 0002, www. starcruises.com), **Silversea Cruises** (www.silversea.com) and **Cunard Line** (www. cunard.com), which operates the *QE2*. Ships dock at the **Singapore Cruise Centre** (6513 2222, www.singapore cruise.com) at HarbourFront, opposite Sentosa.

For ferry services to the nearby Indonesian islands of Bintan and Batam, *see p216*.

Public transport

Singapore's public transport network – combining the MRT underground train network, island-wide bus service and localised tram and monorail systems – is well run, modern, comprehensive and inexpensive. Westerners from major cities with more outdated, underfunded and inefficient networks will be impressed (and jealous).

SMRT (www.smrt.com.sg) runs the MRT and LRT systems, some buses and taxis, while **SBS Transit** (www.sbstransit.com.sg) runs buses – though casual passengers won't be aware of the difference. Both operate customer service hotlines: **SMRT Hotline** (1800 3368 900, open 7.30am-6.30pm Mon-Fri) and **SBS TransitLink Hotline** (1800 2255 663, 8am-6pm daily).

For detailed information on the whole transport network, get a copy of the compact but ultra-detailed *TransitLink Guide* ($2, updated annually), available at most MRT stations and bus interchanges, as well as larger bookshops.

ez-link card

If you're in Singapore for more than a few days or planning to travel mainly by MRT or bus, get an ez-link card, a stored-value smart card. It's more convenient, and cheaper, than buying a ticket for every journey. The adult version – available from ticket offices and passenger service centres at MRT stations and bus interchanges – costs $15 ($5 non-refundable deposit plus $10 credit); children's cards are also available. You can top up the card (minimum $10) at add value machines (AVMs), general ticketing machines (GTMs) and ticket offices, as well as at 7-Eleven convenience shops. When you leave Singapore, return the card to get a refund on any unused value minus the $5 deposit – though frequent visitors should hang on to their card as it's valid for five years from date of purchase. Ez-link cards can also be used at 7-Eleven, McDonald's and the Coffee Bean & Tea Leaf outlets. For more information on the ez-link card, visit **www.transitlink.com.sg**.

Buses

The bus network is efficient and comprehensive, covering most of the island. Most buses are air-conditioned. Services start around 6am and stop by 1am. Single fares are between $0.90 and $1.80; under-7s pay $0.55. The exact fare is required for cash payments. If you're using an ez-link card, you have to swipe it across the electronic reader when getting both on and off. 'Express' buses provide a faster service between the 'heartlands' and the city, with minimal stops. The bus driver will not stop unless you hold out your arm to request a ride or, inside the bus, press the bell to alight.

The free **SMRT Link** shuttle bus service is aimed at shoppers travelling to Chinatown, Dhoby Ghaut and Little India. The service runs every eight to 15 minutes from 11am to 10pm on weekends and public holidays. There are three loop services: Outram Part MRT station to Chinatown (SMRT Link 1); Dhoby Ghaut MRT station to Chinatown (SMRT Link 2); and Dhoby Ghaut MRT station to Little India (SMRT Link 3). Key pick-up points include People's Park Complex, Chinatown Point, Selegie Centre and Tekka Mall.

Two night bus services operate on Friday, Saturday and public holidays only. SMRT's **NightRider** buses (NR1 to NR8) run to and from the city, through key nightspots, every 15 to 30 minutes from 11.30pm-4.35am. SBS Transit's **NiteOwl** services (1N to 8N) run from midnight to 4am, but only from the city to certain suburban housing estates. Rides on both services cost $3.

MRT

Fast, efficient, clean, air-conditioned, cheap: no wonder Singaporeans are proud of their **MRT** (Mass Rapid Transit) system. Three lines cover much of the island: the red **North South Line**, running between Jurong East and Marina Bay; the purple **North East Line**, running between Punggol and HarbourFront, and the green **East West Line**, running between Pasir Ris and Boon Lay, with the Changi Airport Extension at Tanah Merah station ferrying passengers to and from Changi Airport. Trains run underground in the city centre and above ground everywhere else.

The service operates from 5.30am to 12.30am daily, at intervals of roughly three to eight minutes. Route maps on station platforms provide timings between stations. A single ticket costs between

Directory

$0.90 and $1.90, depending on how far you're travelling, plus a $1 refundable deposit. Hang on to the ticket; you'll need to insert it into any general ticketing machine to get your refund (available for up to 30 days from purchase).

The three existing MRT lines cover much of the island, but with certain gaps (Holland Village, for example). Some of these will be plugged by the new **Circle Line**, currently under construction. Fully underground and with 29 stations in an orbit around the city centre, it will interchange with the existing lines. Six stations – Dhoby Ghaut, Museum, Convention Centre, Millennia, Nicoll Highway and Stadium Boulevard – are scheduled to open by 2008, with full completion by 2010.

A Quick Guide to MRT Travel can be obtained from the station control rooms at all MRT stations. For a map of the MRT network, *see p256.*

LRT

LRT (Light Rail Transit) lines operate within the 'heartland' areas of Bukit Panjang, Punggol and Sengkang, providing a link between HDB housing estates and the MRT network. Most casual visitors to Singapore will probably not need to use them.

Sentosa Express

This new monorail system (opened early 2007) provides easy access between HarbourFront MRT station and Sentosa. Trains run every five to eight minutes between 7am and midnight daily; the journey takes eight minutes. The train runs from the third floor of megamall VivoCity to two stops on Sentosa – Imbiah station and Beach station – from where passengers can board the island's free buses and beach trams. The $3

Sentosa Pass allows unlimited travel for 24 hours, and includes admission to Sentosa.

For more information, visit www.sentosa.com.sg or call 1800 736 8672. For other ways to get to Sentosa, *see p84.*

Trishaws

Trishaws are a throwback to colonial times, and a characterful, if touristy, way to tour the streets of Singapore. Trishaws operate outside the Raffles Hotel and along the riverfront; be sure to agree the fare before your journey starts. For information on trishaw tours, *see p55.*

Water transport

Bumboat taxis are available for short hops ($3-$8) along the city-centre stretch of the Singapore River. For river tours and cruises around the Southern Islands, *see p55.*

Taxis

Taxis are plentiful and reasonably priced. You can flag a cab at any time of day along most roads, though on Orchard Road and in the CBD you must go to a designated taxi stand (found in front of shopping malls or major buildings). In less central areas taxis are harder to find; it is best to order one by phone for a fee. Taxis tend to disappear in the city centre at peak evening times (4-8pm, 10pm-midnight). Also watch out for taxis 'changing shift', when the driver will only want to go in one direction.

All taxis have air-conditioning and are fitted with meters; drivers who fail to use their meters are liable for a $500 fine, so fare disputes are rare. A blue or green light on the cab roof means it is free; a red light, or no light, means it's occupied or booked. Seat belts must be worn.

The flag-down fare is usually $2.40 ($2.60 for a premier taxi service). It then costs 10 cents for every 225 metres (0.14 miles) and for every 25 seconds of waiting time. But be prepared for a plethora of surcharges to be added to the fare on the meter. Phone booking fees are $2.50-$4; premier taxi companies charge advance booking surcharges of $6-$8. Staggered surcharges operate between 11.30pm and 6am (peaking at 50 per cent of the total fare between 1am and 6am). You also have to pay an extra $1 for trips originating in the CBD, and an extra $3-$5 for taxis from Changi Airport. ERP (road toll) charges are also included in the fare. Note: taxi drivers do not expect a tip.

Taxi companies
Comfort/Yellow Top 6552 2222
City Cab 6555 8888
Presido/MaxiCab 6552 2222
Prestige 6555 8888
Sovereign 6552 2828

Driving

As in the UK, vehicles drive on the left. The speed limit varies from 40kmh (25mph) in town to 80/90kmh (50/55mph) on highways. Watch out for cars switching lane without signalling, and for speed control cameras. The minimum driving age is 18 years, and visitors need a valid driving licence from their country of residence. An International Driving Permit (IDP) is recommended if your driving licence is not in English, as it can simplify hiring a car and dealing with police; drivers must apply for an IDP in their own country before arriving in Singapore. Foreign residents must convert their national licence (or IDP) into a local licence within 12 months of arrival, and also pass the Basic Theory Test (BTT). Third party insurance is compulsory.

At the time of writing, unleaded petrol cost around $1.65 per litre.

If your car breaks down, call the **Automobile Association of Singapore** (AAS, www.aas.com.sg) on 6748 9911.The **Traffic Police** (6547 0000) have info on road conditions and traffic accidents.

Other rules

Seat belts are compulsory for the driver and front-seat passenger; under-8s must be strapped into a child safety seat. It's illegal to use a mobile phone while driving. The driver's licence and car insurance certificate must be carried in the vehicle, and be presented upon request. The legal Blood Alcohol Content (BAC) limit is 0.08%.

Owning a car

Buying a car is expensive and complicated, owing to government regulations designed to limit the amount of traffic on the land-scarce island (and, some say, generate additional revenue). Anyone buying a car – already priced well above the European average – must bid for a Certificate of Entitlement (COE) in a twice-monthly online auction. The majority succeed, and can then shell out the remaining $75,000 or so required to buy an average family saloon; the rest will have their $10,000 deposit returned.

Parking

At most public car parks you pay on leaving, depending on time expired. Some car parks and streets use coupon parking (usually $1 per hour within the CBD, $0.50 outside it). You can buy coupons at various outlets including URA parking kiosks, Singapore Post offices, 7-Elevens and selected petrol stations. Display the coupon on your dashboard. Avoid parking in season parking lots (identified by red markings and reserved for tenants of offices and flats) and along roads with double yellow lines.

Tolls

The **Electronic Road Pricing Scheme (ERP)**, designed to moderate traffic flow along expressways, busy roads and in the CBD, operates between 7.30am and 10am, noon to 8pm, Monday to Friday. Rates depend on the time and road travelled, but for standard cars are $0.50 to $4.

Cars are fitted with an electronic In-Vehicle Unit (IU), which automatically deducts the appropriate fee using a stored-value cash card, available from a bank, post office or petrol station. Top-ups ($20-$500) are available at any ATM. Cashcards with a sun logo can withstand high temperatures for up to five hours (useful if you park your car in the sun), the other cards tend to melt.

For more information, contact the **Land Transport Authority** (1800 2255 582, www.lta.gov.sg). Or call the ERP hotline on 1800 553 5226.

Tolls to Malaysia

If you drive to Malaysia you have to pay a crossing toll: $3.70 per car (Tuas checkpoint, departing and arriving in Singapore) or $1.20 (Woodlands checkpoint, departure only). To do so, you must purchase toll coupons before you arrive at immigration – from designated petrol stations, post offices, 7-Eleven stores, NTUC Fairprice outlets and the Land Transport Authority. You can pay cash on the return leg. Foreign registered cars also have to pay VEP (Vehicle Entry Permit) charges.

Within Malaysia, the North-South Expressway is dotted with toll booths. Rates are 70 cents per kilometre. Tolls are paid in cash – make sure you have Malaysian ringgits to hand.

Vehicle hire

There are car rental counters at the Ground Transport Centres in the Arrival Halls of Terminals 1 and 2 at Changi Airport, as well as offices in the city. Rates start at around $100 per day, plus five per cent GST (Goods & Sales Tax). You will also need to purchase a cash card for paying ERP toll charges. Contact **Avis** (Terminal 1 6545 0800, Terminal 2 6542 8855, www.avis.com.sg), or **Hertz** (Terminal 2 6542 5300, www.hertz.com.sg).

Walking

Walking is a great way to explore the smaller districts, though the heat and humidity can be tiring (take water and plenty of breaks). The **Singapore Tourist Board** (STB, 1800 736 2000, www.visitsingapore.com) produces free walking guides to various tourist hotspots such as Little India and Chinatown (available at the airport, visitor centres, selected hotels and online). You can also discover interesting nooks and crannies in areas like Katong, Changi Village and Bugis with walking maps created by the **Urban Redevelopment Authority** (URA, 6221 6666, www.ura.gov.sg). These are available at various locations, including the **Singapore City Gallery** (*see p66*), and can be downloaded at www.ura.gov.sg/publications/walking_map.

For guided walking tours, *see p55*. For hiking, *see p195*.

Cycling

Singaporeans tend to cycle for leisure rather than as transport. Favoured cycling spots, with bike rental available, include East Coast Park and the islands of Sentosa and Pulau Ubin. The island-wide Park Connector network links up major parks, nature sites and housing estates; visit the **National Parks Board** website (www.nparks.gov.sg) for full details. Off-road cycling trails in Clementi and Bukit Timah Nature Reserve are popular among hardcore mountain bikers.

For a list of shops where you can buy or rent a bike, visit the website of the **Singapore Mountain Bike Forum** (www.smbf.com.sg).

Directory

Resources A-Z

Addresses

Addresses begin with the block or building number, followed by the street name, unit number and postal code. For example, Blk 595, Pasir Ris Street 51, #04-04, Singapore 519595, in the case of high-rise apartments, or 42 Westbourne Road, Singapore 138950, for regular properties.

Age restrictions

You have to be 18 to buy and consume alcohol and cigarettes, and to get a driver's licence. The minimum age for sex is 16 (for the law on gay sex, *see p224*).

Attitude & etiquette

Singaporeans of different races and backgrounds have been co-existing peacefully for decades, and in a cosmopolitan country like this, it shouldn't be hard to get by. Social mores include taking off your shoes before entering a Singaporean home and greeting older folk, who are generally referred to as 'uncle' and 'auntie'. Don't jump the queue at taxi ranks, especially when a car is within visible reach. In general, Singaporeans are friendly and helpful to visitors, increasingly so as the government works to boost tourist arrivals.

Business

Drawn by Singapore's advanced open economy, low levels of corruption, developed infrastructure and efficiency, around 7,000 multinational corporations make the island a thriving centre of business activity. Corporate culture in Singapore is similar to that of the West. Some social protocols to observe, however, include respecting the chain of command in organisations, especially in government-linked corporations and more traditional companies. Business cards are exchanged using both hands.

Singaporeans are non-confrontational but savvy when it comes to the bottom line. Bring common-sense professionalism to the negotiating table, but be wary of prescribing solutions, and try to cultivate a thorough understanding first.

Conventions & Conferences

The **Singapore Exhibition & Convention Bureau** (SECB, 6736 6622, www.visitsingapore.com/mice) supports business event organisers with planning advice and incentive schemes. More information, including a directory of vendors and suppliers, can be found at **www.visitsingapore.com/businessevents**.

Raffles City Convention Centre
2 Stamford Road, Colonial District (6339 7777/fax 6337 1554/ www.rafflescityhotels.com). City Hall MRT. **Map** p251 K7.

Suntec Singapore International Convention & Exhibition Centre
Suntec City, 1 Raffles Boulevard, Marina (6337 2888/www.suntec singapore.com). City Hall MRT. **Map** p251 M7.

Couriers & shippers

DHL Express
DHL Air Express Centre, 1 Tai Seng Drive, Eunos (1800 285 8888/6285 8888/www.dhl.com.sg). Eunos or Paya Lebar MRT. **Open** 24hrs daily.

Apart from this 24hr express centre, DHL has five other centres around town.

FedEx
#03-14/25 31 Kaki Bukit Road 3, Eunos (1800 743 2626/6743 2626/www.fedex.com.sg). Eunos MRT. **Open** 9am-6pm Mon-Fri; 9am-1pm Sat.

Schenker Logistics
2 Changi South Ave 1, Simei (6245 5226/www.schenker.com.sg). Expo MRT.

Office hire & business centres

Changi Airport has business and internet centres in Terminals 1 and 2, as well as PC connection points and wireless internet access services. Most of the smarter hotels have business centres with workstations, and secretarial services for business travellers. Contact **International Enterprise Singapore** (*see p223*) for immediate occupancy business facilities and secretarial support such as consultation on accounting, financial and legal issues.

For photocopies, most photo developing shops offer copying services. There are numerous copy shops in **Bras Basah Complex** (Block 231, Bain Street) and **Peace Centre** (1 Sophia Road, Orchard Road & Around). Also try **A1 Photocopy & Laminating** (#03-66 Peninsula Plaza, 111 North Bridge Road, 6336 0883), located near City Hall. **Libraries** (*see p227*) offer photocopying services, with cash card payment.

The Enterprise
#02-02 No.1 Science Centre Road, Jurong East (6826 3000/fax 6822 8838/www.smafederation.org.sg). Jurong East MRT. Specially tailored for immediate occupancy, offering innovative and fully serviced offices.

i-Hub

9 Jurong Town Hall Road, Jurong East (1800 568 7000/www.jtc.gov. sg). Jurong East MRT.
Offers ready business space that clusters high-tech start-ups and emerging enterprises under one roof.

Secretarial services

Also check with your hotel business centre.

ACS Management Consultants

#02 59 32 Wallich Street, Chinatown (6883 0881//www.acsmgt.com.sg). Tanjong Pagar MRT. Map p250 I12.
Provides accounting, tax and secretarial services, as well as consulting and advisory services to growing businesses.

Raffles Corporate Consultants

#13-02 105 Cecil Street, CBD (6538 9558/6323 3275/www.raffles corporate.com). Raffles Place MRT. Map p250 J11.
Provides accounting, tax, secretarial, management and other services.

Translators & interpreters

ACTC Translation Centre

#04-03D The Spire, 10 Bukit Batok Crescent, Bukit Batok (6479 0098/ 6426 6789/www.actc.com.sg). Bukit Batok MRT.
Offers fast and accurate translation, interpretation and transcription in more than 40 foreign languages.

Useful organisations

Association of Small & Medium Enterprises (ASME)

6513 0388/6513 0399/ www.asme.org.sg.
A business association for entrepreneurs, ASME facilitates the development of more than 2,500 registered SMEs in Singapore. It provides consultancy services to investors and foreign businesses.

Contact Singapore

www.contactsingapore.org.sg.
Offers professional consultancy services and information on career and educational opportunities in Singapore. Has offices in London, Chennai, Shanghai and Boston.

International Enterprise Singapore

7th Floor, Bugis Junction Office Tower, 230 Victoria Street, Bras Basah & Bugis (6337 6628/ www.iesingapore.com). Bugis MRT. Map p249 L5.
Assists local enterprises and promotes Singapore as a base for foreign businesses. Its IE Resource Centre houses print and electronic business resources with market information, business contacts, trade statistics, export regulations and tariff information.

Singapore International Chamber of Commerce (SICC)

#10-01 6 Raffles Quay, CBD (6224 1255) Raffles Place MRT. Map p251 K11.
The oldest commercial organisation in Singapore, dating from 1837.

Consumer

Complaints can be made to the **Consumers Association of Singapore** (CASE), which protects consumer rights. It also has a mediation centre to settle disputes between businesses and consumers. Walk-in consumer advice and mediation is available from 9am-4pm, Mon-Sat, at their main office.

CASE

#05-01 Ulu Pandan Community Building, 170 Ghim Moh Road, Buona Vista (hotline 6463 1811/ complaints@case.org.sg). Buona Vista MRT. Open 9am-6pm Mon-Fri; 9am-noon Sat.

Customs

There are no restrictions on the amount of currency you can bring into Singapore. Duty-free shoppers are allowed 1 litre of spirits, 1 litre of wine or port and 1 litre of beer, stout or ale each. If you are over 18 years of age and have been outside Singapore for more than 48 hours, you may bring in $300 worth of goods (gifts, food, clothing) without paying duty ($100 if you are below 18). For under 48 hours, the maximum is $150 ($50 for under-18s); and for less than 24 hours, it's $50 (nothing for under-18s).

To buy duty-free goods when entering Singapore, you have to have been away for at least two nights. You can't bring cigarettes into Singapore, but you can buy them on the way out. There are no duty-free concessions on cigarettes or other tobacco items. You are not allowed to bring in chewing gum, firecrackers or pirated video tapes, CDs or DVDS.

For more information, contact the **Immigration & Checkpoints Authority** (www.ica.gov.sg) and **Singapore Customs** (www.customs.gov.sg).

Travel advice

For up to-date information on travel to a specific country – including the latest news on safety and security, health issues, local laws and customs – contact your home country government's department of foreign affairs. Most have websites packed with useful advice for would-be travellers.

Australia
www.smartraveller.gov.au

Canada
www.voyage.gc.ca

New Zealand
www.safetravel.govt.nz

Republic of Ireland
http://foreignaffairs.gov.ie

UK
www.fco.gov.uk/travel

USA
http://travel.state.gov

Directory

Disabled

Public transport systems and buildings have been increasingly equipped with facilities for the disabled over the years, with campaigns raising awareness of those with special needs. Some taxi companies, such as CityCab and SMRT, have wheelchair-accessible cabs. A free accessibility guide is available at www.ncss.org.sg/docs/access.pdf.

Disabled People's Association of Singapore

6899 1220/www.dpa.org.sg. A non-profit advocacy group that campaigns to achieve equal status for disabled people, and promotes independent living.

National Council of Social Services

6210 2500/www.ncss.org.sg. Aims to enhance the quality of social services for the disadvantaged. Services cater to children, families, the elderly and the disabled.

Drugs

Don't do drugs! Importing, selling or using illegal narcotics is absolutely forbidden. The death penalty is automatic for morphine quantities exceeding 3g, heroin 15g, cocaine 30g, marijuana 500g, cannabis 15g, cannabis resin 10g, opium 1.2kg, ketamine 113g or methamphetamines 250g. For smaller quantities (heroin 2g, cocaine 3g, marijuana 15g, hashish 10g, opium 100g or methamphetamines 25g), carriers may still face the death penalty if they cannot disprove the intent to traffic.

Electricity

Singapore voltage is 220-240 volts AC, 50 cycles per second – as in the UK. Most hotels will provide transformers on request to visitors with electrical appliances of a different voltage, such as 110-120 volts, 60 cycles per second. When shopping for electrical appliances, remember to check the voltage of the item against the acceptable voltage in your home country. The power plugs used in Singapore are of the three-pin, square-shaped type. Plug adaptors are available from convenience and electrical stores.

Embassies & consulates

For a full list of foreign missions, check the **Singapore Tourist Board**'s website: www.visitsingapore.com. If you're planning to visit an embassy or consulate, it's a good idea to call first.

Australian High Commission

25 Napier Road, Orchard Road & Around (6836 4100/www.australia. org.sg). Orchard MRT then taxi. **Open** 8.30am-12.30pm, 1.30-5pm Mon-Fri. **Map** p246 A3.

British High Commission

100 Tanglin Road, Orchard Road & Around (6424 4200/www.britain. org.sg). Orchard MRT then taxi. **Open** 8.30am-1pm, 2-5pm Mon-Fri. **Map** p246 B4.

Canadian High Commission

#11-01 One George Street, Chinatown (6854 5900/ www.cic.gc.ca). Clarke Quay MRT. **Open** 8am-12.30pm, 1-4.30pm Mon-Thur; 8am-1.30pm Fri. *Visa office* 8am-12.30pm Mon-Fri. **Map** p250 J10.

Embassy of Ireland

#08-00 Liat Towers, 541 Orchard Road (6238 7616/www.ireland. org.sg). Orchard MRT. **Open** 9.30am-noon, 2.30-4.30pm Mon-Fri. **Map** p247 E3.

New Zealand High Commission

#15-06/10 Tower A, Ngee Ann City, 391 Orchard Road (6235 9966/ 6738 6700/6235 3486/ www.nzembassy.com/contact.cfm). Orchard MRT. **Open** 9.30am-1pm; 2-4pm Mon-Fri. **Map** p247 F4.

South African High Commission

#15-01/06 Odeon Towers, 331 North Bridge Road, Bras Basah & Bugis (6339 3319/www.south africahc.org.sg). Bugis or City Hall MRT. **Open** 8.30am-1pm; 2-5.30pm Mon-Thur; 8.30am-1pm, 2-5pm Fri. **Map** p249 L6.

Embassy of the United States of America

27 Napier Road, Orchard Road & Around (6476 9100/http:// singapore.usembassy.gov). Orchard MRT then taxi. **Open** 8.30am-5.15pm Mon-Fri. *Consular office* 8.30-11.30am Mon-Fri. **Map** p246 B3.

Emergencies

Below is a list of numbers for emergencies. Consult the yellow pages of the Singapore phone book for listings of medical practitioners and private ambulance services. Also *see p225* **Health**.

Emergency Ambulance 995
Non-emergency Ambulance 1777
Fire 995
Police Emergency 999
Police Hotline 1800 255 0000
Singapore General Hospital 1800 321 3591
Civil Defence 1800 286 5555
Ministry of Health Emergency 1800 333 9999
Drugs & Poison 6423 9119
Blackout 1800 7788 888

Gay & lesbian

Gay sex is outlawed under Singapore's penal code, which defines it as 'an act of gross indecency' punishable by a maximum of two years in jail. In reality, there are few prosecutions of consenting adults who are acting in private. But be warned: in the 1990s, police decoys were used to tempt men in a public place; if the unsuspecting party made physical contact, he was fined or imprisoned. And in 2005, four men were arrested and fined for engaging in sexual activity in a sauna. In contrast, prosecution of lesbians is virtually unheard of.

Despite the laws, though, gay and lesbian culture

continues to flourish in Singapore. Gay and lesbian support groups include: the volunteer counselling service **Oogachaga** (www.oogachaga. com); **SgButterfly** (www.sgbutterfly.com), Singapore's first transgender community portal; **Sayoni** (http://blog.sayoni.com), an online resource and forum; **Plume** (http://plume.sg/home), an online platform for LGBT youth; and **Safehaven** (www.oursafehaven.com), a Christian support group for LGBTs. For information on what's on offer to gay and lesbian visitors, *see pp181-184*.

For information on HIV and AIDS, *see p226*.

Health

Singapore has well-qualified professionals providing first-class medical facilities. There are no vaccination requirements to enter the country, but immunisation against diphtheria, tetanus, hepatitis A and B and typhoid is recommended if you're travelling to less developed areas in South-east Asia. Visit the Travellers' Health & Vaccination Clinic in **Tan Tock Seng Hospital** (*see below* **Hospitals**) for advice and vaccinations.

Accident & emergency

A&E services are available at all hospitals. If you're staying in the city area, **Raffles Hospital** (*see p226*) has an A&E ward, 24-hour walk-in clinic and International Patients Centre.

Complementary medicine

Singapore's healthcare services are based on Western medical science, although there are other methods derived from

various Asian traditions. If you're interested in Traditional Chinese Medicine (TCM), a widely accepted form of complementary medicine, you can consult Chinese physicians or visit medical halls all over the island. These serve the older population and an increasing pool of people interested in alternative remedies. Yoga, ayurvedic therapies and the like are increasingly trendy. **Holistic Living** (www.holisticliving. com.sg) has a directory of complementary medicine clinics. *See also p157*.

Contraception & abortion

Contraceptives and legalised abortions are available in Singapore. Birth control pills like Yasmin and Mercilon can be bought at pharmacies, but a doctor's prescription is required for both locals and foreigners, unless you are a foreigner travelling out of Singapore within 24 hours (and can provide proof of travel).

Lien Clinic for Women
#05-03 Mount Elizabeth Medical Centre, 3 Mount Elizabeth, Orchard Road & Around (6736 3331/6635 8833). Orchard MRT. Map p247 F4.

Dentists

There are more than 400 private dental clinics, as well as 13 government-run clinics across the island. The **Singapore Dental Council** (www.sdc.gov.sg) has a comprehensive listing, and the **Ministry of Health** (www.moh.gov.sg) provides a list of clinics.

National Dental Centre
*5 Second Hospital Ave, Chinatown (6324 8910/www.ndc.com.sg). Outram Park MRT. **Open** 8am-5.30pm Mon, Wed-Fri; 8am-5.15pm Tue. **Map** p250 G11.*
A major state-run referral centre for patients needing specialist dental healthcare. Patients who are non-residents of Singapore or are referred

by a private practitioner or are self-referred/walk-ins pay $67-$87 for an initial visit. Subsidised rates (from $32) are available for residents of Singapore already receiving state-subsidised medical treatment.

Doctors

Most hotels have their own doctor on 24-hour call. General practitioners are easy to find in the city and in housing estates. Consultations and medication for minor ailments should cost $25-$35 per visit, more for specialist consultations. For details about how to find a GP, contact the **Singapore Medical Association** (6223 1264, www.sma.org.sg). For a list of GPs by area, go to **www.medicalhub.com.sg**. For private walk-in clinics, **Gleneagles Hospital** offers a 24-hour facility (6470 5688), as does **Mount Elizabeth Hospital** (6731 2218). For both, *see p226*.

Helplines

Alcoholics Anonymous
6475 0890
Pregnancy Crisis Service (Family Life Society)
6339 9770
Samaritans of Singapore
(24hrs) 1800 221 4444
Singapore Anti-Narcotics Association (SANA)
1800 733 4444
Singapore Cancer Society
6221 9578
Teen Challenge 6743 7933

Hospitals

There are government and private hospitals across Singapore. Citizens are heavily subsidised, so make sure you have travel insurance.

Public hospitals
Singapore General Hospital
Outram Road, Chinatown (6222 3322/6224 9221/ www.sgh.com.sg). Outram Park MRT.

Tan Tock Seng Hospital
11 Jalan Tan Tock Seng, Novena (6256 6011/Travellers' Health & Vaccination Centre 6357 2222/ www.ttsh.com.sg). Novena MRT.

Directory

Private hospitals

Gleneagles Hospital *6A Napier Road, Orchard Road & Around (6473 7222/6475 1832/ www.gleneagles.com.sg). Orchard MRT then taxi.* **Map** *p246 A3.*

Mount Elizabeth Hospital *3 Mount Elizabeth Road, Orchard Road & Around (6737 2666/ 6737 1189/www.mountelizabeth. com.sg). Orchard MRT.* **Map** *p247 F4.*

Raffles Hospital *585 North Bridge Road, Bras Basah & Bugis (6311 1111/6311 2390/24hr 6311 1222). Bugis MRT.* **Map** *p249 M5.*

Raffles Hospital International Patients Centre *6311 1666/www.raffleshospital.com.*

Opticians

See p158.

Pharmacies

For over the counter medication, most chemists have registered pharmacists to assist. Stores such as Guardian, NTUC Healthcare and Watson's convenience store are found in shopping centres near MRT stations, and usually stay open until 9.30pm. *See also p158.*

Prescriptions

GPs will prescribe medication after a consultation, but you can also consult a licensed pharmacist. It is a good idea to bring copies of all important prescriptions and medications with you.

STDs, HIV & AIDS

Action for AIDS (21 Norris Road, Little India, 6254 0212, www.afa.org.sg) is the only NGO committed to AIDS prevention, advocacy and support in Singapore. It runs the **Department of Sexually Transmitted Infections Control (DSC) Clinic**, a public clinic for the diagnosis, treatment and control of sexually transmitted infections in Singapore.

DSC Clinic

#01-16 31 Kelantan Lane, Little India (AIDS information 6254 0212/counselling 1800 6252 1324/6294 6300). Little India MRT. **Open** *6.30-8pm Tue, Wed; 1.30-3.30pm Sat.* **Map** *p249 L3.* Anonymous testing is available. Identification or passport numbers are not required, and results are available within 20mins.

ID

Young visitors should bring along photo ID for door checks at some bars and clubs, and also for above-21 movies.

Insurance

Check if your insurance policy has international coverage. If not, take out travel insurance, especially for hospitalisation and unforeseen accidents. There is no reciprocal health agreement with the UK or the US.

Internet

Internet cafés can be found all over the city, with costs of $5-$6 per hour. While many hotels have LAN connection points and wireless access, usage charges can cost up to $25 per day. Changi Airport has a number of cybercafés and free surfing booths in transit lounges. If you have a WiFi-enabled laptop, you can surf for free when you register with the Wireless@SG broadband network, a trial service by the Infocomm Development Authority over the next two years. The service is available in the centre of town, mostly in large malls. Visit **www.ida.gov.sg** for more details.

Language

Singapore has four official languages (English, Chinese, Tamil and Malay, which is also the national language). The national anthem is sung in Malay, but the pledge is recited in English and Mandarin. When the prime minister speaks at the annual National Day Parade, he uses three of the official languages (English, Mandarin, Malay). There are also numerous unofficial languages and dialects, thanks to the multicultural make-up of the nation's inhabitants – for more information, *see pp27-30.*

English is the lingua franca and English-speaking visitors will have no problem communicating. Famously, Singapore also has its very own brand of casual English – Singlish (*see p29* **Got Singlish, lah!**), which is widely spoken, though the government discourages its use through 'Good English' campaigns.

Left luggage

Left luggage facilities are available at **Changi Airport** at the Departure Transit Mall East in Terminal 1 and at Departure Transit Mall South in Terminal 2. Call Harilela International on 6214 1683 or email baggage@airport-hotel.com.sg. Charges per 24hrs start at $3.15 for cabin bags, $4.20 for suitcases and $8.40 for odd-sized items.

Legal help

The **Law Society of Singapore** (6538 2500, www.lawsociety.org.sg) lists legal practices and provides legal aid for low-income foreigners, as does the **Ministry of Law** (6332 8840, www.mlaw.gov.sg), though they do not as a rule provide legal assistance for foreign visitors. Consult your embassy should you need legal advice. Otherwise, check the *Singapore Business Directory* for details of legal practices. For consumer-related complaints, *see p223* **Consumer**.

Directory

Libraries

The National Library Board (NLB) runs a network of public reference and community libraries. Foreigners need to produce their passport and employment, student or dependant's pass. A non-refundable registration fee of $10.50 plus annual membership fee of $10.50 will be charged. Basic members can borrow four library books for three weeks. If you have a WiFi-enabled laptop, free wireless internet access is available at the Victoria Street NLB headquarters.

National Library Building
100 Victoria Street, Bras Basah & Bugis (6332 3255/www.nlb.gov.sg). Bugis MRT. **Open** *Central Lending Library* 10am-9pm daily. **Map** p249 L6.

Library@esplanade
#03-01 Raffles Avenue, Marina (6332 3256). City Hall MRT then 10mins walk. **Open** 11am-9pm daily. **Map** p251 L8.

Library@orchard
#05-22/26 Podium Block, Tower B, Ngee Ann City, 391 Orchard Road (838 5188). Orchard MRT. **Open** 11am-9pm daily. **Map** p247 F4.

Lost property

To lodge a police report, call 1800 255 0000 or contact the nearest police post. If you lose an item at the airport, approach the information and customer service counters, or call 1800 542 9727. For misplaced items on SMRT public buses, call 1800 336 8900. For MRT trains, inform the station staff. For taxis, call the respective operators.

Media

Magazines

Major bookshops and newsstands sell a wide variety of international magazines and their local editions. Popular local magazines for women, fashion and entertainment include *8Days* (also with TV listings), *Her World*, *Female* and *CLEO*. The Singapore edition of *Time Out* magazine launched in early 2007; and there's also free listings mag *I S*. Monthly publications include local men's mag *New Man*, clubbing bible *Juice* and film mag *First*. All are very ad-heavy and 'advertorials' loom large in most print media. Screening and selective 'blacking out' of risqué images in foreign titles has relaxed in recent years. *Playboy* is still banned, as is any publication with copious nudity.

Newspapers

Singapore Press Holdings (SPH), the main print media company, is part-owned by the government, and publishes nearly all the daily newspapers in the four main languages. The *Straits Times*, the flagship English broadsheet, has the widest circulation (about 400,000 copies), and covers local, Asian and foreign news, as well as lifestyle and culture (it also has a Sunday edition, the *Sunday Times*). Other major dailies include afternoon English tabloid the *New Paper* (tame by Western standards, but not above some low-blow muck-raking); self-explanatory the *Business Times*; Chinese-language broadsheet *Lian Zaobao* and its salacious sister-paper *Shin Min Daily*, *Berita Harian* is in Malay, *Tamil Murasu* in Tamil. The only non-SPH managed title is *Today* (published by Mediacorp), a free paper handed out at MRT stations in the morning and lunchtime.

As is to be expected, domestic coverage is heavily skewed in celebration of government policies, although there is the occasional contrary guest-editorial, column or reader's letter (always by local writers – foreign critiques of Singapore are barred), but anything too one-sided or emotionally argued will receive strident rebuttal. As with broadcast media, censorship is largely institutionalised, with a wary management careful to block or tone down any stories that might annoy the PAP.

Radio

Mediacorp dominates the airwaves, with English stations **Gold 90.5FM** (classic hits, the cabbies' favourite), **Class 95FM** (current hits), **Lush 99.5FM** (ambient, pop and electronica), **Symphony 92.4FM** (classical) and **938 LIVE** (news). Mandarin stations include **Y.E.S. 93.3FM** (current hits) and **Capital 95.8FM** (classic hits and, interestingly, the news in Chinese dialects). There's also **Ria 89.7FM** (Malay pop) and **Oli 96.8FM** (Tamil).

SPH invested in a rival radio network, Unionworks, which has two stations: **Radio 91.3** (Western pop) and **Radio 100.3** (Mandarin music and news).

Playlists are strictly top 40, but in the recent past there have been controversies over 'inappropriate' remarks and gags, resulting in hefty fines and a suspensions.

Television

Mediacorp, wholly owned by the government's business arm, has a monopoly over all local terrestrial TV and tightly manages its factory of mostly Chinese 'stars'. Channels are oriented by language: **Channel 8** and **Channel U** are in Mandarin (mainly dramas, some homegrown, others imported and dubbed) and are the most watched by far; **Channel 5** is in English (reality TV, magazine shows, comedy, lots of US imports);

Directory

Suria is in Malay (drama, variety shows); **Vasantham**, in Tamil, gets the daytime slot on **Channel 12** (films, dramas, current affairs), and then becomes **Arts Central** at night (documentaries, films, lifestyle magazine shows). **Channel News Asia** is a 24-hour rolling news network.

Local TV productions are generally mediocre to dreadful: the monolingual channel structure and a ban on Singlish and Chinese dialects means 'real life' in Singapore can hardly be represented; dramas and sitcoms have to be morally edifying; and entire series are created around advertisers' products. Most households opt for cable, and both **National Geographic** and **Discovery** produce content locally. As with terrestial TV, nudity is non-existent on cable, and **HBO** cuts its movies and dramas for Singapore.

Money

Singapore currency is divided into denominations, in notes, of 1, 2, 5, 10, 20, 50, 100, 500, 1,000 and 10,000 dollars. Coins come in 5, 10, 20 and 50 cents and 1 dollar. The US and Australian dollars, yen and British pound are accepted in major shopping centres and big department stores. At the time of writing, Singapore $1 was worth £0.33 and US$0.65.

ATMs

ATMs accept cards from the Cirrus and Plus networks – if your bank/credit card is not attached to one of these, you will probably have to change money in a bank. ATMs are readily available, in shopping malls, MRT stations and along the street. Call your credit card company before departure to check on withdrawal limits, and if there are any fees for overseas withdrawal. Some local banks impose a charge.

Banks

Standard banking hours are 10am to 3pm Monday to Friday, 9.30am to 1pm Saturday, although some stay open until 3pm on Saturday, and open from 9.30am to 3pm on Sunday. Most banks handle travellers' cheques and foreign currency exchange (though not always on Saturdays). Passports are required when cashing travellers' cheques, and a nominal commission may be charged. Bank branches are found throughout the city.

American Express Bank
#03-00 Hitachi Tower, 16 Collyer Quay, CBD (6538 4833). Raffles Place MRT. **Map** p251 K10.

Citibank Singapore
#01-01 Capital Square, 23 Church Street, CBD (6225 5221). Raffles Place MRT. **Map** p250 J10.

Deutsche Bank
#15-08 DBS Building Tower, 6 Shenton Way, CBD (6423 8001). Tanjong Pagar MRT. **Map** p250 J12.

Standard Chartered Bank
6 Battery Road, CBD (6225 8888). Raffles Place MRT. **Map** p251 K10.

Bureaux de change

Besides banks and hotels, you can change money at places that display a 'Licensed Money Changer' sign – present in most shopping malls. Avoid using an unlicensed money changer. At Changi Airport's Terminal 2, an **American Express** foreign exchange office (6543 0671) is open from noon to midnight daily.

Credit cards

Major credit cards (American Express, MasterCard, Visa) are widely accepted in Singapore; Diners' Club and JCB are also common. Should any shop insist on adding a surcharge, contact the respective card company to report the shop owner. Credit card cash advances can be withdrawn from banks and ATMs – make sure you know your PIN number.

American Express
#18-01 The Concourse, 300 Beach Road, Arab Quarter (6880 1333). Bugis MRT then 10mins walk. **Open** 9am-5pm Mon-Fri; 9am-1pm Sat. **Map** p249 N5.

Lost/stolen cards

Block withdrawals from your account the minute you discover a card has been lost or stolen by calling your credit card company. Most card companies also require that you file a report at the nearest police station.

American Express 1800 6737 8188/6299 8133
Diners Card 1800 292 7055/6294 4222
JCB 1800 6734 0096
MasterCard 1800 110 0113/6533 2888
Visa 1800 448 1250/1800 345 1345

Tax

A five per cent **Goods & Services Tax (GST)** is levied on most goods and services in Singapore. Tax refunds are available if you're not a permanent resident of Singapore, and have not been employed in the country in the past six months. You must also have spent $100 or more on goods at shops displaying the Tax-Free Shopping or Premier Tax-Free logos, or at least $300 at shops displaying the Tax Refund logo. Ask for a GST refund form at time of purchase – you'll need your passport. Claims have to be made within two months.

When you leave Singapore, present the GST refund form and shop receipts at the tax refund counters at Changi Airport or Seletar Airport (sea and land departures are not valid). Don't pack the goods in your hold luggage, as you may have to present them too.

A two per cent hike in GST is set to be implemented in the second half of 2007.

Natural hazards

Singaore's sheltered geographic location means it was unaffected by the 2004 tsunami and other disasters that have recently plagued its neighbours. Malaria was wiped out by the 1980s, through government efforts. The country also won praise from the World Health Organisation for exemplary handling of the 2003 SARS epidemic. Although dengue fever persists, cases are few and far between, occurring mostly in residential areas such as Katong and Joo Chiat.

Generally, Singaporeans are a sheltered lot, and air-conditioning protects everyone from the natural hazard of equatorial heat. An unpleasant haze can occur in September/October, caused by illegal land clearing fires in Indonesia (affecting other parts of the region too). Floods may happen in the December rainy season, but mostly in the north.

Opening hours

Standard banking hours are 10am to 3pm Monday to Friday, 9am to 1pm Saturday. Bars tend to stay open until 2am on weekdays and until 3am on Friday and Saturday. Government offices function from 9am to 5pm Monday to Friday. Shops are open 10am to 9pm all week, and have later hours on some public holidays. Post offices are open 8.30am to 5pm Monday to Friday, and 8.30am to 1pm Saturday.

Police stations

The **Singapore Police Force** (www.spf.gov.sg) runs police stations across the island. Below are some central addresses.

Central Police Divisional HQ

#03-112 Police Cantonment Complex, Block A, 391 New Bridge Road, Chinatown (1800 224 0000/ 6220 0877). Outram Park MRT. **Map** p250 G12.

Orchard Neighbourhood Police Centre

51 Killiney Road, Orchard Road & Around (1800 735 9999/6733 1934). Newton MRT. **Map** p247 H5.

Tanglin Police Divisional HQ

21 Kampong Java Road, Orchard Road & Around (1800 391 0000/ 6396 4900). Newtown MRT. **Map** p248 I1.

Postal services

Singapore Post (www.singpost.com.sg) operates a network of more than 1,300 postal outlets, offering a wide range of telecommunication, postal and other services. Most outlets are open from 8.30am-5pm Mon-Fri, and until 1pm on Sat. Postal rates to the UK and USA are $1 for 20g and 35 cents for every 10g thereafter. Poste restante services are available at the Singapore Post Centre on Eunos Road.

Singapore Post Centre

10 Eunos Road 8, Singapore 408600 (6841 2000). Paya Lebar MRT. **Open** 8.30am-9pm Mon-Fri; 8.30am-4pm Sat; 10am-4pm Sun.

Religion

Adherents of Buddhism, Taoism, Islam, Hinduism, Christianity (and other faiths) can be found in Singapore's multiracial population. As religious society, Singaporeans look to the spiritual realm for matters ranging from health to prosperity, examinations and careers. Consult the yellow pages of the Singapore phone book, under 'Churches, Mosques and Temples', for places of worship. *See also pp27-30.*

Safety & security

Singapore has one of the lowest crime rates in the world. Still, be careful with your belongings, and exercise the usual precautions, especially at night and in crowds. Police posts are stationed all over the island if you need help.

Smoking

Smoking is not permitted on public transport, in museums, libraries, lifts, theatres, cinemas, air-conditioned restaurants, hair salons, supermarkets, department stores and government offices. With a hefty penalty of $1,000 for a smoking offence, it's wise to light up where it's safe. Alfresco coffeeshops and cafés have designated smoking areas, indicated by yellow boxes on the ground. Smoking is permitted in air-conditioned pubs, discos, karaoke bars and nightspots, but not in eating places.

Study

Singapore boasts three internationally respected universities. To find out about attending university here, visit the **Singapore Education Services Centre** (*see p230*). It holds talks for foreign students on the last Wednesday of every month and is also home to the **Overseas Students Association** (6831 3764, www.osa.org.sg).

For language schools, try the **Cambridge School of Languages** (#26-04 Peninsular Plaza, 111 North Bridge Road, 6336 5982). The **Goethe-Institut** (#05-01 Winsland House II, 163 Penang Road, 6735 4555) offers German classes, and you can enroll for French lessons at the **Alliance Française** (1 Sarkies Road, 6737 8422, www.alliancefrancaise.org.sg).

Singapore Education Services Centre

#01-01 1 Orchard Road (6831 3764/6337 6322/www.singapore edu.gov.sg). Orchard MRT. **Open** 9am-6.30pm Mon-Fri. **Map** p248 J6.
Provides information on every aspect of education in Singapore, from pre-school to secondary education, from polytechnics to universities. An invaluable resource centre for foreign students.

Universities

National University of Singapore

21 Lower Kent Ridge Road, Singapore 119077 (6516 6666/ www.nus.edu.sg). Clementi or Buona Vista MRT then bus 95, 96.
Founded in 1905, NUS is now one of the top universities in the world, offering a comprehensive field of academic study, including sciences, engineering, technology, law, arts and social sciences and medicine. In a 2006 survey by the *Times Higher Education Supplement*, it was ranked the 19th best university globally, and the third best in Asia. It is among the world's top ten for technology and biomedicine, and in the world's top 30 for science and arts and humanities. And, according to the same survey, it is the best university in Asia for social sciences (11th in the world).

Nanyang Technological University

50 Nanyang Avenue, Singapore 639798 (6791 1744/www.ntu. edu.sg). Boon Lay MRT then bus 179, 199.
NTU was established in 1981 as a polytechnic; it achieved university status in 1991. The initial focus was on engineering and technology, but it has recently expanded to include accountancy, business and communication studies, and humanities and social science. It is a research-based university, with 19,100 undergraduate and 8,600 graduate students, taught by 2,500 staff from more than 40 countries. The *Times Higher Education Supplement* ranked it one of the world's top 20 universities for technology.

Singapore Management University

Administration Building, 81 Victoria Street, Singapore 188065 (6828 0110/www.smu.edu.sg). Bugis MRT. **Map** p248 K6.

Established in 2000, SMU was the first publicly funded private university to focus on business and management programmes. Its educational and administrative structure is modelled on the Wharton School of the University of Pennsylvania, which had a hand in SMU's development. SMU is home to over 4,700 students and comprises five schools: Lee Kong Chian School of Business; School of Accountancy; School of Economics & Social Sciences; School of Information Systems – which has a partnership with IT-renowned Carnegie Mellon University – and a new School of Law, which will open in 2007.

Telephones

Dialling & codes

Singapore's country code is **65**. Land lines begin with a 6, while mobile numbers begin with a 9. Toll-free lines (which work only in Singapore) start with 1800. To make an **international call**, dial the access code, which varies according to the phone company used – 001 using SingTel, 002 using M1 and 008 using StarHub – followed by the relevant country code, area code and telephone number.

The country code for the UK is **44**, for New Zealand **64**, for the US and Canada **1**, for the Republic of Ireland **353** and for South Africa **27**.

For residential **directory enquiries**, call 1609; for business, call 1606. If you need **local operator services**, call 100.

Making a call

Public payphones are found in most shopping malls and MRT stations. You can make local and international calls from stored-value card phones and credit card phones. Local calls are charged at $0.10 per three minutes. Stored-value phonecards in denominations of $3, $5, $10, $20 and $50 can be purchased from post offices and phonecard agents.

For international calls, different phone companies use different access codes (*see above*). International calling cards in denominations of $10, $20 and $50 are available at Changi Airport, post offices, 7-Eleven convenience stores and other retail outlets.

Applications for your own phone line can be made by calling 169 (for residential) and 169 (for business).

For general information contact **SingTel** (6838 3388, www.singtel.com).

Mobile phones

Mobile phones are called hand phones in Singapore; any phone number marked HP is a mobile number. You can use your existing mobile phone in Singapore if your service provider has a roaming service and the roaming function is enabled; however, this is very expensive.

Alternatively, purchase a local pay-as-you-go SIM card, which will give you a local number and allow you to pay local rates; the phone number usually lasts six months from the moment you first top up the card. You can buy pay-as-you-go phone cards from one of the mobile networks at one of their outlets (scattered around Orchard Road and the CBD) or at 7-Eleven stores.

The three major networks are **Starhub** (Plaza Singapura, 68 Orchard Road, 6782 7482, www.starhub.com.sg); **M1** (Paragon, 290 Orchard Road, 6895 1111, www.m1.com.sg); and **SingTel** (#B2-12 Ngee Ann City, 391 Orchard Road, 6838 3388/1626, www.singtel-mobile.com). Most cards start at $15. A passport is required for registration, and some foreign phones will have to be 'unlocked' before they can be used – check with your local provider before departure on whether your phone is suitable for use in Singapore.

Useful phone numbers

Ambulance 995
Police 999
Fire Brigade 995
Flight information
1800 542 4422
(toll-free in Singapore only)
CitySearch
(operator-assisted yellow pages)
1900 777 7777.
International calls 104
Time of day 1711
Weather 6542 7788

Tickets

SISTIC is the main booking
agent for most event tickets –
from concerts to theatre,
sports to entertainment.
Convenient outlets are at
Raffles City Shopping Centre,
the Esplanade, Suntec City
and Wisma Atria Shopping
Centre. Expect to pay booking
fees of $1-$2 per ticket.

Gatecrash

6222 5595/www.gatecrash.com.sg.
Open *Phone bookings* 10am-8pm
Mon-Fri; noon-6pm Sat, Sun.
Credit MC, V.
Gatecrash has the cheapest booking
fees, and also sells tickets via
SingPost post offices and SAM
kiosks.

SISTIC

6348 5555/www.sistic.com.sg.
Open *Phone bookings* 10am-10pm
Mon-Sat; noon-8pm Sun. **Credit**
AmEx, DC, JCB, MC, V.
Sistic also has 25 authorised agents
around the island; check the website
for details.

TicketCharge

6296 2929/www.ticketcharge.com.sg.
Open *Phone bookings* 9am-9pm
Mon-Sat; noon-6pm Sun. **Credit**
AmEx, DC, MC, V.
Plus seven agents.

Time

Singapore operates on
Singapore Standard Time
(GMT plus 8 hours). There
is no daylight savings time.
This means it is usually eight
hours ahead of London, 13
hours ahead of New York and
16 hours ahead of Los Angeles.
It is usually two hours behind
Sydney and one hour behind
Tokyo.

Tipping

Singaporeans don't generally
tip, as hotels and restaurants
levy a 10 per cent service
charge on bills. Note that
tipping is actually prohibited
at Changi Airport.

Toilets

In sanitary Singapore, a clean
and functioning toilet is
always within visible reach.
Singapore has 29,500 public
toilets; New York City, which
is slightly larger in land area,
has fewer than 2,000 public
facilities. Public toilets can be
found in MRT stations, bus
terminals, shopping malls and
commercial buildings. Most
bars and restaurants allow
the public to use their facilities.

The **Restroom
Assocation** (www.toilet.org.
sg) is an advocacy group that
campaigns for clean and
comfortable public toilets and
monitors the island's loos.

Tourist information

The website of the efficient,
well-funded **Singapore
Tourist Board** (STB,
www.visitsingapore.com)
contains massive amounts of
information. It also runs the
24-hour **STB Touristline**
on 1800 736 2000 (toll-free in
Singapore only).

Singapore Visitors Centres@Changi

*Arrival Halls and Transit Halls,
Terminal 1 & 2, Changi Airport.*
Open 6am-2am daily.

Singapore Visitors Centre@Cruise Centre

*Arrival Hall, Singapore Cruise
Centre, HarbourFront.
HarbourFront MRT.* **Open** 9am-
9pm daily. **Map** p252 B1.

Singapore Visitors Centre@Liang Court

*Level 1, Liang Court Shopping
Centre, 177 River Valley Road,
Clarke Quay (6336 2888). Clarke*

Quay MRT. **Open** 10.30am-9.30pm
daily. **Map** p250 I8.

Singapore Visitors Centre@Little India

*Inn Crowd Hostel, 73 Dunlop Street,
Little India (6296 9169). Little India
MRT.* **Open** 10am-10pm daily.
Map p248 K3.

Singapore Visitors Centre@Orchard

*Orchard Road, at Cairnhill Road.
Somerset MRT.* **Open** 8am-10pm
daily. **Map** p247 G4.

Singapore Visitors Centre@Suntec

*The Galleria @ Suntec City Mall,
Marina (6333 3825). City Hall MRT
then 10mins walk.* **Open** 10am-6pm
daily. **Map** p251 M7.

Visas & Immigration

Nationals of most Western
countries do not require a visa
for admission to Singapore,
and if visiting as tourists will
be given 'social visit' passes
valid for up to 30 days upon
arrival (if you come by air; by
sea it is 14 days). Tourists
should make sure they have
passports (with at least six
months' validity), onward/
return tickets, documents
(visas and entry permits) to
their next destination and
sufficient funds for their stay.

A full list of countries
whose nationals do require
a visa to enter Singapore
(including India, Pakistan
and Middle Eastern countries)
can be found at http://app.ica.
gov.sg/travellers/entry/visa_
requirements.asp.

If you need to extend
your stay, apply at the
**Immigration &
Checkpoints Authority**
(see p233). Processing takes
at least one working day.
Women in an advanced state of
pregnancy should make prior
applications at their embassy.
As regulations change from
time to time, visitors are
advised to check the latest
information before departure.

Note that the final decision on whether any person is allowed to enter Singapore rests with the customs officer at the checkpoint.

Immigration & Checkpoints Authority
ICA Building, 10 Kallang Road, Lavender (6391 6100/6298 0843/ www.ica.gov.sg). Lavender MRT.

Weights & measures

Singapore uses the metric system. Distance is measured in kilometres and weight in kilogrammes.

When to go

Rather than having four seasons, the weather in Singapore is summer, summer, and more summer all year round. The heat gets intense mid-year (June, July, August), though with a maximum averaging 31°C to 34°C, it hardly reaches the extremes of Thailand or India. Humidity is high all year round, pushing 90 per cent in the morning – and can be draining, especially for newcomers. Christmas brings its fair share of rain and clouds, though technically, the monsoon season is divided into two. The North-east monsoon (December to early March) is cloudy with afternoon showers, while the South-west monsoon (June to September) is hot and wet.

For weather forecasts, call the **Weather Hotline** on 6542 7788.

For details of Singapore's numerous annual festivals and events, *see pp162-165*.

Public holidays
New Year's Day (1 January); **Lunar New Year** (January or February); **Good Friday**; **Labour Day** (1 May); **Vesak Day** (May); **National Day** (9 August); **Hari Raya Puasa** (October); **Deepavali** (October, November); **Hari Raya Haji** (December, January); **Christmas Day** (25 December).

Women

With one of the lowest crime rates in the world, Singapore is a safe place for women to walk around at night. For information about women's health issues, including contraception, pregnancy and abortion, *see p225*.

Working in Singapore

Singapore woos foreign talent: the expat crowd numbers 750,000. Depending on the type of occupation, your employer has to pay the **Ministry of Manpower** (MOM, *see below*) a levy that varies from $200 to $400. The government tries to encourage **Permanent Residency** (PR) for long-term expats by hiking up medical prices for expats with an Employment Pass. PRs get a five-year renewable pass that doesn't depend on a sponsor/ employer (so you can work for whomever you choose).

Work permits

Professionals and executives earning more than $2,500 a month can apply for an Employment Pass from the Ministry of Manpower, under three categories: P1, P2 and Q Pass. P1 Pass is for applicants earning a monthly salary of more than $7,000, P2 for between $3,500 and $7,000 and the Q Pass for more than $2,500. P and Q Pass holders can apply for the Dependant's Pass for spouses and unmarried children aged under 21, while only P Pass holders can apply for the Long-Term Social Visit Pass for spouses, parents and unmarried daughters aged above 21.

Foreign entrepreneurs can apply for the EntrePass, an employment pass geared specifically towards them. The S Pass is for foreigners who earn a basic monthly salary of at least $1,800. You will need a local sponsor in the form of a Singapore-registered corporation (usually your employer) when applying for the Employment Pass. Application forms are available at the MOM website.

ExpatSingapore
Jurong West Post Office, PO Box 1033 (6226 6062/ www.expatsingapore.com). Information on expat life.

Ministry of Manpower
18 Havelock Road, Chinatown (6438 5122/6534 4840/ www.mom.gov.sg). Clarke Quay MRT. **Map** p250 H9.

Average climate

Month	Temperature (°C/°F)	Rainfall (mm/in)
January	23-30/73-85	238/9.4
February	23-31/73.6-87	165/6.5
March	23-31/73.9-88	174/6.8
April	24-31/75-89	166/6.6
May	24-31/75-88	171/6.7
June	24-31/75-88	163/6.4
July	24-31/75-88	150/5.9
August	24-31/75-88	171/6.7
September	23-31/74-88	163/6.4
October	23-31/74-88	191/7.5
November	23-30/74-87	250/9.8
December	23-29/73-85	269/10.6

Directory

Further Reference

Non-fiction

**Bayly, Christopher
and Harper, Tim**
*Forgotten Armies: Britain's Asian
Empire and the War with Japan*
Of the many books detailing
Singapore's World War II experience,
this takes the widest view, slotting
Singapore into a complex and
compelling jigsaw puzzle.

Bastin, John Sturgus
Travellers' Singapore: An Anthology
Tales from the times when there were
more travellers than Singaporeans.

Brazil, David
Insider's Singapore
Recently updated, well-researched,
punchily written guide to the
backstories and anomalies of
Singapore's urban fabric.

Chua Beng Huat
*Life is Not Complete
Without Shopping*
Named after a quote by then PM
Goh Chok Tong, Singapore's premier
sociologist analyses what locals
are really up to as they browse, buy
and snog on the escalator.

Chan, Margaret
*Ritual is Theatre, Theatre
is Ritual: Tang-ki – Chinese
Spirit Medium Worship*
In-depth but accessible guide to
one of the most arcane and extreme
religious practices that thrive
alongside modern life in Singapore.
Coxford Singlish Dictionary
Put together by the people behind
the popular satirical Talking Cock
website (*see p234*), this guide
celebrates the local pidgin in all
its barbarous, florid and, to the
uninitiated, utterly bizarre variety.

Davison, Julian
*Black and White: The Singapore
House 1898-1941*
Handsome coffeetable book about
this distinctive and stylish colonial
solution to tropical life.

Dobbs, Stephen
*The Singapore River: A
Social History, 1819-2002*
For large parts of its history, the
story of the Singapore River has
been the story of Singapore.

George, Cherian
*The Air-Conditioned Nation:
Essays on the Politics of Comfort
and Control, 1990-2000*
Insightful and informative: required
reading if you want to understand
what makes Singapore tick.

Humphreys, Neil
*Notes From an Even Smaller Island;
Scribbles from the Same Island;
Final Notes from a Great Island*
Affectionate observations from a
Brit journalist who spent ten years

reflecting on details too mundane
for most Singaporeans to notice. He's
no Theroux, though, and the humour
misses as often as hits.

Lam, Dana
*Days of Being Wild: GE2006 –
Walking the Line with the Opposition*
For a fortnight every four years, the
country's staid political scene erupts
into carnival as Singaporeans flock
to opposition rallies and indulge in
a collective fantasy of democratic
participation. This nattily designed
eye-witness account of the 2006
general election chronicles the most
recent such period.

Lau, Albert
*A Moment of Anguish:
Singapore in Malaysia and
the Politics of Disengagement*
Definitive account of the birth
pangs of independent Singapore.

Lee Kuan Yew
*Singapore Story: Memoirs of
Lee Kuan Yew; From Third
World to First: The Singapore
Story 1965-2000*
No man is an island? Think again.
The titles say it all.

Lim, Gerrie
*Invisible Trade: High Class
Sex for Sale in Singapore*
This bestselling exposé is a reminder
that Singapore's once notorious
sex trade never went away: it just
upped its rates.

Lingle, Christopher
*Singapore's Authoritarian Capitalism,
Asian Values, Free Market Illusions
and Political Dependency*
An academic who fell foul of the PAP
in the early 1990s when he raised
questions about the independence
of the judiciary in the press, Lingle's
book remains unavailable in
Singapore. Go figure.

Liu, Gretchen
*Singapore: A Pictorial
History 1819-2000*
Does exactly what it says on the tin.

Makansutra
The bible of hawker food gourmets,
published annually. Works best
when you already know what
you're looking for.

Millet, Raphael
Singapore Cinema
The most thoroughly researched
and clearly presented account of
Singapore's little-understood film
'industry' to date. Fabulous collection
of stills and publicity photos.

Powell, Robert
*Singapore: Architecture
of a Global City*
Local architecture up to 2000.
Look out for other books by Powell,
who writes authoritatively and
perceptively on many aspects of
Singapore's built environment.

Renner, Karen J
Fun 4 Kids in Singapore
A godsend when the appeal of malls
wears thin.

Singapore's Best Restaurants
Published by Singapore *Tatler*,
covers the opposite end of the price
spectrum from *Makansutra*.

**Koh, Tommy; Auger,
Timothy; Yap, Jimmy;
and Ng Wei-Chian (eds)**
Singapore: The Encyclopedia
A local bestseller (published 2006),
this hefty tome is an indispensable
guide to the nooks and crannies of
the place, its cultures and history.

Singapore's 100 Historic Places
Published by the National Heritage
Board. A useful complement to the
book you are currently reading.

Slater, Ben
*Kinda Hot: The Making of
Saint Jack in Singapore*
The book of the film (directed by
Peter Bogdanovich) of the book (by
Paul Theroux), *Kinda Hot* focuses
engagingly on events and characters,
while slyly allowing 1970s Singapore
to emerge in all its local colour.

Seow, Francis
*To Catch a Tartar: A Dissident
in Lee Kuan Yew's Prison*
Former solicitor general turned
detainee and now exile, in this (and
books on the Singapore media and
judiciary), Seow paints a less-than-
flattering picture of the Singapore
system. Unavailable in Singapore.

Carl Trocki
*Singapore: Wealth, Power
and the Culture of Control*
A more conventional academic
history than the title may suggest,
but slyly revisionist in its own way,
suggesting there may be greater
continuity between colonial and
independent Singapore than
normally acknowledged.

Warren, James
*Rickshaw Coolie: A People's History
of Singapore 1880-1940; Ah Ku
and Karayuki-San: Prostitution
in Singapore 1880-1940*
While most history books focus on
war, trade or Great Men, Warren's
detailed narratives tell a wholly
different – and decidedly more
down-to-earth – side of Singapore.

Fiction

Alfian Sa'at
*One Fierce Hour; A History
of Amnesia; Corridor*
Wunderkind poet, playwright and
short story writer. The poems, in
particular, combine biting criticism
of the establishment with disarming
insights into human nature.

Boey Kim Cheng
*After the Fire: New
and Collected Poems*
A Singaporean now living in
Australia, Boey's poems deal with
questions of memory, place and
identity. This includes selections
from his previous three books.
Clavell, James
King Rat
After surviving the Japanese-run
Changi prison in World War II,
Clavell crafted this tough-as-nails
pulp yarn (his debut novel) of
vicious inmate rivalry amid near-
starvation, ritualised punishment
and tropical malady.
Conrad, Joseph
The End of the Tether
Conrad visited Singapore eight times
between 1883-88. While several of
his works were set in South-east Asia
– most notably *Lord Jim* (1900) –
this short story (1902), about a man
doggedly piloting a ship despite
his blindness, makes most explicit
reference to Singapore.
Coward, Noel
Pretty Polly Barlow
Quintessential short tale of
interracial longing and stiff upper
lipness as the sun sets on the British
Empire. Observations from the
lawn at Raffles Hotel by one of its
most famous guests.
Jeyaretnam, Philip
*Tigers in Paradise: Collected
Works of Philip Jeyaretnam*
The prodigiously talented lawyer son
of the legendary opposition politician
JB Jeyaretnam uses his downtime
to create short stories, novels and
essays that reflect on aspirational
living, and dreams gone sour.
Kon, Stella
Emily of Emerald Hill
Much-loved, often revived and
quietly feminist play recounting the
archetypal rags-to-riches-to-relic
story of a Peranakan matriarch.
Kuo Pao Kun
*Images at the Margins; Two Plays by
Kuo Pao Kun: Descendants of the
Eunuch Admiral & The Spirits Play.*
The enduring popularity of these
scripts by the doyen of Singapore
theatre hints at the depths of thought
and feeling that lie beneath their
disconcertingly simple form.
Kwa, Lydia
This Place Called Absence
Parallel lesbian love affairs in
colonial Singapore and contemporary
Vancouver provide the hook for this
exploration of displacement and
memory from this Canadian author.
Lim, Catherine
*The Bondmaid; Following
the Wrong God Home*
Known for occasional run-ins with
the political establishment over her
op-ed pieces, Lim's novels are more
soft-focused affairs, which place
the domestic labours and desires of

Chinese women centre-stage in
historical contexts where they
have often been forgotten.
Loh, Vyvyane
Breaking the Tongue
Harrowing first novel from US-based
Loh. Set during the Japanese
occupation, it uses the torture of its
central character to explore what
happens to national and ethnic
identities and relationships under
extreme pressure.
Tan Hwee Hwee
Foreign Bodies; Mammon Inc
The closest thing Singapore
literature has to an international
bright young thing, Tan's tales of
international bright young things
have been described by one local
critic as 'fascinatingly shallow'.
Theroux, Paul
Saint Jack
Theroux taught in Singapore in the
early 1970s – and hated it. Maybe
that's why *Saint Jack* paints such a
seductive, seedy and cynical picture
of the city state on the brink of the
big clean-up.
Wong, Cyril
Like a Seed with its Singular Purpose
Lyrical angst from the up-and-
coming gay poet, who also founded
and co-edits the online poetry journal
Softblow (www.softblow.com).
Yap, Arthur
*The Space of City Trees:
Selected Poems*
One of Singapore's most respected
poets (who died in 2006), and one of
few local writers who managed to
combine a nuanced and sophisticated
exploration of English with an ear for
the patterns and idioms of Singlish.

Music

Electrico
Hip City
Unambitious but catchy and popular
indie-guitar pop.
Force Vomit
www.myspace.com/forcevomit
Hardy perennials on the local surf
rock scene.
Mark Chan
www.markchan.com
Multi-instrumentalist with an
Asian-flavoured new age aura, who
composes for the stage and releases
his own albums.
The Observatory
www.theobservatory.com.sg
Expansive, atmospheric guitar-based
group with a large local following
and two critically acclaimed albums,
Time of Rebirth and *Blank Walls*.
The Quests
The most famous 1960s Singaporean
band, the Quests' have endured,
largely thanks to a memoir, *Call it
Shanty*, by former drummer Henry
Chua, and two compilation CDs,
Recollecting the Quests Vols 1 and 2.

Ronin
www.roninriot.com
Derivative heavy rock. Very popular,
especially album *Do or Die*.
**sporesac (Singapore
Sonic Arts Collective)**
A loose collective of sound and noise
artists. Notable laptop abusers
include minimalist Ang Song Ming
(www.circadiansongs.com), static
junkie Yuen Chee Wai (www.my
space.com/yuencheewai), and
transcendentalist George Chua
(www.georgechua.com).
Stephanie Sun
Mandarin pop star who spends most
of her time in Taiwan. Crooned her
way through the National Day
anthems in 2002 and 2003, and
continues to release albums of
varying degrees of sucrosity.
The Suns
www.thesunsrock.com
Previously – and notoriously –
known as the Boredphucks (whose
'Banned in Da Singapura' remains
seminal singalong fare for antsy
kids), ska-punk-funksters the Suns
have relocated to Melbourne.
X'Ho
www.xhosux.com
Self-styled enfant terrible of the
Singapore airwaves, DJ, journalist
and sometime rock star Chris Ho
continues to tread a lonely, if
flamboyant, path.

Websites

www.expatsingapore.com
Need to know if you're hanging
around.
www.gov.sg
Guess who.
www.ica.gov.sg
Immigration & Checkpoints
Authority website, with a 'visitor
services' page for visa queries etc.
www.inkpot.com/theatre
Best local site for theatre listings.
www.nac.gov.sg
Information on the local arts scene,
from the National Arts Council.
www.sammyboy.com
Local smut and political cynicism.
www.sg
Officially Singapore.
www.singaporewindow.org
Archives local and international
press coverage of social and political
issues.
www.streetdirectory.com
Find yourself.
www.talkingcock.com
Satirical website 'exercising free
speech in Singapore since 2000' –
including the right to speak Singlish
('talk cock' means 'speak nonsense').
www.visitsingapore.com
The Singapore Tourist Board's
comprehensive website.
www.yawningbread.org
Liberal political commentary.

Directory

Index

Note: page numbers in **bold**
indicate section(s) giving key
information on a topic; *italics*
indicate photographs.

Index

Advertisers' Index

Please refer to relevant sections for addresses and/or telephone numbers

Area name	CHINATOWN
Place of interest and/or entertainment	
Park	
Pedestrian road	
MRT station	
Buddhist temple	
Hindu temple	
Mosque	
Church	

Maps

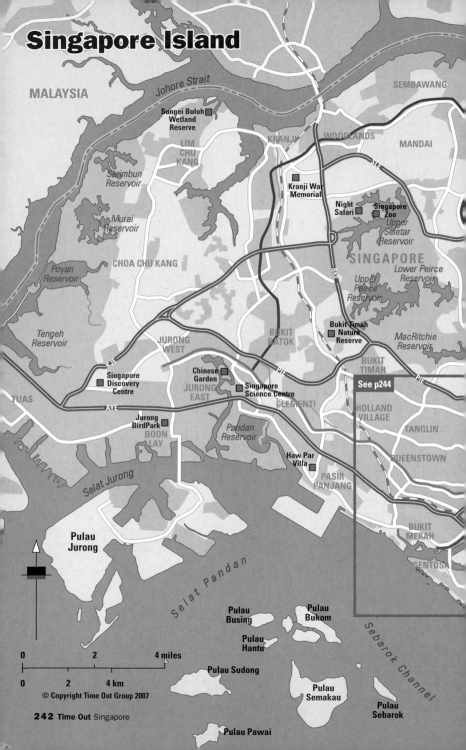

Singapore Island

MALAYSIA

Johore Strait

SEMBAWANG

WOODLANDS

KRANJI

MANDAI

Sungei Buloh
Wetland
Reserve

LIM
CHU
KANG

Sarimbun
Reservoir

Kranji War
Memorial

Murai
Reservoir

Night
Safari

Singapore
Zoo

Upper
Seletar
Reservoir

Poyan
Reservoir

CHOA CHU KANG

SINGAPORE

Lower Peirce
Reservoir

Upper
Peirce
Reservoir

MacRitchie
Reservoir

Tengeh
Reservoir

JURONG
WEST

BUKIT
BATOK

Bukit Timah
Nature
Reserve

BUKIT
TIMAH

Singapore
Discovery
Centre

Chinese
Garden

JURONG
EAST

Singapore
Science Centre

CLEMENTI

See p244

HOLLAND
VILLAGE

TANGLIN

TUAS

AYE

Jurong
BirdPark

BOON
LAY

Pandan
Reservoir

Haw Par
Villa

PASIR
PANJANG

QUEENSTOWN

BUKIT
MERAH

Selat Jurong

Pulau
Jurong

SENTOSA

Selat Pandan

Pulau
Busing

Pulau
Bukom

Sebarok Channel

Pulau
Hantu

Pulau Sudong

Pulau
Semakau

Pulau
Sebarok

0   2   4 miles

0   2   4 km

© Copyright Time Out Group 2007

Pulau Pawai

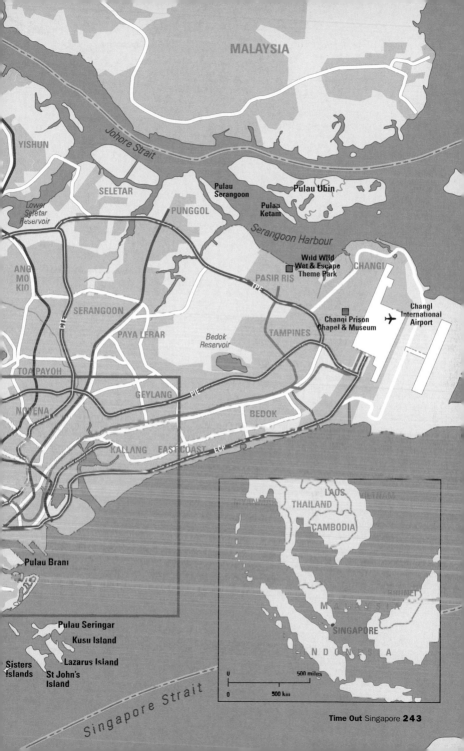

MALAYSIA

YISHUN

SELETAR

Johore Strait

Lower
Seletar
Reservoir

PUNGGOL

Pulau
Serangoon

Pulau Ubin

Pulau
Ketam

ANG
MO
KIO

SERANGOON

PAYA LEBAR

Serangoon Harbour

PASIR RIS

Wild Wild
Wet & Escape
Theme Park

CHANGI

Bedok
Reservoir

TAMPINES

Changi Prison
Chapel & Museum

Changi
International
Airport

TOA PAYOH

GEYLANG

PIE

NOVENA

BEDOK

KALLANG

EAST COAST

ECP

Pulau Brani

Pulau Seringar

Kusu Island

Lazarus Island

Sisters
Islands

St John's
Island

Singapore Strait

MYANMAR

LAOS

VIETNAM

THAILAND

CAMBODIA

MALAYSIA

BRUNEI

SINGAPORE

INDONESIA

0   500 miles

0   500 km

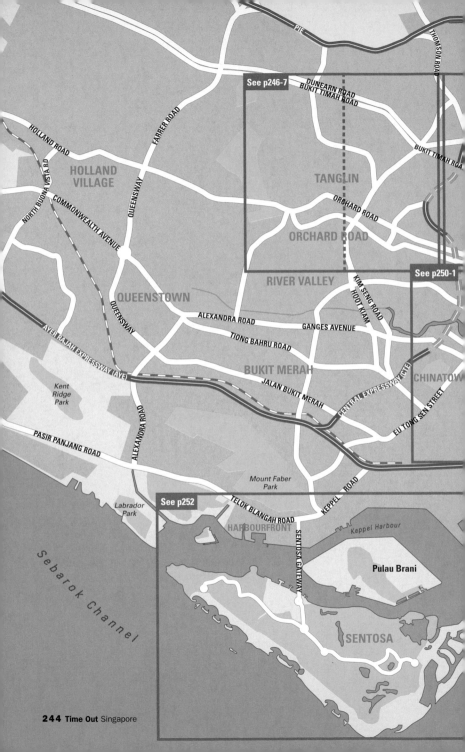

See p246-7

DUNEARN ROAD
BUKIT TIMAH ROAD

See p250-1

See p252

PIE

THOMSON ROAD

HOLLAND ROAD

HOLLAND VILLAGE

FARRER ROAD

TANGLIN

BUKIT TIMAH ROA

ORCHARD ROAD

NORTH BUONA VISTA RD

COMMONWEALTH AVENUE

QUEENSWAY

ORCHARD ROAD

RIVER VALLEY

KIM SENG ROAD

QUEENSTOWN

QUEENSWAY

ALEXANDRA ROAD

GANGES AVENUE

HOOT KIAM

TIONG BAHRU ROAD

AYER RAJAH EXPRESSWAY (AYE)

BUKIT MERAH

JALAN BUKIT MERAH

CENTRAL EXPRESSWAY (CTE)

CHINATOW

Kent Ridge Park

EU TONG SEN STREET

ALEXANDRA ROAD

PASIR PANJANG ROAD

Labrador Park

Mount Faber Park

KEPPEL ROAD

TELOK BLANGAH ROAD

HARBOURFRONT

SENTOSA GATEWAY

Kappel Harbour

Pulau Brani

S e b a r o k   C h a n n e l

SENTOSA

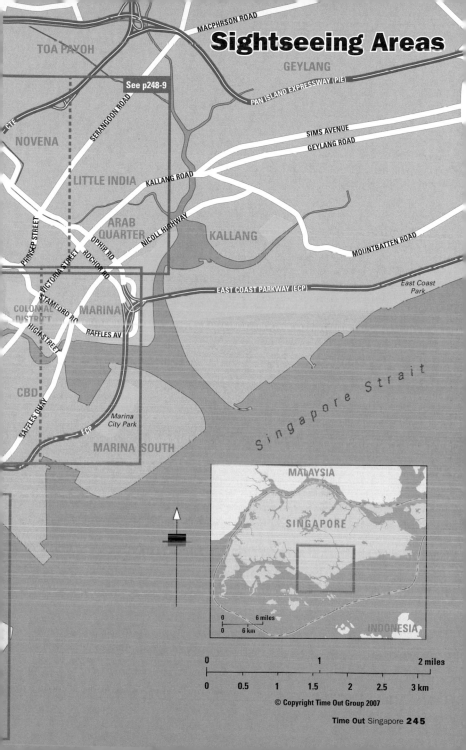

Sightseeing Areas

MACPHERSON ROAD

TOA PAYOH

GEYLANG

CTE

See p248-9

PAN ISLAND EXPRESSWAY (PIE)

NOVENA

SERANGOON ROAD

SIMS AVENUE

GEYLANG ROAD

LITTLE INDIA

KALLANG ROAD

ARAB
QUARTER

NICOLL HIGHWAY

KALLANG

PRINSEP STREET

OPHIR RD

ROCHOR RD

MOUNTBATTEN ROAD

VICTORIA STREET

STAMFORD RD

COLONIAL
DISTRICT

MARINA

East Coast
Park

HIGH STREET

RAFFLES AV

EAST COAST PARKWAY (ECP)

CBD

Singapore Strait

RAFFLES QUAY

ECP

Marina
City Park

MARINA SOUTH

MALAYSIA

SINGAPORE

0   6 miles

0   6 km

INDONESIA

0		1		2 miles
0	0.5	1	1.5	2	2.5	3 km

© Copyright Time Out Group 2007

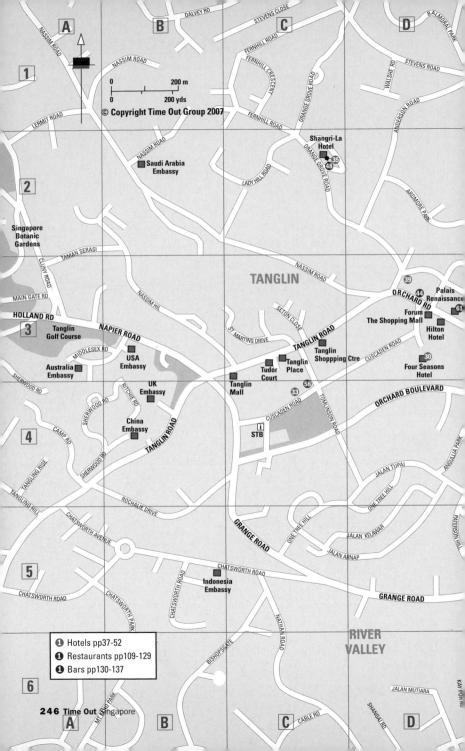

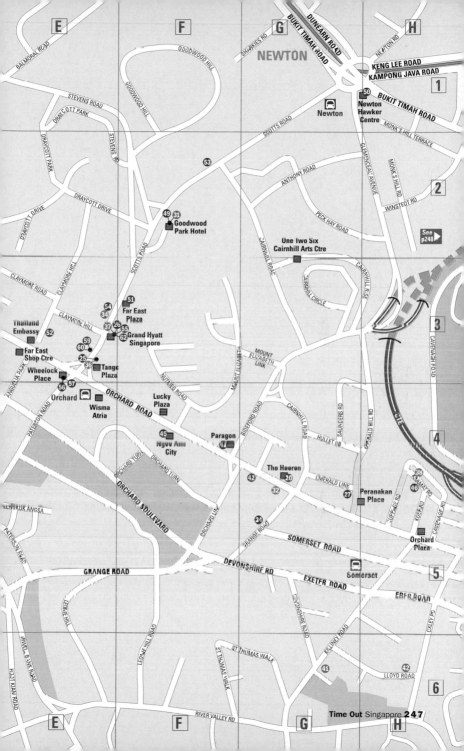

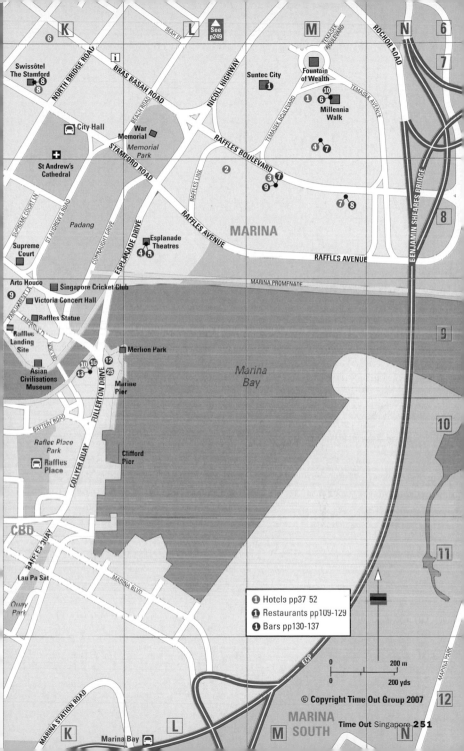

K L M N 6

7

SEAH ST

See p249

Swissôtel
The Stamford 8
8

NORTH BRIDGE ROAD

BRAS BASAH ROAD

i

BEACH ROAD

NICOLL HIGHWAY

TEMASEK BOULEVARD

Suntec City 1

Fountain
of Wealth

1
6 10
Millennia
Walk

TEMASEK AVENUE

City Hall

War
Memorial

Memorial
Park

STAMFORD ROAD

RAFFLES BOULEVARD

4 7

RAFFLES LINK

St Andrew's
Cathedral

SUPREME COURT LN

ST ANDREW'S ROAD

CONNAUGHT DRIVE

Padang

ESPLANADE DRIVE

2

3 7
9

RAFFLES AVENUE

7 8

MARINA

8

Supreme
Court

Esplanade
Theatres
4 5

BENJAMIN SHEARES BRIDGE

Arts House
9

PARLIAMENT LA

EMPRESS PLACE

Singapore Cricket Club

Victoria Concert Hall

Raffles Statue

RAFFLES AVENUE

MARINA PROMENADE

9

Raffles
Landing
Site

Merlion Park

Marina
Bay

Asian
Civilisations
Museum

FULLERTON DRIVE

10 16 12

13 25

Marine
Pier

10

BATTERY ROAD

COLLYER QUAY

Raffles Place
Park

Raffles
Place

Clifford
Pier

CBD

RAFFLES QUAY

Lau Pa Sat

MARINA BLVD

11

Quay
Park

1 Hotels pp37-52
1 Restaurants pp109-129
1 Bars pp130-137

ECP

MARINA PARK

0   200 m
0   200 yds

MARINA STATION ROAD

© Copyright Time Out Group 2007

12

K L M MARINA N
SOUTH

Marina Bay

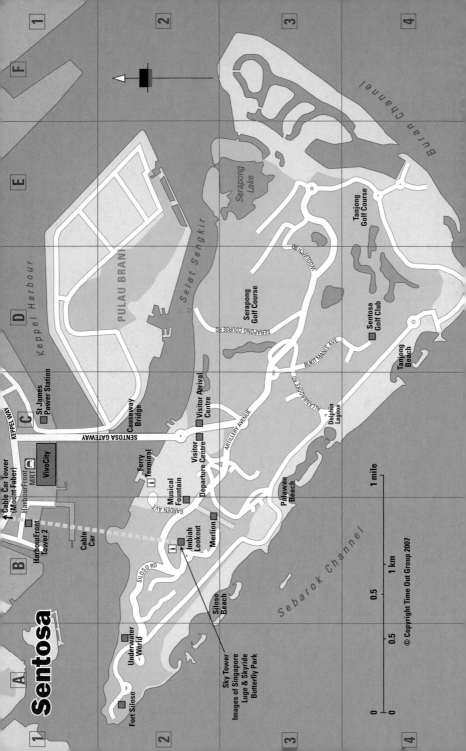

Sentosa

A **B** **C** **D** **E** **F**

1 **2** **3** **4**

Keppel Harbour

PULAU BRANI

Selat Sengkir

Serapong Lake

Buran Channel

Tanjong
Golf Course

Serapong
Golf Course

SERAPONG COURSE RD

WOOMICH RD

Sentosa
Golf Club

Tanjong
Beach

St James
Power Station

Cable Car Tower
(Mount Faber)

KEPPEL WAY

HarbourFront
Tower 2

HarbourFront
MRT

VivoCity

Cable Car

Causeway
Bridge

SENTOSA GATEWAY

Ferry
Terminal

Visitor Arrival
Centre

Visitor
Departure Centre

ARTILLERY AVENUE

BUKIT MANIS AVE

ALLANBROOKE RD

Dolphin
Lagoon

GARDEN AVE

Musical
Fountain

Imbiah
Lookout

Merlion

SILOSO RD

Siloso
Beach

Palawan
Beach

Underwater
World

Fort Siloso

Sky Tower
Images of Singapore
Luge & Skyride
Butterfly Park

Sebarok Channel

0   0.5   1 km

0   0.5   1 mile

© Copyright Time Out Group 2007

© Copyright Time Out Group 2007

Street Index